W9-ANT-691

Bürgr
& de Man on Modernity

All That Is

Marshall Berman

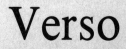

Solid Melts Into Air

The Experience of Modernity

First published by
Simon and Schuster, New York, 1982
© Marshall Berman

This edition first published by
Verso Editions, 15 Greek Street, London W1
1983

ISBN 0 86091 785 1

Printed in Great Britain by
The Thetford Press Ltd., Thetford, Norfolk

(Continued after Index)

In Memory of
Marc Joseph Berman
1975–1980

ACKNOWLEDGMENTS

This is far from a confessional book. Still, as I carried it for years inside me, I felt that in some sense it was the story of my life. It is impossible here to acknowledge all those who lived through the book with me and who helped make it what it is: the subjects would be too many, the predicates too complex, the emotions too intense; the work of making the list would never begin, or else would never end. What follows is no more than a start. For energy, ideas, support and love, my deepest thanks to Betty and Diane Berman, Morris and Lore Dickstein, Sam Girgus, Denise Green, Irving Howe, Leonard Kriegel, Meredith and Corey Tax, Gaye Tuchman, Michael Walzer; to Georges Borchardt and Michel Radomisli; to Erwin Glikes, Barbara Grossman and Susan Dwyer at Simon and Schuster; to Allen Ballard, George Fischer and Richard Wortman, who gave me special help with St. Petersburg; to my students and colleagues at the City College and the City University of New York, and at Stanford and the University of New Mexico; to the members of the Columbia University seminar in Political and Social Thought, and of the NYU seminar in the Culture of Cities; to the National Endowment for the Humanities; to the Purple Circle Day Care Center; to Lionel Trilling and Henry Pachter, who encouraged me to begin this book, and to keep at it, but who did not live to see it in print; and to many others, not named here, but not forgotten, who helped.

Contents

All That Is
Solid Melts
Into Air

Preface

For most of my life, since I learned that I was living in "a modern building" and growing up as part of "a modern family," in the Bronx of thirty years ago, I have been fascinated by the meanings of modernity. In this book I have tried to open up some of these dimensions of meaning, to explore and chart the adventures and horrors, the ambiguities and ironies of modern life. The book moves and develops through a number of ways of reading: of texts —Goethe's *Faust,* the *Communist Manifesto, Notes from Underground,* and many more; but also I try to read spatial and social environments—small towns, big construction sites, dams and power plants, Joseph Paxton's Crystal Palace, Haussmann's Parisian boulevards, Petersburg prospects, Robert Moses' highways through New York; and finally, reading fictional and actual people's lives, from Goethe's time through Marx's and Baudelaire's and into our own. I have tried to show how all these people share, and all these books and environments express, certain distinctively modern concerns. They are moved at once by a will to change—to transform both themselves and their world—and by a terror of disorientation and disintegration, of life falling apart. They all know the thrill and the dread of a world in which "all that is solid melts into air."

To be modern is to live a life of paradox and contradiction. It is to be overpowered by the immense bureaucratic organizations that have the power to control and often to destroy all communities, values, lives; and yet to be undeterred in our determination to face these forces, to fight to change their world and make it our own. It is to be both revolutionary and conservative: alive to new possibil-

13

ities for experience and adventure, frightened by the nihilistic depths to which so many modern adventures lead, longing to create and to hold on to something real even as everything melts. We might even say that to be fully modern is to be anti-modern: from Marx's and Dostoevsky's time to our own, it has been impossible to grasp and embrace the modern world's potentialities without loathing and fighting against some of its most palpable realities. No wonder then that, as the great modernist and anti-modernist Kierkegaard said, the deepest modern seriousness must express itself through irony. Modern irony animates so many great works of art and thought over the past century; at the same time, it infuses millions of ordinary people's everyday lives. This book aims to bring these works and these lives together, to restore the spiritual wealth of modernist culture to the modern man and woman in the street, to show how, for all of us, modernism is realism. This will not resolve the contradictions that pervade modern life; but it should help us to understand them, so that we can be clear and honest in facing and sorting out and working through the forces that make us what we are.

Shortly after I finished this book, my dear son Marc, five years old, was taken from me. I dedicate *All That Is Solid Melts into Air* to him. His life and death bring so many of its ideas and themes close to home: the idea that those who are most happily at home in the modern world, as he was, may be most vulnerable to the demons that haunt it; the idea that the daily routine of playgrounds and bicycles, of shopping and eating and cleaning up, of ordinary hugs and kisses, may be not only infinitely joyous and beautiful but also infinitely precarious and fragile; that it may take desperate and heroic struggles to sustain this life, and sometimes we lose. Ivan Karamazov says that, more than anything else, the death of children makes him want to give back his ticket to the universe. But he does not give it back. He keeps on fighting and loving; he keeps on keeping on.

New York City
January 1981

Introduction
Modernity–Yesterday, Today and Tomorrow

THERE IS a mode of vital experience—experience of space and time, of the self and others, of life's possibilities and perils—that is shared by men and women all over the world today. I will call this body of experience "modernity." To be modern is to find ourselves in an environment that promises us adventure, power, joy, growth, transformation of ourselves and the world—and, at the same time, that threatens to destroy everything we have, everything we know, everything we are. Modern environments and experiences cut across all boundaries of geography and ethnicity, of class and nationality, of religion and ideology: in this sense, modernity can be said to unite all mankind. But it is a paradoxical unity, a unity of disunity: it pours us all into a maelstrom of perpetual disintegration and renewal, of struggle and contradiction, of ambiguity and anguish. To be modern is to be part of a universe in which, as Marx said, "all that is solid melts into air."

People who find themselves in the midst of this maelstrom are apt to feel that they are the first ones, and maybe the only ones, to be going through it; this feeling has engendered numerous nostalgic myths of pre-modern Paradise Lost. In fact, however, great and ever-increasing numbers of people have been going through it for close to five hundred years. Although most of these people have probably experienced modernity as a radical threat to all their history and traditions, it has, in the course of five centuries, developed a rich history and a plenitude of traditions of its own. I want to explore and chart these traditions, to understand the ways in which they can nourish and enrich our own modernity, and the ways in which they may obscure or impoverish our sense of what modernity is and what it can be.

The maelstrom of modern life has been fed from many sources: great discoveries in the physical sciences, changing our images of the universe and our place in it; the industrialization of production, which transforms scientific knowledge into technology, creates new human environments and destroys old ones, speeds up the whole tempo of life, generates new forms of corporate power and class struggle; immense demographic upheavals, severing millions of people from their ancestral habitats, hurtling them halfway across the world into new lives; rapid and often cataclysmic urban growth; systems of mass communication, dynamic in their development, enveloping and binding together the most diverse people and societies; increasingly powerful national states, bureaucratically structured and operated, constantly striving to expand their powers; mass social movements of people, and peoples, challenging their political and economic rulers, striving to gain some control over their lives; finally, bearing and driving all these people and institutions along, an ever-expanding, drastically fluctuating capitalist world market. In the twentieth century, the social processes that bring this maelstrom into being, and keep it in a state of perpetual becoming, have come to be called "modernization." These world-historical processes have nourished an amazing variety of visions and ideas that aim to make men and women the subjects as well as the objects of modernization, to give them the power to change the world that is changing them, to make their way through the maelstrom and make it their own. Over the past century, these visions and values have come to be loosely grouped together under the name of "modernism." This book is a study in the dialectics of modernization and modernism.

In the hope of getting a grip on something as vast as the history of modernity, I have divided it into three phases. In the first phase, which goes roughly from the start of the sixteenth century to the end of the eighteenth, people are just beginning to experience modern life; they hardly know what has hit them. They grope, desperately but half blindly, for an adequate vocabulary; they have little or no sense of a modern public or community within which their trials and hopes can be shared. Our second phase begins with the great revolutionary wave of the 1790s. With the French Revolution and its reverberations, a great modern public abruptly and dramatically comes to life. This public shares the feeling of living in a revolutionary age, an age that generates explosive upheavals in every dimension of personal, social and political life. At the same time, the nineteenth-century modern public can remember what it is like to live, materially and spiritually, in worlds that are not modern at all. From this inner dichotomy, this sense of living in two worlds simultaneously, the ideas of modernization and modernism emerge and unfold. In the twentieth century, our third and final phase, the process of modernization expands to take in virtually the whole world, and the developing world culture of modernism achieves spectacular triumphs in art and thought. On the other hand, as the modern public expands, it shatters into a multitude of fragments, speaking incommensurable private languages; the idea of modernity, conceived in numerous fragmentary ways, loses much of its vividness, resonance and depth, and loses its capacity to organize and give meaning to people's lives. As a result of all this, we find ourselves today in the midst of a modern age that has lost touch with the roots of its own modernity.

If there is one archetypal modern voice in the early phase of modernity, before the American and French revolutions, it is the voice of Jean-Jacques Rousseau. Rousseau is the first to use the word *moderniste* in the ways in which the nineteenth and twentieth centuries will use it; and he is the source of some of our most vital modern traditions, from nostalgic reverie to psychoanalytic self-scrutiny to participatory democracy. Rousseau was, as everyone knows, a deeply troubled man. Much of his anguish springs from sources peculiar to his own strained life; but some of it derives from his acute responsiveness to social conditions that were coming to shape millions of people's lives. Rousseau astounded his contemporaries by proclaiming that European society was "at the edge of the abyss," on the verge of the most explosive revolutionary upheavals. He experienced everyday life in that society—especially in Paris, its capital—as a whirlwind, *le tourbillon social*.[1] How was the self to move and live in the whirlwind?

In Rousseau's romantic novel *The New Eloise*, his young hero, Saint-Preux, makes an exploratory move—an archetypal move for millions of young people in the centuries to come—from the country to the city. He writes to his love, Julie, from the depths of *le tourbillon social*, and tries to convey his wonder and dread. Saint-Preux experiences metropolitan life as "a perpetual clash of groups and cabals, a continual flux and reflux of prejudices and conflicting opinions . . . Everyone constantly places himself in contradiction with himself," and "everything is absurd, but nothing is shocking, because everyone is accustomed to everything." This is a world in which "the good, the bad, the beautiful, the ugly, truth, virtue, have only a local and limited existence." A multitude of new experiences offer themselves; but anyone who wants to enjoy them "must be more pliable than Alcibiades, ready to change his principles with his audience, to adjust his spirit with every step." After a few months in this environment,

> I'm beginning to feel the drunkenness that this agitated, tumultuous life plunges you into. With such a multitude of objects passing before my eyes, I'm getting dizzy. Of all the things that strike me, there is none that holds my heart, yet all of them together disturb my feelings, so that I forget what I am and who I belong to.

He reaffirms his commitment to his first love; yet even as he says it, he fears that "I don't know one day what I'm going to love the next." He longs desperately for something solid to cling to, yet "I see only phantoms that strike my eye, but disappear as soon as I try to grasp them."[2] This atmosphere—of agitation and turbulence, psychic dizziness and drunkenness, expansion of experiential possibilities and destruction of moral boundaries and personal bonds, self-enlargement and self-derangement, phantoms in the street and in the soul—is the atmosphere in which modern sensibility is born.

If we move forward a hundred years or so and try to identify the distinctive rhythms and timbres of nineteenth-century modernity, the first thing we will notice is the highly developed, differentiated and dynamic new landscape in which modern experience takes place. This is a landscape of steam engines, automatic factories, railroads, vast new industrial zones; of teeming cities that have grown overnight, often with dreadful human consequences; of daily newspapers, telegraphs, telephones and other mass media, communicating on an ever wider scale; of increasingly strong national states and multinational aggregations of capital; of mass social movements fighting these modernizations from above with their own modes of modernization from below; of an ever-expanding world market embracing all, capable of the most spectacular growth, capable of appalling waste and devastation, capable of everything except solidity and stability. The great modernists of the nineteenth century all attack this environment passionately, and strive to tear it down or explode it from within; yet all find themselves remarkably at home in it, alive to its possibilities, affirmative even in their radical negations, playful and ironic even in their moments of gravest seriousness and depth.

We can get a feeling for the complexity and richness of nineteenth-century modernism, and for the unities that infuse its diversity, if we listen briefly to two of its most distinctive voices: Nietzsche, who is generally perceived as a primary source of many of the modernisms of our time, and Marx, who is not ordinarily associated with any sort of modernism at all.

Here is Marx, speaking in awkward but powerful English in London in 1856.[3] "The so-called revolutions of 1848 were but poor incidents," he begins, "small fractures and fissures in the dry crust of European society. But they denounced the abyss. Beneath the apparently solid surface, they betrayed oceans of liquid matter, only needing expansion to rend into fragments continents of hard rock." The ruling classes of the reactionary 1850s tell the world that all is solid again; but it is not clear if even they themselves believe it. In fact, Marx says, "the atmosphere in which we live weighs upon everyone with a 20,000-pound force, but do you feel it?" One of Marx's most urgent aims is to make people "feel it"; this is why his ideas are expressed in such intense and extravagant images—abysses, earthquakes, volcanic eruptions, crushing gravitational force—images that will continue to resonate in our own century's modernist art and thought. Marx goes on: "There is one great fact, characteristic of this our nineteenth century, a fact which no party dares deny." The basic fact of modern life, as Marx experiences it, is that this life is radically contradictory at its base:

On the one hand, there have started into life industrial and scientific forces which no epoch of human history had ever suspected. On the other hand, there exist symptoms of decay, far surpassing the horrors of the latter times of the Roman Empire. In our days everything seems pregnant with its contrary. Machinery, gifted with the wonderful power of shortening and fructifying human labor, we behold starving and overworking it. The new-fangled sources of wealth, by some weird spell, are turned into sources of want. The victories of art seem bought by the loss of character. At the same pace that mankind masters nature, man seems to become enslaved to other men or to his own infamy. Even the pure light of science seems unable to shine but on the dark background of ignorance. All our invention and progress seem to result in endowing material forces with intellectual life, and stultifying human life into a material force.

These miseries and mysteries fill many moderns with despair. Some would "get rid of modern arts, in order to get rid of modern conflicts"; others will try to balance progress in industry with a neofeudal or neoabsolutist regression in politics. Marx, however, proclaims a paradigmatically modernist faith: "On our part, we do not mistake the shrewd spirit that continues to mark all these contradictions. We know that to work well . . . the new-fangled forces of society want only to be mastered by new-fangled men—and such are the working men. They are as much the invention of modern time as machinery itself." Thus a class of "new men," men who are thoroughly modern, will be able to resolve the contradictions of modernity, to overcome the crushing pressures, earthquakes, weird spells, personal and social abysses, in whose midst all modern men and women are forced to live. Having said this, Marx turns abruptly playful and connects his vision of the future with the past—with English folklore, with Shakespeare: "In the signs that bewilder the middle class, the aristocracy and the poor prophets of regression, we recognize our brave friend Robin Goodfellow, the old mole that can work in the earth so fast, that worthy pioneer—the Revolution."

Marx's writing is famous for its endings. But if we see him as a modernist, we will notice the dialectical motion that underlies and animates his thought, a motion that is open-ended, and that flows against the current of his own concepts and desires. Thus, in the *Communist Manifesto,* we see that the revolutionary dynamism that will overthrow the modern bourgeoisie springs from that bourgeoisie's own deepest impulses and needs:

> The bourgeoisie cannot exist without constantly revolutionizing
> the instruments of production, and with them the relations of
> production, and with them all the relations of society. . . . Con-
> stant revolutionizing of production, uninterrupted disturbance
> of all social relations, everlasting uncertainty and agitation, distin-
> guish the bourgeois epoch from all earlier ones.

This is probably the definitive vision of the modern environment,
that environment which has brought forth an amazing plenitude
of modernist movements, from Marx's time to our own. The vision
unfolds:

> All fixed, fast-frozen relations, with their train of ancient and
> venerable prejudices and opinions, are swept away, all new-
> formed ones become antiquated before they can ossify. All that is
> solid melts into air, all that is holy is profaned, and men at last
> are forced to face . . . the real conditions of their lives and their
> relations with their fellow men.[4]

Thus the dialectical motion of modernity turns ironically against
its prime movers, the bourgeoisie. But it may not stop turning
there: after all, all modern movements are caught up in this ambience—including Marx's own. Suppose, as Marx supposes, that
bourgeois forms decompose, and that a communist movement
surges into power: what is to keep this new social form from shar-
ing its predecessor's fate and melting down in the modern air?
Marx understood this question and suggested some answers,
which we will explore later on. But one of the distinctive virtues of
modernism is that it leaves its questions echoing in the air long
after the questioners themselves, and their answers, have left the
scene.

If we move a quarter century ahead, to Nietzsche in the 1880s,
we will find very different prejudices, allegiances and hopes, yet a
surprisingly similar voice and feeling for modern life. For
Nietzsche, as for Marx, the currents of modern history were ironic
and dialectical: thus Christian ideals of the soul's integrity and the
will to truth had come to explode Christianity itself. The results
were the traumatic events that Nietzsche called "the death of God"
and "the advent of nihilism." Modern mankind found itself in the
midst of a great absence and emptiness of values and yet, at the
same time, a remarkable abundance of possibilities. Here, in

Nietzsche's *Beyond Good and Evil* (1882), we find, just as we found in Marx, a world where everything is pregnant with its contrary:[5]

> At these turning points in history there shows itself, juxtaposed and often entangled with one another, a magnificent, manifold, jungle-like growing and striving, a sort of tropical tempo in rivalry of development, and an enormous destruction and self-destruction, thanks to egoisms violently opposed to one another, exploding, battling each other for sun and light, unable to find any limitation, any check, any considerateness within the morality at their disposal. . . . Nothing but new "wherefores," no longer any communal formulas; a new allegiance of misunderstanding and mutual disrespect; decay, vice, and the most superior desires gruesomely bound up with one another, the genius of the race welling up over the cornucopias of good and ill; a fateful simultaneity of spring and autumn. . . . Again there is danger, the mother of morality—great danger—but this time displaced onto the individual, onto the nearest and dearest, onto the street, onto one's own child, one's own heart, one's own innermost secret recesses of wish and will.

At times like these, "the individual dares to individuate himself." On the other hand, this daring individual desperately "needs a set of laws of his own, needs his own skills and wiles for self-preservation, self-heightening, self-awakening, self-liberation." The possibilities are at once glorious and ominous. "Our instincts can now run back in all sorts of directions; we ourselves are a kind of chaos." Modern man's sense of himself and his history "really amounts to an instinct for everything, a taste and tongue for everything." So many roads open up from this point. How are modern men and women to find the resources to cope with their "everything"? Nietzsche notes that there are plenty of "Little Jack Horners" around whose solution to the chaos of modern life is to try not to live at all: for them, " 'Become mediocre' is the only morality that makes sense."

Another type of modern throws himself into parodies of the past: he "needs history because it is the storage closet where all the costumes are kept. He notices that none really fits him"—not primitive, not classical, not medieval, not Oriental—"so he keeps trying on more and more," unable to accept the fact that a modern man "can never really look well-dressed," because no social role in modern times can ever be a perfect fit. Nietzsche's own stance toward the perils of modernity is to embrace them all with joy: "We moderns, we half-barbarians. We are in the midst of our bliss only when we are most in danger. The only stimulus that tickles us is the infinite, the immeasurable." And yet Nietzsche is not willing to live in the midst of this danger forever. As ardently as Marx, he asserts his faith in a new kind of man—"the man of tomorrow and the day after tomorrow"—who, "standing in opposition to his today," will have the courage and imagination to "create new values" that modern men and women need to steer their way through the perilous infinities in which they live.

What is distinctive and remarkable about the voice that Marx and Nietzsche share is not only its breathless pace, its vibrant energy, its imaginative richness, but also its fast and drastic shifts in tone and inflection, its readiness to turn on itself, to question and negate all it has said, to transform itself into a great range of harmonic or dissonant voices, and to stretch itself beyond its capacities into an endlessly wider range, to express and grasp a world where everything is pregnant with its contrary and "all that is solid melts into air." This voice resonates at once with self-discovery and self-mockery, with self-delight and self-doubt. It is a voice that knows pain and dread, but believes in its power to come through. Grave danger is everywhere, and may strike at any moment, but not even the deepest wounds can stop the flow and overflow of its energy. It is ironic and contradictory, polyphonic and dialectical, denouncing modern life in the name of values that modernity itself has created, hoping—often against hope—that the modernities of tomorrow and the day after tomorrow will heal the wounds that wreck the modern men and women of today. All the great modernists of the nineteenth century—spirits as diverse as Marx and Kierkegaard, Whitman and Ibsen, Baudelaire, Melville, Carlyle, Stirner, Rimbaud, Strindberg, Dostoevsky, and many more—speak in these rhythms and in this range.

What has become of nineteenth-century modernism in the twentieth century? In some ways it has thrived and grown beyond its own wildest hopes. In painting and sculpture, in poetry and the novel, in theater and dance, in architecture and design, in a whole array of electronic media and a wide range of scientific disciplines that didn't even exist a century ago, our century has produced an amazing plenitude of works and ideas of the highest quality. The twentieth century may well be the most brilliantly creative in the history of the world, not least because its creative energies have burst out in every part of the world. The brilliance and depth of living modernism—living in the work of Grass, Garcia Márquez, Fuentes, Cunningham, Nevelson, di Suvero, Kenzo Tange, Fassbinder, Herzog, Sembene, Robert Wilson, Philip Glass, Richard Foreman, Twyla Tharp, Maxine Hong Kingston, and so many more who surround us—give us a great deal to be proud of, in a world where there is so much to be ashamed and afraid of. And yet, it seems to me, we don't know how to use our modernism; we have missed or broken the connection between our culture and our lives. Jackson Pollock imagined his drip paintings as forests in which spectators might lose (and, of course, find) themselves; but we have mostly lost the art of putting ourselves in the picture, of recognizing ourselves as participants and protagonists in the art and thought of our time. Our century has nourished a spectacular modern art; but we seem to have forgotten how to grasp the modern life from which this art springs. In many ways, modern thought since Marx and Nietzsche has grown and developed; yet our thinking about modernity seems to have stagnated and regressed.

If we listen closely to twentieth-century writers and thinkers about modernity and compare them to those of a century ago, we will find a radical flattening of perspective and shrinkage of imaginative range. Our nineteenth-century thinkers were simultaneously enthusiasts and enemies of modern life, wrestling inexhaustibly with its ambiguities and contradictions; their self-ironies and inner tensions were a primary source of their creative power. Their twentieth-century successors have lurched far more toward rigid polarities and flat totalizations. Modernity is either embraced with a blind and uncritical enthusiasm, or else condemned with a neo-Olympian remoteness and contempt; in either case, it is conceived as a closed monolith, incapable of being shaped or changed by modern men. Open visions of modern life have been supplanted by closed ones, Both/And by Either/Or.

The basic polarizations take place at the very start of our century. Here are the Italian futurists, passionate partisans of modernity in the years before the First World War: "Comrades, we tell you now that the triumphant progress of science makes changes in humanity inevitable, changes that are hacking an abyss between those docile slaves of tradition and us free moderns who are confident in the radiant splendor of our future."[6] There are no ambiguities here: "tradition"—all the world's traditions thrown together—simply equals docile slavery, and modernity equals freedom; there are no loose ends. "Take up your pickaxes, your axes and hammers, and wreck, wreck the venerable cities, pitilessly! Come on! set fire to the library shelves! Turn aside the canals to flood the museums! . . . So let them come, the gay incendiaries with charred fingers! Here they are! Here they are!" Now, Marx and Nietzsche could also rejoice in the modern destruction of traditional structures; but they knew the human costs of this progress, and knew that modernity would have a long way to go before its wounds could be healed.

> We will sing of great crowds excited by work, by pleasure and by riot; we will sing of the multicolored, polyphonic tides of revolution in the modern capitals; we will sing of the nightly fervor of arsenals and shipyards blazing with violent electric moons; greedy railway stations that devour smoke-plumed serpents; factories hung on clouds by the crooked lines of their smoke; bridges that stride the rivers like giant gymnasts, flashing in the sun with a glitter of knives; adventurous steamers . . . deep-chested locomotives . . . and the sleek light of planes [etc., etc.].[7]

Seventy years later, we can still feel stirred by the futurists' youthful verve and enthusiasm, by their desire to merge their energies with modern technology and create the world anew. But so much is left out of this new world! We can see it even in that marvelous metaphor "the multicolored, polyphonic tides of revolution." It is a real expansion of human sensibility to be able to experience political upheaval in an aesthetic (musical, painterly) way. On the other hand, what happens to all the people who get swept away in those tides? Their experience is nowhere in the futurist picture. It appears that some very important kinds of human feeling are dying, even as machines are coming to life. Indeed, in later futurist writing, "we look for the creation of a nonhuman type in whom moral suffering, goodness of heart, affection, and love, those corrosive poisons of vital energy, interrupters of our powerful bodily electricity, will be abolished."[8] On this note, the young futurists ardently threw themselves into what they called "war, the world's only hygiene," in 1914. Within two years, their two most creative spirits—the painter-sculptor Umberto Boccioni, the architect Antonio Sant'Elia—would be killed by the machines they loved. The rest survived to become cultural hacks in Mussolini's mills, pulverized by the dead hand of the future.

The futurists carried the celebration of modern technology to a grotesque and self-destructive extreme, which ensured that their extravagances would never be repeated. But their uncritical romance of machines, fused with their utter remoteness from people, would be reincarnated in modes that would be less bizarre and longer-lived. We find this mode of modernism after World War One in the refined forms of the "machine aesthetic," the technocratic pastorals of the Bauhaus, Gropius and Mies van der Rohe, Le Corbusier and Léger, the *Ballet Mécanique*. We find it again, after another World War, in the spaced-out high-tech rhapsodies of Buckminster Fuller and Marshall McLuhan and in Alvin Toffler's *Future Shock*. Here, in McLuhan's *Understanding Media*, published in 1964,

> The computer, in short, promises by technology a Pentecostal condition of universal understanding and unity. The next logical step would seem to be . . . to bypass languages in favor of a general cosmic consciousness . . . The condition of "weightlessness," that biologists say promises a physical immortality, may be paralleled by the condition of speechlessness that could confer a perpetuity of collective harmony and peace.[9]

This modernism underlay the models of modernization which postwar American social scientists, often working under lavish government and foundation subsidies, developed for export to the Third World. Here, for instance, is a hymn to the modern factory by the social psychologist Alex Inkeles:

> A factory guided by modern management and personnel policies will set its workers an example of rational behavior, emotional balance, open communication, and respect for the opinions, the feelings, and the dignity of the worker, which can be a powerful example of the principles and practices of modern living.[10]

The futurists might deplore the low intensity of this prose, but they would surely be delighted with the vision of the factory as an exemplary human being which men and women should take as a model for their lives. Inkeles' essay is entitled "The Modernization of Man," and is meant to show the importance of human desire and initiative in modern life. But its problem, and the problem of all modernisms in the futurist tradition, is that, with brilliant machines and mechanical systems playing all the leading roles—just as the factory is the subject in the quotation above—there is precious little for modern man to do except to plug in.

If we move to the opposite pole of twentieth-century thought, which says a decisive "No!" to modern life, we find a surprisingly similar vision of what that life is like. At the climax of Max Weber's *The Protestant Ethic and the Spirit of Capitalism,* written in 1904, the whole "mighty cosmos of the modern economic order" is seen as "an iron cage." This inexorable order, capitalistic, legalistic and bureaucratic, "determines the lives of all individuals who are born into this mechanism . . . with irresistible force." It is bound to "determine man's fate until the last ton of fossilized coal is burnt out." Now, Marx and Nietzsche—and Tocqueville and Carlyle and Mill and Kierkegaard and all the other great nineteenth-century critics —also understood the ways in which modern technology and social organization determined man's fate. But they all believed that modern individuals had the capacity both to understand this fate and, once they understood it, to fight it. Hence, even in the midst of a wretched present, they could imagine an open future. Twentieth-century critics of modernity almost entirely lack this empathy with, and faith in, their fellow modern men and women. To Weber, his contemporaries are nothing but "specialists without spirit, sensualists without heart; and this nullity is caught in the delusion that it has achieved a level of development never before attained by mankind."[11] Thus, not only is modern society a cage, but all the people in it are shaped by its bars; we are beings without spirit, without heart, without sexual or personal identity ("this nullity . . . caught in the delusion that *it* has achieved . . .")—we might almost say without being. Here, just as in futurist and techno-pastoral forms of modernism, modern man as a subject— as a living being capable of response, judgment and action in and on the world—has disappeared. Ironically, twentieth-century critics of "the iron cage" adopt the perspective of the cage's keepers: since those inside are devoid of inner freedom or dignity, the cage is not a prison; it merely furnishes a race of nullities with the emptiness they crave and need.*

Weber had little faith in the people, but even less in their ruling classes, whether aristocratic or bourgeois, bureaucratic or revolutionary. Hence his political stance, at least in the last years of his life, was a perpetually embattled liberalism. But when the Weberian remoteness and contempt for modern men and women were split off from Weberian skepticism and critical insight, the result was a politics far to the right of Weber's own. Many twentieth-century thinkers have seen things this way: the swarming masses who press upon us in the street and in the state have no sensitivity, spirituality or dignity like our own; isn't it absurd, then, that these "mass men" (or "hollow men") should have not only the right to govern themselves but also, through their mass majorities, the power to govern us? In the ideas and intellectual gestures of Ortega, Spengler, Maurras, T. S. Eliot and Allen Tate, we see Weber's neo-Olympian perspective appropriated, distorted and magnified by the modern mandarins and would-be aristocrats of the twentieth-century right.

What is more surprising, and more disturbing, is the extent to which this perspective thrived among some of the participatory democrats of the recent New Left. But this is what happened, at least for a time, at the very end of the 1960s, when Herbert Marcuse's "One-Dimensional Man" became the dominant paradigm in critical thought. According to this paradigm, both Marx and Freud are obsolete: not only class and social struggles but also psychological conflicts and contradictions have been abolished by the state of "total administration." The masses have no egos, no ids, their souls are devoid of inner tension or dynamism: their ideas, their needs, even their dreams, are "not their own"; their inner lives are "totally

---

* A more dialectical perspective may be found in some of Weber's later essays, for instance "Politics as a Vocation" and "Science as a Vocation" (in Hans Gerth and C. Wright Mills, editors and translators, *From Max Weber*, Oxford, 1946). Weber's contemporary and friend Georg Simmel intimates, but never really develops, what is probably the closest thing to a twentieth-century dialectical theory of modernity. See, for example, "The Conflict in Modern Culture," "The Metropolis and Mental Life," "Group Expansion and the Development of Individuality," in *Georg Simmel on Individuality and Social Forms*, edited by Donald Levine (University of Chicago, 1971). In Simmel—and later in his youthful followers Georg Lukács, T. W. Adorno and Walter Benjamin—dialectical vision and depth are always entangled, often in the same sentence, with monolithic cultural despair.

administered," programmed to produce exactly those desires that the social system can satisfy, and no more. "The people recognize themselves in their commodities; they find their soul in their automobiles, hi-fi sets, split-level homes, kitchen equipment."[12]

Now this is a familiar twentieth-century refrain, shared by those who love the modern world and those who hate it: modernity is constituted by its machines, of which modern men and women are merely mechanical reproductions. But it is a travesty of the nineteenth-century modern tradition in whose orbit Marcuse claimed to move, the critical tradition of Hegel and Marx. To invoke those thinkers while rejecting their vision of history as restless activity, dynamic contradiction, dialectical struggle and progress, is to retain little but their names. Meanwhile, even as the young radicals of the 1960s fought for changes that would enable the people around them to control their lives, the "one-dimensional" paradigm proclaimed that no change was possible and that, indeed, these people weren't even really alive. Two roads opened up from this point. One was the search for a vanguard that was wholly "outside" modern society: "the substratum of outcasts and outsiders, the exploited and persecuted of other races and other colors, the unemployed and the unemployable."[13] These groups, whether in America's ghettos and prisons or in the Third World, could qualify as a revolutionary vanguard because they were supposedly untouched by modernity's kiss of death. Of course, such a search is doomed to futility; no one in the contemporary world is or can be "outside." For radicals who understood this, yet took the one-dimensional paradigm to heart, it seemed that the only thing left was futility and despair.

The volatile atmosphere of the 1960s generated a large and vital body of thought and controversy over the ultimate meaning of modernity. Much of the most interesting of this thought revolved around the nature of modernism. Modernism in the 1960s can be roughly divided into three tendencies, based on attitudes toward modern life as a whole: affirmative, negative and withdrawn. This division may sound crude, but recent attitudes toward modernity have in fact tended to be cruder and simpler, less subtle and dialectical than those of a century ago.

The first of these modernisms, the one that strives to withdraw from modern life, was proclaimed most forcefully by Roland Barthes in literature and Clement Greenberg in the visual arts.

Greenberg argued that the only legitimate concern of modernist art was art itself; furthermore, the only rightful focus for an artist in any given form or genre was the nature and limits of that genre: the medium is the message. Thus, for instance, the only permissible subject for a modernist painter was the flatness of the surface (canvas, etc.) on which the painting takes place, because "flatness alone is unique and exclusive to the art."[14] Modernism, then, was the quest for the pure, self-referential art object. And that was all it was: the proper relationship of modern art to modern social life was no relationship at all. Barthes put this absence in a positive, even a heroic light: the modern writer "turns his back on society and confronts the world of objects without going through any of the forms of History or social life."[15] Modernism thus appeared as a great attempt to free modern artists from the impurities, vulgarities of modern life. Many artists and writers—and, even more, art and literary critics—have been grateful to this modernism for establishing the autonomy and dignity of their vocations. But very few modern artists or writers have stayed with this modernism for long: an art without personal feelings or social relationships is bound to seem arid and lifeless after a little while. The freedom it confers is the freedom of a beautifully formed, perfectly sealed tomb.

Then there was the vision of modernism as an unending permanent revolution against the totality of modern existence: it was "a tradition of overthrowing tradition" (Harold Rosenberg),[16] an "adversary culture" (Lionel Trilling),[17] a "culture of negation" (Renato Poggioli).[18] The modern work of art was said to "molest us with an aggressive absurdity" (Leo Steinberg).[19] It seeks the violent overthrow of all our values, and cares little about reconstructing the worlds it destroys. This image gained force and credence as the 1960s progressed and the political climate heated up: in some circles, "modernism" became a code word for all the forces in revolt.[20] This obviously tells part of the truth, but it leaves far too much out. It leaves out the great romance of construction, a crucial force in modernism from Carlyle and Marx to Tatlin and Calder, Le Corbusier and Frank Lloyd Wright, Mark di Suvero and Robert Smithson. It leaves out all the affirmative and life-sustaining force that in the greatest modernists is always interwoven with assault and revolt: the erotic joy, natural beauty and human tenderness in D. H. Lawrence, always locked in mortal embrace with his nihilistic rage and despair; the figures in Picasso's

Guernica, struggling to keep life itself alive even as they shriek their death; the triumphant last choruses of Coltrane's *A Love Supreme;* Alyosha Karamazov, in the midst of chaos and anguish, kissing and embracing the earth; Molly Bloom bringing the archetypal modernist book to an end with "yes I said yes I will Yes."

There is a further problem with the idea of modernism as nothing but trouble: it tends to posit a model of modern society as one that is in itself devoid of trouble. It leaves out all the "uninterrupted disturbances of all social relations, everlasting uncertainty and agitation" that have for two hundred years been basic facts of modern life. When students at Columbia University rebelled in 1968, some of their conservative professors described their action as "modernism in the streets." Presumably those streets would have been calm and orderly—in the middle of Manhattan, yet!— if only modern culture could somehow have been kept off them, and confined to university classrooms and libraries and Museums of Modern Art.[21] Had the professors learned their own lessons, they would have remembered how much of modernism—Baudelaire, Boccioni, Joyce, Mayakovsky, Léger, et al.—has nourished itself on the real trouble in the modern streets, and transformed their noise and dissonance into beauty and truth. Ironically, the radical image of modernism as pure subversion helped to nourish the neoconservative fantasy of a world purified of modernist subversion. "Modernism has been the seducer," Daniel Bell wrote in *The Cultural Contradictions of Capitalism.* "The modern movement disrupts the unity of culture," "shatters the 'rational cosmology' that underlay the bourgeois world view of an ordered relation between space and time," etc., etc.[22] If only the modernist snake could be expelled from the modern garden, space, time and the cosmos would straighten themselves out. Then, presumably, a techno-pastoral golden age would return, and men and machines could lie down together happily forevermore.

The affirmative vision of modernism was developed in the 1960s by a heterogeneous group of writers, including John Cage, Lawrence Alloway, Marshall McLuhan, Leslie Fiedler, Susan Sontag, Richard Poirier, Robert Venturi. It coincided loosely with the emergence of pop art in the early 1960s. Its dominant themes were that we must "wake up to the very life we're living" (Cage), and "cross the border, close the gap" (Fiedler).[23] This meant, for one thing, breaking down the barriers between "art" and other human activities, such as commercial entertainment, industrial technology, fashion and design, politics. It also encouraged writers, painters, dancers, composers and filmmakers to break down the boundaries of their specializations and work together on mixed-media productions and performances that would create richer and more multivalent arts.

For modernists of this variety, who sometimes called themselves "post-modernists," the modernism of pure form and the modernism of pure revolt were both too narrow, too self-righteous, too constricting to the modern spirit. Their ideal was to open oneself to the immense variety and richness of things, materials and ideas that the modern world inexhaustibly brought forth. They breathed fresh air and playfulness into a cultural ambience which in the 1950s had become unbearably solemn, rigid and closed. Pop modernism recreated the openness to the world, the generosity of vision, of some of the great modernists of the past—Baudelaire, Whitman, Apollinaire, Mayakovsky, William Carlos Williams. But if this modernism matched their imaginative sympathy, it never learned to recapture their critical bite. When a creative spirit like John Cage accepted the support of the Shah of Iran, and performed modernist spectacles a few miles from where political prisoners shrieked and died, the failure of moral imagination was not his alone. The trouble was that pop modernism never developed a critical perspective which might have clarified the point where openness to the modern world has got to stop, and the point where the modern artist needs to see and to say that some of the powers of this world have got to go.*

* For pop nihilism in its most insouciant form, consider this black-comic monologue by the architect Philip Johnson, who is being interviewed by Susan Sontag for the BBC in 1965:

> SONTAG: I think, I think in New York your aesthetic sense is in a curious, very modern way more developed than anywhere else. If you are experiencing things morally one is in a state of continual indignation and horror, but [they laugh] but if one has a very modern kind of . . .
> JOHNSON: Do you suppose that will change the sense of morals, the fact that we can't use morals as a means of judging this city because we couldn't stand it? And that we're changing our whole moral system to suit the fact that we're living in a ridiculous way?
> SONTAG: Well I think we are learning the limitations of, of moral experience of things. I think it's possible to be aesthetic. . . .
> JOHNSON: To merely, to enjoy things as they are—we see entirely different beauty from what [Lewis] Mumford could possibly see.
> SONTAG: Well, I think, I see for myself that I just now see things in a kind of split-level way, both morally and . . .

All the modernisms and anti-modernisms of the 1960s, then, were seriously flawed. But their sheer plenitude, along with their intensity and liveliness of expression, generated a common language, a vibrant ambience, a shared horizon of experience and desire. All these visions and revisions of modernity were active orientations toward history, attempts to connect the turbulent present with a past and a future, to help men and women all over the contemporary world to make themselves at home in this world. These initiatives all failed, but they sprang from a largeness of vision and imagination, and from an ardent desire to seize the day. It was the absence of these generous visions and initiatives that made the 1970s such a bleak decade. Virtually no one today seems to want to make the large human connections that the idea of modernity entails. Hence discourse and controversy over the meaning of modernity, so lively a decade ago, have virtually ceased to exist today.

Many artistic and literary intellectuals have immersed themselves in the world of structuralism, a world that simply wipes the question of modernity—along with all other questions about the self and history—off the map. Others have embraced a mystique of post-modernism, which strives to cultivate ignorance of modern history and culture, and speaks as if all human feeling, expressiveness, play, sexuality and community have only just been invented —by the post-modernists—and were unknown, even inconceivable, before last week.[24] Meanwhile, social scientists, embarrassed by critical attacks on their techno-pastoral models, have fled from the task of building a model that might be truer to modern life. Instead, they have split modernity into a series of separate components—industrialization, state-building, urbanization, development of markets, elite formation—and resisted any attempt to integrate them into a whole. This has freed them from extravagant generalizations and vague totalities—but also from thought that might engage their own lives and works and their place in his-

---

JOHNSON: What good does it do you to believe in good things?
SONTAG: Because I . . .
JOHNSON: It's feudal and futile. I think it much better to be nihilistic and forget it all. I mean, I know I'm attacked by my moral friends, er, but really, don't they shake themselves up over nothing?

Johnson's monologue goes on and on, interspersed with perplexed stammers by Sontag, who, although she clearly wants to play, can't quite bring herself to kiss morality goodbye. Quoted in Jencks, *Modern Movements in Architecture*, 208–10.

tory.[25] The eclipse of the problem of modernity in the 1970s has meant the destruction of a vital form of public space. It has hastened the disintegration of our world into an aggregation of private material and spiritual interest groups, living in windowless monads, far more isolated than we need to be.

Just about the only writer of the past decade who has had anything substantial to say about modernity is Michel Foucault. And what he has to say is an endless, excruciating series of variations on the Weberian themes of the iron cage and the human nullities whose souls are shaped to fit the bars. Foucault is obsessed with prisons, hospitals, asylums, with what Erving Goffman has called "total institutions." Unlike Goffman, however, Foucault denies the possibility of any sort of freedom, either outside these institutions or within their interstices. Foucault's totalities swallow up every facet of modern life. He develops these themes with obsessive relentlessness and, indeed, with sadistic flourishes, clamping his ideas down on his readers like iron bars, twisting each dialectic into our flesh like a new turn of the screw.

Foucault reserves his most savage contempt for people who imagine that it is possible for modern mankind to be free. Do we think we feel a spontaneous rush of sexual desire? We are merely being moved by "the modern technologies of power that take life as their object," driven by "the deployment of sexuality by power in its grip on bodies and their materiality, their forces, their energies, sensations and pleasures." Do we act politically, overthrow tyrannies, make revolutions, create constitutions to establish and protect human rights? Mere "juridical regression" from the feudal ages, because constitutions and bills of rights are merely "the forms that [make] an essentially normalizing power acceptable."[26] Do we use our minds to unmask oppression—as Foucault appears to be trying to do? Forget it, because all forms of inquiry into the human condition "merely refer individuals from one disciplinary authority to another," and hence only add to the triumphant "discourse of power." Any criticism rings hollow, because the critic himself or herself is "in the panoptic machine, invested by its effects of power, which we bring to ourselves, since we are part of its mechanism."[27]

After being subjected to this for a while, we realize that there is no freedom in Foucault's world, because his language forms a seamless web, a cage far more airtight than anything Weber ever dreamed of, into which no life can break. The mystery is why so many of today's intellectuals seem to want to choke in there with him. The answer, I suspect, is that Foucault offers a generation of refugees from the 1960s a world-historical alibi for the sense of passivity and helplessness that gripped so many of us in the 1970s. There is no point in trying to resist the oppressions and injustices of modern life, since even our dreams of freedom only add more links to our chains; however, once we grasp the total futility of it all, at least we can relax.

In this bleak context, I want to bring the dynamic and dialectical modernism of the nineteenth century to life again. A great modernist, the Mexican poet and critic Octavio Paz, has lamented that modernity is "cut off from the past and continually hurtling forward at such a dizzy pace that it cannot take root, that it merely survives from one day to the next: it is unable to return to its beginnings and thus recover its powers of renewal."[28] The argument of this book is that, in fact, the modernisms of the past can give us back a sense of our own modern roots, roots that go back two hundred years. They can help us connect our lives with the lives of millions of people who are living through the trauma of modernization thousands of miles away, in societies radically different from our own—and with millions of people who lived through it a century or more ago. They can illuminate the contradictory forces and needs that inspire and torment us: our desire to be rooted in a stable and coherent personal and social past, and our insatiable desire for growth—not merely for economic growth but for growth in experience, in pleasure, in knowledge, in sensibility—growth that destroys both the physical and social landscapes of our past, and our emotional links with those lost worlds; our desperate allegiances to ethnic, national, class and sexual groups which we hope will give us a firm "identity," and the internationalization of everyday life—of our clothes and household goods, our books and music, our ideas and fantasies—that spreads all our identities all over the map; our desire for clear and solid values to live by, and our desire to embrace the limitless possibilities of modern life and experience that obliterate all values; the social and political forces that propel us into explosive conflicts with other people and other peoples, even as we develop a deeper sensitivity and empathy toward our ordained enemies and come to realize, sometimes too late, that they are not so different from us after all. Experiences like these unite us with the nineteenth-century modern world: a world where, as Marx said, "everything is pregnant with its contrary" and "all that is solid melts into air"; a world where, as Nietzsche said, "there is danger, the mother of morality—great danger . . . displaced onto the individual, onto the nearest and dearest, onto the street, onto one's own child, one's own heart, one's own innermost secret recesses of wish and will." Modern machines have changed a great deal in the years between the nineteenth-century modernists and ourselves; but modern men and women, as Marx and Nietzsche and Baudelaire and Dostoevsky saw them then, may only now be coming fully into their own.

Marx, Nietzsche and their contemporaries experienced modernity as a whole at a moment when only a small part of the world was truly modern. A century later, when the processes of modernization have cast a net that no one, not even in the remotest corner of the world, can escape, we can learn a great deal from the first modernists, not so much about their age as about our own. We have lost our grip on the contradictions that they had to grasp with all their strength, at every moment in their everyday lives, in order to live at all. Paradoxically, these first modernists may turn out to understand us—the modernization and modernism that constitute our lives—better than we understand ourselves. If we can make their visions our own, and use their perspectives to look at our own environments with fresh eyes, we will see that there is more depth in our lives than we thought. We will feel our community with people all over the world who have been struggling with the same dilemmas as our own. And we will get back in touch with a remarkably rich and vibrant modernist culture that has grown out of these struggles: a culture that contains vast resources of strength and health, if only we come to know it as our own.

It may turn out, then, that going back can be a way to go forward: that remembering the modernisms of the nineteenth century can give us the vision and courage to create the modernisms of the twenty-first. This act of remembering can help us bring modernism back to its roots, so that it can nourish and renew itself, to confront the adventures and dangers that lie ahead. To appropriate the modernities of yesterday can be at once a critique of the modernities of today and an act of faith in the modernities—and in the modern men and women—of tomorrow and the day after tomorrow.

I

Goethe's *Faust:* The Tragedy of Development

Modern bourgeois society, a society that has conjured up such gigantic means of production and exchange, is like the sorcerer who is no longer able to control the powers of the underworld that he has called up by his spells.

> —*Communist Manifesto*

Good God! . . . the long-haired boys have lost control!

> —**An army officer at Alamogordo, New Mexico, just after the explosion of the first atom bomb in July 1945**

We are a Faustian age determined to meet the Lord or the Devil before we are done, and the ineluctable ore of the authentic is our only key to the lock.

> —**Norman Mailer, 1971**

FOR AS long as there has been a modern culture, the figure of Faust has been one of its culture heroes. In the four centuries since Johann Spiess's *Faustbuch* of 1587 and Christopher Marlowe's *Tragical History of Doctor Faustus* a year later, the story has been retold endlessly, in every modern language, in every known medium from operas to puppet plays and comic books, in every literary form from lyrical poetry to theologico-philosophical tragedy to vulgar farce; it has proven irresistible to every type of modern artist all over the world. Though the figure of Faust has taken many forms, he is virtually always a "long-haired boy"—an intellectual nonconformist, a marginal and suspicious character. In all versions, too, the tragedy or comedy comes when Faust "loses control" of the energies of his mind, which then proceed to take on a dynamic and highly explosive life of their own.

Almost four hundred years after his debut, Faust continues to grip the modern imagination. Thus *The New Yorker* magazine, in an anti-nuclear editorial just after the accident at Three Mile Island, indicts Faust as a symbol of scientific irresponsibility and indifference to life: "The Faustian proposal that the experts make to us is to let them lay their fallible human hands on eternity, and it is not acceptable."[1] Meanwhile, at the other end of the cultural spectrum, a recent issue of *Captain America* comics features "the Deadly Designs of . . . DOCTOR FAUSTUS!" This villain, who strikingly resembles Orson Welles, soars over New York Harbor in a giant dirigible. "Even as we watch," he tells two bound and helpless victims, "those canisters containing my ingenious mind-gas are being affixed to special hookups within the dirigible's exhaust system. At my command, these loyal [robotized] National Force agents will begin flooding the city with it, bringing every man, woman and child in New York under my absolute MENTAL CONTROL!" This means trouble: the last time Dr. Faustus passed through, he confused the minds of all Americans, leading them to paranoiacally suspect and denounce their neighbors, and generating McCarthyism. Who knows what he will be up to now? A reluctant Captain America comes out of retirement to confront this enemy. "And, unfashionable as it may sound," he tells his jaded 1970s readers, "I've got to do it for the nation. America could never be the land of the free once Faustus got it in his slimy grip!" When the Faustian villain is finally thwarted, the terrified Statue of Liberty feels free to smile again.[2]

Goethe's *Faust* surpasses all others in the richness and depth of its historical perspective, in its moral imagination, its political intelligence, its psychological sensitivity and insight. It opens up new dimensions in the emerging modern self-awareness that the Faust myth has always explored. Its sheer immensity, not only in scope and ambition but in genuine vision, led Pushkin to call it "an Iliad of modern life."[3] Goethe's work on the Faust theme began around 1770, when he was twenty-one, and continued intermittently for the next sixty years; he did not consider the work finished until 1831, a year before his death at the age of eighty-three, and it did not appear as a whole until after he was dead.[4] Thus the work was in process all through one of the most turbulent and revolutionary eras in the history of the world. Much of its strength springs from this history: Goethe's hero and the characters around him experience, with great personal intensity, many of the world-historical dramas and traumas that Goethe and his contemporaries went through; the whole movement of the work enacts the larger movement of Western society.

Faust begins in an epoch whose thought and sensibility are modern in a way that twentieth-century readers can recognize at once, but whose material and social conditions are still medieval; the work ends in the midst of the spiritual and material upheavals of an industrial revolution. It starts in an intellectual's lonely room, in an abstracted and isolated realm of thought; it ends in the midst of a far-reaching realm of production and exchange, ruled by giant corporate bodies and complex organizations, which Faust's thought is helping to create, and which are enabling him to create more. In Goethe's version of the Faust theme, the subject and object of transformation is not merely the hero, but the whole world. Goethe's *Faust* expresses and dramatizes the process by which, at the end of the eighteenth century and the start of the nineteenth, a distinctively modern world-system comes into being.

The vital force that animates Goethe's *Faust*, that marks it off from its predecessors, and that generates much of its richness and dynamism, is an impulse that I will call the desire for *development*. Goethe's Faust tries to explain this desire to his devil; it isn't all that easy to explain. Earlier incarnations of Faust have sold their souls in exchange for certain clearly defined and universally desired good things of life: money, sex, power over others, fame and glory. Goethe's Faust tells Mephistopheles that, yes, he wants these things, but these things aren't in themselves what he wants.

> Do you not hear, I have no thought of joy!
> The reeling whirl I seek, the most painful excess,
> Enamored hate and quickening distress.
> > . . . my mind
> Shall not be henceforth closed to any pain,
> And what is portioned out to all mankind,
> I shall enjoy deep within myself, contain
> Within my spirit summit and abyss,
> Pile on my breast their agony and bliss,
> And let my own self grow into theirs unfettered,
> Till as they are, at last I, too, am shattered. [1765–75][5]

What this Faust wants for himself is a dynamic process that will include every mode of human experience, joy and misery alike, and that will assimilate them all into his self's unending growth; even the self's destruction will be an integral part of its development.

One of the most original and fruitful ideas in Goethe's *Faust* is the idea of an affinity between the cultural ideal of *self*-development and the real social movement toward *economic* development. Goethe believes that these two modes of development must come together, must fuse into one, before either of these archetypally modern promises can be fulfilled. The only way for modern man to transform himself, Faust and we will find out, is by radically transforming the whole physical and social and moral world he lives in. Goethe's hero is heroic by virtue of liberating tremendous repressed human energies, not only in himself but in all those he touches, and eventually in the whole society around him. But the great developments he initiates—intellectual, moral, economic, social—turn out to exact great human costs. This is the meaning of Faust's relationship with the devil: human powers can be developed only through what Marx called "the powers of the underworld," dark and fearful energies that may erupt with a horrible force beyond all human control. Goethe's *Faust* is the first, and still the best, *tragedy of development*.

The Faust story can be traced through three metamorphoses: he first emerges as The Dreamer, then, through Mephisto's mediation, transforms himself into The Lover, and finally, long after the tragedy of love is over, he will reach his life's climax as The Developer.

First Metamorphosis: The Dreamer

As THE curtain rises,[6] we find Faust alone in his room, late at night, feeling trapped. "Ach! am I still stuck in this jail? this God-damned dreary hole in the wall. . . . Anyway! there's a wide world outside!" (398–99, 418) This scene should ring a bell for us: Faust is part of a long line of modern heroes and heroines whom we find talking to themselves in the middle of the night. Usually, however, the speaker is youthful, impoverished, inexperienced—indeed, forcibly deprived of experience by the class or sexual or racial barriers of a cruel society. Faust is not only middle-aged (he is one of the first middle-aged heroes in modern literature; Captain Ahab may be the next), he is about as successful as a middle-aged man in his world can be. He is recognized and esteemed as a doctor, a lawyer, a theologian, philosopher, scientist, professor and college administrator. We find him surrounded by rare and beautiful books and manuscripts, paintings and diagrams and scientific instruments—all the paraphernalia of a successful life of the mind. And yet everything he has achieved rings hollow, everything around him looks like a pile of junk. He talks endlessly to himself and says he hasn't lived at all.

What makes Faust's triumphs feel like traps to him is that up to now they have all been triumphs of inwardness. For years, through both meditation and experimentation, through reading books and taking drugs—he is a humanist in the truest sense; nothing human is alien to him—he has done all he could do to cultivate his capacity for thought and feeling and vision. And yet the further his mind has expanded, the deeper his sensitivity has grown, the more he has isolated himself, and the more impoverished have become his relationships to life outside—to other people, to nature, even to his own needs and active powers. His culture has developed by detaching itself from the totality of life.

We see Faust call up his magical powers, and a marvelous cosmic vision unfolds before his (and our) eyes. But he turns away from the visionary gleam: "A great show! Yes, but only a show." Contemplative vision, whether mystical or mathematical (or both), keeps the visionary in his place, the place of a passive spectator. Faust craves a connection with the world that will be more vital, at once more erotic and more active.

> Infinite nature, how can I grasp you?
> Where are your breasts, those sources of all life . . .
> Toward which my dry breast strains? [455–60]

The powers of his mind, in turning inward, have turned against him and turned into his prison. He is straining to find a way for the abundance of his inner life to overflow, to express itself through action in the world outside. Leafing through his magical book, he encounters the symbol of the Earth Spirit; and all at once,

> I look and feel my powers growing,
> As if I'd drunk new wine I'm glowing.
> I feel the courage to plunge into the world,
> To bear all earthly grief, all earthly joy;
> To wrestle with the storm, to grapple and clinch,
> To enter the jaws of the shipwreck and never to flinch. [462–67]

He invokes the Earth Spirit and, when it appears, asserts his kinship with it; but the spirit laughs at him and his cosmic aspirations and tells him he will have to find a spirit closer to his real size. Before the Earth Spirit fades from Faust's vision, it flings at him a derisive epithet that will have much resonance in the culture of the centuries to come: *Übermensch*, "Superman." Whole books could be written about the metamorphoses of this symbol; what matters here is the metaphysical and moral context in which it first arises. Goethe brings the *Übermensch* into being not so much to express modern man's titanic strivings but rather to suggest that much of the striving is misplaced. Goethe's Earth Spirit is saying to Faust, Why don't you strive to become a *Mensch*—an authentic human being—instead.

Faust's problems are not his alone; they dramatize larger tensions that agitated all European societies in the years before the French and Industrial Revolutions. The social division of labor in early modern Europe, from the Renaissance and Reformation to Goethe's own time, has produced a large class of relatively independent producers of culture and ideas. These artistic and scientific, legal and philosophical specialists have created, over three centuries, a brilliant and dynamic modern culture. And yet the very division of labor that has enabled this modern culture to live and thrive has also kept its new discoveries and perspectives, its potential wealth and fruitfulness, locked away from the world around it. Faust participates in, and helps to create, a culture that has opened up a range and depth of human desires and dreams far beyond classical and medieval frontiers. At the same time, he is part of a stagnant and closed society that is still encrusted in medieval and feudal social forms: forms like the guild specialization that keeps him and his ideas locked away. As the bearer of a dynamic culture within a stagnant society, he is torn between inner and outer life. In the sixty years it takes Goethe to finish *Faust*, modern intellectuals will find striking new ways to break out of their isolation. These years will see the birth of a new social division of labor in the West, and with it new relationships—adventurous and, as we will see, tragic relationships—between thought and political and social life.

The split I have described in Goethe's Faust is pervasive in European society, and it will be one of the primary sources of international romanticism. But it has a special resonance in countries that are socially, economically and politically "underdeveloped." German intellectuals in Goethe's age were the first to see their society this way when they compared it with England, with France, with expanding America. This "underdeveloped" identity was sometimes a source of shame, at other times (as in German romantic conservatism) a source of pride, most often a volatile mixture of both. This mixture will next occur in nineteenth-century Russia, which we will examine in detail later on. In the twentieth century, intellectuals in the Third World, bearers of avant-garde cultures in backward societies, have experienced the Faustian split with a special intensity. Their inner anguish has often inspired revolutionary visions, actions and creations—as it will for Goethe's Faust at the close of *Part Two*. Just as often, however, it has led only to blind alleys of futility and despair—as it does for Faust at first in the solitary depths of "Night."

As Faust sits up through the night, the cave of his inwardness grows darker and deeper, till at last he resolves to kill himself, to seal himself up once and for all in the tomb his inner space has become. He grasps a flask of poison. But just at the point of his darkest negation, Goethe rescues him and floods him with light and affirmation. The whole room shakes, there is a tremendous pealing of bells outside, the sun comes up and a great angelic choir bursts into song: for it is Easter Sunday. "Christ is arisen, from the womb of decay!" they say. "Burst from your prison, rejoice in the day!" The angels sing soaringly on, the flask drops from the condemned man's lips and he is saved. This miracle has always struck many readers as a crude gimmick, an arbitrary *deus ex machina;* but it is more complex than it seems. What saves Goethe's Faust is not Jesus Christ: he laughs off the manifest Christian content of what he hears. What strikes him is something else:

> And yet, I know this sound so well, from childhood,
> That even now it calls me back to life. [769–70]

These bells, like the apparently random but luminous sights and sounds and sensations that Proust and Freud will explore a century later, bring Faust into touch with the whole buried life of his childhood. Floodgates of memory are thrown open in his mind, waves of lost feeling rush in on him—love, desire, tenderness, unity—and he is engulfed by the depths of a childhood world that his whole adulthood has forced him to forget. Like a drowning man giving himself up to be carried away, Faust has inadvertently opened himself up to a whole lost dimension of his being, and so put himself in touch with sources of energy that can renew him. As he remembers that in his childhood the Easter bells made him cry with joy and yearning, he finds himself crying again, for the first time since he grew up. Now the flow becomes an overflow, and he can emerge from the cave of his study into the spring sunlight; in touch with his deepest springs of feeling, he is ready to start a new life in the world outside.[7]

This moment of Faust's rebirth, composed in 1799 or 1800 and published in 1808, is one of the high points of European Romanticism. (Goethe's *Faust* contains several of these points, and we will explore some of them.) It is easy to see how this scene prefigures some of the great achievements of twentieth-century modernist art and thought: the most obvious links are to Freud, Proust and their various followers. But it may not be clear what Faust's rediscovery of childhood has to do with our other central theme, and the theme of *Faust, Part Two:* modernization. Indeed, many nineteenth- and twentieth-century writers would see Faust's last metamorphosis, his role as an industrial developer, as the very negation of the emotional freedom he has found here. The whole conservative–radical tradition, from Burke through D. H. Lawrence, sees the development of industry as a radical negation of the development of feeling.[8] In Goethe's vision, however, the psychic breakthroughs of Romantic art and thought—in particular the rediscovery of childhood feelings—can liberate tremendous human energies, which may then generate much of the power and initiative for the project of social reconstruction. Thus the importance of the bell scene to the development of Faust—and of *Faust* —reveals the importance of the Romantic project of psychic liberation in the historical process of modernization.

At first, Faust is thrilled to be back in the world. It is Easter Sunday now, and thousands of people are streaming out of the city gates to enjoy their short time in the sun. Faust merges with the crowd—a crowd he has avoided all his adult life—and feels vivified by its liveliness and color and human variety. He gives us a lovely lyrical celebration (903–40) of life—of natural life in the spring, of divine life in the Easter Resurrection, of human and social life (most strikingly the life of the oppressed lower classes) in the public joy of the holiday, of his own emotional life in his return to childhood. Now he feels a connection between his own closeted, esoteric sufferings and strivings and those of the poor urban working people all around him. Before long, individual people emerge from this crowd; although they have not seen Faust for years, they recognize him at once, greet him affectionately and stop to chat and reminisce. Their memories reveal to us another buried dimension of Faust's life. We learn that Doctor Faust began his career as a medical doctor, and his life as a physician's son, practicing medicine and public health among the poor people of this district. At first he is happy to be back in his old neighborhood, grateful for the good feelings of the people he grew up with. But soon his heart sinks; as more memories return, he remembers why he left his old home behind. His father's work, he came to feel, was ignorant patchwork. Practicing medicine as a traditional medieval small craft, they groped randomly and blindly in the dark; although the people loved them, he is sure they killed more people than they saved, and the guilt he has blocked out comes back. It was to overcome this fatal inheritance, he remembers now, that he withdrew from all practical work with people and set out on his solitary intellectual quest, the quest that has led both to knowledge and to intensified isolation, and that almost led him to his death last night.

Faust began the day with a new hope, only to find himself thrown into a new form of despair. He knows he cannot fall back on the claustral comforts of his childhood home—though he also knows he can't let himself drift as far from home as he has been for all these years. He needs to make a connection between the solidity and warmth of life with people—everyday life lived within the matrix of a concrete community—and the intellectual and cultural revolution that has taken place in his head. This is the point of his famous lament "Two souls, alas, are living in my breast." He cannot go on living as a disembodied mind, bold and brilliant in a vacuum; he cannot go on living mindlessly in the world he left. He must participate in society in a way that will give his adventurous spirit room to soar and grow. But it will take "the powers of the underworld" to pull these polarities together, to make such a synthesis work.

In order to bring about the synthesis he craves, Faust will have to embrace a whole new order of paradoxes, paradoxes that are crucial to the structure of both the modern psyche and the modern economy. Goethe's Mephistopheles materializes as the master of these paradoxes—a modern complication of his traditional Christian role as the father of lies. In a typically Goethean irony, he appears to Faust just when Faust feels closest to God. Faust has come back to his solitary study once again to meditate on the human condition. He opens the Bible to the beginning of the Gospel of John: "In the beginning was the Word." He considers this beginning cosmically inadequate, casts about for an alternative and finally chooses and writes a new beginning: "In the beginning was the Deed." He is elated at the idea of a God who defines himself through action, through the primal act of creating the world; he lights up with enthusiasm for the spirit and power of this God; he declares himself ready to reconsecrate his life to creative worldly deeds. His God will be the God of the Old Testament, of the Book of Genesis, who defines himself and proves his divinity by creating the heavens and the earth.*

It is at this point—to work out the meaning of Faust's new revelation and to give him the power to imitate the God he conceives —that the devil appears. Mephistopheles explains that his function is to personify the dark side not only of creativity but of divinity itself. He explicates the subtext of the Judeo-Christian myth of creation: Can Faust be so naive as to think that God really created the world "out of nothing"? In fact, nothing comes from nothing; it is only by virtue of "everything that *you* call sin, destruction, evil" that any sort of creation can go on. (God's creation of the world itself "usurped the ancient rank and realm of Mother Night.") Thus, says Mephisto,

> I am the spirit that negates all!
> And rightly so, for all that comes to be
> Deserves to perish wretchedly . . .

And yet, at the same time he is "part of the power that would / Do nothing but evil, and yet creates the good." (1335ff.) Paradoxically, just as God's creative will and action are cosmically destructive, so the demonic lust for destruction turns out to be creative. Only if

---

* Conflict between Old and New Testament gods, between the God of the Word and the God of the Deed, played an important symbolic role in all nineteenth-century German culture. This conflict, which is articulated in German writers and thinkers from Goethe and Schiller to Rilke and Brecht, was in fact a veiled debate about the modernization of Germany: Should German society throw itself into "Jewish" material and practical activity, that is, into economic development and construction, along with liberal political reform, in the manner of England, France and America? Or, alternately, should it hold aloof from such "worldly" concerns and cultivate an inward-looking "German-Christian" way of life? German philo- and anti-Semitism should be seen in the context of this symbolism, which equated the nineteenth-century Jewish community with the Old Testament God, and equated both with modern modes of activism and worldliness. Marx, in his first Thesis on Feuerbach (1845), points out an affinity between the radical humanist Feuerbach and his reactionary "German-Christian" opponents: both parties "regard . . . only the theoretical attitude as the truly human attitude, while practice is understood only in its dirty-Jewish form"—i.e., the form of the Jewish God who gets his hands dirty making the world. Jerrold Seigel, in *Marx's Fate* (Princeton, 1978), 112–19, offers a perceptive discussion of the equation of Jewishness with practical life in Marx's thought. What needs to be done now is to explore this symbolism in the larger context of modern German history.

Faust works with and through these destructive powers will he be able to create anything in the world: in fact, it is only by working with the devil, and willing "nothing but evil," that he can end up on God's side and "create the good." The road to heaven is paved with bad intentions. Faust yearned to tap the sources of all creativity; now he finds himself face to face with the power of destruction instead. The paradoxes go even deeper: he won't be able to create anything unless he's prepared to let everything go, to accept the fact that all that has been created up to now—and, indeed, all that he may create in the future—must be destroyed to pave the way for more creation. This is the dialectic that modern men must embrace in order to move and live; and it is the dialectic that will soon envelop and move the modern economy, state and society as a whole.*

Faust's fears and scruples are powerful. Years before, remember, he not only left the practice of medicine but withdrew from all practical activity because he and his father were inadvertently killing people. Mephisto's message is not to blame oneself for the casualties of creation, for that is just the way life is. Accept destructiveness as part of your share of divine creativity, and you can throw off your guilt and act freely. No longer need you be inhibited by the moral question *Should I* do it? Out on the open road to self-development, the only vital question is *How to* do it? As a start, Mephisto will show Faust how; later, as the hero lives and grows, he will learn to do it on his own.

How to do it? Mephisto gives some fast advice:

> Hell! you've got hands and feet,
> And head and arse are yours alone;
> If I can find delight in things,
> Does that make them any less my own?
> If I can buy myself six steeds,
> Then aren't all their powers mine?

* Lukács, in *Goethe and His Age*, 197–200, claims that "this new form of the dialectic of good and evil was first perceived by the most penetrating observers of the development of capitalism." Lukács attaches special importance to Bernard de Mandeville, who had argued in his *Fable of the Bees* (1714) that private vice—particularly the economic vice of avarice—would, if pursued by everybody, generate public virtue. Here, as elsewhere, Lukács is valuable in emphasizing the concrete economic and social context of the Faustian tragedy, but mistaken, I believe, in defining this context too narrowly, as a purely capitalist affair. My own perspective emphasizes the contradiction and tragedy in *all* forms of modern enterprise and creativity.

> I can race along, and be a real man,
> As if their two dozen legs were mine. [1820–28]

Money will work as one of the crucial mediators: as Lukacs says, "money as an extension of man, as his power over men and circumstances"; "magical enlargement of the radius of human action by means of money." It is obvious here that capitalism is one of the essential forces in Faust's development.[9] But there are several Mephistophelean themes here that go beyond the scope of the capitalist economy. First, the idea evoked in the first quatrain that man's body and mind, and all their capacities, are there to be *used*, either as tools for immediate application or as resources for long-range development. Body and soul are to be exploited for a maximum return—not, however, in money, but in experience, intensity, felt life, action, creativity. Faust will be glad to use money to pursue these aims (Mephisto will supply him), but the accumulation of money is not itself one of his aims. He will become a sort of symbolic capitalist, but his capital, which he will throw incessantly into circulation and seek endlessly to expand, will be himself. This will make his aims complex and ambiguous in all sorts of ways that the capitalist bottom line is not. Thus, Faust says,

> . . . my mind
> Will not henceforth be closed to any pain,
> And what is portioned out to all mankind,
> I will enjoy deep in myself; contain
> Within my spirit summit and abyss,
> Pile on my breast their agony and bliss,
> And let myself grow into theirs, unfettered,
> Till, as they are, I too will be shattered. [1768–75]

We have here an emerging economy of self-development that can transform even the most shattering human loss into a source of psychic gain and growth.

Mephisto's economics are cruder, more conventional, closer to the crudities of the capitalist economy itself. But there is nothing inherently bourgeois about the experiences he wants Faust to buy. The "six steeds" quatrain suggests that the most valuable commodity, from Mephisto's perspective, is *speed*. First of all, speed has its uses: anyone who wants to do great things in the world will need to move around and through it fast. Beyond this, however, speed generates a distinctively sexual aura: the faster Faust can "race along," the more of a "real man"—the more masculine, the more sexy—he can be. This equation of money, speed, sex and power is far from exclusive to capitalism. It is equally central to the collectivist mystiques of twentieth-century socialism, and to the various populist mythologies of the Third World: the huge posters and sculptural groups in the public squares evoking whole peoples on the move, their bodies straining and heaving as one as they surge forward to overtake the effete and declining West. These aspirations are universally modern, regardless of the ideology under which modernization takes place. Universally modern, too, are the Faustian pressures to use every part of ourselves, and of everybody else, to push ourselves and others as far as we can go.

There is one more universally modern problem here: Where, ultimately, are we supposed to be going? At one point, the point at which he makes his bargain, Faust feels that the crucial thing is to keep moving: "If I stand fast [*Wie ich beharre*], I shall be a slave" (1692–1712); he is willing to give up his soul to the devil the minute he wants to rest—even in contentment. He rejoices at the chance to "plunge into time's whirl, into the torrent of events," and says that what matters is the process, not the result: "it's restless activity that proves a man." (1755–60) And yet, a few moments later, he is worried about what kind of man he is going to prove to be. There must be some sort of ultimate goal to human life; and

> Alas, what am I, if I cannot
> Reach mankind's crown, which merely mocks
> Our senses' craving like a star? [1802–05)]

Mephistopheles answers him in a typically cryptic and equivocal way: "You are in the end—what you are." Faust carries this ambiguity out the door and into the world with him as he goes.

Second Metamorphosis: The Lover

ALL THROUGH the nineteenth century, the "Gretchen tragedy" that concludes *Part One* of *Faust* was seen as the heart of the work; it was instantly canonized and repeatedly celebrated as one of the great love stories of the ages. Contemporary readers and audiences, however, are apt to be skeptical and impatient with this story for some of the very reasons that our ancestors loved it: Goethe's heroine seems simply too good to be true—or to be interesting. Her simple innocence and spotless purity belong more to the world of sentimental melodrama than to tragedy. I want to argue that Gretchen is in fact a more dynamic, interesting and genuinely tragic figure than she is usually made out to be. Her depth and power will come across more vividly, I think, if we focus on Goethe's *Faust* as a story, and a tragedy, of development. This segment of the tragedy will turn out to have three protagonists: Gretchen herself, Faust, and the "little world"—the closed world of the devoutly religious small town from which Gretchen emerges. This was the world of Faust's childhood, the world that in his first metamorphosis he couldn't fit into, although, at his moment of his deepest despair, its bells brought him back to life; it is the world that in his last metamorphosis he will utterly destroy. Now, in his second metamorphosis, he will find a way to confront this world actively, to interact with it; at the same time, he will awaken Gretchen into modes of action and interaction that are distinctively her own. Their love affair will dramatize the tragic impact—at once explosive and implosive—of modern desires and sensibilities on a traditional world.

Before we can fathom the tragedy that lies at the story's end, we must grasp a basic irony that infuses this story from its start: in the course of working with and through the devil, Faust develops into a genuinely better man. The way in which Goethe makes this happen is worth special notice. Like many middle-aged men and women who experience a kind of rebirth, Faust first feels his new powers as sexual powers; erotic life is the sphere in which he first learns to live and act. After a little while in Mephisto's company, Faust becomes radiant and exciting. Some of the changes come through artificial aids: chic and dashing clothes (he has never given a thought to how he looks; all his discretionary income till now has gone for books and equipment) and drugs from the Witch's Kitchen that make Faust look and feel thirty years younger. (This last item will have a special poignancy for those—particularly those of middle age—who lived through the 1960s.)

Besides this, Faust's social status and role change significantly: furnished with easy money and mobility, he is free now to drop out of academic life (as he says he has been dreaming of doing for years) and to move fluidly through the world, a wandering handsome stranger whose very marginality makes him a figure of mystery and romance. But the most important of the devil's gifts is the least artificial, the deepest and most enduring: he encourages Faust to "trust himself"; once Faust learns to do this, he overflows with charm and self-assurance that, along with his native brilliance and energy, are enough to sweep women off their feet. Victorian moralists like Carlyle and G. H. Lewes (Goethe's first great biographer, and George Eliot's lover) gritted their teeth at this metamorphosis and urged their readers to endure it bravely for the sake of ultimate transcendence. But Goethe's own view of Faust's transformation is far more affirmative. Faust is not about to turn into a Don Juan, as Mephistopheles urges him to do now that he has the looks, money and equipment. He is too serious a person to play with bodies and souls, other people's or his own. Indeed, he is even more serious than before, because the scope of his concerns has enlarged. After a life of increasingly narrow self-absorption, he suddenly finds himself interested in other people, sensitive to what they feel and need, ready not only for sex but for love. If we fail to see the real and admirable human growth he goes through, we will be unable to comprehend the human costs of that growth.

We began with Faust intellectually detached from the traditional world he grew up in, but physically still in its grip. Then, through the mediation of Mephisto and his money, he was able to become physically as well as spiritually free. Now he is clearly disengaged from "the little world"; he can return to it as a stranger, survey it as a whole from his emancipated perspective—and, ironically, fall in love with it. Gretchen—the young girl who becomes Faust's first lay, then his first love, finally his first casualty—strikes him first of all as a symbol of everything most beautiful in the world he has left and lost. He is enthralled with her childlike innocence, her small-town simplicity, her Christian humility.

There is a scene (2679–2804) in which he prowls about her room, a neat but shabby room in a poor family's cottage, preparing to leave her a secret gift. He caresses the furniture, celebrates the room as "a shrine," the cottage as "a kingdom of heaven," the armchair he sits in as "a patriarchal throne."

> What sense of calm embraces me,
> Of order and complete content!
> What bounty in this poverty,
> And in this prison, ah, what ravishment! [2691–94]

Faust's voyeuristic idyll is almost unbearably uncomfortable for us because we know—in ways that at this point he cannot know—that his very homage to her room (read: her body, her life) is part of a design on it, the first step in a process that is bound to destroy it. And not out of any malice on his part: it is only by shattering her peaceable kingdom that he will be able to win her love or express his own. On the other hand, he would not be able to subvert her world if she were as happily at home in it as he thinks. We will see that in fact she is as restless here as Faust was in his study, though she lacks the vocabulary to express her discontent until he comes along. If she lacked this inner restlessness, she would be imperme-able to Faust; there would be nothing he could give her. Their tragic romance could not develop if they were not kindred spirits from the start.

Gretchen enters, feeling strange stirrings, and sings to herself a haunting lyric of love and death. Then she discovers the gift—jewels, procured for Faust by Mephisto; she puts them on and looks in the mirror. As she muses to herself, we see that she is more sophisticated in the ways of the world than Faust expects. She knows all about men who bestow rich gifts on poor girls: what they are after, how the story usually ends. She knows, too, how much the poor people around her covet such things. It is a bitter fact of life that, despite the air of pious moralism that chokes this cramped town, a rich man's mistress still counts for more than a

hungry saint. "For gold contend, / On gold depend / All things
. . . Woe to us poor!" (2802–04) Still, for all her wariness, something real and genuinely valuable is happening to her. No one has
ever given her anything; she has grown up poor in love as well as
in money; she has never thought of herself as worthy of gifts or of
the emotions that gifts are supposed to convey. Now, as she looks
at herself in the mirror—maybe for the first time in her life—a
revolution takes place inside her. All at once she becomes self-
reflective; she grasps the possibility of becoming something different, of changing herself—of *developing*. If she was ever at home in
this world, she will never fit in here again.

As the affair unfolds, Gretchen learns to feel both wanted and
loved, both lustful and loving, she is forced to develop a new sense
of herself in a hurry. She mourns that she is not clever. Faust tells
her it doesn't matter, he loves her for her sweet meekness, "supreme among the gifts of nature"; but in fact Goethe shows her
becoming smarter from moment to moment, because it is only
through intelligence that she can cope with the emotional upheavals she is going through. Her innocence must go—not merely her
virginity but, far more important, her naiveté—for she has to
build up and maintain a double life against the surveillance of
family, neighbors, priests, against all the suffocating pressures of
the closed small-town world. She has to learn to defy her own
guilty conscience, a conscience that has the power to terrorize her
far more violently than any external force. As her new feelings
clash with her old social role, she comes to believe that her own
needs are legitimate and important, and to feel a new kind of self-
respect. The angelic child Faust loves disappears before his eyes;
love makes her grow up.

Faust is thrilled to see her grow; he does not see that her growth
is precarious because it has no social underpinning, and receives
no sympathy or confirmation except from Faust himself. At first
her desperation comes across as frenzied passion, and he is delighted. But before long her ardor dissolves into hysteria, and it is
more than he can handle. He loves her, but his love comes in the
context of a full life, surrounded by a past and a future and a wide
world that he is determined to explore; while her love for him has
no context at all, it constitutes her only hold on life. Forced to face
the desperate intensity of her need, Faust panics and leaves town.

Faust's first flight leads him to a romantic "Forest and Cavern," where he meditates alone, in lovely romantic lyrics, on the richness and beauty and beneficence of Nature. The only thing that shakes his serenity here is the presence of Mephistopheles, who reminds him of desires that disturb his peace. Mephisto delivers a caustic critique of Faust's typically romantic Nature worship. This Nature, desexualized, dehumanized, drained of all conflict, subject only to calm contemplation, is a cowardly lie. The desires that drew him to Gretchen are as genuinely natural as anything in this idyllic landscape. If Faust really wants to unite with Nature, he had better confront the human consequences of his own emerging nature. While he makes poetry, the woman whose "naturalness" he loved, and made love to, is coming apart without him. Faust torments himself with guilt. Indeed, he even exaggerates his guilt, minimizing Gretchen's own freedom and initiative in their romance.

Goethe uses this occasion to suggest how self-protective and self-deceptive an emotion guilt can be. If he is an utterly despicable person, hated and mocked by all the gods, what possible good can he do her? The devil, surprisingly, acts as his conscience here, and drags him down into the world of human responsibility and mutuality. But he is soon off again, this time on a more exciting flight. He comes to feel that Gretchen, by giving him all she can give, has made him hungry for more than she can give. He takes a night flight into the Harz Mountains with Mephisto to celebrate Walpurgisnacht, an orgiastic Witches' Sabbath. There Faust enjoys women who are far more experienced and shameless, drugs that are headier, strange and marvelous conversations that are trips in themselves. This scene, the delight of adventurous choreographers and set designers since the 1800s, is one of Goethe's great set pieces; and the reader or onlooker, as much as Faust himself, is bound to be diverted. It is only at the very end of the night that he has an ominous flash, asks after the girl he left behind, and is told the worst.

While Faust was away expanding himself beyond Gretchen's embrace, the "little world" he plucked her out of—that world of "order and complete content" that he found so sweet—has crashed in on her. As word of her new life has got around, her old friends and neighbors have begun to turn on her with a barbaric cruelty and vindictive fury. We hear Valentine, her brother, a vain, mean soldier, tell how he once put her on a pedestal, boasting of her virtue in bars; now, however, every scamp can laugh at him, and he hates her with all his heart. As we listen—and Goethe protracts his diatribes so we will be sure to get the point—we realize that he never noticed her then, any more than he notices her now. Then she was a symbol of heaven, now a symbol of hell, but always a prop for his status and vanity, never a person in her own right— thus Goethe on family feeling in the "little world." Valentine attacks Faust in the street, they fight, Faust wounds him mortally (with Mephisto's help) and runs for his life. With his last breath, Valentine curses his sister obscenely, blames her for his death and urges the townspeople to lynch her. Next, her mother dies, and again she is blamed. (Mephisto is the guilty party here, but neither Gretchen nor her persecutors know.) Next, she has a baby— Faust's baby—and cries for vengeance mount. The townspeople, glad to find a scapegoat for their own guilty lusts, lust for her death. With Faust absent, she is utterly unprotected—in a still-feudal world where not only status but survival depends on the protection of people more powerful than oneself. (Faust, of course, has had excellent protection all along.)

Gretchen takes her sorrows to the cathedral, hoping to find comfort there. Faust, remember, was able to do just that: the church bells called him back from death. But then, Faust could relate to Christianity as he has related to everything and everybody else, including Gretchen herself: he could take what he needed for his own development and leave the rest. Gretchen is too earnest and honest to be selective in this way. Hence the Christian message, which he could interpret as a symbol of life and joy, confronts her with a crushing literalism: "The day of wrath, that day shall dissolve the world in fire," is what she hears. Torment and dread are all her world has to offer her: the bells that saved her lover's life now toll her doom. She feels it all close in: the organ is stifling her, the choir dissolves her heart, the stony pillars imprison her, the vaulted roof is crushing her. She screams, falls to the floor in delirium and delusion. This terrifying scene (3776–3834), expressionistic in its dark and stark intensity, constitutes a particularly scathing judgment on the whole Gothic world—a world that conservative thinkers would idealize extravagantly, especially in Germany, in the century to come. Once, perhaps, the Gothic vision might have offered mankind an ideal of life and activity, of heroic striving toward heaven; now, however, as Goethe presents it at the end of the eighteenth century, all it has to offer is dead weight pressing down on its subjects, crushing their bodies and strangling their souls.

The end comes fast: Gretchen's baby dies, she is thrown in a dungeon, tried as a murderess, condemned to death. In a heart-rending last scene, Faust comes to her cell in the middle of the night. At first she does not know him. She takes him for the executioner and, in a mad but horribly apt gesture, offers up her body to him for the final blow. He swears his love and urges her to escape with him. Everything can be arranged: she need only step out the door and she will be free. She is moved, but she will not move. She says his embrace is cold, he doesn't really love her. And there is some truth here: although he does not want her to die, neither does he want to live with her anymore. Drawn impatiently toward new realms of experience and action, he has come to feel her needs and fears as more and more of a drag. But she does not mean to blame him: even if he really did want her, even if she could bring herself to go, "What good to flee? They lie in wait for me." (4545) They lie inside her. Even as she imagines freedom, the image of her mother rises up, sitting on a rock (the Church? the abyss?), shaking her head, barring the way. Gretchen stays where she is and dies.

Faust is sick with grief and guilt. In an empty field on a dismal day, he confronts Mephisto and cries out against her doom. What kind of a world is it where things can happen this way? At such a point, even poetry dies: Goethe frames this one scene in stark, gnarled prose. The devil's first response is terse and cruel: "Why do you make a community [*Gemeinschaft*] with us if you can't go through with it? You want to fly, but you get dizzy." Human growth has its human costs; anyone who wants it must pay the price, and the price runs high. But then he says something else that, although it sounds harsh, turns out to contain a certain comfort: "She is not the first." If devastation and ruin are built into the process of human development, Faust is at least partially absolved of personal guilt. What could he have done? Even if he had been willing to settle down with Gretchen and stop being "Faustian"— and even if the devil had let him stop (contrary to the original terms of their deal)—he could never have fit into her world. His one direct encounter with a representative of that world, Valentine, erupted into lethal violence. Clearly there is no room for dialogue between an open man and a closed world.

But the tragedy has another dimension. Even if, somehow, Faust had been willing and able to fit himself into Gretchen's world, she herself was no longer willing or able to fit into that world. In moving so dramatically into her life, Faust set her in motion on a course of her own. But her trajectory was bound to end in disaster, for reasons that Faust should have foreseen: reasons of sex and reasons of class. Even in a world of feudal enclaves, a man with lots of money and no attachment to land, family or occupation has virtually unlimited freedom to move. A woman who is poor and embedded in family life has no room to move at all. She is bound to find herself at the mercy of men who have no mercy for a woman who doesn't know her place. In her closed world, madness and martyrdom may be the only places she has to go. Faust, if he learns anything from her fate, learns that if he wants to get involved with other people for the sake of his development, he must take some sort of responsibility for their development—or else be responsible for their doom.

And yet, in fairness to Faust, we must recognize how deeply Gretchen wants to be doomed. There is something dreadfully willful about the way she dies: she brings it on herself. Maybe her self-annihilation is mad, but there is something strangely heroic about it as well. The willfulness and activism of her death confirm her as more than a helpless victim, either of her lover or of her society: she is a tragic protagonist in her own right. Her self-destruction is a form of self-development as authentic as Faust's own. She, as much as he, is trying to move beyond the rigid enclosures of family, church and town, a world where blind devotion and self-abasement are the only roads to virtue. But where his way out of the medieval world is to try to create new values, her way is to take the old values seriously, to really live up to them. Although she rejects the conventions of her mother's world as empty forms, she grasps and embraces the spirit that underlies these forms: a spirit of active dedication and commitment, a spirit that has the moral courage to give up everything, even life, out of faith in its deepest and dearest beliefs. Faust fights the old world, the world he has cut himself loose from, by transforming himself into a new type of person, one who asserts and knows himself, indeed who *becomes* himself through restless, endless self-expansion. Gretchen clashes just as radically with that world by asserting its noblest human qualities: pure concentration and commitment of the self in the name of love. Her way is surely more beautiful, but Faust's is finally more fruitful: it can help the self to survive, to confront the old world more successfully as time goes by.

It is this old world that is the final protagonist in the Gretchen tragedy. When Marx in the *Communist Manifesto* sets out to describe the bourgeoisie's authentic revolutionary achievements, the first achievement on his list is that it has "put an end to all feudal, patriarchal, idyllic conditions." The first part of *Faust* takes place at a moment when, after centuries, these feudal, patriarchal social conditions are breaking down. The vast majority of people still live in "little worlds" like Gretchen's, and those worlds, as we have seen, are formidable enough. Nevertheless, these cellular small towns are beginning to crack: first of all, through contact with explosive marginal figures from outside—Faust and Mephisto, bursting with money, sexuality and ideas, are the classical "outside agitators" so dear to conservative mythology—but more important, through implosion, ignited by the volatile inner developments that their own children, like Gretchen, are going through. Their draconic response to Gretchen's sexual and spiritual deviation is, in effect, a declaration that they will not adapt to their children's will to change. Gretchen's successors will get the point: where she stayed and died, they will leave and live. In the two centuries between Gretchen's time and ours, thousands of "little worlds" will be emptied out, transformed into hollow shells, while their young people head for great cities, for open frontiers, for new nations, in search of freedom to think and love and grow. Ironically, then, the destruction of Gretchen by the little world will turn out to be a crucial phase in the destruction of the little world itself. Unwilling or unable to develop along with its children, the closed town will become a ghost town. Its victims' ghosts will be left with the last laugh.*

* In recent years, as social historians have developed both the demographic tools and the psychological sensitivities to grasp the currents of change in sexual and family life, it has become possible to see with increasing clarity the social realities that underlay the Faust-Gretchen romance. Edward Shorter, in *The Making of The Modern Family* (Basic Books, 1975), especially in Chapters 4 and 6, and Lawrence Stone, in *The Family, Sex and Marriage in England, 1500–1800* (Harper & Row, 1978), especially Chapters 6 and 12, argue that "affective individualism" (Stone's term) played a crucial role in subverting the "feudal, patriarchal, idyllic conditions" of European rural life. Both historians, building on the work of many others, argue that in the late eighteenth and early nineteenth centuries significant numbers of young people were forming intimate bonds that violated traditional family, class,

Our century has been prolific in constructing idealized fantasies of life in tradition-bound small towns. The most popular and influential of these fantasies is elaborated in Ferdinand Toennies' *Gemeinschaft und Gesellschaft* (*Community and Society*, 1887). Goethe's Gretchen tragedy gives us what must be the most devastating portrait in all literature of a *Gemeinschaft*. His portrait should etch in our minds forever the cruelty and brutality of so many of the forms of life that modernization has wiped out. So long as we remember Gretchen's fate, we will be immune to nostalgic yearning for the worlds we have lost.

Third Metamorphosis: The Developer

MOST INTERPRETATIONS and adaptations of Goethe's *Faust* come to an end with the end of *Part One*. After Gretchen's condemnation and redemption, human interest tends to flag. *Part Two*, written between 1825 and 1831, contains much brilliant intellectual play, but its life is suffocated under ponderous allegorical weight. For more than 5000 lines very little happens. It is only in Acts Four

---

religious and occupational boundaries. In virtually all cases, if the man deserted (as Faust did), the woman (like Gretchen) was lost. But if the couple managed to stick together, they could usually marry—often on pretext of premarital pregnancy—and, especially in England, be accepted and integrated into normal life. On the Continent, where small towns were apt to be less tolerant, these couples were more likely to leave in search of environments more supportive of their love. Thus they contributed to the great nineteenth-century demographic movements to cities and new nations and, with their children (born on the move and frequently out of wedlock), established the type of mobile nuclear family that has come to pervade the industrial world today.

For a Jewish version of the Gretchen story, set a century later in the late-developing countryside of Eastern Europe, see Sholem Aleichem's story cycle *Tevye and His Daughters*. These stories, which, like *Faust*, emphasize the liberating but tragic initiatives of young women, end in (partially voluntary, partially forced) emigration to America, and they have played an important part in American Jews' self-awareness. *Tevye and His Daughters* has been recently sweetened for mass (and non-Jewish) consumption in the musical *Fiddler on the Roof*, but the tragic resonances of modern love are still there to be seen and felt.

and Five that dramatic and human energies revive: here Faust's story comes to its climax and its end. Now Faust takes on what I call his third and final metamorphosis. In his first phase, as we saw, he lived alone and dreamed. In his second period, he intertwined his life with the life of another person, and learned to love. Now, in his last incarnation, he connects his personal drives with the economic, political and social forces that drive the world; he learns to build and to destroy. He expands the horizon of his being from private to public life, from intimacy to activism, from communion to organization. He pits all his powers against nature and society; he strives to change not only his own life but everyone else's as well. Now he finds a way to act effectively against the feudal and patriarchal world: to construct a radically new social environment that will empty the old world out or break it down.

Faust's last metamorphosis begins at a point of deep impasse. He and Mephistopheles find themselves alone on a jagged mountain peak staring blankly into cloudy space, going nowhere. They have taken exhausting trips through all history and mythology, explored endless experiential possibilities, and now find themselves at point zero, or even behind that point, for they feel less energetic than they were at the story's start. Mephisto is even more dejected than Faust, for he seems to have run out of temptations; he makes a few desultory suggestions, but Faust only yawns. Gradually, however, Faust begins to stir. He contemplates the sea and evokes lyrically its surging majesty, its primal and implacable power, so impervious to the works of man.

So far this is a typical theme of romantic melancholy, and Mephisto hardly notices. It's nothing personal, he says; the elements have always been this way. But now, suddenly, Faust springs up enraged: Why should men let things go on being the way they have always been? Isn't it about time for mankind to assert itself against nature's tyrannical arrogance, to confront natural forces in the name of "the free spirit that protects all rights"? (10202–05) Faust has begun to use post-1789 political language in a context that no one has ever thought of as political. He goes on: It is outrageous that, for all the vast energy expended by the sea, it merely surges endlessly back and forth—"and nothing is achieved!" This seems natural enough to Mephisto, and no doubt to most of Goethe's audience, but not to Faust himself:

> This drives me near to desperate distress!
> Such elemental power unharnessed, purposeless!
> There dares my spirit soar past all it knew;
> Here I would fight, this I would subdue! [10218–21]

Faust's battle with the elements appears as grandiose as King Lear's, or, for that matter, as King Midas' whipping of the waves. But the Faustian enterprise will be less quixotic and more fruitful, because it will draw on nature's own energy and organize that energy into the fuel for new collective human purposes and projects of which the archaic kings could hardly have dreamt.

As Faust's new vision unfolds, we see him come to life again. Now, however, his visions take on a radically new form: no longer dreams and fantasies, or even theories, but concrete programs, operational plans for transforming earth and sea. "And it is possible! . . . Fast in my mind, plan upon plan unfolds." (10222ff.) Suddenly the landscape around him metamorphoses into a site. He outlines great reclamation projects to harness the sea for human purposes: man-made harbors and canals that can move ships full of goods and men; dams for large-scale irrigation; green fields and forests, pastures and gardens, a vast and intensive agriculture; waterpower to attract and support emerging industries; thriving settlements, new towns and cities to come—and all this to be created out of a barren wasteland where human beings have never dared to live. As Faust unfolds his plans, he notices that the devil is dazed, exhausted. For once he has nothing to say. Long ago, Mephisto called up the vision of a speeding coach as a paradigm of the way for a man to move through the world. Now, however, his protégé has outgrown him: Faust wants to move the world itself.

We suddenly find ourselves at a nodal point in the history of modern self-awareness. We are witnessing the birth of a new social division of labor, a new vocation, a new relationship between ideas and practical life. Two radically different historical movements are converging and beginning to flow together. A great spiritual and cultural ideal is merging into an emerging material and social reality. The romantic quest for self-development, which has carried Faust so far, is working itself out through a new form of romance, through the titanic work of economic development. Faust is transforming himself into a new kind of man, to suit himself to a new occupation. In his new work, he will work out some of the most creative and some of the most destructive potentialities of modern life; he will be the consummate wrecker and creator, the dark and deeply ambiguous figure that our age has come to call "the developer."

Goethe is aware that the issue of development is necessarily a political issue. Faust's projects will require not only a great deal of capital but control over a vast extent of territory and a large number of people. Where can he get this power? The bulk of Act Four provides a solution. Goethe appears uncomfortable with this political interlude: his characters here are uncharacteristically pale and flaccid, and his language loses much of its normal force and intensity. He does not feel at home with any of the existing political options and wants to get through this part fast. The alternatives, as they are defined in Act Four, are: on one side, a crumbling multinational empire left over from the Middle Ages, ruled by an emperor who is pleasant but venal and utterly inept; on the other side, challenging him, a gang of pseudo-revolutionaries out for nothing but power and plunder, and backed by the Church, which Goethe sees as the most voracious and cynical force of all. (The idea of the Church as a revolutionary vanguard has always struck readers as farfetched, but recent events in Iran suggest that Goethe may have been onto something.)

We should not belabor Goethe's travesty of modern revolution. Its main function is to give Faust and Mephisto an easy rationale for the political bargain they make: they lend their minds and their magic to the Emperor, to help him make his power newly solid and efficient. He, in exchange, will give them unlimited rights to develop the whole coastal region, including carte blanche to exploit whatever workers they need and displace whatever indigenous people are in their way. "Goethe could not seek the path of democratic revolution," Lukacs writes. The Faustian political bargain shows Goethe's vision of "another way" to progress: "Unrestricted and grandiose development of productive forces will render political revolution superfluous."[10] Thus Faust and Mephisto help the Emperor prevail, Faust gets his concession, and, with great fanfare, the work of development begins.

Faust throws himself passionately into the task at hand. The pace is frenzied—and brutal. An old lady, whom we will meet again, stands at the edge of the construction site and tells the story:

> Daily they would vainly storm,
> Pick and shovel, stroke for stroke;
> Where the flames would nightly swarm
> Was a dam when we awoke.
> Human sacrifices bled,
> Tortured screams would pierce the night,
> And where blazes seaward spread
> A canal would greet the light. [11123–30]

The old lady feels that there is something miraculous and magical about all this, and some commentators think that Mephistopheles must be operating behind the scenes for so much to be accomplished so fast. In fact, however, Goethe assigns Mephisto only the most peripheral role in this project. The only "forces of the underworld" at work here are the forces of modern industrial organization. We should note, too, that Goethe's Faust—unlike some of his successors, especially in the twentieth century—makes no striking scientific or technological discoveries: his men seem to use the same picks and shovels that have been in use for thousands of years. The key to his achievement is a visionary, intensive and systematic organization of labor. He exhorts his foremen and overseers, led by Mephisto, to "use every possible means / To get crowds and crowds of workers here. / Spur them on with enjoyment, or be severe, / Pay them well, allure or repress!" (11551–54) The crucial point is to spare nothing and no one, to overleap all boundaries: not only the boundary between land and sea, not only traditional moral limits on the exploitation of labor, but even the primary human dualism of day and night. All natural and human barriers fall before the rush of production and construction.

Faust revels in his new power over people: it is, specifically, to use an expression of Marx's, a power over labor-power.

> Up from your beds, my servants! Every man!
> Let happy eyes behold my daring plan.
> Take up your tools, stir shovel now and spade!
> What has been staked must at once be made.

He has found, at last, a fulfilling purpose for his mind:

> What I have thought, I hasten to fulfill;
> The master's word alone has real might! . . .

> To consummate the greatest work,
> One mind for a thousand hands will do. [11501–10]

But if he drives his workers hard, so he drives himself. If church bells called him back to life long ago, it is the sound of shovels that vivifies him now. Gradually, as the work comes together, we see Faust radiant with real pride. He has finally achieved a synthesis of thought and action, used his mind to transform the world. He has helped mankind assert its rights over the anarchic elements, "bringing the earth back to itself, / Setting the waves a boundary, / Putting a ring around the ocean." (11541–43) And it is a collective victory that mankind will be able to enjoy once Faust himself is gone. Standing on an artificial hill created by human labor, he overlooks the whole new world that he has brought into being, and it looks good. He knows he has made people suffer ("Human sacrifices bled, / Tortured screams would pierce the night . . ."). But he is convinced that it is the common people, the mass of workers and sufferers, who will benefit most from his great works. He has replaced a barren, sterile economy with a dynamic new one that will "open up space for many millions / To live, not securely, but free for action [tätig-frei]." It is a physical and natural space, but one that has been created through social organization and action.

> Green are the meadows, fertile; and in mirth,
> Both men and herds live on this newest earth,
> Settled along the edges of a hill
> Raised by the masses' bold, industrious will.
> A veritable paradise inside,
> Then let the dams be licked by the raging tide,
> And as it gnaws, to rush in with full force,
> Communal will fills gaps and checks its course.
> This is the highest wisdom that I own,
> The best that mankind ever knew;
> Freedom and life are earned by those alone
> Who conquer them each day anew.
> Surrounded by such danger, each one thrives,
> Childhood, manhood and age lead active lives.
> In such a crowd I would be glad to be,
> To walk on free ground with people who are free! [11563–80]

Walking the earth with the pioneers of his new settlement, Faust feels far more at home than he ever felt with the friendly but narrow folk of his home town. These are new men, as modern as Faust himself. Emigrants and refugees from a hundred Gothic villages and towns—from the world of *Faust, Part One*—they have moved here in search of action, adventure, an environment in which they can be, like Faust himself, *tätig-frei*, free to act, freely active. They have come together to form a new kind of community: a community that thrives not on the repression of free individuality in order to maintain a closed social system, but on free constructive action in common to protect the collective resources that enable every individual to become *tätig-frei*.

These new men feel at home in their community and proud of it: they are eager to pit their communal will and spirit against the sea's own energy, confident they will win. In the midst of such men —men whom he has helped to come into their own—Faust can fulfill a hope he has cherished ever since he has left his father's side: to belong to an authentic community, to work with and for people, to use his mind in action in the name of a general will and welfare. Thus the process of economic and social development generates new modes of self-development, ideal for men and women who can grow into the emerging new world. Finally, too, it generates a home for the developer himself.

Thus Goethe sees the modernization of the material world as a sublime spiritual achievement; Goethe's Faust, in his activity as "the developer" who puts the world on its new path, is an archetypal modern hero. But the developer, as Goethe conceives him, is tragic as well as heroic. In order to understand the developer's tragedy, we must judge his vision of the world not only by what it sees—by the immense new horizons it opens up for mankind— but also by what it does not see: what human realities it refuses to look at, what potentialities it cannot bear to face. Faust envisions, and strives to create, a world where personal growth and social progress can be had without significant human costs. Ironically, his tragedy will stem precisely from his desire to eliminate tragedy from life.

As Faust surveys his work, the whole region around him has been renewed, and a whole new society created in his image. Only one small piece of ground along the coast remains as it was before. This is occupied by Philemon and Baucis, a sweet old couple who have been there from time out of mind. They have a little cottage on the dunes, a chapel with a little bell, a garden full of linden trees. They offer aid and hospitality to shipwrecked sailors and wanderers. Over the years they have become beloved as the one source of life and joy in this wretched land. Goethe borrows their name and situation from Ovid's *Metamorphoses,* in which they alone offer hospitality to Jupiter and Mercury in disguise, and, accordingly, they alone are saved when the gods flood and destroy the whole land. Goethe gives them more individuality than they have in Ovid, and endows them with distinctively Christian virtues: innocent generosity, selfless devotion, humility, resignation. Goethe invests them, too, with a distinctively modern pathos. They are the first embodiments in literature of a category of people that is going to be very large in modern history: people who are in the way—in the way of history, of progress, of development; people who are classified, and disposed of, as obsolete.

Faust becomes obsessed with this old couple and their little piece of land: "That aged couple should have yielded, / I want their lindens in my grip, / Since these few trees that are denied me / Undo my worldwide ownership. . . . Hence is our soul upon the rack, / To feel, amid plenty, what we lack." (11239–52) They must go, to make room for what Faust comes to see as the culmination of his work: an observation tower from which he and his public can "gaze out into the infinite" at the new world they have made. He offers Philemon and Baucis a cash settlement, or else resettlement on a new estate. But what should they do with money at their age? And how, after living their whole long lives here, and approaching the end of life here, can they be expected to start new lives somewhere else? They refuse to move. "Resistance and such stubbornness / Thwart the most glorious success, / Till in the end, to one's disgust, / One soon grows tired of being just." (11269–72)

At this point, Faust commits his first self-consciously evil act. He summons Mephisto and his "mighty men" and orders them to get the old people out of the way. He does not want to see it, or to know the details of how it is done. All that interests him is the end result: he wants to see the land cleared next morning, so the new construction can start. This is a characteristically modern style of evil: indirect, impersonal, mediated by complex organizations and institutional roles. Mephisto and his special unit return in "deep night" with the good news that all has been taken care of. Faust,

suddenly concerned, asks where the old folks have been moved—
and learns that their house has been burned to the ground and
they have been killed. Faust is aghast and outraged, just as he was
at Gretchen's fate. He protests that he didn't say anything about
violence; he calls Mephisto a monster and sends him away. The
prince of darkness departs gracefully, like the gentleman he is; but
he laughs before he leaves. Faust has been pretending not only to
others but to himself that he could create a new world with clean
hands; he is still not ready to accept responsibility for the human
suffering and death that clear the way. First he contracted out all
the dirty work of development; now he washes his hands of the
job, and disavows the jobber once the work is done. It appears that
the very process of development, even as it transforms a wasteland
into a thriving physical and social space, recreates the wasteland
inside the developer himself. This is how the tragedy of development works.

But there is still an element of mystery about Faust's evil act.
Why, finally, does he do it? Does he really need that land, those
trees? Why is his observation tower so important? And why are
those old people so threatening? Mephisto sees no mystery in it:
"Here, too, occurs what long occurred: / Of Naboth's vineyard you
have heard." (11286–87) Mephisto's point, in invoking King
Ahab's sin in 1 Kings 21, is that there is nothing new about Faust's
acquisition policy: the narcissistic will to power, most rampant in
those who are most powerful, is the oldest story in the world. No
doubt he is right; Faust does get increasingly carried away by the
arrogance of power. But there is another motive for the murder
that springs not merely from Faust's personality, but from a collective, impersonal drive that seems to be endemic to modernization:
the drive to create a homogeneous environment, a totally modernized space, in which the look and feel of the old world have disappeared without a trace.

To point to this pervasive modern need, however, is only to
widen the mystery. We are bound to be in sympathy with Faust's
hatred for the closed, repressive, vicious Gothic world where he
began—the world that destroyed Gretchen, and she was not the
first. But at this point in time, the point where he becomes obsessed with Philemon and Baucis, he has already dealt the Gothic
world a death blow: he has opened up a vibrant and dynamic new
social system, a system oriented toward free activity, high produc-

tivity, long-distance trade and cosmopolitan commerce, abundance for all; he has cultivated a class of free and enterprising workers who love their new world, who will risk their lives for it, who are willing to pit their communal strength and spirit against any threat. It is clear, then, that there is no real danger of reaction. So why is Faust threatened by even the slightest traces of the old world? Goethe unravels, with extraordinary penetration, the developer's deepest fears. This old couple, like Gretchen, personify all the best that the old world has to give. They are too old, too stubborn, maybe even too stupid, to adapt and to move; but they are beautiful people, the salt of the earth where they are. It is their beauty and nobility that make Faust so uneasy. "My realm is endless to the eye, behind my back I hear it mocked." He comes to feel that it is terrifying to look back, to look the old world in the face. "And if I'd rest there from the heat, their shadows would fill me with fear." If he were to stop, something dark in those shadows might catch up with him. "That little bell rings, and I rage!" (11235–55)

Those church bells, of course, are the sound of guilt and doom and all the social and psychic forces that destroyed the girl he loved: who could blame him for wanting to silence that sound forever? Yet church bells were also the sound that, when he was ready to die, called him back to life. There is more of him in those bells, and in that world, than he likes to think. The magical power of the bells on Easter morning was their power to put Faust in touch with his childhood. Without that vital bond with his past— the primary source of spontaneous energy and delight in life—he could never have developed the inner strength to transform the present and future. But now that he has staked his whole identity on the will to change, and on his power to fulfill that will, his bond with his past terrifies him.

> That bell, those lindens' sweet perfume
> Enfolds me like a church or tomb.

For the developer, to stop moving, to rest in the shadows, to let the old people enfold him, is death. And yet, to such a man, working under the explosive pressures of development, burdened by the guilt it brings him, the bells' promise of peace must sound like bliss. Precisely because Faust finds the bells so sweet, the woods so lovely, dark and deep, he drives himself to wipe them out.

Commentators on Goethe's *Faust* rarely grasp the dramatic and human resonance of this episode. In fact, it is central to Goethe's historical perspective. Faust's destruction of Philemon and Baucis turns out to be the ironic climax of his life. In killing the old couple, he turns out to be pronouncing a death sentence on himself. Once he has obliterated every trace of them and their world, there is nothing left for him to do. Now he is ready to pronounce the words that seal his life in fulfillment and deliver him over to death: *Verweile doch, du bist so schoen!* Why should Faust die now? Goethe's reasons refer not only to the structure of *Faust, Part Two,* but to the whole structure of modern history. Ironically, once this developer has destroyed the pre-modern world, he has destroyed his whole reason for being in the world. In a totally modern society, the tragedy of modernization—including its tragic hero—comes naturally to an end. Once the developer has cleared all the obstacles away, he himself is in the way, and he must go. Faust turns out to have been speaking truer than he knew: Philemon and Baucis' bells were tolling for him after all. Goethe shows us how the category of obsolete persons, so central to modernity, swallows up the man who gave it life and power.

Faust almost grasps his own tragedy—almost, but not quite. As he stands on his balcony at midnight and contemplates the smoldering ruins that will be cleared for construction in the morning, the scene suddenly and jarringly shifts: from the concrete realism of the construction site, Goethe plunges us into the symbolist ambience of Faust's inner world. Suddenly four spectral women in gray hover toward him, and proclaim themselves: they are Need, Want, Guilt, and Care. All these are forces that Faust's program of development has banished from the outer world; but they have crept back as specters inside his mind. Faust is disturbed but adamant, and he drives the first three specters away. But the fourth, the vaguest and deepest one, Care, continues to haunt him. Faust says, "I have not fought my way through to freedom yet." He means by this that he is still beset by witchcraft, magic, ghosts in the night. Ironically, however, the threat to Faust's freedom springs not from the presence of these dark forces but from the absence that he soon forces on them. His problem is that he cannot look these forces in the face and live with them. He has striven mightily to create a world without want, need or guilt; he does not even feel guilty about Philemon and Baucis—though he does feel sad. But he cannot banish care from his mind. This might turn out to be a source of inner strength, if only he could face the fact. But he cannot bear to confront anything that might cast shadows on his brilliant life and works. Faust banishes care from his mind, as he banished the devil not long before. But before she departs, she breathes on him—and with her breath strikes him blind. As she touches him, she tells him that he has been blind all along; it is out of inner darkness that all his visions and all his actions have grown. The care he would not admit has stricken him to depths far past his understanding. He destroyed those old people and their little world—his own childhood world—so that his scope of vision and activity could be infinite; in the end, the infinite "Mother Night," whose power he refused to face, is all he sees.

Faust's sudden blindness gives him, in his last scene on earth, an archaic and mythical grandeur: he appears as a peer of Oedipus and Lear. But he is a distinctively modern hero, and his wound only drives him to drive himself and his workers harder, to finish the job fast:

> Deep night now seems to fall more deeply still,
> Yet inside me there shines a brilliant light;
> What I have thought I hasten to fulfill;
> The master's word alone has real might! [11499ff.]

And so it goes. It is at this point, amid the noise of construction, that he declares himself fully alive, and hence ready to die. Even in the dark his vision and energy go on thriving; he goes on striving, developing himself and the world around him to the very end.

Epilogue: The Faustian and Pseudo-Faustian Age

WHOSE TRAGEDY is this? Where does it belong in the long-term history of modern times? If we try to place the particular type of modern environment Faust creates, we may at first be perplexed. The clearest analogue seems to be the tremendous surge of industrial expansion that England had been going through since the 1760s. Lukacs makes this connection, and argues that the last act of *Faust* is a tragedy of "capitalist development" in its early industrial phase.[11] The trouble with this scenario is that, if we pay attention to the text, Faust's motives and aims are clearly not capitalistic. Goethe's Mephisto, with his eye for the main chance, his celebration of selfishness and his genial lack of scruple, conforms pretty well to one type of capitalist entrepreneur; but Goethe's Faust is worlds away. Mephisto is constantly pointing out money-making opportunities in Faust's development schemes; but Faust himself couldn't care less. When he says that he means "to open to the millions living-space / not danger-proof, but free to run their race," it's clear that he is not building for his own short-term profit but rather for the long-range future of mankind, for the sake of public freedom and happiness that will come to fruition only long after he is gone. If we try to cut the Faustian project to fit the capitalist bottom line, we will cut out what is noblest and most original in it and, moreover, what makes it genuinely tragic. Goethe's point is that the deepest horrors of Faustian development spring from its most honorable aims and its most authentic achievements.

If we want to locate Faustian visions and designs in the aged Goethe's time, the place to look is not in the economic and social realities of that age but in its radical and Utopian dreams; and, moreover, not in the capitalism of that age, but in its socialism. In the late 1820s, when the last sections of *Faust* were being composed, Goethe's favorite reading included the Parisian newspaper *Le Globe*, one of the organs of the Saint-Simonian movement, and the place where the word *socialisme* was coined just before Goethe's death in 1832.[12] The *Conversations with Eckermann* are full of admiring references to the young writers of *Le Globe*, who included many scientists and engineers, and who seem to have appreciated Goethe as much as he appreciated them. One of the standard features of *Le Globe*, as of all Saint-Simonian writings, was a constant stream of proposals for long-range development projects on an enormous scale. These projects were far beyond both the financial and the imaginative resources of early nineteenth-century capitalists, who—especially in England, where capitalism was then

most dynamic—were oriented primarily toward the individual entrepreneur, the quick conquest of markets, the pursuit of immediate profits. Neither were those capitalists much interested in the
social benefits that the Saint-Simonians claimed wholesale development would bring: steady jobs and decent incomes for "the most
numerous and the poorest class," abundance and welfare for all,
new modes of community that would synthesize medieval organi-
cism with modern energy and rationality.

It was no surprise that the Saint-Simonian projects were almost
universally dismissed as "Utopian." But it was precisely this Uto-
pianism that captured the old Goethe's imagination. Here he is, in
1827, effusive over proposals for a Panama Canal, and thrilled by
the prospect of a glorious future opening up for America. "I
should be amazed if the United States were to let an opportunity
of getting such a work into their own hands escape. It may be
foreseen that this young state, with its decided predilection to the
West, will in thirty or forty years have occupied and peopled the
large tract of land beyond the Rocky Mountains."

Looking further ahead, Goethe is confident "that along the Pa-
cific Ocean, where nature has already formed the most capacious
and secure harbors, important commercial towns will gradually
arise, for the furtherance of a great intercourse between China
and the East Indies and the United States." With the emergence
of a sphere of transpacific activity, "more rapid communication
between the Eastern and Western shores of North America . . .
would be not only desirable, but absolutely indispensable." A canal
between the seas, either at Panama or farther north, will play a
leading role in this development. "All this is reserved for the future, and for an enterprising spirit." Goethe is certain that "innumerable benefits would result to the whole human race." He
dreams, "Would that I might live to see it! but I shall not." (He is
seventy-eight, five years from death.) Goethe then conjures up two
more enormous development projects, also Saint-Simonian favor-
ites: a canal connecting the Danube and the Rhine, and another
across the Isthmus of Suez. "Would I could live to see these great
works! it would well be worth the trouble to last some fifty years
more for the purpose."[13] We see Goethe in the process of transforming Saint-Simonian proposals and programs into poetic vision, the vision that will be realized and dramatized in Faust's last
act.

Goethe synthesizes these ideas and hopes into what I will call the "Faustian model" of development. This model gives top priority to gigantic energy and transportation projects on an international scale. It aims less for immediate profits than for long-range development of productive forces, which it believes will produce the best results for everyone in the end. Instead of letting entrepreneurs and workers waste themselves in piecemeal and fragmentary and competitive activities, it will strive to integrate them all. It will create a historically new synthesis of private and public power, symbolized by the union of Mephistopheles, the private freebooter and predator who executes much of the dirty work, and Faust, the public planner who conceives and directs the work as a whole. It will open up an exciting and ambiguous world-historical role for the modern intellectual—Saint-Simon called this figure "the organizer"; I have favored "the developer"—who can bring material, technical and spiritual resources together, and transform them into new structures of social life. Finally, the Faustian model will present a new mode of authority, authority that derives from the leader's capacity to satisfy modern people's persistent need for adventurous, open-ended, ever-renewed development.

Many of the youthful Saint-Simonians of *Le Globe* went on to distinguish themselves, mostly under Napoleon III, as brilliant innovators in finance and industry. They organized the French railway system; established the Crédit Mobilier, an international investment bank to finance the emerging world energy industry; and realized one of Goethe's fondest dreams, the Suez Canal. But their visionary style and scale were generally disparaged in a century when development tended to be private and piecemeal, governments remained in the background (and often masked their economic activity), and public initiative, long-range planning and systematic regional development were scorned as vestiges of the despised mercantilist age. It is only in the twentieth century that Faustian development has come into its own. In the capitalist world it has emerged most vividly in the proliferation of "public authorities" and superagencies designed to organize immense construction projects, especially in transportation and energy: canals and railroads, bridges and highways, dams and irrigation systems, hydroelectric power plants, nuclear reactors, new towns and cities, the exploration of outer space.

In the last half century, and particularly since World War Two, these authorities have brought about a "changing balance of public and private power" that has been a crucial force in capitalist success and growth.[14] Faustian developers as diverse as David Lilienthal, Robert Moses, Hyman Rickover, Robert McNamara and Jean Monnet have utilized this balance to make contemporary capitalism far more imaginative and resilient than the capitalism of a century ago. But Faustian development has been an equally potent force in the socialist states and economies that have emerged since 1917. Thomas Mann, writing in 1932, in the midst of the first Soviet Five-Year Plan, was right to place Goethe at the nodal point where "the bourgeois attitude passes over . . .—if one takes the word broadly enough and is willing to understand it undogmatically—into communism."[15] We can find visionaries and authorities in power all over the world today, both in the most advanced state capitalist and social democratic countries, and in dozens of nations which, regardless of their reigning ideology, see themselves as "underdeveloped" and see rapid, heroic development as the first order of the day. The distinctive environment that formed the stage for Faust's last act—the immense construction site, stretching out boundlessly in every direction, constantly changing and forcing the characters in the foreground themselves to change—has become the stage for world history in our time. Faust the Developer, still only marginal in Goethe's world, would be completely at home in our own.

Goethe presents a model of social action around which advanced and backward societies, capitalist and socialist ideologies, converge. But Goethe insists that it is a terrible and tragic convergence, sealed with victims' blood, undergirded with their bones, which come in the same forms and colors everywhere. The process of development that the creative spirits of the nineteenth century conceived as a great human adventure has become in our own era a life-and-death necessity for every nation and every social system in the world. As a result, development authorities everywhere have accumulated powers that are enormous, uncontrolled and all too often lethal.

In so-called underdeveloped countries, systematic plans for rapid development have generally meant systematic repression of the masses. This has generally taken two forms, distinct though generally interfused. The first form has involved squeezing every last drop of labor power out of the masses—Faust's "human sacrifices bled, / tortured screams would pierce the night"—in order to build up the forces of production, and at the same time drastically restricting mass consumption so as to create a surplus for reinvestment in the economy. The second form entails seemingly gratuitous acts of destruction—Faust's destruction of Philemon and Baucis and their bells and trees—not to create any material utility but to make the symbolic point that the new society must burn all its bridges so there can be no turning back.

The first Soviet generation, especially during the Stalin years, provides vivid illustrations of both these horrors. Stalin's first showcase development project, the White Sea Canal (1931–33), sacrificed hundreds of thousands of workers, more than enough to leave any contemporary capitalist project behind. And Philemon and Baucis could stand all too well for the millions of peasants who were killed between 1932 and 1934 because they stood in the way of the state's plan to collectivize the land they had won in the Revolution barely a decade before.

But what makes these projects pseudo-Faustian rather than Faustian, and less tragedy than theater of cruelty and absurdity, is the heartbreaking fact—often forgotten in the West—that *they didn't work.* The Nixon-Brezhnev wheat deal of 1972 should be enough to remind us that the Stalinist attempt to collectivize the land not only killed millions of people but dealt Russian agriculture a crippling blow from which it has never recovered. As for the canal, Stalin seems to have been so intent on creating a highly visible *symbol* of development that he pushed and squeezed the project in ways that only retarded the *reality* of development. Thus the workers and engineers were never allowed the time, money or equipment necessary to build a canal that would be deep enough and safe enough to carry twentieth-century cargoes; consequently, the canal has never played any significant role in Soviet commerce or industry. All the canal could support, apparently, were tourist steamers, which in the 1930s were abundantly stocked with Soviet and foreign writers who obligingly proclaimed the glories of the work. The canal was a triumph of publicity; but if half the care that went into the public relations campaign had been devoted to the work itself, there would have been far fewer victims and far more real development—and the project would have been a genuine tragedy, rather than a brutal farce in which real people were killed by pseudo-events.*

It should be noted that in the pre-Stalin 1920s it was still possible to talk about the human costs of progress in an honest and searching way. Isaac Babel's stories, for example, are full of tragic losses. In "Froim Grach" (rejected by the censors), a Falstaffian old scoundrel is summarily killed for no particular reason by the Cheka. When the narrator, himself a member of the political police, protests indignantly, the killer replies, "Tell me as a Chekist, tell me as a revolutionary: What good was this man for the society of the future?" The heartbroken narrator can think of no retort, but resolves to commit to paper his vision of the flawed but good lives that the Revolution has destroyed. This story, although set in the recent past (the Civil War), was a dire and apt prophecy of the future, including Babel's own.[16]

What makes the Soviet case especially depressing is that its pseudo-Faustian enormities have been enormously influential in the Third World. So many contemporary ruling classes, right-wing colonels and left-wing commissars alike, have shown a fatal weakness (more fatal to their subjects, alas, than to themselves) for grandiose projects and campaigns that incarnate all Faust's gigantism and ruthlessness without any of his scientific and technical ability, organizational genius or political sensitivity to people's real desires and needs. Millions of people have been victimized by disastrous development policies, megalomaniacally conceived, shoddily and insensitively executed, which in the end have developed little but the rulers' own fortunes and powers. The pseudo-Fausts of the Third World have in barely a generation become remarkably adept at manipulating images and symbols of progress—the public relations of pseudo-development has become a major worldwide industry, thriving from Tehran to Peking—but notoriously inept at generating real progress to compensate for the real misery and devastation they bring. From time to time, a people manages to overthrow its pseudo-developers—like that world-class

* Solzhenitsyn devotes some of his most scathingly brilliant pages to the canal. He shows how the technical imperatives of the work were systematically violated from the start, in the rush to prove to the world that modernization could be accomplished overnight by force of revolutionary will alone. He is particularly trenchant on the readiness of writers, including some of the very best, to embrace and to transmit techno-pastoral lies, even as the bodies lay under their feet. *The Gulag Archipelago*, translated by Thomas Whitney (Harper & Row, 1975), II, 85–102.

pseudo-Faustian, the Shah of Iran. Then, for a little while—rarely for more than a little while—the people may be able to take their development into their own hands. If they are shrewd and fortunate, they will create and enact their own tragedies of development, simultaneously playing the Faustian and the Gretchen / Philemon-Baucis roles. If they are less than lucky, their brief moments of revolutionary action will lead only to new suffering that leads nowhere at all.

In the world's more advanced industrial countries, development has followed more authentically Faustian forms. Here the tragic dilemmas that Goethe defined have remained urgently in force. It has turned out—and Goethe could have predicted it—that under the pressures of the modern world economy the process of development must itself go through perpetual development. Where it does, all people, things, institutions and environments that are innovative and avant-garde at one historical moment will become backward and obsolescent in the next. Even in the most highly developed parts of the world, all individuals, groups and communities are under constant relentless pressure to reconstruct themselves; if they stop to rest, to be what they are, they will be swept away. The climactic clause in Faust's contract with the devil—that if ever he stops and says to the moment, *"Verweile doch, du bist so schoen,"* he will be destroyed—is played out to the bitter end in millions of lives every day.

In the past generation, even through the economic slumps of the 1970s, the process of development has spread, often at a frantic pace, into the most remote, isolated and backward sectors of advanced societies. It has transformed innumerable pastures and cornfields into chemical plants, corporate headquarters, suburban shopping centers— How many orange groves are left in California's Orange County? It has transformed thousands of urban neighborhoods into freeways and parking lots, or into World Trade Centers and Peachtree Plazas, or into abandoned, burnt-out wilderness—where, ironically, grass has come to grow again amid the rubble, while small bands of brave homesteaders stake out new frontiers—or, in the standard urban success story of the 1970s, into glossy airbrushed antique-stained parodies of their old selves. From abandoned New England mill towns to ravaged strip-mined Appalachian hills to the South Bronx to the Love Canal, insatiable development has left spectacular devastation in its wake.

The shovels that made Faust feel alive, and that made the last sound he heard as he died, have become gigantic earth movers capped with dynamite today. Even yesterday's Fausts may find themselves today's Philemons and Baucises, buried under debris where their lives used to be, even as today's enthusiastic young Gretchens are crushed in the gears or blinded by the light.

Within these advanced industrial countries, the Faust myth has served as a kind of prism over the past two decades for a great array of visions of our lives and times. Norman O. Brown's *Life Against Death* (1959) offered a fascinating critique on the Faustian ideal of development: "The Faustian restlessness of man in history shows that men are not satisfied by the satisfaction of their conscious desires." Brown hoped that psychoanalytic thought, radically interpreted, might "offer a way out of the nightmare of endless 'progress' and endless Faustian discontent, a way out of the human neurosis, a way out of history." Brown saw Faust primarily as a symbol of historical action and anguish: "Faustian man is history-making man." But if sexual and psychic repression could somehow be overcome—this was Brown's hope—then "man would be ready to live instead of making history." Then "the restless career of Faustian man would come to an end, because he would be satisfied and could say, *Verweile doch, du bist so schoen.*"[17] Like Marx after *The Eighteenth Brumaire of Louis Bonaparte,* and Joyce's Stephen Dedalus, Brown experienced history as a nightmare from which he longed to awaken; only his nightmare, unlike theirs, was not any particular historical situation but historicity as such. Nevertheless, intellectual initiatives like Brown's helped many of his contemporaries to develop a critical perspective on their historical period, the comfortably anxious Eisenhower Age. Even though Brown professed to detest history, to take on Faust was a historical gesture of great audacity—indeed, a Faustian act in its own right. As such, it both prefigured and nourished the radical initiatives of the decade to come.

Faust went on to play important symbolic roles in the 1960s. A Faustian vision can be said to have animated some of the primary radical movements and *journées* of the decade. It was dramatized very powerfully, for instance, in the mass march on the Pentagon in October 1967. This demonstration, immortalized in Norman Mailer's *Armies of the Night,* featured a symbolic exorcism conducted in the name of a vast syncretistic assemblage of familiar and strange gods, with the intention of driving the Pentagon's structural demons out. (Liberated from the weight, the exorcists proclaimed, the building would levitate and float or fly away.) For participants in this remarkable event, the Pentagon appeared as an apotheosis of Faustian construction gone awry, construction that had built up the world's most virulent engines of destruction. Our demonstration, and our peace movement as a whole, appeared to us as an indictment of America's Faustian visions and designs. And yet this demonstration was a spectacular construction in its own right, one of the American left's few chances to express its own Faustian longings and aptitudes. The weird ambivalences of the whole affair made themselves felt as we got closer and closer to the building—one could get closer forever, it seemed, without ever getting there: it was a perfect Kafkaesque environment—and some of the little figures inside it, framed by their windows far away (windows are ultra-Faustian, Spengler said), pointed, waved and even reached out their arms to embrace us, as if to recognize us as kindred spirits, to tempt or welcome us in. Before long, soldiers' clubs and tear gas would clarify the distance between us; but the clarification was a relief when it came, and there were some troubled moments before it did. Mailer may have had that day in mind when he wrote, at the decade's very end, "We are a Faustian age determined to meet the Lord or the Devil before we are done, and the ineluctable ore of the authentic is the only key to the lock." [18]

Faust occupied an equally important place in the very different 1960s vision that we might call "pastoral." His role in the 1960s pastoral was, specifically, to be put out to pasture. His desires, drives and abilities had enabled mankind to make great scientific discoveries and create magnificent art, to transform the natural and human environment, and to create the economy of abundance that advanced industrial societies had recently come to enjoy. Now, however, by virtue of his very success, "Faustian Man" had rendered himself historically obsolete. This argument was developed by the molecular biologist Gunther Stent in a book called *The Coming of the Golden Age: A View of the End of Progress*. Stent used the breakthroughs in his own science, specifically the recent discovery of DNA, to argue that the achievements of modern culture left that culture fulfilled but exhausted, with nowhere to go. Modern economic development and overall social evolution had, by a similar process, reached the end of the road. History had brought us to a point where "economic well-being [is] taken for granted," and there is nothing significant left to do:

> And here we can perceive an internal contradiction of progress. Progress depends on the exertion of Faustian Man, whose motivational mainspring is the idea of the will to power. But when progress has proceeded far enough to provide an ambiance of economic security for Everyman, the resulting social ethos works against the transmission of the will to power in childrearing, and hence aborts the development of Faustian Man.

Through a process of natural selection, Faustian Man was being gradually phased out of the environment he had created.

The younger generation, who had grown up in this new world, clearly felt no desire for action or achievement, power or change; they cared only to say *Verweile doch, du bist so schoen,* and to keep on saying it till the end of their days. These children of the future could even now be seen happily lolling, singing, dancing, making love and getting high in the California sunshine. Lucas Cranach's painting of the Golden Age, which Stent reproduced as his frontispiece, was "nothing other than a prophetic vision of a hippie Be-In in Golden Gate State Park."

The coming consummation of history would be "a period of general stasis"; art, science and thought might continue to exist, but they would do little but mark time and enjoy life. "The Faustian Man of the Iron Age will view with distaste the prospect of his affluent successors devoting their abundance of leisure time to sensual pleasures. . . . But Faustian Man had better face up to the fact that it is precisely *this* Golden Age that is the fruit of all his frantic efforts, and that it does no good now to wish it otherwise." Stent ended on a rueful, almost elegiac note: "Millennia of doing arts and sciences will finally transform the tragicomedy of life into a happening."[19] But nostalgia for a Faustian life was the surest sign of obsolescence. Stent had seen the future, and it played.*

* This book took on a new half-life in the 1970s, when it helped to shape the rhetoric, and perhaps the sensibility, of California Governor Jerry Brown. Brown distributed copies widely among his aides, and referred reporters to it for clues to his thinking.

It is hard to reread these 1960s pastorals without feeling nostalgic sadness, not so much for the hippies of yesterday as for the virtually unanimous belief—shared by those upright citizens who most despised hippies—that a life of stable abundance, leisure and well-being was here to stay. There have in fact been many continuities between the 1960s and the 1970s; but the economic euphoria of those years—John Brooks, in his account of Wall Street in the 1960s, called them "the go-go years"—now seems to belong to some wholly other world. Within a remarkably short time, the buoyant confidence was utterly wiped away. The gathering energy crisis of the 1970s, with all its ecological and technological, economic and political dimensions, generated waves of disenchantment, bitterness and perplexity, sometimes extending to panic and hysterical despair; inspired healthy and trenchant cultural self-scrutiny, which, however, often degenerated into morbid self-laceration and self-hate.

Now, for many people, the whole centuries-long project of modernization appeared as a disastrous mistake, an act of cosmic hubris and evil. And the figure of Faust now appeared in a new symbolic role, as the demon who had wrenched mankind out of its primal unity with nature and propelled us all along the road to catastrophe. "There is a sense of desperation in the air," a cultural anthropologist named Bernard James wrote in 1973, "a sense that . . . man has been pitchforked by science and technology into a new and precarious age." In this age, "the final period of decay of our Western world, the predicament is clear. We live on an over-crowded and pillaged planet, and we must stop the pillage or perish." James's book had a typical 1970s-apocalyptic title, *The Death of Progress*. His lethal force, which would have to be killed before it killed all mankind, was "the modern progress culture," and its number-one culture hero was Faust. James did not appear quite ready to denounce and renounce all modern scientific discoveries and technological innovations. (He showed a special tenderness for computers.) But he did say that "the need to know, as we understand it today, may be a lethal cultural sport," which would have to be radically restricted, if not abolished root and branch. After painting vivid pictures of possible nuclear disasters, and of monstrous forms of biological warfare and genetic engineering, James insisted that these horrors flowed quite naturally from "the laboratory-born lust to commit the sin of Faust."[20] Thus the Faustian villain, dear to the Captain America comics and *New*

Yorker editorials of the late 1970s, reared his head. It is remarkable to see 1960s-pastoral and 1970s-apocalypse come together in the behalf that in order for mankind to prevail—to live the good life (1960s) or to live any life at all (1970s)—"Faustian Man" must go.

As debate intensified through the 1970s on the desirability and limits of economic growth, and on the best ways to produce and conserve energy, ecologists and anti-growth writers typecast Faust as the primal "Growthman," who would tear the whole world apart for the sake of insatiable expansion, without asking or caring what unlimited growth would do to nature or to man. I need not say that this is an absurd distortion of the Faust story, flattening tragedy into melodrama. (It does, however, resemble the Faustian puppet plays that Goethe saw as a child.) What seems to me more important is to point out the intellectual vacuum that emerges when Faust is removed from the scene. The various advocates of solar, wind and water power, of small and decentralized sources of energy, of "intermediate technologies," of the "steady-state economy," are virtually all enemies of large-scale planning, of scientific research, of technological innovation, of complex organization.[21] And yet, in order for any of their visions or plans to be actually adopted by any substantial number of people, the most radical redistribution of economic and political power would have to take place. And even this—which would mean the dissolution of General Motors, Exxon, Con Edison and their peers, and the redistribution of all their resources to the people—would be only a prelude to the most extensive and staggeringly complex reorganization of the whole fabric of everyday life. Now there is nothing bizarre about the anti-growth or soft-energy arguments in themselves, and, indeed, they are full of ingenious and imaginative ideas. What is bizarre is that, given the magnitude of the historical tasks before them, they should exhort us, in E. F. Schumacher's words, to "think small." The paradoxical reality which escapes most of these writers is that in modern society only the most extravagant and systematic "thinking big" can open up channels for "thinking small."[22] Thus the advocates of energy shrinkage, limited growth and decentralization, instead of damning Faust, should embrace him as their man of the hour.

The one contemporary group that has not only used the Faustian myth but grasped its tragic depth is the collectivity of nuclear scientists. The nuclear pioneers who experienced the blinding flash of light at Alamogordo ("Good God! . . . the long-haired boys have lost control!") never learned how to exorcise that dreaded Earth Spirit that had sprung from the creativity of their minds. The "concerned scientists" of the postwar era established a distinctively Faustian style of science and technology, driven by guilt and care, by anguish and contradiction. This was radically opposed to the Panglossian mode of science prevalent in military, industrial and political ruling circles then as now, which assures the world that any trouble is fortuitous and transient and that everything works out for the best in the end. At a time when all governments were systematically lying to their peoples about the dangers of nuclear arms and nuclear war, it was above all the haunted veterans of the Manhattan Project (Leo Szilard was the most heroic) who lucidly explained the truth, and who began the fight for civilian control of atomic energy, for restrictions on nuclear tests and for international arms control.[23] Their project helped to keep a Faustian awareness alive, and to refute the Mephistophelean claim that men could do great things in the world only by blotting out their sense of guilt and care. They showed how these emotions can lead to action that may be supremely creative in organizing the survival of mankind.

In recent years, the debates over nuclear power have generated new metamorphoses of Faust. In 1971, Alvin Weinberg, a brilliant physicist and administrator, and for many years the director of the Oak Ridge Laboratory, invoked Faust at the climax of a much-discussed address on "Social Institutions and Nuclear Energy":

> We nuclear people [Weinberg said] have made a Faustian bargain with society. On the one hand, we offer—in the catalytic nuclear burner—an inexhaustible source of energy . . . But the price we demand of society for this magical energy source is both a vigilance and a longevity of social institutions that we are quite unaccustomed to.

In order to support this "all but infinite source of cheap and clean energy," the men, societies and nations of the future would have to maintain an "eternal vigilance" against grave dangers which might be not only technological—this might in fact be the least of it—but social and political.

Now this book is no place to argue the merits and demerits of

Weinberg's disturbing and deeply problematical nuclear bargain. But it is a place to take note of what he does to Faust. The decisive point here is that the scientists ("we nuclear people") are no longer playing the Faustian part. Instead, they fill the role of the party that offers the deal—that is, Mephistopheles, "the spirit that negates all"! A strange, richly ambiguous self-image, not likely to win public relations awards, but appealing in its (perhaps unconscious) candor. But it is the corollary to this piece of casting that matters most: Weinberg's Faustian protagonist, who must decide to accept or reject the deal, is "the society"—that is, all of us. His implicit point is that the Faustian drive for development has come to animate all modern men and women. As a result, "The society must make the choice, and this is a choice that we nuclear people have no right to dictate."[24] This means that, whatever Faustian bargains are made—or not made—we have not only the right but the obligation to be in on their making.* We cannot hand over the responsibility for development to any cadre of experts—precisely because, in the project of development, we are all experts. If scientific and technological cadres have accumulated vast powers in modern society, it is only because their visions and values have echoed, amplified and realized our own. They have only created means to fulfill ends embraced by the modern public: open-ended development of self and society, incessant transformation of the whole inner and outer world. As members of modern society, we are responsible for the directions in which we develop, for our goals and achievements, for their human costs. Our society will never be able to control its eruptive "powers of the underworld" if it pretends that its scientists are the only ones out of control. One of the basic facts of modern life is that we are all "long-haired boys" today.

Modern men and women in search of self-knowledge might well begin with Goethe, who gave us in *Faust* our first tragedy of devel-

* Unfortunately, much of the force of Weinberg's Faustian insight was undermined by his other central paradigm: the endlessly quoted image of a "nuclear priesthood." This secular holy order, whose founding father Weinberg apparently hoped to be, would protect mankind against the risks of nuclear energy, and vanquish forever its diabolical potentialities. Weinberg obviously did not grasp the radical contradiction between his Faustian vision and his ecclesiastical aspirations. Some acquaintance with Goethe's *Faust,* and especially with Goethe's treatment of the Church and priests, might have made this antinomy clear.

opment. It is a tragedy that nobody wants to confront—neither advanced nor backward countries, neither capitalist nor socialist ideologues—but that everybody continues to re-enact. Goethe's perspectives and visions can help us see how the fullest and deepest critique of modernity may come from those who most ardently embrace its adventure and romance. But if *Faust* is a critique, it is also a challenge—to our world even more than to Goethe's own—to imagine and to create new modes of modernity, in which man will not exist for the sake of development, but development for the sake of man. Faust's unfinished construction site is the vibrant but shaky ground on which we must all stake out and build up our lives.

All That Is Solid Melts Into Air: Marx, Modernism and Modernization

*There followed on the birth of mechanization and modern industry
. . . a violent encroachment like that of an avalanche in its intensity
and its extent. All bounds of morals and nature, of age and sex, of day
and night, were broken down. Capital celebrated its orgies.*
                              —*Capital*, **Volume One**

I am the spirit that negates all.
                              —**Mephistopheles in** *Faust*

Innovative Self-Destruction!
                              —**Ad for Mobil Oil, 1978**

*In the research racks at Shearson Hayden Stone, Inc., a commodity
letter bears this quotation from Heraclitus: "All is flux, nothing stays
still."*
                              —**"Shearson Chief Builds a New Wall Street
                              Giant," story in** *New York Times*, **1979**

. . . that apparent disorder that is in actuality the highest degree of
bourgeois order.
                              —Dostoevsky in London, 1862

WE HAVE seen how Goethe's *Faust,* universally regarded as a prime
expression of the modern spiritual quest, reaches its fulfillment—
but also its tragic catastrophe—in the transformation of modern
material life. We will soon see how the real force and originality of
Marx's "historical materialism" is the light it sheds on modern
spiritual life. Both writers share a perspective that was far more
widely shared in their time than it is in our own: a belief that
"modern life" comprises a coherent whole. This sense of wholeness underlies Pushkin's judgment of *Faust* as "an *Iliad* of modern
life." It presupposes a unity of life and experience that embraces
modern politics and psychology, modern industry and spirituality,
the modern ruling classes and the modern working classes. This
chapter will attempt to recover and reconstruct Marx's vision of
modern life as a whole.

It is worth noting that this sense of wholeness goes against the
grain of contemporary thought. Current thinking about modernity is broken into two different compartments, hermetically
sealed off from one another: "modernization" in economics and
politics, "modernism" in art, culture and sensibility. If we try to
locate Marx amid this dualism, we will find that, not surprisingly,
he bulks large in the literature on modernization. Even writers
who claim to refute him generally recognize his work as a primary
source and point of reference for their own.[1] On the other hand,
in the literature on modernism, Marx is not recognized in any way
at all. Modernist culture and consciousness are often traced back
to his generation, the generation of the 1840s—to Baudelaire,
Flaubert, Wagner, Kierkegaard, Dostoevsky—but Marx himself
does not rate even a branch in the genealogical tree. If he is even
mentioned in this company, it is as a foil, or sometimes as a survival
of an earlier and more innocent age—the Enlightenment, say—
whose clear vistas and solid values modernism has supposedly destroyed. Some writers (like Vladimir Nabokov) depict Marxism as
a dead weight that crushes the modernist spirit; others (like Georg
Lukács in his communist years) see Marx's outlook as far saner,
healthier and more "real" than those of the modernists; but everybody seems to agree that he and they are worlds apart.[2]

And yet, the closer we get to what Marx actually said, the less this dualism makes sense. Take an image like this: "All that is solid melts into air." The cosmic scope and visionary grandeur of this image, its highly compressed and dramatic power, its vaguely apocalyptic undertones, the ambiguity of its point of view—the heat that destroys is also superabundant energy, an overflow of life—all these qualities are supposed to be hallmarks of the modernist imagination. They are just the sort of thing we are prepared to find in Rimbaud or Nietzsche, Rilke or Yeats—"Things fall apart, the center does not hold." In fact, this image comes from Marx, and not from any esoteric long-hidden early manuscript, but from the heart of the *Communist Manifesto*. It comes as the climax of Marx's description of "modern bourgeois society." The affinities between Marx and the modernists are even clearer if we look at the whole of the sentence from which our image is drawn: "All that is solid melts into air, all that is holy is profaned, and men at last are forced to face with sober senses the real conditions of their lives and their relations with their fellow men."[3] Marx's second clause, which proclaims the destruction of everything holy, is more complex and more interesting than the standard nineteenth-century materialist assertion that God does not exist. Marx is moving in the dimension of time, working to evoke an ongoing historical drama and trauma. He is saying that the aura of holiness is suddenly missing, and that we cannot understand ourselves in the present until we confront what is absent. The final clause—"and men at last are forced to face . . ."—not only describes a confrontation with a perplexing reality but acts it out, forces it on the reader—and, indeed, on the writer too, for "men," *die Menschen* as Marx says, are all in it together, at once subjects and objects of the pervasive process that melts everything solid into air.

If we follow this modernist "melting" vision, we will find it throughout Marx's works. Everywhere it pulls like an undertow against the more "solid" Marxian visions we know so well. It is especially vivid and striking in the *Communist Manifesto*. Indeed, it opens up a whole new perspective on the *Manifesto* as the archetype of a century of modernist manifestos and movements to come. The *Manifesto* expresses some of modernist culture's deepest insights and, at the same time, dramatizes some of its deepest inner contradictions.

At this point it would not be unreasonable to ask, Aren't there already more than enough interpretations of Marx? Do we really need a modernist Marx, a kindred spirit of Eliot and Kafka and Schoenberg and Gertrude Stein and Artaud? I think we do, not only because he's there, but because he has something distinctive and important to say. Marx, in fact, can tell us as much about modernism as it can tell us about him. Modernist thought, so brilliant in illuminating the dark side of everyone and everything, turns out to have some repressed dark corners of its own, and Marx can shine new light on these. Specifically, he can clarify the relationship between modernist culture and the bourgeois economy and society—the world of "modernization"—from which it has sprung. We will see that they have far more in common than either modernists or bourgeoisie would like to think. We will see Marxism, modernism and the bourgeoisie caught up in a strange dialectical dance, and if we follow their movements we can learn some important things about the modern world we all share.

I.

The Melting Vision and Its Dialectic

THE CENTRAL drama for which the *Manifesto* is famous is the development of the modern bourgeoisie and proletariat, and the struggle between them. But we can find a play going on within this play, a struggle inside the author's consciousness over what is really going on and what the larger struggle means. We might describe this conflict as a tension between Marx's "solid" and his "melting" visions of modern life.

The *Manifesto*'s first section, "Bourgeois and Proletarians" (473–83), sets out to present an overview of what is now called the process of modernization, and sets the stage for what Marx believes will be its revolutionary climax. Here Marx describes the solid institutional core of modernity. First of all, there is the emergence of a world market. As it spreads, it absorbs and destroys whatever local and regional markets it touches. Production and consumption—and human needs—become increasingly international and cosmopolitan. The scope of human desires and demands is enlarged far beyond the capacities of local industries, which consequently collapse. The scale of communications becomes worldwide, and technologically sophisticated mass media emerge. Capital is concentrated increasingly in a few hands. Independent peasants and artisans cannot compete with capitalist mass production, and they are forced to leave the land and close their workshops. Production is increasingly centralized and rationalized in highly automated factories. (It is no different in the country, where farms became "factories in the field," and the peasants who do not leave the countryside are transformed into agricultural proletarians.) Vast numbers of the uprooted poor pour into cities, which grow almost magically—and cataclysmically—overnight. In order for these great changes to go on with relative smoothness, some legal, fiscal and administrative centralization must take place; and it does take place wherever capitalism goes. National states arise and accumulate great power, although that power is continually undermined by capital's international scope. Meanwhile, industrial workers gradually awaken to some sort of class consciousness and activate themselves against the acute misery and chronic oppression in which they live. As we read this, we find ourselves on familiar ground; these processes are still going on around us, and a century of Marxism has helped to establish a language in which they make sense.

As we read on, however, if we read with our full attention, strange things begin to happen. Marx's prose suddenly becomes luminous, incandescent; brilliant images succeed and blend into one another; we are hurtled along with a reckless momentum, a breathless intensity. Marx is not only describing but evoking and enacting the desperate pace and frantic rhythm that capitalism imparts to every facet of modern life. He makes us feel that we are part of the action, drawn into the stream, hurtled along, out of control, at once dazzled and menaced by the onward rush. After a few pages of this, we are exhilarated but perplexed; we find that the solid social formations around us have melted away. By the time Marx's proletarians finally appear, the world stage on which they were supposed to play their part has disintegrated and meta-morphosed into something unrecognizable, surreal, a mobile con-struction that shifts and changes shape under the players' feet. It is as if the innate dynamism of the melting vision has run away with Marx and carried him—and the workers, and us—far beyond the range of his intended plot, to a point where his revolutionary script will have to be radically reworked.

The paradoxes at the heart of the *Manifesto* are manifest almost at its very start: specifically, from the moment Marx starts to de-scribe the bourgeoisie. "The bourgeoisie," he begins, "has played a most revolutionary role in history." What is startling about Marx's next few pages is that he seems to have come not to bury the bourgeoisie, but to praise it. He writes an impassioned, enthu-siastic, often lyrical celebration of bourgeois works, ideas and achievements. Indeed, in these pages he manages to praise the bourgeoisie more powerfully and profoundly than its members have ever known how to praise themselves.

What have the bourgeois done to deserve Marx's praise? First of all, they have "been the first to show what man's activity can bring about." Marx does not mean that they have been the first to cele-brate the idea of *vita activa,* an activistic stance toward the world. This has been a central theme of Western culture since the Renais-sance; it has taken on new depths and resonances in Marx's own century, in the age of romanticism and revolution, of Napoleon and Byron and Goethe's *Faust.* Marx himself will develop it in new directions,[4] and it will go on evolving into our own era. Marx's point is that what modern poets, artists and intellectuals have only dreamed of the modern bourgeoisie has actually done. Thus it has "accomplished wonders that far surpass Egyptian pyramids, Roman aqueducts, Gothic cathedrals"; it has "conducted expedi-tions that put all former migrations of nations and crusades in the shade." Its genius for activity expresses itself first in great projects of physical construction—mills and factories, bridges and canals, railroads, all the public works that constitute Faust's final achieve-ment—these are the pyramids and cathedrals of the modern age. Next there are the immense movements of peoples—to cities, to frontiers, to new lands—which the bourgeoisie has sometimes in-spired, sometimes brutally enforced, sometimes subsidized, and always exploited for profit. Marx, in a stirring, evocative para-graph, transmits the rhythm and drama of bourgeois activism:

The bourgeoisie, in its reign of barely a hundred years, has created more massive and more colossal productive power than have all previous generations put together. Subjection of nature's forces to man, machinery, application of chemistry to agriculture and industry, steam navigation, railways, electric telegraphs, clearing of whole continents for cultivation, canalization of rivers, whole populations conjured out of the ground—what earlier century had even an intimation that such productive power slept in the womb of social labor? [473–75]

Marx is neither the first nor the last writer to celebrate the triumphs of modern bourgeois technology and social organization. But his paean is distinctive both in what it emphasizes and in what it leaves out. Although Marx identifies himself as a materialist, he is not primarily interested in the things that the bourgeoisie creates. What matters to him is the processes, the powers, the expressions of human life and energy: men working, moving, cultivating, communicating, organizing and reorganizing nature and themselves—the new and endlessly renewed modes of activity that the bourgeoisie brings into being. Marx does not dwell much on particular inventions and innovations in their own right (in the tradition that runs from Saint-Simon through McLuhan); what stirs him is the active and generative process through which one thing leads to another, dreams metamorphose into blueprints and fantasies into balance sheets, the wildest and most extravagant ideas get acted on and acted out ("whole populations conjured out of the ground") and ignite and nourish new forms of life and action.

The irony of bourgeois activism, as Marx sees it, is that the bourgeoisie is forced to close itself off from its richest possibilities, possibilities that can be realized only by those who break its power. For all the marvelous modes of activity the bourgeoisie has opened up, the only activity that really means anything to its members is making money, accumulating capital, piling up surplus value; all their enterprises are merely means to this end, in themselves of no more than transient and intermediary interest. The active powers and processes that mean so much to Marx appear as mere incidental by-products in the minds of their producers. Nevertheless, the bourgeois have established themselves as the first ruling class whose authority is based not on who their ancestors were but on what they themselves actually do. They have produced vivid new images and paradigms of the good life as a life of action. They have proved that it is possible, through organized and concerted action, to really change the world.

Alas, to the bourgeois' embarrassment, they cannot afford to look down the roads they have opened up: the great wide vistas may turn into abysses. They can go on playing their revolutionary role only by denying its full extent and depth. But radical thinkers and workers are free to see where the roads lead, and to take them. If the good life is a life of action, why should the range of human activities be limited to those that are profitable? And why should modern men, who have seen what man's activity can bring about, passively accept the structure of their society as it is given? Since organized and concerted action can change the world in so many ways, why not organize and work together and fight to change it still more? The "revolutionary activity, practical-critical activity" that overthrows bourgeois rule will be an expression of the active and activistic energies that the bourgeoisie itself has set free. Marx began by praising the bourgeoisie, not by burying it; but if his dialectic works out, it will be the virtues for which he praised the bourgeoisie that will bury it in the end.

The second great bourgeois achievement has been to liberate the human capacity and drive for development: for permanent change, for perpetual upheaval and renewal in every mode of personal and social life. This drive, Marx shows, is embedded in the everyday workings and needs of the bourgeois economy. Everybody within reach of this economy finds himself under pressure of relentless competition, whether from across the street or across the world. Under pressure, every bourgeois, from the pettiest to the most powerful, is forced to innovate, simply in order to keep his business and himself afloat; anyone who does not actively change on his own will become a passive victim of changes draconically imposed by those who dominate the market. This means that the bourgeoisie, taken as a whole, "cannot exist without constantly revolutionizing the means of production." But the forces that shape and drive the modern economy cannot be compartmentalized and cut off from the totality of life. The intense and relentless pressure to revolutionize production is bound to spill over and transform what Marx calls "conditions of production" (or, alternately, "productive relationships") as well, "and, with them, all social conditions and relationships."*

At this point, propelled by the desperate dynamism he is striving to grasp, Marx makes a great imaginative leap:

> Constant revolutionizing of production, uninterrupted disturbance of all social relations, everlasting uncertainty and agitation, distinguish the bourgeois epoch from all earlier times. All fixed, fast-frozen relationships, with their train of venerable ideas and opinions, are swept away, all new-formed ones become obsolete before they can ossify. All that is solid melts into air, all that is holy is profaned, and men at last are forced to face with sober senses the real conditions of their lives and their relations with their fellow men. [338]

skepti-cism

Where does all this leave us, the members of "modern bourgeois society"? It leaves us all in strange and paradoxical positions. Our lives are controlled by a ruling class with vested interests not merely in change but in crisis and chaos. "Uninterrupted disturbance, everlasting uncertainty and agitation," instead of subverting this society, actually serve to strengthen it. Catastrophes are transformed into lucrative opportunities for redevelopment and renewal; disintegration works as a mobilizing and hence an integrating force. The one specter that really haunts the modern ruling class, and that really endangers the world it has created in its image, is the one thing that traditional elites (and, for that matter, traditional masses) have always yearned for: prolonged solid stability. In this world, stability can only mean entropy, slow death, while our sense of progress and growth is our only way of knowing for sure that we are alive. To say that our society is falling apart is only to say that it is alive and well.

What kinds of people does this permanent revolution produce? In order for people, whatever their class, to survive in modern society, their personalities must take on the fluid and open form of this society. Modern men and women must learn to yearn for change: not merely to be open to changes in their personal and social lives, but positively to demand them, actively to seek them

---

* The German word here is *Verhältnisse*, which can be translated as "conditions," "relations," "relationships," "circumstances," "affairs," and so on. At different points in this essay it will be translated in different ways, whichever seems most apt in context.

out and carry them through. They must learn not to long nostalgically for the "fixed, fast-frozen relationships" of the real or fantasized past, but to delight in mobility, to thrive on renewal, to look forward to future developments in their conditions of life and their relations with their fellow men.

Marx absorbs this developmental ideal from the German humanist culture of his youth, from the thought of Goethe and Schiller and their romantic successors. This theme and its development, still very much alive in our own day—Erik Erikson is its most distinguished living exponent—may be Germany's deepest and most lasting contribution to world culture. Marx is perfectly clear about his links to these writers, whom he is constantly citing and alluding to, and to their intellectual tradition. But he understands, as most of his predecessors did not—the crucial exception is the aged Goethe, the author of *Faust, Part Two*—that the humanistic ideal of self-development grows out of the emerging reality of bourgeois economic development. Thus, for all Marx's invective against the bourgeois economy, he embraces enthusiastically the personality structure that this economy has produced. The trouble with capitalism is that, here as elsewhere, it destroys the human possibilities it creates. It fosters, indeed forces, self-development for everybody; but people can develop only in restricted and distorted ways. Those traits, impulses and talents that the market can use are rushed (often prematurely) into development and squeezed desperately till there is nothing left; everything else within us, everything nonmarketable, gets draconically repressed, or withers away for lack of use, or never has a chance to come to life at all.[5]

The ironic and happy solution to this contradiction will occur, Marx says, when "the development of modern industry cuts from under its feet the very grounds on which the bourgeoisie produces and appropriates products." The inner life and energy of bourgeois development will sweep away the class that first brought it to life. We can see this dialectical movement as much in the sphere of personal as in economic development: in a system where all relationships are volatile, how can capitalist forms of life—private property, wage labor, exchange value, the insatiable pursuit of profit—alone hold still? Where the desires and sensibilities of people in every class have become open-ended and insatiable, attuned to permanent upheavals in every sphere of life, what can possibly keep them fixed and frozen in their bourgeois roles? The more furiously bourgeois society agitates its members to grow or die, the more likely they will be to outgrow it itself, the more furiously they will eventually turn on it as a drag on their growth, the more implacably they will fight it in the name of the new life it has forced them to seek. Thus capitalism will be melted by the heat of its own incandescent energies. After the Revolution, "in the course of development," after wealth is redistributed, class privileges are wiped away, education is free and universal, and workers control the ways in which work is organized, then—so Marx prophesies at the *Manifesto*'s climactic moment—then, at last,

> In place of the old bourgeois society, with its classes and class antagonisms, we will have an association in which the free development of each will be the condition for the free development of all. [353]

Then the experience of self-development, released from the demands and distortions of the market, can go on freely and spontaneously; instead of the nightmare that bourgeois society has made it, it can be a source of joy and beauty for all.

I want to step back from the *Communist Manifesto* for a moment to emphasize how crucial the developmental ideal is to Marx, from his earliest writings to his last. His youthful essay on "Estranged Labor" (or "Alienated Labor"), written in 1844, proclaims, as the truly human alternative to estranged labor, work that will enable the individual to "freely develop his physical and spiritual [or mental] energies."[6] In *The German Ideology* (1845–46), the goal of communism is "the development of a totality of capacities in the individuals themselves." For "only in community with others has each individual the means of cultivating his gifts in all directions; only in the community, therefore, is personal freedom possible."[7] In Volume One of *Capital*, in the chapter on "Machinery and Modern Industry," it is essential to communism that it transcend the capitalist division of labor:

> . . . the partially developed individual, who is merely the bearer of one specialized social function, must be replaced by the fully developed individual, fit for a variety of labors, ready to face any change in production, for whom the different social functions he

performs are only so many modes of giving free scope to his own natural and acquired powers.[8]

This vision of communism is unmistakably modern, first of all in its individualism, but even more in its ideal of development as the form of the good life. Here Marx is closer to some of his bourgeois and liberal enemies than he is to traditional exponents of communism, who, since Plato and the Church Fathers, have sanctified self-sacrifice, distrusted or loathed individuality and yearned for a still point at which all strife and all striving will reach an end. Once again we find Marx more responsive to what is going on in bourgeois society than are the members and supporters of the bourgeoisie themselves. He sees in the dynamics of capitalist development—both the development of each individual and of society as a whole—a new image of the good life: not a life of definitive perfection, not the embodiment of prescribed static essences, but a process of continual, restless, open-ended, unbounded growth. Thus he hopes to heal the wounds of modernity through a fuller and deeper modernity.[9]

→ perfectionism?

2.

Innovative Self-Destruction

WE CAN see now why Marx gets so excited and enthusiastic about the bourgeoisie and the world it has made. Now we must confront something even more perplexing: next to the *Communist Manifesto*, the whole body of capitalist apologetics, from Adam Ferguson to Milton Friedman, is remarkably pale and empty of life. The celebrants of capitalism tell us surprisingly little of its infinite horizons, its revolutionary energy and audacity, its dynamic creativity, its adventurousness and romance, its capacity to make men not merely more comfortable but more alive. The bourgeoisie and its ideologists have never been known for their humility or modesty, yet they seem strangely determined to hide much of their light under a bushel. The reason, I think, is that there is a dark side to this light that they cannot blot out. They are dimly aware of this, and deeply embarrassed and frightened by it, to the point that they will ignore or deny their own strength and creativity rather than look their virtues in the face and live with them.

What is it that the members of the bourgeoisie are afraid to recognize in themselves? Not their drive to exploit people, to treat them purely as means or (in economic rather than moral language) as commodities. The bourgeoisie, as Marx sees it, doesn't lose much sleep over this. After all, they do it to one another, and even to themselves, so why shouldn't they do it to everybody else? The real source of trouble is the bourgeois claim to be the "Party of Order" in modern politics and culture. The immense amounts of money and energy put into building, and the self-consciously monumental character of so much of this building—indeed, throughout Marx's century, every table and chair in a bourgeois interior resembled a monument—testify to the sincerity and seriousness of this claim. And yet, the truth of the matter, as Marx sees, is that everything that bourgeois society builds is built to be torn down. "All that is solid"—from the clothes on our backs to the looms and mills that weave them, to the men and women who work the machines, to the houses and neighborhoods the workers live in, to the firms and corporations that exploit the workers, to the towns and cities and whole regions and even nations that embrace them all —all these are made to be broken tomorrow, smashed or shredded or pulverized or dissolved, so they can be recycled or replaced next week, and the whole process can go on again and again, hopefully forever, in ever more profitable forms.

The pathos of all bourgeois monuments is that their material strength and solidity actually count for nothing and carry no weight at all,[10] that they are blown away like frail reeds by the very forces of capitalist development that they celebrate. Even the most beautiful and impressive bourgeois buildings and public works are disposable, capitalized for fast depreciation and planned to be obsolete, closer in their social functions to tents and encampments than to "Egyptian pyramids, Roman aqueducts, Gothic cathedrals."*

---

* Engels, just a few years before the *Manifesto*, in *The Condition of the Working Class in England in 1844*, was appalled to find that workers' housing, built by speculators for fast profits, was constructed to last for only forty years. He little suspected that this would become the archetypal pattern of construction in bourgeois society. Ironi-

If we look behind the sober scenes that the members of our bourgeoisie create, and see the way they really work and act, we see that these solid citizens would tear down the world if it paid. Even as they frighten everyone with fantasies of proletarian rapacity and revenge, they themselves, through their inexhaustible dealing and developing, hurtle masses of men, materials and money up and down the earth, and erode or explode the foundations of everyone's lives as they go. Their secret—a secret they have managed to keep even from themselves—is that, behind their facades, they are the most violently destructive ruling class in history. All the anarchic, measureless, explosive drives that a later generation will baptize by the name of "nihilism"—drives that Nietzsche and his followers will ascribe to such cosmic traumas as the Death of God—are located by Marx in the seemingly banal everyday working of the market economy. He unveils the modern bourgeois as consummate nihilists on a far vaster scale than modern intellectuals can conceive.* But these bourgeois have alienated themselves

cally, even the most splendid mansions of the richest capitalists would be gone in less than forty years—not in Manchester alone, but in virtually every capitalist city —leased or sold off to developers, pulled down by the same insatiable drives that threw them up. (New York's Fifth Avenue is a vivid example, but these modern instances are everywhere.) Considering the rapidity and brutality of capitalist development, the real surprise is not that so much of our architectural and constructed heritage has been destroyed but that there is anything still left to preserve.

It is only recently that Marxist thinkers have begun to explore this theme. The economic geographer David Harvey, for example, tries to show in detail how the repeated intentional destruction of the "built environment" is integral to the accumulation of capital. Harvey's writings are widely scattered; for a lucid introduction and analysis, see Sharon Zukin, "Ten Years of the New Urban Sociology," in *Theory and Society,* July 1980, 575–601.

Ironically, communist states have done far better than capitalist ones in preserving the substance of the past in their great cities: Leningrad, Prague, Warsaw, Budapest, etc. But this policy springs less from respect for beauty and human achievement than from the desire of autocratic governments to mobilize traditionalist loyalties by creating a sense of continuity with the autocracies of the past.

*Actually, the term "nihilism" springs from Marx's own generation: it was coined by Turgenev as a motto for his radical hero Bazarov in *Fathers and Sons* (1861), and elaborated in a far more serious way by Dostoevsky in *Notes from Underground* (1864) and *Crime and Punishment* (1866–67). Nietzsche explores the sources and meanings of nihilism most profoundly in *The Will to Power* (1885–88), especially in Book One, "European Nihilism." It is rarely mentioned, but worth noting, that Nietzsche considered modern politics and economics profoundly nihilistic in their own right. See Section 1, an inventory of the roots of contemporary nihilism. Some of Nietzsche's images and analyses here have a surprisingly Marxistic ring. See Section 63 on the spiritual consequences, both negative and positive, of "the fact of credit, of world-wide trade and means of transportation"; 67 on "the breaking up of landed prop-

from their own creativity because they cannot bear to look into the moral, social and psychic abyss that their creativity opens up.

Some of Marx's most vivid and striking images are meant to force us all to confront that abyss. Thus, "Modern bourgeois society, a society that has conjured up such mighty means of production and exchange, is like the sorcerer who can no longer control the powers of the underworld that he has called up by his spells." (478) This image evokes the spirits of that dark medieval past that our modern bourgeoisie is supposed to have buried. Its members present themselves as matter-of-fact and rational, not magical; as children of the Enlightenment, not of darkness. When Marx depicts the bourgeois as sorcerers—remember, too, their enterprise has "conjured whole populations out of the ground," not to mention "the specter of communism"—he is pointing to depths they deny. Marx's imagery projects, here as ever, a sense of wonder over the modern world: its vital powers are dazzling, overwhelming, beyond anything the bourgeoisie could have imagined, let alone calculated or planned. But Marx's images also express what must accompany any genuine sense of wonder: a sense of dread. For this miraculous and magical world is also demonic and terrifying, swinging wildly out of control, menacing and destroying blindly as it moves. The members of the bourgeoisie repress both wonder and dread at what they have made: these possessors don't want to know how deeply they are possessed. They learn only at moments of personal and general ruin—only, that is, when it is too late.

Marx's bourgeois sorcerer descends from Goethe's Faust, of course, but also from another literary figure who haunted the imagination of his generation: Mary Shelley's Frankenstein. These mythical figures, striving to expand human powers through science and rationality, unleash demonic powers that erupt irrationally, beyond human control, with horrifying results. In the second part of Goethe's *Faust*, the consummate underworld power, which finally makes the sorcerer obsolete, is a whole modern social

---

erty . . . newspapers (in place of daily prayers), railway, telegraph. Centralization of a tremendous number of interests in a single soul, which for that reason must be very strong and protean." (Translated by Walter Kaufmann and R. J. Hollingdale, Vintage, 1968.) But these connections between the modern soul and the modern economy are never worked out by Nietzsche, and (with very rare exceptions) never even noticed by his followers.

system. Marx's bourgeoisie moves within this tragic orbit. He places its underworld in a worldly context and shows how, in a million factories and mills, banks and exchanges, dark powers work in broad daylight, social forces are driven in dreadful directions by relentless market imperatives that not even the most powerful bourgeois can control. Marx's vision brings this abyss close to home.

Thus, in the first part of the *Manifesto*, Marx lays out the polarities that will shape and animate the culture of modernism in the century to come: the theme of insatiable desires and drives, permanent revolution, infinite development, perpetual creation and renewal in every sphere of life; and its radical antithesis, the theme of nihilism, insatiable destruction, the shattering and swallowing up of life, the heart of darkness, the horror. Marx shows how both these human possibilities are infused into the life of every modern man by the drives and pressures of the bourgeois economy. In the course of time, modernists will produce a great array of cosmic and apocalyptic visions, visions of the most radiant joy and the bleakest despair. Many of the most creative modernist artists will be simultaneously possessed by both and driven endlessly from pole to pole; their inner dynamism will reproduce and express the inward rhythms by which modern capitalism moves and lives. Marx plunges us into the depths of this life process, so that we feel ourselves charged with a vital energy that magnifies our whole being—and are simultaneouly seized by shocks and convulsions that threaten at every instant to annihilate us. Then, by the power of his language and thought, he tries to entice us to trust his vision, to let ourselves be swept along with him toward a climax that lies just ahead.

The sorcerer's apprentices, the members of the revolutionary proletariat, are bound to wrest control of modern productive forces from the Faustian-Frankensteinian bourgeoisie. When this is done, they will transform these volatile, explosive social forces into sources of beauty and joy for all, and bring the tragic history of modernity to a happy end. Whether or not this ending should ever really come to pass, the *Manifesto* is remarkable for its imaginative power, its expression and grasp of the luminous and dreadful possibilities that pervade modern life. Along with everything else that it is, it is the first great modernist work of art.

But even as we honor the *Manifesto* as an archetype of modernism, we must remember that archetypal models serve to typify not only truths and strengths but also inner tensions and strains. Thus, both in the *Manifesto* and in its illustrious successors, we will find that, against the creator's intentions and probably without his awareness, the vision of revolution and resolution generates its own immanent critique, and new contradictions thrust themselves through the veil that this vision weaves. Even as we let ourselves be carried along by Marx's dialectical flow, we feel ourselves being carried away by uncharted currents of uncertainty and unease. We are caught up in a series of radical tensions between Marx's intentions and his insights, between what he wants and what he sees.

Take, for instance, Marx's theory of crises: "crises that by their periodic return put the existence of the whole bourgeois society in question, each time more threateningly." (478) In these recurrent crises "a great part, not only of existing products, but of previously created productive forces, are repeatedly destroyed." Marx appears to believe that these crises will increasingly cripple capitalism and eventually destroy it. And yet, his own vision and analysis of bourgeois society show how well this society can thrive on crisis and catastrophe: "on one hand, by enforced destruction of a mass of productive forces; on the other, by conquest of new markets and more thorough exploitation of the old ones." The crises can annihilate people and companies that are, by the market's definitions, relatively weak and inefficient; they can open up empty spaces for new investment and redevelopment; they can force the bourgeoisie to innovate, expand and combine more intensively and ingeniously than ever: thus they may act as unexpected sources of capitalist strength and resiliency. It may be true that, as Marx says, these forms of adaptation only "pave the way for more extensive and more destructive crises." But, given the bourgeois capacity to make destruction and chaos pay, there is no apparent reason why these crises can't spiral on endlessly, smashing people, families, corporations, towns, but leaving the structures of bourgeois social life and power intact.

Next we might take Marx's vision of the revolutionary community. Its foundations will be laid, ironically, by the bourgeoisie itself. "The progress of industry, whose inadvertent promoter is the bourgeoisie, replaces the isolation of the workers through competition with their union through association." (483) The immense productive units inherent in modern industry will throw large numbers of workers together, will force them to depend on each other and to cooperate in their work—the modern division of labor requires intricate cooperation from moment to moment on a vast scale—and so will teach them to think and act collectively. The workers' communal bonds, generated inadvertently by capitalist production, will generate militant political institutions, unions that will oppose and finally overthrow the private, atomistic framework of capitalist social relations. So Marx believes.

And yet, if his overall vision of modernity is true, why should the forms of community produced by capitalist industry be any more solid than any other capitalist product? Might not these collectivities turn out to be, like everything else here, only temporary, provisional, built for obsolescence? Marx in 1856 will speak of the industrial workers as "new-fangled men. . . . as much an invention of modern times as machinery itself." But if this is so, then their solidarity, however impressive at any given moment, may turn out to be as transient as the machines they operate or the products they turn out. The workers may sustain each other today on the assembly line or the picket line, only to find themselves scattered tomorrow among different collectivities with different conditions, different processes and products, different needs and interests. Once again the abstract forms of capitalism seem to subsist—capital, wage labor, commodities, exploitation, surplus value—while their human contents are thrown into perpetual flux. How can any lasting human bonds grow in such loose and shifting soil?

Even if the workers do build a successful communist *movement*, and even if that movement generates a successful revolution, how, amid the flood tides of modern life, will they ever manage to build a solid communist *society*? What is to prevent the social forces that melt capitalism from melting communism as well? If all new relationships become obsolete before they can ossify, how can solidarity, fraternity and mutual aid be kept alive? A communist government might try to dam the flood by imposing radical restrictions, not merely on economic activity and enterprise (every socialist government has done this, along with every capitalist welfare state), but on personal, cultural and political expression. But insofar as such a policy succeeded, wouldn't it betray the Marxist aim of free development for each and all? Marx looked forward to communism as the fulfillment of modernity; but how can communism entrench itself in the modern world without suppressing those very modern energies that it promises to set free? On the other hand, if it gave these energies free rein, mightn't the spontaneous flow of popular energy sweep away the new social formation itself?[11]

Thus, simply by reading the *Manifesto* closely and taking its vision of modernity seriously, we arrive at serious questions about Marx's answers. We can see that the fulfillment Marx sees just around the bend may be a long time coming, if it comes at all; and we can see that even if it does come, it may be only a fleeting, transitory episode, gone in a moment, obsolete before it can ossify, swept away by the same tide of perpetual change and progress that brought it briefly within our reach, leaving us endlessly, helplessly floating on. We can see, too, how communism, in order to hold itself together, might stifle the active, dynamic and developmental forces that have brought it into being, might betray many of the hopes that have made it worth fighting for, might reproduce the inequities and contradictions of bourgeois society under a new name. Ironically, then, we can see Marx's dialectic of modernity re-enacting the fate of the society it describes, generating energies and ideas that melt it down into its own air.

3.

Nakedness: The Unaccommodated Man

NOW THAT we have seen Marx's "melting" vision in action, I want to use it to explicate some of the *Manifesto*'s most powerful images of modern life. In the passage below, Marx is trying to show how capitalism has transformed people's relationships with each other and with themselves. Although, in Marx's syntax, "the bourgeoisie" is the subject—in its economic activities that bring the big changes about—modern men and women of every class are objects, for all are changed:

> The bourgeoisie has torn apart the many feudal ties that bound men to their "natural superiors," and left no other bond between man and man than naked interest, than callous cash payment. It has drowned the heavenly ecstasies of pious fanaticism, of chivalrous enthusiasm, of philistine sentimentalism, in the icy water of egoistical calculation. . . . The bourgeoisie has stripped of its halo every occupation hitherto honored and looked up to with reverent awe. . . . The bourgeoisie has torn away from the family its sentimental veil, and turned the family relation into a pure money relation. . . . In place of exploitation veiled by religious and political illusions, it has put open, shameless, direct, naked exploitation. [475–76]

Marx's basic opposition here is between what is open or naked and what is hidden, veiled, clothed. This polarity, perennial in Eastern as well as Western thought, symbolizes everywhere a distinction between a "real" world and an illusory one. In most ancient and medieval speculative thought, the whole world of sensuous experience appears illusory—the Hindu "veil of Maya"—and the true world is thought to be accessible only through transcendence of bodies, space and time. In some traditions, reality is accessible through religious or philosophical meditation; in others, it will be available to us only in a future existence after death—the Pauline "for now we see through a glass darkly, but then face to face."

The modern transformation, beginning in the age of the Renaissance and Reformation, places both these worlds on earth, in space and time, filled with human beings. Now the false world is seen as a historical past, a world we have lost (or are in the process of losing), while the true world is in the physical and social world that exists for us here and now (or is in the process of coming into being). At this point a new symbolism emerges. Clothes become an emblem of the old, illusory mode of life; nakedness comes to signify the newly discovered and experienced truth; and the act of taking off one's clothes becomes an act of spiritual liberation, of becoming real. Modern erotic poetry elaborates this theme, as generations of modern lovers have experienced it, with playful irony; modern tragedy penetrates its awesome and fearsome depths. Marx thinks and works in the tragic tradition. For him, the clothes are ripped off, the veils are torn away, the stripping process is violent and brutal; and yet, somehow, the tragic movement of modern history is supposed to culminate in a happy end.

The dialectic of nakedness that culminates in Marx is defined at the very start of the modern age, in Shakespeare's *King Lear*. For Lear, the naked truth is what a man is forced to face when he has lost everything that other men can take away, except life itself. We see his voracious family, aided by his own blind vanity, tear away its sentimental veil. Stripped not only of political power but of even the barest traces of human dignity, he is thrown out of doors in the middle of the night at the height of a torrential and terrifying storm. This, he says, is what human life comes down to in the end: the solitary and poor abandoned in the cold, while the nasty and brutish enjoy all the warmth that power can provide. Such knowledge seems to be too much for us: "man's nature cannot carry / Th' affliction, nor the fear." But Lear is not broken by the storm's icy blasts, neither does he flee them; instead, he exposes himself to the storm's full fury, looks it in the face and affirms himself against it even as it tosses and tears him. As he wanders with his royal fool (Act III, Scene 4), they meet Edgar, disguised as a crazy beggar, stark naked, apparently even more wretched than he. "Is man no more than this?" Lear demands. "Thou art the thing itself: unaccommodated man . . ." Now, at the climactic moment of the play, he tears off his royal robes—"Off, off you lendings"—and joins "poor Tom" in naked authenticity. This act, which Lear believes has placed him at the very nadir of existence —"a poor, bare, forked animal"—turns out, ironically, to be his first step toward a full humanity, because, for the first time, he recognizes a connection between himself and another human being. This recognition enables him to grow in sensitivity and insight, and to move beyond the bounds of his self-absorbed bitterness and misery. As he stands and shivers, it dawns on him that his kingdom is full of people whose whole lives are consumed by the abandoned, defenseless suffering that he is going through right now. When he was in power he never noticed, but now he stretches his vision to take them in:

> Poor naked wretches, wheresoe'er you are,
> That bide the pelting of this pitiless storm,
> How shall your houseless heads and unfed sides,

> Your loop'd and window'd raggedness defend you
> From seasons such as these? O, I have ta'en
> Too little care of this! Take physic, pomp;
> Expose thyself to feel what wretches feel,
> That thou mayst shake the superflux to them,
> And show the heavens more just. [III, 4, 28–36]

It is only now that Lear is fit to be what he claims to be, "every inch a king." His tragedy is that the catastrophe that redeems him humanly destroys him politically: the experience that makes him genuinely qualified to be a king makes it impossible for him to be one. His triumph lies in becoming something he never dreamt of being, a human being. Here a hopeful dialectic lights up the tragic bleakness and blight. Alone in the cold and the wind and the rain, Lear develops the vision and courage to break out of his loneliness, to reach out to his fellow men for mutual warmth. Shakespeare is telling us that the dreadful naked reality of the "unaccommodated man" is the point from which accommodation must be made, the only ground on which real community can grow.

In the eighteenth century, the metaphors of nakedness as truth and stripping as self-discovery take on a new political resonance. In Montesquieu's *Persian Letters,* the veils that Persian women are forced to wear symbolize all the repressions that traditional social hierarchies inflict on people. By contrast, the absence of veils in the streets of Paris symbolizes a new kind of society where "liberty and equality reign," and where, as a consequence, "everything speaks out, everything is visible, everything is audible. The heart shows itself as clearly as the face."[12] Rousseau, in his *Discourse on the Arts and Sciences,* denounces "the uniform and deceptive veil of politeness" that covers his age, and says that "the good man is an athlete who loves to wrestle stark naked; he despises all those vile ornaments that cramp the use of his powers."[13] Thus the naked man will be not only a freer and happier man but a better man. The liberal revolutionary movements that bring the eighteenth century to a climax act out this faith: if hereditary privileges and social roles are stripped away, so that all men can enjoy an unfettered freedom to use all their powers, they will use them for the good of all mankind. We find here a striking absence of worry as to what the naked human being will do or be. The dialectical complexity and wholeness that we found in Shakespeare have faded away, and narrow polarizations have taken their place. The counter-revolutionary thought of this period shows the same narrowing and flattening of perspective. Here is Burke on the French Revolution:

> But now all is to be changed. All the pleasing illusions that made power gentle, and obedience liberal, which harmonized the different shades of life . . . are to be dissolved by this new conquering empire of light and reason. All the decent drapery of life is to be rudely torn off. All the super-added ideas, which the heart owns, and the understanding ratifies, as necessary to cover the defects of our weak and shivering nature, and to raise it to a dignity in our own estimation, are to be exploded as a ridiculous, absurd and antiquated fashion.[14]

The *philosophes* imagined nakedness as idyllic, opening new vistas of beauty and happiness for all; for Burke it is counter-idyllic, an unmitigated disaster, a fall into nothingness from which nothing and no one can rise. Burke cannot imagine that modern men might learn something, as Lear learns, from their mutual vulnerability in the cold. Their only hope lies in lies: in their capacity to construct mythic draperies heavy enough to stifle their dreadful knowledge of who they are.

For Marx, writing in the aftermath of bourgeois revolutions and reactions, and looking forward to a new wave, the symbols of nakedness and unveiling regain the dialectical depth that Shakespeare gave them two centuries before. The bourgeois revolutions, in tearing away veils of "religious and political illusion," have left naked power and exploitation, cruelty and misery, exposed like open wounds; at the same time, they have uncovered and exposed new options and hopes. Unlike the common people of all ages, who have been endlessly betrayed and broken by their devotion to their "natural superiors," modern men, washed in "the icy water of egoistical calculation," are free from deference to masters who destroy them, animated rather than numbed by the cold. Because they know how to think of, by, and for themselves, they will demand a clear account of what their bosses and rulers are doing for them—and doing to them—and be ready to resist and rebel where they are getting nothing real in return.

Marx's hope is that once the unaccommodated men of the working class are "forced to face . . . the real conditions of their lives and their relations with their fellow men," they will come together to overcome the cold that cuts through them all. Their union will generate the collective energy that can fuel a new communal life. One of the *Manifesto*'s primary aims is to point the way out of the cold, to nourish and focus the common yearning for communal warmth. Because the workers can come through the affliction and the fear only by making contact with the self's deepest resources, they will be prepared to fight for collective recognition of the self's beauty and value. Their communism, when it comes, will appear as a kind of transparent garment, at once keeping its wearers warm and setting off their naked beauty, so that they can recognize themselves and each other in all their radiance.

Here, as so often in Marx, the vision is dazzling but the light flickers if we look hard. It isn't hard to imagine alternate endings to the dialectic of nakedness, endings less beautiful than Marx's but no less plausible. Modern men and women might well prefer the solitary pathos and grandeur of the Rousseauean unconditioned self, or the collective costumed comforts of the Burkean political masque, rather than the Marxian attempt to fuse the best of both. Indeed, the sort of individualism that scorns and fears connections with other people as threats to the self's integrity, and the sort of collectivism that seeks to submerge the self in a social role, may be more appealing than the Marxian synthesis, because they are intellectually and emotionally so much easier.

There is a further problem that might keep the Marxian dialectic from even getting under way. Marx believes that the shocks and upheavals and catastrophes of life in bourgeois society enable moderns, by going through them, as Lear does, to discover who they "really are." But if bourgeois society is as volatile as Marx thinks it is, how can its people ever settle on any real selves? With all the possibilities and necessities that bombard the self and all the desperate drives that propel it, how can anyone define definitively which ones are essential and which merely incidental? The nature of the newly naked modern man may turn out to be just as elusive and mysterious as that of the old, clothed one, maybe even more elusive, because there will no longer be any illusion of a real self underneath the masks. Thus, along with community and society, individuality itself may be melting into the modern air.

4.

The Metamorphosis of Values

THE PROBLEM of nihilism emerges again in Marx's next line: "The bourgeoisie has resolved all personal honor and dignity into exchange-value; and in place of all the freedoms that men have fought for, it has put one unprincipled freedom—free trade." The first point here is the immense power of the market in modern men's inner lives: they look to the price list for answers to questions not merely economic but metaphysical—questions of what is worthwhile, what is honorable, even what is real. When Marx says that other values are "resolved into" exchange value, his point is that bourgeois society does not efface old structures of value but subsumes them. Old modes of honor and dignity do not die; instead, they get incorporated into the market, take on price tags, gain a new life as commodities. Thus, any imaginable mode of human conduct becomes morally permissible the moment it becomes economically possible, becomes "valuable"; anything goes if it pays. This is what modern nihilism is all about. Dostoevsky, Nietzsche and their twentieth-century successors will ascribe this predicament to science, rationalism, the death of God. Marx would say that its basis is far more concrete and mundane: it is built into the banal everyday workings of the bourgeois economic order—an order that equates our human value with our market price, no more, no less, and that forces us to expand ourselves in pushing our price up as far as we can make it go.

Marx is appalled by the destructive brutalities that bourgeois nihilism brings to life, but he believes that it has a hidden tendency to transcend itself. The source of this tendency is the paradoxically "unprincipled" principle of free trade. Marx believes that the bourgeois really believe in this principle—that is, in an incessant, unrestricted flow of commodities in circulation, a continuous meta-morphosis of market values. If, as he believes, the members of the bourgeoisie really do want a free market, they will have to enforce the freedom of new products to enter the market. This in turn means that any full-fledged bourgeois society must be a genuinely open society, not only economically but politically and culturally as well, so that people will be free to shop around and seek the best deals, in ideas, associations, laws and social policies, as well as in things. The unprincipled principle of free trade will force the bourgeoisie to grant even communists the basic right that all busi-nessmen enjoy, the right to offer and promote and sell their goods to as many customers as they can attract.

Thus, by virtue of what Marx calls "free competition within the realm of knowledge" (489), even the most subversive works and ideas—like the *Manifesto* itself—must be allowed to appear, on the grounds that they may sell. Marx is confident that once the ideas of revolution and communism become accessible to the masses they *will* sell, and communism as a "self-conscious, independent movement of the immense majority" (482) will come into its own. Thus he can live with bourgeois nihilism in the long run, because he sees it as active and dynamic, what Nietzsche would call a nihil-ism of strength.* Propelled by its nihilistic drives and energies, the bourgeoisie will open the political and cultural floodgates through which its revolutionary nemesis will flow.

This dialectic presents several problems. The first concerns the bourgeoisie's commitment to the unprincipled principle of free trade, whether in economics, politics or culture. In fact, in bour-geois history this principle has generally been more honored in the breach than in the observance. The members of the bourgeoi-sie, especially the most powerful, have generally fought to restrict, manipulate and control their markets. Indeed, much of their cre-ative energy over the centuries has gone into arrangements for doing this—chartered monopolies, holding companies, trusts, car-tels and conglomerates, protective tariffs, price-fixing, open or

---

* See the crucial distinction in *The Will to Power*, Sections 22–23: "Nihilism. It is ambiguous: A. Nihilism as a sign of increased power of the spirit: as *active* nihilism. B. Nihilism as decline and recession of the power of the spirit: as *passive* nihilism." In Type A, "the spirit may have grown so strong that previous goals (convictions, articles of faith) have become incommensurate . . . It reaches its maximum of rela-tive strength as a violent force of destruction—as active nihilism." Marx understood far better than Nietzsche the nihilistic strength of modern bourgeois society.

hidden subsidies from the state—all accompanied by paeans in praise of the free market. Moreover, even among the few who really do believe in free exchange, there are fewer still who would extend free competition to ideas as well as things.* Wilhelm von Humboldt, J. S. Mill, Justices Holmes and Brandeis and Douglas and Black have been still, small voices in bourgeois society, embattled and marginal at best. A more typical bourgeois pattern is to praise freedom when in opposition and to repress it when in power. Here Marx may be in danger—a surprising danger for him—of getting carried away by what bourgeois ideologues say, and losing touch with what the men with money and power actually do. This is a serious problem, because if the members of the bourgeoisie really don't give a damn about freedom, then they will work to keep the societies they control closed against new ideas, and it will be harder than ever for communism to take root. Marx would say that their need for progress and innovation will force them to open up their societies even to ideas they dread. Yet their ingenuity might avoid this through a truly insidious innovation: a consensus of mutually enforced mediocrity, designed to protect each individual bourgeois from the risks of competition, and bourgeois society as a whole from the risks of change.†

Another problem in Marx's dialectic of the free market is that it

* The most trenchant statement of this principle—that free trade and competition entail free thought and culture—may be found, surprisingly, in Baudelaire. His Preface to the *Salon of 1846,* dedicated "To the Bourgeois," asserts a special affinity between modern enterprise and modern art: both are striving "to realize the idea of the future in its most diverse forms—political, industrial, artistic"; both are thwarted by "the aristocrats of thought, the monopolists of things of the mind," who would stifle the energy and progress of modern life. (*Art in Paris, 1845–62,* translated and edited by Jonathan Mayne, Phaidon, 1965, 41–43.) Baudelaire will be discussed at length in the following chapter. But it is worth noting here that arguments like Baudelaire's make perfect sense to large numbers of people in dynamic and progressive periods like the 1840s—or the 1960s. On the other hand, in periods of reaction and stagnation, like the 1850s or the 1970s, this sort of argument is apt to sound unthinkably bizarre, if not monstrous, to many bourgeois who embraced it enthusiastically just a few years before.

† In the climactic chapter of the first volume of *Capital,* "The Historical Tendency of Capitalist Accumulation," Marx says that when a system of social relations acts as a fetter on "the free development of productive forces," that social system has simply got to go: "It must be annihilated; it is annihilated." But what would happen if, somehow, it didn't get annihilated? Marx lets himself imagine this for barely an instant, only to dismiss the possibility. "To perpetuate" such a social system, he says, would be "to decree universal mediocrity." (*MER* 437) This is perhaps the one thing that Marx is utterly incapable of imagining.

entails a strange collusion between bourgeois society and its most radical opponents. This society is driven by its unprincipled principle of free exchange to open itself to movements for radical change. The enemies of capitalism may enjoy a great deal of freedom to do their work—to read, write, speak, meet, organize, demonstrate, strike, elect. But their freedom to move transforms their movement into an enterprise, and they find themselves cast in the paradoxical role of merchants and promoters of revolution, which necessarily becomes a commodity like everything else. Marx does not seem to be disturbed by the ambiguities of this social role—maybe because he is sure that it will become obsolete before it can ossify, that the revolutionary enterprise will be put out of business by its rapid success. A century later, we can see how the business of promoting revolution is open to the same abuses and temptations, manipulative frauds and wishful self-deceptions, as any other promotional line.

Finally, our skeptical doubts about promoters' promises must lead us to question one of the primary promises in Marx's work: the promise that communism, while upholding and actually deepening the freedoms that capitalism has brought us, will free us from the horrors of bourgeois nihilism. If bourgeois society is really the maelstrom Marx thinks it is, how can he expect all its currents to flow only one way, toward peaceful harmony and integration? Even if a triumphant communism should someday flow through the floodgates that free trade opens up, who knows what dreadful impulses might flow in along with it, or in its wake, or impacted inside? It is easy to imagine how a society committed to the free development of each and all might develop its own distinctive varieties of nihilism. Indeed, a communist nihilism might turn out to be far more explosive and disintegrative than its bourgeois precursor—though also more daring and original—because, while capitalism cuts the infinite possibilities of modern life with the limits of the bottom line, Marx's communism might launch the liberated self into immense unknown human spaces with no limits at all.[15]

5.

The Loss of a Halo

ALL THE ambiguities in Marx's thought are crystallized in one of his most luminous images, the last one we will explore here: "The bourgeoisie has stripped of its halo every activity hitherto honored and looked up to with reverent awe. It has transformed the doctor, the lawyer, the priest, the poet, the man of science [*Mann der Wissenschaft**], into its paid wage-laborers." (476) The halo, for Marx, is a primary symbol of religious experience, the experience of something holy. For Marx, as for his contemporary Kierkegaard, experience, rather than belief or dogma or theology, forms the core of religious life. The halo splits life into sacred and profane: it creates an aura of holy dread and radiance around the figure who wears it; the sanctified figure is torn from the matrix of the human condition, split off inexorably from the needs and pressures that animate the men and women who surround it.

Marx believes that capitalism tends to destroy this mode of experience for everybody: "all that is holy is profaned"; nothing is sacred, no one is untouchable, life becomes thoroughly desanctified. In some ways, Marx knows, this is frightful: modern men and women may well stop at nothing, with no dread to hold them back; free from fear and trembling, they are free to trample down everyone in their way if self-interest drives them to it. But Marx also sees the virtue of a life without auras: it brings about a condition of spiritual equality. Thus the modern bourgeoisie may hold vast material powers over the workers and everybody else, but it will

* The word *Wissenschaft* may be translated in many ways, narrowly as "science" or more broadly as "knowledge," "learning," "scholarship" or any sustained and serious intellectual pursuit. Whatever word we use, it is crucial to remember that Marx is talking here about the predicament of his own group, and hence about himself.

I have intermittently used the word "intellectuals" as shorthand for the diverse occupational groups Marx brings together here. I realize the word is anachronistic to Marx's time—it stems from Nietzsche's generation—but it has the advantage of bringing together, as Marx aims to do, people in diverse occupations who, despite their differences, all work with their minds.

never achieve the spiritual ascendancy that earlier ruling classes could take for granted. For the first time in history, all confront themselves and each other on a single plane of being.

We must remember that Marx is writing at a historical moment when, especially in England and France (the *Manifesto* really has more to do with them than with the Germany of Marx's time), disenchantment with capitalism is pervasive and intense, and almost ready to flare up in revolutionary forms. In the next twenty years or so, the bourgeoisie will prove remarkably inventive in constructing haloes of its own. Marx will try to strip these away in the first volume of *Capital*, in his analysis of "The Fetishism of Commodities"—a mystique that disguises the intersubjective relations between men in a market society as purely physical, "objective," unalterable relations between things.[16] In the climate of 1848, this bourgeois pseudo-religiosity had not yet established itself. Marx's targets here are, for both him and us, a lot closer to home: those professionals and intellectuals—"the doctor, the lawyer, the priest, the poet, the man of science"—who think they have the power to live on a higher plane than ordinary humanity, to transcend capitalism in life and work.

Why does Marx place that halo on the heads of modern professionals and intellectuals in the first place? To bring out one of the paradoxes of their historical role: even though they tend to pride themselves on their emancipated and thoroughly secular minds, they turn out to be just about the only moderns who really believe that they are called to their vocations and that their work is holy. It is obvious to any reader of Marx that in his commitment to his work he shares this faith. And yet he is suggesting here that in some sense it is a bad faith, a self-deception. This passage is so arresting because, as we see Marx identifying himself with the critical force and insight of the bourgeoisie, and reaching out to tear the haloes from modern intellectuals' heads, we realize that in some sense it is his own head he is laying bare.

The basic fact of life for these intellectuals, as Marx sees them, is that they are "paid wage-laborers" of the bourgeoisie, members of "the modern working class, the proletariat." They may deny this identity—after all, who wants to belong to the proletariat?—but they are thrown into the working class by the historically defined conditions under which they are forced to work. When Marx describes intellectuals as wage earners, he is trying to make us see modern culture as part of modern industry. Art, physical science, social theory like Marx's own, all are modes of production; the bourgeoisie controls the means of production in culture, as in everything else, and anyone who wants to create must work in the orbit of its power.

Modern professionals, intellectuals and artists, insofar as they are members of the proletariat,

> live only so long as they find work, and . . . find work only so long as their labor increases capital. These workers, who must sell themselves piecemeal, are a commodity like every other article of commerce, and are consequently exposed to all the vicissitudes of competition, to all the fluctuations of the market. [479]

Thus they can write books, paint pictures, discover physical or historical laws, save lives, only if someone with capital will pay them. But the pressures of bourgeois society are such that no one will pay them unless it pays to pay them—that is, unless their works somehow help to "increase capital." They must "sell themselves piecemeal" to an employer willing to exploit their brains for profit. They must scheme and hustle to present themselves in a maximally profitable light; they must compete (often brutally and unscrupulously) for the privilege of being bought, simply in order to go on with their work. Once the work is done they are, like all other workers, separated from the products of their labor. Their goods and services go on sale, and it is "the vicissitudes of competition, the fluctuations of the market," rather than any intrinsic truth or beauty or value—or, for that matter, any lack of truth or beauty or value—that will determine their fate. Marx does not expect that great ideas and works will fall stillborn for want of a market: the modern bourgeoisie is remarkably resourceful in wringing profit out of thought. What will happen instead is that creative processes and products will be used and transformed in ways that will dumfound or horrify their creators. But the creators will be powerless to resist, because they must sell their labor power in order to live.

Intellectuals occupy a peculiar position in the working class, one that generates special privileges, but also special ironies. They are beneficiaries of the bourgeois demand for perpetual innovation, which vastly expands the market for their products and skills, often stimulates their creative audacity and imagination, and—if they are shrewd enough and lucky enough to exploit the need for brains—enables them to escape the chronic poverty in which most workers live. On the other hand, because they are personally involved in their work—unlike most wage laborers, who are alienated and indifferent—the fluctuations of the market place strike them in a far deeper way. In "selling themselves piecemeal," they are selling not merely their physical energy but their minds, their sensibilities, their deepest feelings, their visionary and imaginative powers, virtually the whole of themselves. Goethe's *Faust* gave us the archetype of a modern intellectual forced to "sell himself" in order to make a difference in the world. Faust also embodied a complex of needs endemic to intellectuals: they are driven not only by a need to live, which they share with all men, but by a desire to communicate, to engage in dialogue with their fellow men. But the cultural commodity market offers the only media in which dialogue on a public scale can take place: no idea can reach or change moderns unless it can be marketed and sold to them. Hence they turn out to be dependent on the market not for bread alone but for spiritual sustenance—a sustenance they know the market cannot be counted on to provide.

It is easy to see why modern intellectuals, trapped in these ambiguities, would imagine radical ways out: in their situation, revolutionary ideas would spring from the most direct and intense personal needs. But the social conditions that inspire their radicalism also serve to frustrate it. We saw that even the most subversive ideas must manifest themselves through the media of the market. Insofar as these ideas attract and arouse people, they will expand and enrich the market, and so "increase capital." Now, if Marx's vision of bourgeois society is at all accurate, there is every reason to think that it will generate a market for radical ideas. This system requires constant revolutionizing, disturbance, agitation; it needs to be perpetually pushed and pressed in order to maintain its elasticity and resilience, to appropriate and assimilate new energies, to drive itself to new heights of activity and growth. This means, however, that men and movements that proclaim their enmity to capitalism may be just the sort of stimulants capitalism needs. Bourgeois society, through its insatiable drive for destruction and development, and its need to satisfy the insatiable needs it creates, inevitably produces radical ideas and movements that aim to destroy it. But its very capacity for development enables it to negate its own inner negations: to nourish itself and thrive on opposition, to become stronger amid pressure and crisis than it could ever be in peace, to transform enmity into intimacy and attackers into inadvertent allies.

In this climate, then, radical intellectuals encounter radical obstacles: their ideas and movements are in danger of melting into the same modern air that decomposes the bourgeois order they are working to overcome. To surround oneself with a halo in this climate is to try to destroy danger by denying it. The intellectuals of Marx's time were particularly susceptible to this sort of bad faith. Even as Marx was discovering socialism in the Paris of the 1840s, Gautier and Flaubert were developing their mystique of "art for art's sake," while the circle around Auguste Comte was constructing its own parallel mystique of "pure science." Both these groups—sometimes in conflict with each other, sometimes interfused—sanctified themselves as avant-gardes. They were at once perceptive and trenchant in their critiques of capitalism, and, at the same time, absurdly complacent in their faith that they had the power to transcend it, that they could live and work freely beyond its norms and demands.[17]

Marx's point in tearing the haloes from their heads is that nobody in bourgeois society can be so pure or safe or free. The networks and ambiguities of the market are such that everybody is caught up and entangled in them. Intellectuals must recognize the depths of their own dependence—spiritual as well as economic dependence—on the bourgeois world they despise. It will never be possible to overcome these contradictions unless we confront them directly and openly. This is what stripping away the haloes means.[18]

This image, like all the great images in the history of literature and thought, contains depths that its creator could not have foreseen. First of all, Marx's indictment of the nineteenth-century artistic and scientific avant-gardes cuts just as deeply against the twentieth-century Leninist "vanguards" who make an identical—and equally groundless—claim to transcend the vulgar world of need, interest, egoistical calculation and brutal exploitation. Next, however, it raises questions about Marx's own romantic image of the working class. If being a paid wage laborer is the antithesis of having a halo, how can Marx speak of the proletariat as a class of new men, uniquely equipped to transcend the contradictions of modern life? Indeed, we can carry this questioning a step further. If we have followed Marx's unfolding vision of modernity, and confronted all its endemic ironies and ambiguities, how can we expect *anybody* to transcend all this?

Once again we encounter a problem we have met before: the tension between Marx's critical insights and his radical hopes. My emphases in this essay have leaned toward the skeptical and self-critical undercurrents in Marx's thought. Some readers may be inclined to take only the criticism and self-criticism to heart, and throw out the hopes as Utopian and naive. To do this, however, would be to miss what Marx saw as the essential point of critical thinking. Criticism, as he understood it, was part of an ongoing dialectical process. It was meant to be dynamic, to drive and inspire the person criticized to overcome both his critics and himself, to propel both parties toward a new synthesis. Thus, to unmask phony claims of transcendence is to demand and fight for real transcendence. To give up the quest for transcendence is to erect a halo around one's own stagnation and resignation, and to betray not only Marx but ourselves. We need to strive for the precarious, dynamic balance that Antonio Gramsci, one of the great communist writers and leaders of our century, described as "pessimism of the intellect, optimism of the will." [19]

Conclusion: Culture and the Contradictions of Capitalism

I HAVE been trying in this essay to define a space in which Marx's thought and the modernist tradition converge. First of all, both are attempts to evoke and to grasp a distinctively modern experience. Both confront this realm with mixed emotions, awe and elation fused with a sense of horror. Both see modern life as shot through with contradictory impulses and potentialities, and both embrace a vision of ultimate or ultramodernity—Marx's "new-fan-gled men . . . as much the invention of modern time as machinery itself"; Rimbaud's *"Il faut être absolument moderne"*—as the way through and beyond these contradictions.

In the spirit of convergence, I have tried to read Marx as a modernist writer, to bring out the vividness and richness of his language, the depth and complexity of his imagery—clothes and nakedness, veils, haloes, heat, cold—and to show how brilliantly he develops the themes by which modernism will come to define itself: the glory of modern energy and dynamism, the ravages of modern disintegration and nihilism, the strange intimacy between them; the sense of being caught in a vortex where all facts and values are whirled, exploded, decomposed, recombined; a basic uncertainty about what is basic, what is valuable, even what is real; a flaring up of the most radical hopes in the midst of their radical negations.

At the same time, I have tried to read modernism in a Marxist way, to suggest how its characteristic energies, insights and anxieties spring from the drives and strains of modern economic life: from its relentless and insatiable pressure for growth and progress; its expansion of human desires beyond local, national and moral bounds; its demands on people to exploit not only their fellow men but also themselves; the volatility and endless metamorphosis of all its values in the maelstrom of the world market; its pitiless destruction of everything and everyone it cannot use—so much of the pre-modern world, but so much of itself and its own modern world as well—and its capacity to exploit crisis and chaos as a springboard for still more development, to feed itself on its own self-destruction.

I don't pretend to be the first to bring Marxism and modernism together. In fact, they have come together on their own at several points over the past century, most dramatically at moments of historical crisis and revolutionary hope. We can see their fusion in Baudelaire, Wagner, Courbet, as well as Marx, in 1848; in the expressionists, futurists, dadaists and constructivists of 1914–25; in the ferment and agitation in Eastern Europe after Stalin's death; in the radical initiatives of the 1960s, from Prague to Paris and throughout the U.S.A. But as revolutions have been suppressed or betrayed, radical fusion has given way to fission; both Marxism and modernism have congealed into orthodoxies and gone their separate and mutually distrustful ways.* So-called orthodox Marxists have at best ignored modernism, but all too often worked to repress it, out of fear, perhaps, that (in Nietzsche's phrase) if they kept looking into the abyss the abyss would start looking back into them.[20] Orthodox modernists, meanwhile, have spared no expense of spirit in refashioning for themselves the halo of an unconditioned "pure" art, free from society and history. This essay tries to close off an exit route for orthodox Marxists by showing how the abyss they fear and flee opens up within Marxism itself. But Marxism's strength has always lain in its willingness to start from frightening social realities, to work through them and work them through; to abandon this primary source of strength leaves Marxism with little but the name. As for the orthodox modernists who avoid Marxist thought for fear that it might strip them of their haloes, they need to learn that it could give them back something better in exchange: a heightened capacity to imagine and express the endlessly rich, complex and ironic relationships between them and the "modern bourgeois society" that they try to deny or defy. A fusion of Marx with modernism should melt the too-solid body of Marxism—or at least warm it up and thaw it out —and, at the same time, give modernist art and thought a new solidity and invest its creations with an unsuspected resonance and depth. It would reveal modernism as the realism of our time.

I want in this concluding section to bring the ideas I have developed here to bear on some contemporary debates concerning Marx, modernism and modernization. I will begin by considering the conservative indictments of modernism that developed at the end of the 1960s, and that have flourished in the reactionary ambience of the past decade. According to Daniel Bell, the most serious of these polemicists, "Modernism has been the seducer," enticing contemporary men and women (and even children) to desert their moral, political and economic stations and duties. Capitalism, for writers like Bell, is wholly innocent in this affair: it is

* Marxism and modernism may also come together as a Utopian fantasy in a period of political quiescence: cf. the surrealism of the 1920s and the work of American thinkers like Paul Goodman and Norman O. Brown in the 1950s. Herbert Marcuse spans both generations, especially in his most original work, *Eros and Civilization* (1955). Another sort of convergence pervades the works of men like Mayakovsky, Brecht, Benjamin, Adorno and Sartre, who experience modernism as a spiritual maelstrom, Marxism as *ein'feste Burg* of solid rock, and who spend their lives plunging between them, but who often create brilliant syntheses in spite of themselves.

portrayed as a kind of Charles Bovary, unexciting but decent and dutiful, working hard to fulfill his wayward wife's insatiable desires and to pay her insupportable debts. This portrait of capitalist innocence has a fine pastoral charm; but no capitalist could afford to take it seriously if he hoped to survive for even a week in the real world that capitalism has made. (On the other hand, capitalists can certainly enjoy this picture as a fine piece of public relations, and laugh all the way to the bank.) Then, too, we must admire Bell's ingenuity in taking one of the most persistent of modernist orthodoxies—the autonomy of culture, the artist's superiority to all the norms and needs that bind the ordinary mortals around him—and turning it against modernism itself.[21]

But what is masked here, by modernists and anti-modernists alike, is the fact that these spiritual and cultural movements, for all their eruptive power, have been bubbles on the surface of a social and economic cauldron that has been teeming and boiling for more than a hundred years. It is modern capitalism, not modern art and culture, that has set and kept the pot boiling—reluctant as capitalism may be to face the heat. The drug-crazed nihilism of William Burroughs, a favorite *bête noire* in anti-modernist polemics, is a pale reproduction of his ancestral trust, whose profits financed his avant-garde career: the Burroughs Adding Machine Company, now Burroughs International, sober nihilists of the bottom line.

In addition to these polemical attacks, modernism has always elicited objections of a very different order. Marx in the *Manifesto* took up Goethe's idea of an emerging "world literature," and explained how modern bourgeois society was bringing a world culture into being:

> In place of the old wants, satisfied by the productions of the country, we find new wants, requiring for their satisfaction the products of distant lands and climes. In place of the old local and national self-sufficiency, we have intercourse in every direction, universal interdependence. And as in material, so in spiritual [*geistige*] production. The spiritual creations of individual nations become common property. National one-sidedness and narrowmindedness become more and more impossible, and from the numerous national and local literatures there arises a world literature. [476–77]

Marx's scenario can serve as a perfect program for the international modernism that has flourished from his era to our own: a culture that is broad-minded and many-sided, that expresses the universal scope of modern desires, and that, despite the mediations of the bourgeois economy, is the "common property" of mankind. But what if this culture were not universal after all, as Marx thought it would be? What if it turned out to be an exclusively and parochially Western affair? This possibility was first proposed in the middle of the nineteenth century by various Russian populists. They argued that the explosive atmosphere of modernization in the West—the breakdown of communities and the psychic isolation of the individual, mass impoverishment and class polarization, a cultural creativity that sprang from desperate moral and spiritual anarchy—might be a cultural peculiarity rather than an iron necessity inexorably awaiting the whole of mankind. Why should not other nations and civilizations achieve more harmonious fusions of traditional ways of life with modern potentialities and needs? In short—sometimes this belief was expressed as a complacent dogma, sometimes as a desperate hope—it was only in the West that "all that is solid melts into air."

The twentieth century has seen a great variety of attempts to realize nineteenth-century populist dreams, as revolutionary regimes have come to power all over the underdeveloped world. These regimes have all tried, in many different ways, to achieve what nineteenth-century Russians called the leap from feudalism to socialism: in other words, by heroic exertions, to attain the heights of modern community without ever going through the depths of modern fragmentation and disunity. This is no place to explore the many different modes of modernization that are available in the world today. But it is relevant to point out the fact that, in spite of the enormous differences among political systems today, so many seem to share a fervent desire to wipe modern culture off their respective maps. Their hope is that, if only the people can be protected from this culture, then they can be mobilized in a solid front to pursue common national aims, instead of going off in a multitude of directions to pursue volatile and uncontrollable aims of their own.

Now it would be stupid to deny that modernization can proceed along a number of different roads. (Indeed, the whole point of modernization theory is to chart these roads.) There is no reason that every modern city must look and think like New York or Los Angeles or Tokyo. Nevertheless, we need to scrutinize the aims and interests of those who would protect their people from modernism for their own good. If this culture were really exclusively Western, and hence as irrelevant to the Third World as most of its governments say, would these governments need to expend as much energy repressing it as they do? What they are projecting onto aliens, and prohibiting as "Western decadence," is in fact their own people's energies and desires and critical spirit. When government spokesmen and propagandists proclaim their various countries to be free of this alien influence, what they really mean is merely that they have managed to keep a political and spiritual lid on their people so far. When the lid comes off, or is blown off, the modernist spirit is one of the first things to come out: it is the return of the repressed.

It is this spirit, at once lyrical and ironical, corrosive and committed, fantastic and realistic, that has made Latin American literature the most exciting in the world today—though it is also this spirit that forces Latin American writers to write from European or North American exile, on the run from their own censors and political police. It is this spirit that speaks from the dissident wall posters in Peking and Shanghai, proclaiming the rights of free individuality in a country that—so we were told only yesterday by China's Maoist mandarins and their comrades in the West—isn't even supposed to have a word for individuality. It is the culture of modernism that inspires the hauntingly intense electronic rock music of the Plastic People of Prague, music that is played in thousands of barricaded rooms on bootlegged cassettes even as the musicians languish in prison camps. It is modernist culture that keeps critical thought and free imagination alive in much of the non-Western world today.

Governments don't like it, but it is likely that in the long run they can't help it. So long as they are forced to sink or swim in the maelstrom of the world market, forced to strive desperately to accumulate capital, forced to develop or disintegrate—or rather, as it generally turns out, to develop *and* disintegrate—so long as they are, as Octavio Paz says, "condemned to modernity," they are bound to produce cultures that will show them what they are doing and what they are. Thus, as the Third World is increasingly caught up in the dynamics of modernization, modernism, far from exhausting itself, is only just beginning to come into its own.*

In closing, I want to comment briefly on two indictments of Marx, by Herbert Marcuse and Hannah Arendt, which raise some of the central issues of this book. Marcuse and Arendt formulated their critiques in America in the 1950s, but seem to have conceived them in the 1920s, in the milieu of German romantic existentialism. In a sense their arguments go back to the debates between Marx and the Young Hegelians in the 1840s; nevertheless, the issues they raise are as relevant as ever today. The basic premise is that Marx uncritically celebrates the values of labor and production, and neglects other human activities and modes of being that are ultimately at least as important.† Marx is reproached here, in other words, for a failure of moral imagination.

Marcuse's most trenchant criticism of Marx occurs in *Eros and Civilization,* in which Marx's presence is evident on every page, but strangely never mentioned by name. However, in a passage like the one that follows, where Marx's favorite culture hero, Prometheus, is attacked, it is obvious what is being said between the lines:

> Prometheus is the culture-hero of toil, productivity, and progress through repression . . . the trickster and (suffering) rebel against the gods, who creates culture at the price of perpetual pain. He symbolizes productiveness, the unceasing effort to master life. . . . Prometheus is the archetypal hero of the performance-principle.

Marcuse proceeds to nominate alternate mythological figures, whom he considers more worthy of idealization: Orpheus, Narcissus, and Dionysus—and Baudelaire and Rilke, whom Marcuse sees as their modern votaries.

> [They] stand for a very different reality. . . . Theirs is the image of joy and fulfillment, the voice that does not command but sings, the deed which is peace and ends the labor of conquest: the

---

* *Alternating Current,* 196–98. Paz argues that the Third World desperately needs the imaginative and critical energy of modernism. Without it, "the revolt of the Third World . . . has degenerated into different varieties of frenzied Caesarism, or languishes beneath the stranglehold of bureaucracies that are both cynical and fuzzy-minded."

† This criticism might best be summed up by T. W. Adorno's remark (which he never put in print) that Marx wanted to turn the whole world into a giant workhouse.[22]

liberty from time that unites man with god, man with nature . . .
the redemption of pleasure, the halt of time, the absorption of
death: silence, sleep, night, paradise—the Nirvana-principle not
as death but life.[23]

What the Promethean/Marxian vision fails to see is the joys of
peacefulness and passivity, sensual languor, mystical rapture, a
state of oneness with nature rather than achieved mastery over it.

There is something to this—certainly *"luxe, calme et volupté"* is
far from the center of Marx's imagination—but less than there
may at first seem to be. If Marx is fetishistic about anything, it is
not work and production but rather the far more complex and
comprehensive ideal of *development*—"the free development of
physical and spiritual energies" (1844 manuscripts); "development
of a totality of capacities in the individuals themselves" (*German
Ideology*); "the free development of each will be the condition
for the free development of all" (*Manifesto*); "the universality of
individual needs, capacities, pleasures, productive forces, etc."
(*Grundrisse*); "the fully developed individual" (*Capital*). The
experiences and human qualities that Marcuse values would certainly be included in this agenda, though there is no guarantee
that they would head the list. Marx wants to embrace Prometheus
and Orpheus; he considers communism worth fighting for, because for the first time in history it could enable men to have both.
He might also argue that it is only against a background of Promethean striving that Orphic rapture gains moral or psychic value;
"luxe, calme et volupté" by themselves are merely boring, as Baudelaire knew well.

Finally, it is valuable for Marcuse to proclaim, as the Frankfurt
School has always proclaimed, the ideal of harmony between man
and nature. But it is equally important for us to realize that, whatever the concrete content of this balance and harmony might be
—a difficult enough question in its own right—it would take an
immense amount of Promethean activity and striving to create it.
Moreover, even if it could be created, it would still have to be
maintained; and given the dynamism of the modern economy,
mankind would have to work incessantly—like Sisyphus, but constantly striving to develop new measures and new means—to keep
its precarious balance from being swept away and melting in foul
air.

Arendt, in *The Human Condition*, understands something that liberal critics of Marx generally miss: the real problem in his thought is not a draconic authoritarianism but its radical opposite, the lack of a basis for any authority at all. "Marx predicted correctly, though with an unjustified glee, the 'withering away' of the public realm under the conditions of the unhampered development of 'the productive forces of society.'" The members of his communist society would find themselves, ironically, "caught in the fulfillment of needs that nobody can share and which nobody can fully communicate." Arendt understands the depth of the individualism that underlies Marx's communism, and understands, too, the nihilistic directions in which that individualism may lead. In a communist society where the free development of each is the condition for the free development of all, what is going to hold these freely developing individuals together? They might share a common quest for infinite experiential wealth; but this would be "no true public realm, but only private activities displayed in the open." A society like this might well come to feel a sense of collective futility: "the futility of a life which does not fix or realize itself in any permanent subject that endures after its labor is past."[24]

This critique of Marx poses an authentic and urgent human problem. But Arendt comes no closer than Marx to resolving the problem. Here, as in many of her works, she weaves a splendid rhetoric of public life and action, but leaves it quite unclear what this life and action are supposed to consist of—except that political life is *not* supposed to include what people do all day, their work and production relationships. (These are consigned to "the cares of the household," a subpolitical realm which Arendt considers to be devoid of the capacity to create human value.) Arendt never makes it clear what, besides lofty rhetoric, modern men can or ought to share. She is right to say that Marx never developed a theory of political community, and right that this is a serious problem. But the problem is that, given the nihilistic thrust of modern personal and social development, it is not at all clear what political bonds modern men can create. Thus the trouble in Marx's thought turns out to be a trouble that runs through the whole structure of modern life itself.

I have been arguing that those of us who are most critical of modern life need modernism most, to show us where we are and where we can begin to change our circumstances and ourselves. In search of a place to begin, I have gone back to one of the first and greatest of modernists, Karl Marx. I have gone to him not so much for his answers as for his questions. The great gift he can give us today, it seems to me, is not a way out of the contradictions of modern life but a surer and deeper way into these contradictions. He knew that the way beyond the contradictions would have to lead through modernity, not out of it. He knew we must start where we are: psychically naked, stripped of all religious, aesthetic, moral haloes and sentimental veils, thrown back on our individual will and energy, forced to exploit each other and ourselves in order to survive; and yet, in spite of all, thrown together by the same forces that pull us apart, dimly aware of all we might be together, ready to stretch ourselves to grasp new human possibilities, to develop identities and mutual bonds that can help us hold together as the fierce modern air blows hot and cold through us all.

‖‖‖

Baudelaire: Modernism in the Streets

But now imagine a city like Paris . . . imagine this metropolis of the world . . . where history confronts us on every street corner.
                              —Goethe to Eckermann, 3 May 1827

It is not merely in his use of imagery of common life, not merely in the imagery of the sordid life of a great metropolis, but in the elevation of such imagery to first intensity—presenting it as it is, and yet making it represent something beyond itself—that Baudelaire has created a mode of release and expression for other men.
                              —T. S. Eliot, "Baudelaire," 1930

since 1950 or so

IN THE past three decades, an immense amount of energy has been expended all over the world in exploring and unraveling the meanings of modernity. Much of this energy has fragmented itself in perverse and self-defeating ways. Our vision of modern life tends to split into material and spiritual planes: some people devote themselves to "modernism," which they see as a species of pure spirit, evolving in accord with its autonomous artistic and

131

intellectual imperatives; other people work within the orbit of "modernization," a complex of material structures and processes —political, economic, social—which, supposedly, once it has got under way, runs on its own momentum with little or no input from human minds or souls. This dualism, pervasive in contemporary culture, cuts us all off from one of the pervasive facts of modern life: the interfusion of its material and spiritual forces, the intimate unity of the modern self and the modern environment. But the first great wave of writers and thinkers about modernity—Goethe, Hegel and Marx, Stendhal and Baudelaire, Carlyle and Dickens, Herzen and Dostoevsky—had an instinctive feeling for this unity; it gave their visions a richness and depth that contemporary writing about modernity sadly lacks.

This chapter is built around Baudelaire, who did more than anyone in the nineteenth century to make the men and women of his century aware of themselves as moderns. Modernity, modern life, modern art—these terms occur incessantly in Baudelaire's work; and two of his great essays, the short "Heroism of Modern Life" and the longer "Painter of Modern Life" (1859–60, published in 1863), have set agendas for a whole century of art and thought. In 1865, when Baudelaire was living in poverty, illness and obscurity, the youthful Paul Verlaine tried to revive interest in him by stressing his modernity as a primary source of his greatness: "Baudelaire's originality is to portray, powerfully and originally, modern man . . . as the refinements of an excessive civilization have made him, modern man with his acute and vibrant senses, his painfully subtle spirit, his brain saturated with tobacco, his blood burning with alcohol. . . . Baudelaire portrays this sensitive individual as a type, a *hero*." [1] The poet Theodore de Banville developed this theme two years later in a moving tribute at Baudelaire's grave:

> He accepted modern man in his entirety, with his weaknesses, his aspirations and his despair. He had thus been able to give beauty to sights that did not possess beauty in themselves, not by making them romantically picturesque, but by bringing to light the portion of the human soul hidden in them; he had thus revealed the sad and often tragic heart of the modern city. That was why he haunted, and would always haunt, the minds of modern men, and move them when other artists left them cold. [2]

Baudelaire's reputation in the century since his death has developed along the lines de Banville suggests: the more seriously Western culture is concerned with the issue of modernity, the more we appreciate Baudelaire's originality and courage as a prophet and pioneer. If we had to nominate a first modernist, Baudelaire would surely be the man.

And yet, one salient quality of Baudelaire's many writings on modern life and art is that the meaning of the modern is surprisingly elusive and hard to pin down. Take, for instance, one of his most famous dicta, from "The Painter of Modern Life": "By 'modernity' I mean the ephemeral, the contingent, the half of art whose other half is eternal and immutable." The painter (or novelist or philosopher) of modern life is one who concentrates his vision and energy on "its fashions, its morals, its emotions," on "the passing moment and all the suggestions of eternity that it contains." This concept of modernity is meant to cut against the antiquarian classical fixations that dominate French culture. "We are struck by a general tendency among artists to dress all their subjects in the garments of the past." The sterile faith that archaic costumes and gestures will produce eternal verities leaves French art stuck in "an abyss of abstract and indeterminate beauty," and deprives it of "originality," which can only come from "the seal that Time imprints on all our generations."* We can see what Baudelaire is driving at here; but this purely formal criterion for modernity—whatever is unique about any period—in fact takes him directly away from where he wants to go. By this criterion, as Baudelaire says, "Every old master has his own modernity," insofar as he captures the look and feeling of his own era. But this empties the idea of modernity of all its specific weight, its concrete historical content. It makes any and all times "modern times"; ironically, by spreading modernity through all history, it leads us away from the special qualities of our own modern history.[3]

The first categorical imperative of Baudelaire's modernism is to

* Marx, in the same decade, was complaining, in terms surprisingly similar to Baudelaire's, about classical and antique fixations in the politics of the left: "The tradition of all the dead generations weighs like a nightmare on the brain of the living. And just when men seem engaged in revolutionizing themselves and things, in creating something entirely new . . . they anxiously conjure up the spirits of the past and borrow from them names, battle slogans and costumes in order to present the new scene of world history in this time-honored disguise and this borrowed language." *The Eighteenth Brumaire of Louis Bonaparte, 1851–52, MER*, 595.

orient ourselves toward the primary forces of modern life; but Baudelaire does not make it immediately clear what these forces are, or what our stance toward them is supposed to be. Nevertheless, if we go through Baudelaire's work, we will find that it contains several distinctive visions of modernity. These visions often seem to be violently opposed to one another, and Baudelaire does not always seem to be aware of the tensions between them. Still, he presents them all with verve and brilliance, and often elaborates them with great originality and depth. Moreover, all of Baudelaire's modern visions, and all his contradictory critical attitudes toward modernity, have taken on lives of their own, long past his death and into our own time.

This essay will start from Baudelaire's most simplistic and uncritical interpretations of modernity: his lyrical celebrations of modern life that created distinctively modern modes of pastoral; his vehement denunciations of modernity, which generated modern forms of counter-pastoral. Baudelaire's pastoral visions of modernity would be elaborated in our century under the name of "modernolatry"; his counter-pastorals would turn into what the twentieth century would call "cultural despair."[4] From these limited visions, we will move on, for most of the essay, to a Baudelairean perspective that is far deeper and more interesting— though probably less well known and less influential—a perspective that resists all final resolutions, aesthetic or political, that wrestles boldly with its own inner contradictions, and that can illuminate not only Baudelaire's modernity but our own.

I.

Pastoral and Counter-Pastoral Modernism

LET US start with Baudelaire's modern pastorals. The earliest version occurs in the Preface to Baudelaire's "Salon of 1846," his critical review of the year's showing of new art. This preface is entitled "To the Bourgeois."[5] Contemporary readers who are accustomed to think of Baudelaire as a lifelong sworn enemy of the bourgeois and all their works are in for a shock.[6] Here Baudelaire not only celebrates the bourgeois, but even flatters them, for their intelligence, willpower and creativity in industry, trade and finance. It is not entirely clear of whom this class is meant to consist: "You are the majority—in number and intelligence; therefore you are the power—which is justice." If the bourgeoisie constitutes a majority of the population, what has become of the working class, let alone the peasantry? However, we must remind ourselves, we are in a pastoral world. In this world, when the bourgeois undertake immense enterprises—"you have combined together, you have formed companies, you have raised loans"—it is not, as some might think, to make lots of money, but for a far loftier purpose: "to realize the idea of the future in all its diverse forms—political, industrial, artistic." The fundamental bourgeois motive here is the desire for infinite human progress, not just in the economy, but universally, in the spheres of politics and culture as well. Baudelaire is appealing to what he sees as their innate creativity and universality of vision: since they are animated by the drive for progress in industry and politics, it would be unworthy of their dignity to stand still and accept stagnation in art.

Baudelaire also appeals, as Mill will appeal a generation later (and even Marx in the *Communist Manifesto*), to the bourgeois belief in free trade, and demands that this ideal be extended to the sphere of culture: just as chartered monopolies are (presumably) a drag on economic life and energy, so "the aristocrats of thought, the monopolists of things of the mind," will suffocate the life of the spirit, and deprive the bourgeoisie of the rich resources of modern art and thought. Baudelaire's faith in the bourgeoisie neglects all the darker potentialities of its economic and political drives—that is why I call it a pastoral vision. Nevertheless, the naiveté of "To the Bourgeois" springs from a fine openness and generosity of spirit. It will not—it could not—survive June 1848 or December 1851; but, in a spirit as bitter as Baudelaire's, it is lovely while it lasts. In any case, this pastoral vision proclaims a natural affinity between material and spiritual modernization; it holds that the groups that are most dynamic and innovative in economic and political life will be most open to intellectual and artistic creativity—"to realize the idea of the future in all its diverse forms"; it sees both economic and cultural change as unproblematical progress for mankind.[7]

Baudelaire's 1859–60 essay "The Painter of Modern Life" presents a very different mode of pastoral: here modern life appears as a great fashion show, a system of dazzling appearances, brilliant facades, glittering triumphs of decoration and design. The heroes of this pageant are the painter and illustrator Constantin Guys, and Baudelaire's archetypal figure of the Dandy. In the world Guys portrays, the spectator "marvels at the . . . amazing harmony of life in capital cities, a harmony so providentially maintained amid the turmoil of human freedom." Readers familiar with Baudelaire will be startled to hear him sound like Dr. Pangloss; we wonder what's the joke, until we conclude ruefully that there isn't any. "The kind of subject preferred by our artist . . . is the pageantry of life [*la pompe de la vie*] as it is to be seen in the capitals of the civilized world; the pageantry of military life, of fashion, and of love [*la vie militaire, la vie élégante, la vie galante*]." If we turn to Guys's slick renderings of the "beautiful people" and their world, we will see only an array of dashing costumes, filled by lifeless mannequins with empty faces. However, it isn't Guys's fault that his art resembles nothing so much as Bonwit's or Bloomingdale's ads. What is really sad is that Baudelaire has written pages of prose that go only too well with them:

> He [the painter of modern life] delights in fine carriages and proud horses, the dazzling smartness of the grooms, the expertness of the footmen, the sinuous gait of the women, the beauty of the children, happy to be alive and well dressed—in a word, he delights in universal life. If a fashion or the cut of a garment has been slightly modified, if bows and curls have been supplanted by cockades, if bavolets have been enlarged and chignons have dropped a fraction toward the nape of the neck, if waists have been raised and skirts have become fuller, be very sure that his eagle eye will have spotted it.[8]

If this is, as Baudelaire says, "universal life," what is universal death? Those who love Baudelaire will think it a pity that, as long as he was writing advertising copy, he couldn't arrange to get paid for it. (He could have used the money, though of course he would never have done it for money.) But this mode of pastoral plays an important role not merely in Baudelaire's own career but in the century of modern culture between his time and our own. There is an important body of modern writing, often by the most serious writers, that sounds a great deal like advertising copy. This writing sees the whole spiritual adventure of modernity incarnated in the latest fashion, the latest machine, or—and here it gets sinister—the latest model regiment.

> A regiment passes, on its way, as it may be, to the ends of the earth, tossing into the air of the boulevards its trumpet-calls as winged and stirring as hope; and in an instant Monsieur G. will already have seen, examined and analyzed the bearing of the external aspect of that company. Glittering equipment, music, bold, determined glances, heavy, solemn mustaches—he absorbs it all pell-mell, and in a few moments the resulting "poem" will be virtually composed. See how his soul lives with the soul of that regiment, marching like a single animal, a proud image of joy and obedience.[9]

These are the soldiers who killed 25,000 Parisians in June 1848 and who opened the way for Napoleon III in December of 1851. On both those occasions Baudelaire went into the streets to fight against—and could easily have been killed by—the men whose animal-like "joy in obedience" so thrills him now.[10] The passage above should alert us to a fact of modern life that students of poetry and art could easily forget: the tremendous importance of military display—psychological as well as political importance—and its power to captivate even the freest spirits. Armies on parade, from Baudelaire's time to our own, play a central role in the pastoral vision of modernity: glittering hardware, gaudy colors, flowing lines, fast and graceful movements, modernity without tears.

Perhaps the strangest thing about Baudelaire's pastoral vision —it typifies his perverse sense of irony, but also his peculiar integrity—is that the vision leaves him out. All the social and spiritual dissonances of Parisian life have been cleaned off these streets. Baudelaire's own turbulent inwardness, anguish and yearning—and his whole creative achievement in representing what Banville called "modern man in his entirety, with his weakness, his aspirations and his despair"—are completely out of this world. We should be able to see now that, when Baudelaire chooses Constantin Guys, rather than Courbet or Daumier or Manet (all of whom he knew and loved), as the archetypal "painter of modern life," it is not merely a lapse in taste but a profound rejection and abasement of himself. His encounter with Guys, pathetic as it is, does convey something true and important about modernity: its power to generate forms of "outward show," brilliant designs, glamorous spectacles, so dazzling that they can blind even the most incisive self to the radiance of its own darker life within.

Baudelaire's most vivid counter-pastoral images of modernity belong to the late 1850s, the same period as "The Painter of Modern Life": if there is a contradiction between the two visions, Baudelaire is wholly unaware of it. The counter-pastoral theme first emerges in an 1855 essay "On the Modern Idea of Progress as Applied to the Fine Arts."[11] Here Baudelaire uses familiar reactionary rhetoric to pour scorn not merely on the modern idea of progress but on modern thought and life as a whole:

> There is yet another and very fashionable error which I am anxious to avoid like the very devil. I refer to the idea of "progress." This obscure beacon, invention of present-day philosophizing, licensed without guarantee of Nature or God—this modern lantern throws a stream of chaos on all objects of knowledge; liberty melts away, punishment [*châtiment*] disappears. Anyone who wants to see history clearly must first of all put out this treacherous light. This grotesque idea, which has flowered on the soil of modern fatuity, has discharged each man from his duty, has delivered the soul from responsibility, has released the will from all the bonds imposed on it by the love of beauty. . . . Such an infatuation is a symptom of an already too visible decadence.

Here beauty appears as something static, unchanging, wholly external to the self, demanding rigid obedience and imposing punishments on its recalcitrant modern subjects, extinguishing all forms of Enlightenment, functioning as a kind of spiritual police in the service of a counter-revolutionary Church and State.

Baudelaire resorts to this reactionary bombast because he is worried about an increasing "confusion of material order with spiritual order" that the modern romance of progress spreads. Thus,

Take any good Frenchman who reads *his* newspaper in *his* cafe, and ask him what he understands by progress, and he will answer that it is steam, electricity and gaslight, miracles unknown to the Romans, whose discovery bears full witness to our superiority over the ancients. Such is the darkness that has gathered in that unhappy brain!

Baudelaire is perfectly reasonable in fighting the confusion of material progress with spiritual progress—a confusion that persists in our century, and becomes especially rampant in periods of economic boom. But he is as silly as the straw man in the cafe when he leaps to the opposite pole, and defines art in a way that seems to have no connection with the material world at all:

> The poor man has become so Americanized by zoöcratic and industrial philosophies that he has lost all notion of the differences between the phenomena of the physical world and those of the moral world, between the natural and the supernatural.

This dualism bears some resemblance to the Kantian dissociation of the noumenal and phenomenal realms, but it goes a lot further than Kant, for whom noumenal experiences and activities—art, religion, ethics—still operate in a material world of time and space. It is not at all clear where, or on what, this Baudelairean artist can work. Baudelaire goes further: he disconnects his artist not only from the material world of steam, electricity and gas, but even from the whole past and future history of art. Thus, he says, it is wrong to even think about an artist's forerunners or the influences on him. "Every efflorescence [in art] is spontaneous, individual. . . . The artist stems only from himself. . . . He stands security only for himself. He dies childless. He has been his own king, his own priest, his own God."[12] Baudelaire leaps into a transcendence that leaves Kant far behind: this artist becomes a walking *Ding-an-sich*. Thus, in Baudelaire's mercurial and paradoxical sensibility, the counter-pastoral image of the modern world generates a remarkably pastoral vision of the modern artist who floats, untouched, freely above it.

The dualism first sketched here—counter-pastoral vision of the modern world, pastoral vision of the modern artist and his art—is extended and deepened in Baudelaire's famous 1859 essay, "The

Modern Public and Photography."[13] Baudelaire begins by complaining that "the exclusive taste for the True (so noble a thing when limited to its proper applications) oppresses the taste for the Beautiful." This is the rhetoric of balance, resisting exclusive emphases: truth is essential, only it shouldn't stifle the desire for beauty. But the sense of balance doesn't last long: "Where one should see nothing but Beauty (I mean in a beautiful painting) our public looks only for Truth." Because photography has the capacity to reproduce reality more precisely than ever before—to show the "Truth"—this new medium is "art's mortal enemy"; and insofar as the development of photography is a product of technological progress, then "Poetry and progress are like two ambitious men who hate each other. When they meet on the same road, one or the other must give way."

But why this mortal enmity? Why should the presence of reality, of "truth" in a work of art, undermine or destroy its beauty? The apparent answer, which Baudelaire believes so vehemently (at least he believes it at this moment) that he doesn't even think of saying it clearly, is that modern reality is utterly loathsome, empty not only of beauty but of even the potential for beauty. A categorical, nearly hysterical contempt for modern men and their life animates statements like these: "The idolatrous mob demanded an ideal appropriate to itself and worthy of its nature." From the moment that photography was developed, "our squalid society, Narcissus to a man, rushed to gaze at its trivial image on a scrap of metal." Baudelaire's serious critical discussion of the representation of reality in modern art is crippled here by an uncritical loathing for the real modern people around him. This leads him once more to a pastoral conception of art: it is "useless and tedious to represent what exists, because nothing that exists satisfies me. . . . I prefer the monsters of my fantasy to what is positively trivial." Even worse than the photographers, Baudelaire says, are the modern painters who are influenced by photography: more and more, the modern painter "is given to painting not what he dreams, but what he sees." What makes this pastoral, and uncritical, is the radical dualism, and the utter lack of awareness that there can be rich and complex relations, mutual influences and interfusions, between what an artist (or anyone else) dreams and what he sees.

Baudelaire's polemic against photography was extremely influential in defining a distinctive mode of aesthetic modernism, pervasive in our century—e.g., in Pound, Wyndham Lewis, and their many followers—in which modern people and life are endlessly abused, while modern artists and their works are exalted to the skies, without any suspicion that these artists may be more human, and more deeply implicated in *la vie moderne,* than they would like to think. Other twentieth-century artists like Kandinsky and Mondrian have created marvelous works out of the dream of a dematerialized, unconditioned, "pure" art. (Kandinsky's 1912 manifesto, *Concerning the Spiritual in Art,* is full of echoes of Baudelaire.) But one artist whom this vision wholly leaves out, alas, is Baudelaire himself. For his poetic genius and achievement, as much as any poet before or after him, is bound up with a particular material reality: the everyday life—and night life—of the streets, cafes, cellars and garrets of Paris. Even his visions of transcendence are rooted in a concrete time and place. One thing that marks Baudelaire off radically from his romantic precursors, and from his symbolist and twentieth-century successors, is the way in which what he dreams is inspired by what he sees.

Baudelaire must have known this, at least unconsciously; whenever he is in the midst of sealing off modern art from modern life, he keeps reaching out to trip himself up and bring the two together again. Thus he stops in the midst of the 1855 "Progress" essay to tell a story, which he says is "an excellent lesson in criticism":

> The story is told of M. Balzac (and who would not listen with respect to any anecdote, no matter how trivial, concerning that great genius?) that one day he found himself in front of a beautiful picture—a melancholy winter-scene, heavy with hoarfrost and thinly sprinkled with cottages and mean-looking peasants; and that after gazing at a little house from which a thin wisp of smoke was rising, "How beautiful it is!" he cried, "But what are they doing in that cottage? What are their thoughts? What are their sorrows? Has it been a good harvest? *No doubt they have bills to pay?*" [Baudelaire's emphasis]

The lesson for Baudelaire, which we will unfold in the following sections of this essay, is that modern life has a distinctive and authentic beauty, which, however, is inseparable from its innate misery and anxiety, from the bills that modern man has to pay. A couple of pages later, in the midst of fulminating complacently against the modern idiots who think themselves capable of spiritual progress, he becomes suddenly serious and cuts sharply from a patronizing certainty that the modern idea of progress is illusory into an intense anxiety over the possibility that this progress is real. There follows a brief and brilliant meditation on the real terror that progress creates:

> I leave aside the question of whether, by continually refining humanity in proportion to the new enjoyments it offers, indefinite progress might not be its most cruel and ingenious torture; whether, proceeding as it does by a negation of itself, it would not turn out to be a perpetually renewed form of suicide, and whether, shut up in the fiery circle of divine logic, it would not be like the scorpion that stings itself with its own tail—progress, that eternal desideratum that is its own eternal despair! [14]

Here Baudelaire is intensely personal, yet close to universal. He wrestles with paradoxes that engage and enrage all modern men, and envelop their politics, their economic activities, their most intimate desires, and whatever art they create. This sentence has a kinetic tension and excitement that re-enact the modern condition it describes; the reader who arrives at the end of this sentence feels he has really been somewhere. This is what Baudelaire's best writing on modern life, far less well-known than his pastorals, is like. We are now ready for more of it.

2.

The Heroism of Modern Life

AT THE very end of his review of the Salon of 1845, Baudelaire complains that the painters of the day are too inattentive to the present: "and yet the heroism of modern life surrounds and presses in on us." He goes on:

> There is no lack of subjects, or of colors, to make epics. The true painter we're looking for will be one who can snatch from the life of today its epic quality, and make us feel how great and poetic we are in our cravats and our patent-leather boots. Next year let's hope that the true seekers may grant us the extraordinary delight of celebrating the advent of the *new!* [15]

These thoughts are not very well developed, but two things are worth noting here. First, Baudelaire's irony in the "cravats" passage: some people might think that the juxtaposition of heroism with cravats is a joke; it is, but the joke is precisely that modern men really are heroic, despite their lack of the paraphernalia of heroism; indeed, they are all the more heroic without paraphernalia to puff up their bodies and souls.* Second, the tendency of modernity to make all things new: next year's modern life will look and feel different from this year's; still, both will be part of the same modern age; but the fact that you can't step into the same modernity twice will make modern life especially elusive and hard to grasp.

Baudelaire goes deeper into modern heroism a year later in his short essay of that name. [16] Here he gets more concrete: "The spectacle of fashionable life [*la vie élégante*] and the thousands of floating existences—criminals and kept women—that drift about in the underworlds [*souterrains*] of a great city; the *Gazette des Tribunaux* and the *Moniteur* all prove to us that we need only open our eyes to recognize our heroism." The fashionable world is here, just as it will be in the essay on Guys; only here it appears in a decidedly nonpastoral form, linked with the underworld, with dark desires and deeds, with crime and punishment; it has a human depth far more arresting than the pallid fashion plates of "The Painter of Modern Life." The crucial point about modern heroism, as Bau-

---

* See Baudelaire's comments, in the "Heroism" essay, on the gray or black suit that was becoming the standard modern man's outfit: it expresses "not only political beauty, which is an expression of universal equality, but also poetic beauty, an expression of the public soul." The emerging standard outfit is "the necessary garb of our suffering age, which wears the symbol of perpetual mourning on its thin black shoulders."(118)

delaire sees it here, is that it emerges in *conflict*, in situations of conflict that pervade everyday life in the modern world. Baudelaire gives examples from bourgeois life as well as from the fashionable high and low life: the heroic politician, the government minister in the Assembly beating back the opposition with a searing and stirring speech, vindicating his policies and himself; the heroic businessman, like Balzac's perfumer Birotteau, fighting the specter of bankruptcy, striving to rehabilitate not only his credit but his life, his whole personal identity; respectable rascals like Rastignac, capable of anything—of the meanest as well as the noblest actions—as he fights his way to the top; Vautrin, who inhabits the heights of the government as well as the depths of the underworld, and who shows the essential intimacy of these two *métiers*. "All these exude a new and special beauty, which is neither that of Achilles nor yet that of Agamemnon." Indeed, Baudelaire says— in rhetoric guaranteed to outrage the neoclassical sensibility of many of his French readers—"the heroes of the Iliad are as pygmies compared to you, Vautrin, Rastignac, Birotteau . . . and you, Honoré de Balzac, you, the most heroic, the most extraordinary, most romantic and most poetic of all the characters you have produced from your womb." In general, contemporary Parisian life "is rich in poetic and marvelous subjects. The marvelous envelops and soaks us like an atmosphere, but we don't see it."

There are several important things to notice here. First, the wide range of Baudelaire's sympathy and generosity, so different from the standard image of an avant-garde snob who exudes nothing but scorn for ordinary people and their travails. We should note in this context that Balzac, the one artist in Baudelaire's gallery of modern heroes, is not one who strives to distance himself from ordinary people, but rather the one who has plunged deeper into their life than any artist has ever done before, and who has come up with a vision of that life's hidden heroism. Finally, it is crucial to note Baudelaire's use of fluidity ("floating existences") and gaseousness ("envelops and soaks us like an atmosphere") as symbols for the distinctive quality of modern life. Fluidity and vaporousness will become primary qualities in the self-consciously modernist painting, architecture and design, music and literature, that will emerge at the end of the nineteenth century. We will encounter them, too, in the thought of the deepest moral and social thinkers of Baudelaire's generation and after—Marx, Kierkegaard, Dostoevsky, Nietzsche—for whom the basic fact of modern life is the fact that, as the *Communist Manifesto* says, "all that is solid melts into air."

Baudelaire's "Painter of Modern Life" is undermined by its pastoral romance with the vapidities of the *vie élégante*. Nevertheless, it offers some brilliant and arresting images, poles away from pastoral, of what modern art should seek to capture in modern life. First of all, he says, the modern artist should "set up his house in the heart of the multitude, amid the ebb and flow of motion, in the midst of the fugitive and the infinite," in the midst of the metropolitan crowd. "His passion and his profession are *to become one flesh with the crowd*"—"*épouser la foule.*" Baudelaire gives special emphasis to this strange, haunting image. This "lover of universal life" must "enter into the crowd as though it were an immense reservoir of electrical energy. . . . Or we might compare him to a kaleidoscope gifted with consciousness." He must "express at once the attitude and the gesture of living beings, whether solemn or grotesque, and their luminous *explosion* in space." Electrical energy, the kaleidoscope, explosion: modern art must recreate for itself the immense transformations of matter and energy that modern science and technology—physics, optics, chemistry, engineering—have brought about.

The point is not that the artist should utilize these innovations (though, in his "Photography" essay, Baudelaire says he approves this—so long as the new techniques are kept in their subordinate place). The real point for the modern artist is to re-enact these processes, to put his own soul and sensibility through these transformations, and to bring these explosive forces to life in his work. But how? I don't think Baudelaire, or anyone else in the nineteenth century, had a clear grasp of how to do this. Not until the early twentieth century will these images begin to realize themselves—in cubist painting, collage and montage, the cinema, the stream of consciousness in the novel, the free verse of Eliot and Pound and Apollinaire, futurism, vorticism, constructivism, dada, poems that accelerate like cars, paintings that explode like bombs. And yet Baudelaire knows something that his twentieth-century modernist successors tend to forget. It is suggested in the extraordinary emphasis he gives to the verb *épouser,* as a primary symbol for the relationship between the artist and the people around him. Whether this word is used in its literal sense, to marry, or in a figurative sense, to sexually embrace, it is one of the most ordinary of human experiences, and one of the most universal: it is, as the songs say, what makes the world go round. One of the fundamental problems of twentieth-century modernism is the way this art tends to lose touch with people's everyday lives. This is not, of course, universally true—Joyce's *Ulysses* may be the noblest exception—but it is true enough to be noticed by everyone who cares about modern life and art. For Baudelaire, however, an art that is not *épousé* with the lives of men and women in the crowd is not properly modern art at all.

Baudelaire's richest and deepest thought about modernity begins just after "The Painter of Modern Life," in the early 1860s, and continues through the decade until the point, not long before his death in 1867, when he became too ill to write. This work is contained in a series of prose poems that he planned to bring out under the title of *Paris Spleen*. Baudelaire did not live to finish the series or publish it as a whole, but he did complete fifty of these poems, plus a Preface and an Epilogue, and they appeared in 1868, just after his death.

Walter Benjamin, in his series of brilliant essays on Baudelaire and Paris, was the first to grasp the great depth and richness of these prose poems.[18] All my work is in the vein Benjamin opened up, though I have found different elements and compounds from the ones he brought out. Benjamin's Parisian writings constitute a remarkable dramatic performance, surprisingly similar to Greta Garbo's in *Ninotchka*. His heart and his sensibility draw him irresistibly toward the city's bright lights, beautiful women, fashion, luxury, its play of dazzling surfaces and radiant scenes; meanwhile his Marxist conscience wrenches him insistently away from these temptations, instructs him that this whole glittering world is decadent, hollow, vicious, spiritually empty, oppressive to the proletariat, condemned by history. He makes repeated ideological resolutions to forsake the Parisian temptation—and to forbear leading his readers into temptation—but he cannot resist one last look down the boulevard or under the arcade; he wants to be saved, but not yet. These inner contradictions, acted out on page after page, give Benjamin's work a luminous energy and poignant charm. Ernst Lubitsch, *Ninotchka*'s scenarist and director, came out of the same Berlin Jewish bourgeois world as Benjamin, and also sympathized with the left; he would have appreciated the drama and the charm, but would doubtless have rewarded it with a happier denouement than Benjamin's own. My own work in this vein is less compelling as drama, but perhaps more coherent as history. Where Benjamin lurches between total merger of the modern self (Baudelaire's, his own) with the modern city, and total alienation from it, I try to recapture the more constant currents of metabolic and dialectical flow.

In the following two sections, I want to read, in detail and in depth, two of Baudelaire's late prose poems: "The Eyes of the Poor" (1864) and "The Loss of a Halo" (1865).[19] We will see at once, from these poems, why Baudelaire is universally acclaimed as one of the great urban writers. In *Paris Spleen,* the city of Paris plays a central role in his spiritual drama. Here Baudelaire belongs to a great tradition of Parisian writing that reaches back to Villon, runs through Montesquieu and Diderot, Restif de la Bretonne and Sebastien Mercier, and into the nineteenth century with Balzac and Hugo and Eugène Sue. But Baudelaire also expresses a radical break in this tradition. His best Parisian writing belongs to the precise historical moment when, under the authority of Napoleon III and the direction of Haussmann, the city was being systematically torn apart and rebuilt. Even as Baudelaire worked in Paris, the work of its modernization was going on alongside him and over his head and under his feet. He saw himself not only as a spectator, but as a participant and a protagonist in this ongoing work; his own Parisian work expresses its drama and trauma. Baudelaire shows us something that no other writer sees so well: how the modernization of the city at once inspires and enforces the modernization of its citizens' souls.

It is important to note the form in which the prose poems of *Paris Spleen* first appeared: as feuilletons that Baudelaire composed for the daily or weekly mass-circulation Paris press. The feuilleton was roughly equivalent to an Op-Ed piece in the newspapers of today. It normally appeared on the paper's first or center page, just below or opposite the editorial, and it was meant to be one of the very first things the reader would read. It was generally written by an outsider, in an evocative or reflective tone, intended as a contrast to the editorial's combativeness—though the piece might well be chosen to reinforce (often subliminally) the editor's polemical point. By Baudelaire's time, the feuilleton was an extremely popular urban genre, featured in hundreds of European and American newspapers. Many of the greatest nineteenth-century writers used this form to present themselves to a mass public: Balzac, Gogol and Poe in the generation before Baudelaire; Marx and Engels, Dickens, Whitman and Dostoevsky in his own generation. It is crucial to remember that the poems in *Paris Spleen* do not present themselves as verse, an established art form, but as prose, in the format of news.[20]

In the Preface to *Paris Spleen,* Baudelaire proclaims that *la vie moderne* requires a new language: "a poetic prose, musical without rhythm and without rhyme, supple enough and rugged enough to adapt itself to the soul's lyrical impulses, the undulations of reverie, the leaps and jolts of consciousness [*soubresauts de conscience*]." He emphasizes that "it was above all from the exploration of enormous cities and from the convergence of their innumerable connections [*du croisement de leurs innombrables rapports*] that this obsessive ideal was born." What Baudelaire communicates in this language, above all, is what I will call primal modern scenes: experiences that arise from the concrete everyday life of Bonaparte's and Haussmann's Paris but carry a mythic resonance and depth that propel them beyond their place and time and transform them into archetypes of modern life.

3.

The Family of Eyes

OUR FIRST primal scene emerges in "The Eyes of the Poor." (*Paris Spleen* #26) This poem takes the form of a lover's complaint: the narrator is explaining to the woman he loves why he feels distant and bitter toward her. He reminds her of an experience they recently shared. It was the evening of a long and lovely day that they had spent alone together. They sat down on the terrace "in front of a new cafe that formed the corner of a new boulevard." The boulevard was "still littered with rubble," but the cafe "already displayed proudly its unfinished splendors." Its most splendid quality was a flood of new light: "The cafe was dazzling. Even the gas burned with the ardor of a debut; with all its power it lit the blinding whiteness of the walls, the expanse of mirrors, the gold cornices and moldings." Less dazzling was the decorated interior that the gaslight lit up: a ridiculous profusion of Hebes and Ganymedes, hounds and falcons; "nymphs and goddesses bearing piles of fruits, patés and game on their heads," a mélange of "all history and all mythology pandering to gluttony." In other circumstances the narrator might recoil from this commercialized grossness; in love, however, he can laugh affectionately, and enjoy its vulgar appeal—our age would call it Camp.

As the lovers sit gazing happily into each other's eyes, suddenly they are confronted with other people's eyes. A poor family dressed in rags—a graybearded father, a young son, and a baby —come to a stop directly in front of them and gaze raptly at the bright new world that is just inside. "The three faces were extraordinarily serious, and those six eyes contemplated the new cafe fixedly with an equal admiration, differing only according to age." No words are spoken, but the narrator tries to read their eyes. The father's eyes seem to say, "How beautiful it is! All the gold of the poor world must have found its way onto these walls." The son's eyes seem to say, "How beautiful it is! But it is a house where only people who are not like us can go." The baby's eyes "were too fascinated to express anything but joy, stupid and profound." Their fascination carries no hostile undertones; their vision of the gulf between the two worlds is sorrowful, not militant, not resentful but resigned. In spite of this, or maybe because of it, the narrator begins to feel uneasy, "a little ashamed of our glasses and decanters, too big for our thirst." He is "touched by this family of eyes," and feels some sort of kinship with them. But when, a moment later, "I turned my eyes to look into yours, dear love, to read *my* thoughts there" (Baudelaire's italics), she says, "Those people with their great saucer eyes are unbearable! Can't you go tell the manager to get them away from here?"

This is why he hates her today, he says. He adds that the incident has made him sad as well as angry: he sees now "how hard it is for people to understand each other, how incommunicable thought is"—so the poem ends—"even between people in love."

What makes this encounter distinctively modern? What marks it off from a multitude of earlier Parisian scenes of love and class struggle? The difference lies in the urban space where our scene takes place: "Toward evening you wanted to sit down in front of a new cafe that formed the corner of a new boulevard, still piled with rubble but already displaying its unfinished splendors." The difference, in one word, is the *boulevard:* the new Parisian boulevard was the most spectacular urban innovation of the nineteenth century, and the decisive breakthrough in the modernization of the traditional city.

In the late 1850s and through the 1860s, while Baudelaire was working on *Paris Spleen,* Georges Eugène Haussmann, the Prefect of Paris and its environs, armed with the imperial mandate of Napoleon III, was blasting a vast network of boulevards through the heart of the old medieval city.[21] Napoleon and Haussmann envisioned the new roads as arteries in an urban circulatory system. These images, commonplace today, were revolutionary in the context of nineteenth-century urban life. The new boulevards would enable traffic to flow through the center of the city, and to move straight ahead from end to end—a quixotic and virtually unimaginable enterprise till then. In addition, they would clear slums and open up "breathing space" in the midst of layers of darkness and choked congestion. They would stimulate a tremendous expansion of local business at every level, and thus help to defray the immense municipal demolition, compensation and construction costs. They would pacify the masses by employing tens of thousands of them—at times as much as a quarter of the city's labor force—on long-term public works, which in turn would generate thousands more jobs in the private sector. Finally, they would create long and broad corridors in which troops and artillery could move effectively against future barricades and popular insurrections.

The boulevards were only one part of a comprehensive system of urban planning that included central markets, bridges, sewers, water supply, the Opéra and other cultural palaces, a great network of parks. "Let it be said to Baron Haussmann's eternal credit" —so wrote Robert Moses, his most illustrious and notorious successor, in 1942—"that he grasped the problem of step-by-step large-scale city modernization." The new construction wrecked hundreds of buildings, displaced uncounted thousands of people, destroyed whole neighborhoods that had lived for centuries. But it opened up the whole of the city, for the first time in its history, to all its inhabitants. Now, at last, it was possible to move not only within neighborhoods, but through them. Now, after centuries of life as a cluster of isolated cells, Paris was becoming a unified physical and human space.*

The Napoleon-Haussmann boulevards created new bases—economic, social, aesthetic—for bringing enormous numbers of people together. At the street level they were lined with small businesses and shops of all kinds, with every corner zoned for restaurants and terraced sidewalk cafes. These cafes, like the one where Baudelaire's lovers and his family in rags come to look, soon came to be seen all over the world as symbols of *la vie parisienne*. Haussmann's sidewalks, like the boulevards themselves, were extravagantly wide, lined with benches, lush with trees.[22] Pedestrian islands were installed to make crossing easier, to separate local from through traffic and to open up alternate routes for promenades. Great sweeping vistas were designed, with monuments at the boulevards' ends, so that each walk led toward a dramatic climax. All these qualities helped to make the new Paris a uniquely enticing spectacle, a visual and sensual feast. Five generations of modern painters, writers and photographers (and, a little later, filmmakers), starting with the impressionists in the 1860s, would nourish themselves on the life and energy that flowed along the boulevards. By the 1880s, the Haussmann pattern was generally

* In *Laboring Classes and Dangerous Classes*, cited in note 21, Louis Chevalier, the venerable historian of Paris, gives a horrific, excruciatingly detailed account of the ravages to which the old central neighborhoods in the pre-Haussmann decades were subjected: demographic bombardment, which doubled the population while the erection of luxury housing and government buildings sharply reduced the overall housing stock; recurrent mass unemployment, which in a pre-welfare era led directly to starvation; dreadful epidemics of typhus and cholera, which took their greatest toll in the old *quartiers*. All this suggests why the Parisian poor, who fought so bravely on so many fronts in the nineteenth century, put up no resistance to the destruction of their neighborhoods: they may well have been willing to go, as Baudelaire said in another context, anywhere out of their world.

The little-known essay by Robert Moses, also cited in note 21, is a special treat for all those who savor the ironies of urban history. In the course of giving a lucid and balanced overview of Haussmann's accomplishments, Moses crowns himself as his successor, and implicitly bids for still more Haussmann-type authority to carry out even more gigantic projects after the war. The piece ends with an admirably incisive and trenchant critique that anticipates, with amazing precision and deadly accuracy, the criticism that would be directed a generation later against Moses himself, and that would finally help to drive Haussmann's greatest disciple from public life.

acclaimed as the very model of modern urbanism. As such, it was soon stamped on emerging and expanding cities in every corner of the world, from Santiago to Saigon.

What did the boulevards do to the people who came to fill them? Baudelaire shows us some of the most striking things. For lovers, like the ones in "The Eyes of the Poor," the boulevards created a new primal scene: a space where they could be private in public, intimately together without being physically alone. Moving along the boulevard, caught up in its immense and endless flux, they could feel their love more vividly than ever as the still point of a turning world. They could display their love before the boulevard's endless parade of strangers—indeed, within a generation Paris would be world-famous for this sort of amorous display—and draw different forms of joy from them all. They could weave veils of fantasy around the multitude of passers-by: who were these people, where did they come from and where were they going, what did they want, whom did they love? The more they saw of others and showed themselves to others—the more they participated in the extended "family of eyes"—the richer became their vision of themselves.

In this environment, urban realities could easily become dreamy and magical. The bright lights of street and cafe only heightened the joy; in the next generations, the coming of electricity and neon would heighten it still more. Even the most blatant vulgarities, like those cafe nymphs with fruits and patés on their heads, turned lovely in this romantic glow. Anyone who has ever been in love in a great city knows the feeling, and it is celebrated in a hundred sentimental songs. In fact, these private joys spring directly from the modernization of public urban space. Baudelaire shows us a new private and public world at the very moment when it is coming into being. From this moment on, the boulevard will be as vital as the boudoir in the making of modern love.

But primal scenes, for Baudelaire as later on for Freud, cannot be idyllic. They may contain idyllic material, but at the climax of the scene a repressed reality creaks through, a revelation or discovery takes place: "a new boulevard, still littered with rubble . . . displayed its unfinished splendors." Alongside the glitter, the rubble: the ruins of a dozen inner-city neighborhoods—the city's oldest, darkest, densest, most wretched and most frightening neighborhoods, home to tens of thousands of Parisians—razed to the ground. Where would all these people go? Those in charge of demolition and reconstruction did not particularly concern themselves. They were opening up vast new tracts for development on the northern and eastern fringes of the city; in the meantime, the poor would make do, somehow, as they always did. Baudelaire's family in rags step out from behind the rubble and place themselves in the center of the scene. The trouble is not that they are angry or demanding. The trouble is simply that they will not go away. They, too, want a place in the light.

This primal scene reveals some of the deepest ironies and contradictions in modern city life. The setting that makes all urban humanity a great extended "family of eyes" also brings forth the discarded stepchildren of that family. The physical and social transformations that drove the poor out of sight now bring them back directly into everyone's line of vision. Haussmann, in tearing down the old medieval slums, inadvertently broke down the self-enclosed and hermetically sealed world of traditional urban poverty. The boulevards, blasting great holes through the poorest neighborhoods, enable the poor to walk through the holes and out of their ravaged neighborhoods, to discover for the first time what the rest of their city and the rest of life is like. And as they see, they are seen: the vision, the epiphany, flows both ways. In the midst of the great spaces, under the bright lights, there is no way to look away. The glitter lights up the rubble, and illuminates the dark lives of the people at whose expense the bright lights shine.* Balzac had compared those old neighborhoods to the darkest jungles of Africa; for Eugène Sue they epitomized "The Mysteries of Paris." Haussmann's boulevards transform the exotic into the immediate; the misery that was once a mystery is now a fact.

The manifestation of class divisions in the modern city opens up new divisions within the modern self. How should the lovers regard the ragged people who are suddenly in their midst? At this point, modern love loses its innocence. The presence of the poor

---

* See Engels, in his pamphlet *The Housing Question* (1872), on "the method called 'Haussmann' . . . I mean the practice, which has now become general, of making breaches in working-class quarters of our big cities, especially in those that are centrally situated. . . . The result is everywhere the same: the most scandalous alleys and lanes disappear, to the accompaniment of lavish self-glorification by the bourgeoisie on account of this tremendous success—but they appear at once somewhere else, and often in the immediate neighborhood." *Marx-Engels Selected Works*, 2 volumes (Moscow, 1955), I, 559, 606–9.

casts an inexorable shadow over the city's luminosity. The setting
that magically inspired romance now works a contrary magic, and
pulls the lovers out of their romantic enclosure, into wider and less
idyllic networks. In this new light, their personal happiness appears as class privilege. The boulevard forces them to react politically. The man's response vibrates in the direction of the liberal
left: he feels guilty about his happiness, akin to those who can see
but cannot share it; he wishes, sentimentally, to make them part of
his family. The woman's affinities—in this instant, at least—are
with the right, the Party of Order: we have something, they want
it, so we'd better "*prier le maître*," call somebody with the power to
get rid of them. Thus the distance between the lovers is not merely
a gap in communication, but a radical opposition in ideology and
politics. Should the barricades go up on the boulevard—as in fact
they will in 1871, seven years after the poem's appearance, four
years after Baudelaire's death—the lovers could well find themselves on opposite sides.

That a loving couple should find themselves split by politics is
reason enough to be sad. But there may be other reasons: maybe,
when he looked deeply into her eyes, he really did, as he hoped to
do, "read *my* thoughts there." Maybe, even as he nobly affirms his
kinship in the universal family of eyes, he shares her nasty desire
to deny the poor relations, to put them out of sight and out of
mind. Maybe he hates the woman he loves because her eyes have
shown him a part of himself that he hates to face. Maybe the
deepest split is not between the narrator and his love but within
the man himself. If this is so, it shows us how the contradictions
that animate the modern city street resonate in the inner life of
the man on the street.

Baudelaire knows that the man's and the woman's responses,
liberal sentimentality and reactionary ruthlessness, are equally futile. On one hand, there is no way to assimilate the poor into any
family of the comfortable; on the other hand, there is no form of
repression that can get rid of them for long—they'll always be
back. Only the most radical reconstruction of modern society could
even begin to heal the wounds—personal as much as social
wounds—that the boulevards bring to light. And yet, too often,
the radical solution seems to be dissolution: tear the boulevards
down, turn off the bright lights, expel and resettle the people, kill
the sources of beauty and joy that the modern city has brought

into being. We can hope, as Baudelaire sometimes hoped, for a future in which the joy and beauty, like the city lights, will be shared by all. But our hope is bound to be suffused by the self-ironic sadness that permeates Baudelaire's city air.

4.

The Mire of the Macadam

OUR NEXT archetypal modern scene is found in the prose poem "Loss of a Halo" (*Paris Spleen* #46), written in 1865 but rejected by the press and not published until after Baudelaire's death. Like "The Eyes of the Poor," this poem is set on the boulevard; it presents a confrontation that the setting forces on the subject; and it ends (as its title suggests) in a loss of innocence. Here, however, the encounter is not between one person and another, or between people of different social classes, but rather between an isolated individual and social forces that are abstract yet concretely dangerous. Here, the ambience, imagery and emotional tone are puzzling and elusive; the poet seems intent on keeping his readers off balance, and he may be off balance himself.

"Loss of a Halo" develops as a dialogue between a poet and an "ordinary man" who bump into each other in *un mauvais lieu*, a disreputable or sinister place, probably a brothel, to the embarrassment of both. The ordinary man, who has always cherished an exalted idea of the artist, is aghast to find one here:

"What! you here, my friend? you in a place like this? you, the eater of ambrosia, the drinker of quintessences! I'm amazed!"

The poet then proceeds to explain himself:

"My friend, you know how terrified I am of horses and vehicles? Well, just now as I was crossing the boulevard in a great hurry, splashing through the mud, in the midst of a moving chaos, with death galloping at me from every side, I made a sudden move [*un mouvement brusque*], and my halo slipped off my head and fell into the mire of the macadam. I was much too scared to pick it up. I thought it was less unpleasant to lose my insignia than to get my bones broken. Besides, I said to myself, every cloud has a silver lining. Now I can walk around incognito, do low things, throw myself into every kind of filth [*me livrer à la crapule*], just like ordinary mortals [*simples mortels*]. So here I am, just as you see me, just like yourself!"

The straight man plays along, a little uneasily:

"But aren't you going to advertise for your halo? or notify the police?"

No: the poet is triumphant in what we recognize as a new self-definition:

"God forbid! I like it here. You're the only one who's recognized me. Besides, dignity bores me. What's more, it's fun to think of some bad poet picking it up and brazenly putting it on. What a pleasure to make somebody happy! especially somebody you can laugh at. Think of X! Think of Z! Don't you see how funny it will be?"

It is a strange poem, and we are apt to feel like the straight man, knowing something's happening here but not knowing what it is.

One of the first mysteries here is that halo itself. What's it doing on a modern poet's head in the first place? It is there to satirize and to criticize one of Baudelaire's own most fervent beliefs: belief in the holiness of art. We can find a quasi-religious devotion to art throughout his poetry and prose. Thus, in 1855: "The artist stems only from himself. . . . He stands security only for himself. . . . He dies childless. He has been his own king, his own priest, his own God."[23] "Loss of a Halo" is about how Baudelaire's own God fails. But we must understand that this God is worshipped not only by artists but equally by many "ordinary people" who believe that art and artists exist on a plane far above them. "Loss of a Halo" takes place at the point at which the world of art and the ordinary world converge. This is not only a spiritual point but a physical one, a point in the landscape of the modern city. It is the point where the history of modernization and the history of modernism fuse into one.

Walter Benjamin seems to have been the first to suggest the deep affinities between Baudelaire and Marx. Although Benjamin does not make this particular connection, readers familiar with Marx will notice the striking similarity of Baudelaire's central image here to one of the primary images of the *Communist Manifesto:* "The bourgeoisie has stripped of its halo every activity hitherto honored and looked up to with reverent awe. It has transformed the doctor, the lawyer, the priest, the poet, the man of science, into its paid wage-laborers."[24] For both men, one of the crucial experiences endemic to modern life, and one of the central themes for modern art and thought, is *desanctification.* Marx's theory locates this experience in a world-historical context; Baudelaire's poetry shows how it feels from inside. But the two men respond to this experience with rather different emotions. In the *Manifesto,* the drama of desanctification is terrible and tragic: Marx looks back to, and his vision embraces, heroic figures like Oedipus at Colonnus, Lear on the heath, contending against the elements, stripped and scorned but not subdued, creating a new dignity out of desolation. "Eyes of the Poor" contains its own drama of desanctification, but there the scale is intimate rather than monumental, the emotions are melancholy and romantic rather than tragic and heroic. Still, "Eyes of the Poor" and the *Manifesto* belong to the same spiritual world. "Loss of a Halo" confronts us with a very different spirit: here the drama is essentially comic, the mode of expression is ironic, and the comic irony is so successful that it masks the seriousness of the unmasking that is going on. Baudelaire's denouement, in which the hero's halo slips off his head and rolls through the mud—rather than being torn off with a violent *grand geste,* as it was for Marx (and Burke and Blake and Shakespeare)—evokes vaudeville, slapstick, the metaphysical pratfalls of Chaplin and Keaton. It points forward to a century whose heroes will come dressed as anti-heroes, and whose most solemn moments of truth will be not only described but actually experienced as clown shows, music-hall or nightclub routines—shticks. The setting plays the same sort of decisive role in Baudelaire's black comedy that it will play in Chaplin's and Keaton's later on.

"Loss of a Halo" is set on the same new boulevard as "Eyes of the Poor." But although the two poems are separated physically by only a few feet, spiritually they spring from different worlds. The gulf that separates them is the step from the sidewalk into the gutter. On the sidewalk, people of all kinds and all classes know themselves by comparing themselves to each other as they sit or walk. In the gutter, people are forced to forget what they are as they run for their lives. The new force that the boulevards have brought into being, the force that sweeps the hero's halo away and drives him into a new state of mind, is modern *traffic*.

When Haussmann's work on the boulevards began, no one understood why he wanted them so wide: from a hundred feet to a hundred yards across. It was only when the job was done that people began to see that these roads, immensely wide, straight as arrows, running on for miles, would be ideal speedways for heavy traffic. Macadam, the surface with which the boulevards were paved, was remarkably smooth, and provided perfect traction for horses' hooves. For the first time, riders and drivers in the heart of the city could whip their horses up to full speed. Improved road conditions not only speeded up previously existing traffic but—as twentieth-century highways would do on a larger scale—helped to generate a volume of new traffic far greater than anyone, apart from Haussmann and his engineers, had anticipated. Between 1850 and 1870, while the central city population (excluding newly incorporated suburbs) grew by about 25 percent, from about 1.3 million to 1.65 million, inner-city traffic seems to have tripled or quadrupled. This growth exposed a contradiction at the heart of Napoleon's and Haussmann's urbanism. As David Pinkney says in his authoritative study, *Napoleon III and the Rebuilding of Paris,* the arterial boulevards "were from the start burdened with a dual function: to carry the main streams of traffic across the city and to serve as major shopping and business streets; and as the volume of traffic increased, the two proved to be ill-compatible." The situation was especially trying and terrifying to the vast majority of Parisians who walked. The macadam pavements, a source of special pride to the Emperor—who never walked—were dusty in the dry months of summer, and muddy in the rain and snow. Haussmann, who clashed with Napoleon over macadam (one of the few things they ever fought about), and who administratively sabotaged imperial plans to cover the whole city with it, said that this surface required Parisians "either to keep a carriage or to walk on stilts." [25] Thus the life of the boulevards, more radiant and exciting than urban life had ever been, was also more risky and frightening for the multitudes of men and women who moved on foot.

This, then, is the setting for Baudelaire's primal modern scene: "I was crossing the boulevard, in a great hurry, in the midst of a moving chaos, with death galloping at me from every side." The archetypal modern man, as we see him here, is a pedestrian thrown into the maelstrom of modern city traffic, a man alone contending against an agglomeration of mass and energy that is heavy, fast and lethal. The burgeoning street and boulevard traffic knows no spatial or temporal bounds, spills over into every urban space, imposes its tempo on everybody's time, transforms the whole modern environment into a "moving chaos." The chaos here lies not in the movers themselves—the individual walkers or drivers, each of whom may be pursuing the most efficient route for himself—but in their interaction, in the totality of their movements in a common space. This makes the boulevard a perfect symbol of capitalism's inner contradictions: rationality in each individual capitalist unit, leading to anarchic irrationality in the social system that brings all these units together.*

The man in the modern street, thrown into this maelstrom, is driven back on his own resources—often on resources he never knew he had—and forced to stretch them desperately in order to survive. In order to cross the moving chaos, he must attune and adapt himself to its moves, must learn to not merely keep up with it but to stay at least a step ahead. He must become adept at *soubresauts* and *mouvements brusques*, at sudden, abrupt, jagged twists and shifts—and not only with his legs and his body, but with his mind and his sensibility as well.

Baudelaire shows how modern city life forces these new moves on everyone; but he shows, too, how in doing this it also paradoxically enforces new modes of freedom. A man who knows how to

---

* Street traffic was not, of course, the only mode of organized motion known to the nineteenth century. The railroad had been around on a large scale since the 1830s, and a vital presence in European literature since Dickens' *Dombey and Son* (1846–48). But the railroad ran on a fixed schedule along a prescribed route, and so, for all its demonic potentialities, became a nineteenth-century paradigm of order.

We should note that Baudelaire's experience of "moving chaos" antedates the traffic light, an innovation developed in America around 1905, and a wonderful symbol of early state attempts to regulate and rationalize the chaos of capitalism.

move in and around and through the traffic can go anywhere, down any of the endless urban corridors where traffic itself is free to go. This mobility opens up a great wealth of new experiences and activities for the urban masses.

Moralists and people of culture will condemn these popular urban pursuits as low, vulgar, sordid, empty of social or spiritual value. But when Baudelaire's poet lets his halo go and keeps moving, he makes a great discovery. He finds to his amazement that the aura of artistic purity and sanctity is only incidental, not essential, to art, and that poetry can thrive just as well, and maybe even better, on the other side of the boulevard, in those low, "unpoetic" places like *un mauvais lieu* where this poem itself is born. One of the paradoxes of modernity, as Baudelaire sees it here, is that its poets will become more deeply and authentically poetic by becoming more like ordinary men. If he throws himself into the moving chaos of everyday life in the modern world—a life of which the new traffic is a primary symbol—he can appropriate this life for art. The "bad poet" in this world is the poet who hopes to keep his purity intact by keeping off the streets, free from the risks of traffic. Baudelaire wants works of art that will be born in the midst of the traffic, that will spring from its anarchic energy, from the incessant danger and terror of being there, from the precarious pride and exhilaration of the man who has survived so far. Thus "Loss of a Halo" turns out to be a declaration of something gained, a rededication of the poet's powers to a new kind of art. His *mouvements brusques*, those sudden leaps and swerves so crucial for everyday survival in the city streets, turn out to be sources of creative power as well. In the century to come, these moves will become paradigmatic gestures of modernist art and thought.*

Ironies proliferate from this primal modern scene. They unfold in Baudelaire's nuances of language. Consider a phrase like *la fange du macadam,* "the mire of the macadam." *La fange* in French is not only a literal word for mud; it is also a figurative word for mire, filth, vileness, corruption, degradation, all that is foul and

* Forty years later, with the coming (or rather the naming) of the Brooklyn Dodgers, popular culture will produce its own ironic version of this modernist faith. The name expresses the way in which urban survival skills—specifically, skill at dodging traffic (they were at first called the *Trolley* Dodgers)—can transcend utility and take on new modes of meaning and value, in sport as in art. Baudelaire would have loved this symbolism, as many of his twentieth-century successors (e.e. cummings, Marianne Moore) did.

loathsome. In classical oratorical and poetic diction, it is a "high" way of describing something "low." As such, it entails a whole cosmic hierarchy, a structure of norms and values not only aesthetic but metaphysical, ethical, political. *La fange* might be the nadir of the moral universe whose summit is signified by *l'auréole*. The irony here is that, so long as the poet's halo falls into *"la fange,"* it can never be wholly lost, because, so long as such an image still has meaning and power—as it clearly has for Baudelaire—the old hierarchical cosmos is still present on some plane of the modern world. But it is present precariously. The meaning of macadam is as radically destructive to *la fange* as to *l'auréole:* it paves over high and low alike.

We can go deeper into the macadam: we will notice that the word isn't French. In fact, the word is derived from John McAdam of Glasgow, the eighteenth-century inventor of modern paving surface. It may be the first word in that language that twentieth-century Frenchmen have satirically named *Franglais:* it paves the way for *le parking, le shopping, le weekend, le drugstore, le mobile-home,* and far more. This language is so vital and compelling because it is the international language of modernization. Its new words are powerful vehicles of new modes of life and motion. The words may sound dissonant and jarring, but it is as futile to resist them as to resist the momentum of modernization itself. It is true that many nations and ruling classes feel—and have reason to feel—threatened by the flow of new words and things from other shores.* There is a wonderful paranoid Soviet word that expresses this fear: *infiltrazya*. We should notice, however, that what nations have normally done, from Baudelaire's time to our own, is, after a wave (or at least a show) of resistance, not only to accept the new thing but to create their own word for it, in the hope of blotting out embarrassing memories of underdevelopment. (Thus the Académie Française, after refusing all through the 1960s to admit *le parking meter* to the French language, coined and quickly canonized *le parcmetre* in the 1970s.)

Baudelaire knew how to write in the purest and most elegant

---

* In the nineteenth century the main transmitter of modernization was England, in the twentieth century it has been the U.S.A. Power maps have changed, but the primacy of the English language—the least pure, the most elastic and adaptable of modern languages—is greater than ever. It might well survive the decline of the American empire.

classical French. Here, however, with the "Loss of a Halo," he projects himself into the new, emerging language, to make art out of the dissonances and incongruities that pervade—and, paradoxically, unite—the whole modern world. "In place of the old national seclusion and self-sufficiency," the *Manifesto* says, modern bourgeois society brings us "intercourse in every direction, universal interdependence of nations. And, as in material, so in intellectual production. The spiritual creations of nations become"—note this image, paradoxical in a bourgeois world—"common property." Marx goes on: "National one-sidedness and narrow-mindedness become more and more impossible, and from the numerous local and national literatures, there arises a world literature." The mire of the macadam will turn out to be one of the foundations from which this new world literature of the twentieth century will arise.[26]

There are further ironies that arise from this primal scene. The halo that falls into the mire of the macadam is endangered but not destroyed; instead, it is carried along and incorporated into the general flow of traffic. One salient feature of the commodity economy, as Marx explains, is the endless metamorphosis of its market values. In this economy, anything goes if it pays, and no human possibility is ever wiped off the books; culture becomes an enormous warehouse in which everything is kept in stock on the chance that someday, somewhere, it might sell. Thus the halo that the modern poet lets go (or throws off) as obsolete may, by virtue of its very obsolescence, metamorphose into an icon, an object of nostalgic veneration for those who, like the "bad poets" X and Z, are trying to escape from modernity. But alas, the anti-modern artist—or thinker or politician—finds himself on the same streets, in the same mire, as the modernist one. This modern environment serves as both a physical and a spiritual lifeline—a primary source of material and energy—for both.

The difference between the modernist and the anti-modernist, so far as they are concerned, is that the modernist makes himself at home here, while the anti-modern searches the streets for a way out. So far as the traffic is concerned, however, there is no difference between them at all: both alike are hindrances and hazards to the horses and vehicles whose paths they cross, whose free movement they impede. Then, too, no matter how closely the anti-modernist may cling to his aura of spiritual purity, he is bound to lose it, more likely sooner than later, for the same reason that the modernist lost it: he will be forced to discard balance and measure and decorum and to learn the grace of brusque moves in order to survive. Once again, however opposed the modernist and the anti-modernist may think they are, in the mire of the macadam, from the viewpoint of the endlessly moving traffic, the two are one.

Ironies beget more ironies. Baudelaire's poet hurls himself into a confrontation with the "moving chaos" of the traffic, and strives not only to survive but to assert his dignity in its midst. But his mode of action seems self-defeating, because it adds yet another unpredictable variable to an already unstable totality. The horses and their riders, the vehicles and their drivers, are trying at once to outpace each other and to avoid crashing into each other. If, in the midst of all this, they are also forced to dodge pedestrians who may at any instant dart out into the road, their movements will become even more uncertain, and hence more dangerous than ever. Thus, by contending against the moving chaos, the individual only aggravates the chaos.

But this very formulation suggests a way that might lead beyond Baudelaire's irony and out of the moving chaos itself. What if the multitudes of men and women who are terrorized by modern traffic could learn to confront it *together*? This will happen just six years after "Loss of a Halo" (and three years after Baudelaire's death), in the days of the Commune in Paris in 1871, and again in Petersburg in 1905 and 1917, in Berlin in 1918, in Barcelona in 1936, in Budapest in 1956, in Paris again in 1968, and in dozens of cities all over the world, from Baudelaire's time to our own—the boulevard will be abruptly transformed into the stage for a new primal modern scene. This will not be the sort of scene that Napoleon or Haussmann would like to see, but nonetheless one that their mode of urbanism will have helped to make.

As we reread the old histories, memoirs and novels, or regard the old photos or newsreels, or stir our own fugitive memories of 1968, we will see whole classes and masses move into the street together. We will be able to discern two phases in their activity. At first the people stop and overturn the vehicles in their path, and set the horses free: here they are avenging themselves on the traffic by decomposing it into its inert original elements. Next they incorporate the wreckage they have created into their rising barricades: they are recombining the isolated, inanimate elements into vital new artistic and political forms. For one luminous moment, the multitude of solitudes that make up the modern city come together in a new kind of encounter, to make a *people*. "The streets belong to the people": they seize control of the city's elemental matter and make it their own. For a little while the chaotic modernism of solitary brusque moves gives way to an ordered modernism of mass movement. The "heroism of modern life" that Baudelaire longed to see will be born from his primal scene in the street. Baudelaire does not expect this (or any other) new life to last. But it will be born again and again out of the street's inner contradictions. It may burst into life at any moment, often when it is least expected. This possibility is a vital flash of hope in the mind of the man in the mire of the macadam, in the moving chaos, on the run.

5.

The Twentieth Century: The Halo and the Highway

IN MANY ways, the modernism of Baudelaire's primal modern scenes is remarkably fresh and contemporary. In other ways, his street and his spirit seem almost exotically archaic. This is not because our epoch has resolved the conflicts that give *Paris Spleen* its life and energy—class and ideological conflicts, emotional conflicts between intimates, conflicts between the individual and social forces, spiritual conflicts within the self—but rather because our epoch has found new ways to mask and mystify conflict. One of the great differences between the nineteenth and twentieth centuries is that our century has created a network of new haloes to replace the ones that Baudelaire's and Marx's century stripped away.

Nowhere is this development clearer than in the realm of urban space. If we picture the newest urban spatial complexes we can think of—all those that have been developed, say, since the end of the Second World War, including all our newer urban neighborhoods and new towns—we should find it hard to imagine Baudelaire's primal encounters happening here. This is no accident: in fact, for most of our century, urban spaces have been systematically designed and organized to ensure that collisions and confrontations will not take place here. The distinctive sign of nineteenth-century urbanism was the boulevard, a medium for bringing explosive material and human forces together; the hallmark of twentieth-century urbanism has been the highway, a means for putting them asunder. We see a strange dialectic here, in which one mode of modernism both energizes and exhausts itself trying to annihilate another, all in modernism's name.

What makes twentieth-century modernist architecture especially intriguing to us here is the very precisely Baudelairean point from which it starts out—a point that it soon does its best to blot out. Here is Le Corbusier, possibly the greatest twentieth-century architect and certainly the most influential, in *L'Urbanisme* (translated as *The City of Tomorrow*), his great modernist manifesto of 1924. His Preface evoked a concrete experience from which, so he tells us, his great vision arose.[27] We shouldn't take him literally, but rather understand his narrative as a modernist parable, formally similar to Baudelaire's. It began on a boulevard—specifically, on the Champs Elysées—on an Indian summer evening in 1924. He had gone for a peaceful walk in the evening twilight, only to find himself driven off the street by traffic. This is half a century after Baudelaire, and the automobile has arrived on the boulevards full force: "it was as if the world had suddenly gone mad." From moment to moment, he felt, "the fury of the traffic grew. Every day increased its agitation." (Here the time frame and the dramatic intensity are somewhat broken.) Le Corbusier felt himself threatened and vulnerable in the most direct way: "To leave our house meant that, once we had crossed our threshhold, we were in danger of being killed by the passing cars." Shocked and disoriented, he contrasts the street (and the city) of his middle age with that of his youth before the Great War: "I think back twenty years, to my youth as a student: *the road belonged to us then;* we sang in it, we argued in it, while the horse-bus flowed softly by." (Emphasis mine.) He is expressing a plaintive sadness and bitterness as old as culture itself, and one of poetry's perennial themes: *Où sont les neiges d'antan?* Whither hath fled the visionary gleam? But his feeling for the textures of urban space and historical time make his nostalgic vision fresh and new. "The road belonged to us then." The young students' relation to the street was their relation to the world: it was—at least it seemed to be—open to them, theirs to move through, at a pace that could accommodate both argument and song; men, animals and vehicles could coexist peaceably in a kind of urban Eden; Haussmann's enormous vistas spread out before them all, leading to the Arc de Triomphe. But now the idyll is over, the streets belong to the traffic, and the vision must flee for its life.

How can the spirit survive this change? Baudelaire showed us one way: transform the *mouvements brusques* and *soubresauts* of modern city life into the paradigmatic gestures of a new art that can bring modern men together. At the ragged edge of Baudelaire's imagination we glimpsed another potential modernism: revolutionary protest that transforms a multitude of urban solitudes into a people, and reclaims the city street for human life. Le Corbusier will present a third strategy that will lead to a third, extremely powerful mode of modernism. After fighting his way through the traffic, and just barely surviving, he makes a sudden daring leap: he identifies himself totally with the forces that have been bearing down on him:

> On that 1st of October, 1924, I was assisting in the titanic rebirth [*renaissance*] of a new phenomenon . . . traffic. Cars, cars, fast, fast! One is seized, filled with enthusiasm, with joy . . . the joy of power. The simple and naive pleasure of being in the midst of power, of strength. One participates in it. One takes part in this society that is just dawning. One has confidence in this new society: it will find a magnificent expression of its power. One believes in it.

This Orwellian leap of faith is so fast and so dazzling (just like that traffic) that Le Corbusier hardly seems to notice that he has made it. One moment he is the familiar Baudelairean man in the street, dodging and fighting the traffic; a moment later his point of view has shifted radically, so that now he lives and moves and speaks from *inside* the traffic. One moment he is speaking about himself, about his own life and experience—"I think back twenty years . . . the road belonged to us then"; the next moment the personal voice utterly disappears, dissolved in a flood of world-historical processes; the new subject is the abstract and impersonal *on*, "one," who is filled with life by the new world power. Now, instead of being menaced by it, he can be in the midst of it, a believer in it, a part of it. Instead of the *mouvements brusques* and *soubresauts* that Baudelaire saw as the essence of everyday modern life, Le Corbusier's modern man will make one big move that will make further moves unnecessary, one great leap that will be the last. The man in the street will incorporate himself into the new power by becoming the man in the car.

The perspective of the new man in the car will generate the paradigms of twentieth-century modernist urban planning and design. The new man, Le Corbusier says, needs "a new type of street" that will be "a machine for traffic," or, to vary the basic metaphor, "a factory for producing traffic." A truly modern street must be "as well equipped as a factory."[28] In this street, as in the modern factory, the best-equipped model is the most thoroughly automated: no people, except for people operating machines; no unarmored and unmechanized pedestrians to slow the flow. "Cafes and places of recreation will no longer be the fungus that eats up the pavements of Paris."[29] In the city of the future, the macadam will belong to the traffic alone.

From Le Corbusier's magic moment on the Champs Elysées, a vision of a new world is born: a fully integrated world of high-rise towers surrounded by vast expanses of grass and open space— "the tower in the park"—linked by aerial superhighways, serviced by subterranean garages and shopping arcades. This vision had a clear political point, stated as the last words of *Towards a New Architecture:* "Architecture or Revolution. Revolution can be avoided."

The political connections were not fully grasped at the time—it is not clear whether Le Corbusier entirely grasped them himself —but we should be able to understand them now. *Thesis,* a thesis asserted by urban people starting in 1789, all through the nineteenth century, and in the great revolutionary uprisings at the end of World War One: the streets belong to the people. *Antithesis,* and here is Le Corbusier's great contribution: no streets, no People. In the post-Haussmann city street, the fundamental social and psychic contradictions of modern life converged and perpetually threatened to erupt. But if this street could only be wiped off the map—Le Corbusier said it very clearly in 1929: "We must kill the street!" [30]—then maybe these contradictions need never come to a head. Thus modernist architecture and planning created a modernized version of pastoral: a spatially and socially segmented world—people here, traffic there; work here, homes there; rich here, poor there; barriers of grass and concrete in between, where haloes could begin to grow around people's heads once again.*

This form of modernism has left deep marks on all our lives. The city development of the last forty years, in capitalist and socialist countries alike, has systematically attacked, and often successfully obliterated, the "moving chaos" of nineteenth-century urban life. In the new urban environment—from Lefrak City to Century City, from Atlanta's Peachtree Plaza to Detroit's Renaissance Center—the old modern street, with its volatile mixture of people and traffic, businesses and homes, rich and poor, is sorted out and split up into separate compartments, with entrances and exits strictly monitored and controlled, loading and unloading behind the scenes, parking lots and underground garages the only mediation.

All these spaces, and all the people who fill them, are far more ordered and protected than any place or anybody in Baudelaire's city could be. The anarchic, explosive forces that urban modernization once brought together, a new wave of modernization, backed by an ideology of developing modernism, has pulled apart. New York is now one of the very few American cities in which Baudelaire's primal scenes can still take place. And these old cities or segments of cities are under pressures far more threatening than the ones that gripped them in Baudelaire's day. They are economically and politically condemned as obsolete, beset by

---

* Le Corbusier was never able to make much headway in his indefatigable schemes for destroying Paris. But many of his most grotesque visions were realized in the Pompidou era, when elevated highways cleft the Right Bank, the great markets of Les Halles were demolished, dozens of thriving streets were razed, and substantial and venerable neighborhoods were turned over to *"les promoteurs"* and obliterated without a trace. See Norma Evenson, *Paris: A Century of Change, 1878–1978* (Yale, 1979); Jane Kramer, "A Reporter in Europe: Paris," *The New Yorker,* 19 June 1978; Richard Cobb, "The Assassination of Paris," *New York Review of Books,* 7 February 1980; and several of Godard's later films, particularly *Two or Three Things I Know About Her* (1973).

chronic blight, sapped by disinvestment, cut off from opportunities for growth, constantly losing ground in competition with areas that are considered more "modern." The tragic irony of modernist urbanism is that its triumph has helped to destroy the very urban life it hoped to set free.*

Corresponding in a most curious way to this flattening out of the urban landscape, the twentieth century has also produced a dismal flattening out of social thought. Serious thinking about modern life has polarized itself into two sterile antitheses, which may be called, as I suggested earlier, "modernolatry" and "cultural despair." For modernolators, from Marinetti and Mayakovsky and Le Corbusier to Buckminster Fuller and the later Marshall McLuhan and Herman Kahn, all the personal and social dissonances of modern life can be resolved by technological and administrative means; the means are all at hand, and the only thing needful is leaders with the will to use them. For the visionaries of cultural despair, from T. E. Hulme and Ezra Pound and Eliot and Ortega, onward to Ellul and Foucault, Arendt and Marcuse, all of modern life seems uniformly hollow, sterile, flat, "one-dimensional," empty of human possibilities: anything that looks or feels like freedom or

---

* This needs to be qualified. Le Corbusier dreamt of an ultramodernity that could heal the modern city's wounds. More typical of the modernist movement in architecture was an intense and unqualified hatred for the city, and a fervent hope that modern design and planning could wipe it out. One of the primary modernist clichés was the comparison of the metropolis to the stagecoach or (after World War One) to the horse and buggy. A typical modernist orientation toward the city can be found in *Space, Time and Architecture*, a monumental work by Le Corbusier's most articulate disciple, and the book that, more than any other, was used for two generations to define the modernist canon. The book's original edition, composed in 1938–39, concludes with a celebration of Robert Moses' new network of urban highways, which Giedion sees as the ideal model for the planning and construction of the future. The highway demonstrates that "there is no longer any place for the city street, with heavy traffic running between rows of houses; it cannot possibly be permitted to persist." (832) This idea comes directly out of *The City of Tomorrow;* what is different, and disturbing, is the tone. Le Corbusier's lyrical, visionary enthusiasm has been replaced by the truculent and threatening impatience of the commissar. "Cannot possibly be permitted to persist": can the police be far behind? Even more ominous is what comes next: the urban highway complex "looks forward to the time when, after the necessary surgery has been performed, the artificial city will be reduced to its natural size." This passage, which has the chilling effect of a marginal note by Mr. Kurtz, suggests how, for two generations of planners, the campaign against the street was only one phase of a wider war against the modern city itself.

The antagonism between modern architecture and the city is explored sensitively by Robert Fishman, *Urban Utopias in the Twentieth Century* (Basic Books, 1977).

beauty is really only a screen for more profound enslavement and horror. We should note, first of all, that both these modes of thought cut across the political divisions of left and right; second, that many people have clung to both these poles at different points in their lives, and some have even tried to cling to both at once. We can find both polarities in Baudelaire, who, indeed (as I suggested in Section 2), might lay claim to having invented both. But we can also find in Baudelaire something that is missing in most of his successors: a will to wrestle to the end of his energy with modern life's complexities and contradictions, to find and create himself in the midst of the anguish and beauty of its moving chaos.

It is ironic that both in theory and in practice the mystification of modern life and the destruction of some of its most exciting possibilities have gone on in the name of progressive modernism itself. And yet in spite of everything that old moving chaos has kept—or perhaps has renewed—its hold on a great many of us. The urbanism of the past two decades has conceptualized and consolidated this hold. Jane Jacobs wrote the prophetic book of this new urbanism: *The Death and Life of Great American Cities*, published in 1961. Jacobs argued brilliantly, first, that the urban spaces created by modernism were physically clean and orderly, but socially and spiritually dead; second, that it was only the vestiges of nineteenth-century congestion, noise and general dissonance that kept contemporary urban life alive; third, that the old urban "moving chaos" was in fact a marvelously rich and complex human order, unnoticed by modernism only because its paradigms of order were mechanical, reductive and shallow; and finally, that what still passed for modernism in 1960 might turn out to be evanescent and already obsolete.* In the last two decades, this

---

* "It is disturbing to think that men who are young today, men who are being trained now for their careers, should accept, *on the grounds that they should be modern in their thinking*, conceptions about cities and traffic which are not only unworkable, but also to which nothing new of any significance has been added since their fathers were children." *Death and Life of Great American Cities* (Random House and Vintage, 1961), 371; Jacobs' emphasis. The Jacobs perspective is developed interestingly in Richard Sennett, *The Uses of Disorder: Personal Identity and City Life* (Knopf, 1970), and in Robert Caro, *The Power Broker: Robert Moses and the Fall of New York* (Knopf, 1974). There is also a rich European literature in this vein. See, for instance, Felizitas Lenz-Romeiss, *The City: New Town or Home Town*, 1970, translated from the German by Edith Kuestner and Jim Underwood (Praeger, 1973).

Within the architectural profession, the critique of Le Corbusier's mode of modernism, and of the sterilities of the International Style as a whole, begins with Robert

perspective has gathered widespread and enthusiastic assent, and masses of Americans have worked steadfastly to save their neighborhoods and cities from the ravages of motorized modernization. Every movement to stop the construction of a highway is a movement to give the old moving chaos a new lease on life. Despite sporadic local successes, no one has had the power to break the accumulated power of the halo and the highway. But there have been enough people with enough passion and dedication to create a strong undertow, to give city life a new tension and excitement and poignancy while it lasts. And there are signs that it may last longer than anyone—even those who loved it most—would have thought. Amid the fears and anxieties of the contemporary energy crisis, the motorized pastoral appears to be breaking down. As it does, the moving chaos of our nineteenth-century modern cities looks more orderly and more up-to-date every day. Thus Baudelaire's modernism, as I have portrayed it here, may turn out to be even more relevant in our time than it was in his own; the urban men and women of today may be the ones to whom he was truly, in his image, *épousé*.

All this suggests that modernism contains its own inner contradictions and dialectics; that forms of modernist thought and vision may congeal into dogmatic orthodoxies and become archaic; that other modes of modernism may be submerged for generations, without ever being superseded; and that the deepest social and psychic wounds of modernity may be repeatedly sealed, without ever being really healed. The contemporary desire for a city that is openly troubled but intensely alive is a desire to open up old but distinctively modern wounds once more. It is a desire to live openly with the split and unreconciled character of our lives, and to draw energy from our inner struggles, wherever they may lead us in the end. If we learned through one modernism to construct haloes around our spaces and ourselves, we can learn from another modernism—one of the oldest but also, we can see now, one of the newest—to lose our haloes and find ourselves anew.

Venturi, *Complexity and Contradiction in Architecture*, with an Introduction by Vincent Scully (Museum of Modern Art, 1966). In the past decade it has come not only to be generally accepted but to generate an orthodoxy of its own. This is codified most clearly in Charles Jencks, *The Language of Post-Modern Architecture* (Rizzoli, 1977).

Petersburg: The Modernism of Underdevelopment

. . . the fleeting twilight of the northern summer, where the sun rolls like a flaming chariot over the somber forests which crown the horizon, and its rays, reflected by the windows of the palaces, give the spectator the impression of an immense conflagration.

—Joseph de Maistre, *Evenings of St. Petersburg*

We have little sense of personal dignity, of necessary egoism . . . Are there many Russians who have discovered what their real activity is? . . . It's then that what is known as dreaminess arises in characters who are eager for activity. And do you know what a Petersburg dreamer is, gentlemen? . . .

In the streets he walks, with a drooping head, paying little attention to his surroundings . . . but if he does notice something, even the most ordinary trifle, the most insignificant fact assumes a fantastic coloring in his mind. Indeed, his mind seems attuned to perceive the fantastic elements in everything.

. . . These gentlemen are no good at all in the civil service, though they sometimes get jobs.

—Dostoevsky, in the *Petersburg News*, 1847

Toward a history of the modern eclipse: the state nomads (civil servants, etc.) without home.
　　　　　　　　　—Nietzsche, *The Will to Power*

I've been to Paris and London . . . it's not customary to mention that our capital city belongs to the land of spirits when reference books are compiled. Karl Baedeker keeps mum about it. A man from the provinces who hasn't been informed of this takes only the visible administrative apparatus into account; he has no shadow passport.
　　　　　　　　　—Andrei Biely, *Petersburg*, 1913–16

It always seemed to me that in Petersburg something very splendid and very solemn was bound to happen.
　　　　　　　　　—Osip Mandelstam, *The Noise of Time*, 1925

It is terrifying to think that our life is a tale without a plot or a hero, made up out of desolation and glass, out of the feverish babble of constant digressions, out of the delirium of the Petersburg influenza.
　　　　　　　　　—Mandelstam, *The Egyptian Stamp*, 1928

WE HAVE been exploring some of the ways in which writers of the nineteenth century drew on the unfolding process of modernization, and used it as a source of creative material and energy. Marx, Baudelaire and many others strove to grasp this world-historical process and appropriate it for mankind: to transform the chaotic energies of economic and social change into new forms of meaning and beauty, of freedom and solidarity; to help their fellow men and help themselves to become the subjects as well as objects of modernization. We have seen how—from the fusion of empathy and irony, romantic surrender and critical perspective—modernist art and thought came into being. At least, this is the way it happened in the great cities of the West—in London, Paris, Berlin, Vienna, New York—where, all through the nineteenth century, the upheavals of modernization were going on.

But what happened in areas outside the West, where, despite the pervasive pressures of the expanding world market, and despite the growth of a modern world culture that was unfolding along with it—modern mankind's "common property," as Marx said in the *Communist Manifesto*—modernization was *not* going on? It is obvious that the meanings of modernity would have to be more complex, elusive and paradoxical there. This was the situation in Russia for most of the nineteenth century. One of the crucial facts about modern Russian history is that the economy of the Russian Empire was stagnating, and in some ways even regressing, at the very moment when the economies of the Western nations were taking off and surging spectacularly ahead. Thus, until the dramatic industrial upsurge of the 1890s, Russians of the nineteenth century experienced modernization mainly as something that was *not* happening; or else as something that was happening far away, in realms that Russians, even when they traveled there, experienced more as fantastic anti-worlds than as social actualities; or else, where it was happening at home, as something that was happening only in the most jagged, halting, blatantly abortive or weirdly distorted ways. The anguish of backwardness and underdevelopment played a central role in Russian politics and culture, from the 1820s well into the Soviet period. In that hundred years or so, Russia wrestled with all the issues that African, Asian and Latin American peoples and nations would confront at a later date. Thus we can see nineteenth-century Russia as an archetype of the emerging twentieth-century Third World.[1]

One of the remarkable features of Russia's age of underdevelopment is that in the span of barely two generations it produced one of the world's great literatures. Moreover, it produced some of the most powerful and enduring myths and symbols of modernity: the Little Man, the Superfluous Man, the Underground, the Vanguard, the Crystal Palace, and finally the Workers' Council or Soviet. Throughout the nineteenth century, the clearest expression of modernity on Russian soil was the imperial capital of St. Petersburg. I want to examine here the ways in which this city, this environment, Petersburg, inspired a series of brilliant explorations of modern life. I will work chronologically and historically, moving from the age when Petersburg developed a distinctive mode of literature to the age when it developed a distinctive mode of revolution.

I should acknowledge, at the start, some of the relevant and important things that this essay will not be doing. First of all, it will not be discussing the Russian countryside, even though the vast majority of Russians lived there, and even though it went through major transformations of its own in the nineteenth century. Second, I will not discuss, except in passing, the endlessly rich symbolism that developed around the polarity of Petersburg and

Moscow: Petersburg representing all the foreign and cosmopolitan forces that flowed through Russian life, Moscow signifying all the accumulated indigenous and insular traditions of the Russian *narod;* Petersburg as the Enlightenment, and Moscow as anti-Enlightenment; Moscow as purity of blood and soil, Petersburg as pollution and miscegenation; Moscow as sacred, Petersburg as secular (or perhaps atheistic); Petersburg as Russia's head, Moscow as its heart. This dualism, one of the central axes of modern Russian history and culture, has been discussed in great detail and depth.[2] Rather than re-examine the contradictions between Petersburg and Moscow, or between Petersburg and the countryside, I have chosen to explore the internal contradictions that pervaded the life of Petersburg itself. I will portray Petersburg in two ways: as the clearest realization of the Russian mode of modernization, and, simultaneously, as the archetypal "unreal city" of the modern world.*

I.

The Real and Unreal City

"Geometry Has Appeared": The City in the Swamps

THE BUILDING of St. Petersburg is probably the most dramatic instance in world history of modernization conceived and imposed draconically from above.[3] Peter I began it in 1703, in the swamps where the Neva ("Mud") River disgorges the waters of Lake Ladoga into the Gulf of Finland, leading to the Baltic Sea. He envisioned it as a combined naval base—he had worked as an apprentice in the Dutch shipyards, and his first achievement as Tsar was to establish Russia as a naval power—and trading center. The city was to be, as an early Italian visitor said, "a window to

---

* I do not know the Russian language, though I have read in Russian history and literature for years. This section owes a special debt to George Fischer, Allen Ballard and Richard Wortman, though they are not responsible for my mistakes.

Europe": in physical terms—for Europe was now accessible as it had never been—but, equally important, in symbolic language. First of all, Peter insisted on establishing Russia's capital here in this new city, with a window open to Europe, and scrapping Moscow, with all its centuries of tradition and its religious aura. He was saying, in effect, that Russian history must have a new beginning, on a clean slate. The inscriptions on this slate were to be exclusively European: thus Petersburg's construction was planned, designed and organized entirely by foreign architects and engineers, imported from England, France, Holland and Italy.

Like Amsterdam and Venice, the city was laid out as a system of islands and canals, with the civic center along the waterfront. Its pattern was geometric and rectilinear, standard in Western urban planning since the Renaissance, but unprecedented in Russia, whose cities were unorganized agglomerations of twisted, winding medieval streets. The official corrector of books wrote a poem that expressed a typical amazement at the new order:

> geometry has appeared,
> land surveying encompasses everything.
> Nothing on earth lies beyond measurement.

On the other hand, important features of the new city were distinctively Russian. No ruler in the West had the power to build on such a vast scale. Within a decade there were 35,000 buildings in the midst of these swamps; within two decades there were close to 100,000 people, and Petersburg had become, virtually overnight, one of the great metropolises of Europe.* Louis XIV's move from Paris to Versailles constituted a sort of precedent; but Louis was seeking to control the old capital from a point just outside it, not to reduce it to political insignificance.

Other features were equally inconceivable in the West. Peter commanded every stonemason in the whole Russian Empire to relocate to the new construction site, and forbade building in stone

---

* Petersburg's population reached 220,000 by 1800. At that point it was still slightly behind Moscow (250,000), but it would soon overtake the old capital. It grew to 485,000 in 1850, 667,000 in 1860, 877,000 in 1880, surpassed a million in 1890, and 2 million on the eve of World War One. It was, through the nineteenth century, the fourth or fifth largest city in Europe, behind London, Paris and Berlin, and in step with Vienna. *European Historical Statistics, 1750–1970*, edited by B. R. Mitchell (Columbia University Press, 1975), 76–78.

anywhere else; he ordered a large proportion of noblemen not only to move to the new capital but to build palaces there, or forfeit their titles. Finally, in a serf society where the vast majority of people were property either of noble landowners or of the state, Peter had total power over a virtually infinite labor force. He forced these captives to work breathlessly to cut through the growth, drain the swamps, dredge the river, dig canals, raise earthen dams and embankments, drive piles into the soft ground, and build the city at breakneck speed. The human sacrifices were immense: within three years the new city had devoured an army of close to 150,000 workers—physically wrecked or dead—and the state had to reach into the Russian interior, inexhaustibly, for more. In his will and his power to destroy his subjects en masse for the sake of construction, Peter was closer to the Oriental despots of ancient times—the Pharaohs with their pyramids, for instance —than to his fellow absolute monarchs in the West. Petersburg's horrific human costs, the dead men's bones mixed into its grandest monuments, immediately became central to the city's folklore and mythology, even for those who loved it most.

In the course of the eighteenth century, Petersburg became at once the home and the symbol of a new secular official culture. Peter and his successors encouraged and imported mathematicians and engineers, jurists and political theorists, manufacturers and political economists, an Academy of Sciences, a state-supported system of technical education. Leibniz and Christian Wolff, Voltaire and Diderot, Bentham and Herder, all enjoyed imperial patronage; they were translated and consulted, subsidized and often invited to St. Petersburg by a series of emperors and empresses, climaxing in Catherine the Great, who hoped to construct rational and utilitarian facades for their power. At the same time, especially under the Empresses Anna, Elizabeth and Catherine, the new capital was lavishly decorated and embellished, using Western architecture and design—classic perspective and symmetry, Baroque monumentality, Rococo extravagance and playfulness—to turn the whole city into a political theater, and everyday urban life into a spectacle. Two of the crucial landmarks were Bartolomeo Rastrelli's Winter Palace (1754–62), the first permanent imperial residence in the new capital, and Etienne Falconet's enormous equestrian statue of Peter the Great, the *Bronze Horseman* (installed 1782) in Senate Square, overlooking the Neva, at one of the city's focal points. Standard Western facades were required for all construction (traditional Russian styles, with wooden walls and onion domes, were explicitly forbidden), and 2:1 or 4:1 ratios of street width to building height were prescribed, so as to give the cityscape a look of infinite horizontal expanse. On the other hand, the use of space behind the building facades was completely unregulated, so that, especially as the city grew, imposing exteriors could conceal festering slums—"mantles of civilization," as Peter Chadaaev said about Russia as a whole, civilized on the outside alone.

There was nothing new about this political use of culture: princes, kings and emperors from Piedmont to Poland were enlisting art and science to buttress and legitimize their regimes. (This is the object of Rousseau's scathing criticism in his 1750 *Discourse on the Arts and Sciences.*) What was different in St. Petersburg was, first, its immensity of scale; second, the radical disparity, both environmentally and ideologically, between the capital and the rest of the country, a disparity that generated violent resistance and long-term polarization; finally, the extreme instability and volatility of a culture that sprang from the needs and fears of despotic rulers. The Petersburg pattern throughout the eighteenth century was for innovators to be sponsored and encouraged from the throne, only to find themselves suddenly disgraced and imprisoned—like Ivan Pososhkov, Russia's first political economist, and Dmitri Golytsin, its first secular political theorist—and left to rot in the Peter-Paul Fortress, Petersburg's Bastille, whose tower dominated the city's skyline (and still does today); for thinkers to be imported from the West, feted and flattered, only to be deported on short notice; for young noblemen to be sent abroad for education at the Sorbonne or in Glasgow or Germany, and then abruptly recalled and forbidden to learn more; of monumental intellectual projects begun with great fanfare and then broken off brusquely—as the Russian edition and translation of Diderot's *Encyclopédie,* in progress at the time of the Pugachev peasant uprising, was stopped short at the letter K, never to be resumed.

Catherine the Great and her successors recoiled in horror from the revolutionary waves that swept over Europe after 1789. Except for the brief period of rapprochement between Alexander I and Napoleon, which nourished liberal and constitutional initiatives from within the imperial bureaucracy, Russia's political role throughout the nineteenth century was to be the vanguard of European counter-revolution. But this role contained paradoxes. First, it meant enlisting the ablest and most dynamic of reactionary thinkers—de Maistre and a whole spectrum of German Romantics —but this only entangled Russia more deeply in those Western impulses and energies that the government was trying to blot out. Next, the *levée-en-masse* against Napoleon in 1812, although it created waves of hysteria, xenophobia, obscurantism and persecution, ironically, by its very success, swept a generation of Russians— most important, a generation of young nobles and officers—into the streets of Paris, and infused the returning veterans (the protagonists of Tolstoy's *War and Peace)* with the very ardor for reform that they had been sent West to blot out. De Maistre, as we quoted him at the head of this chapter, sensed something of this paradox: on one hand, he felt, or wanted to feel, that the serene magnificence of the palaces at the city center promised shelter from the storm; on the other hand, he feared that all he had fled might be pursuing him here, not only reflected but magnified in scope by the city's vast scene. To try to escape revolution here might turn out to be as futile as trying to escape the sun.

The first spark was ignited on December 14, 1825, just after the death of Alexander I, when hundreds of reformist members of the imperial guards—the "Decembrists"—assembled around Peter's statue in Senate Square and staged a large, confused demonstration in favor of the Grand Duke Constantine and constitutional reform. The demonstration, planned as the first phase of a liberal coup d'etat, petered out fast. The demonstrators had never been able to agree on a unified program—for some, the crucial issue was a constitution and the rule of law; for others, it was federalism in the form of home rule for Poland, Lithuania, the Ukraine; for still others, the emancipation of the serfs—and they had done nothing to attract support beyond their own aristocratic and military circles. Their humiliation and martyrdom—show trials, executions, mass imprisonment and Siberian exile, a whole generation decimated—ushered in thirty years of organized brutality and stupidity under the new Tsar Nicholas I. Herzen and Ogarev, as teenagers, took a "Hannibalic oath" to avenge the fallen heroes, and kept their luster burning bright throughout the 19th century.

Twentieth-century historians and critics take a more skeptical view, emphasizing the Decembrists' inchoate or muddled aims, their commitment to autocracy and reform from above, the hermetically sealed aristocratic world they shared with the government they attacked. But if we look at December 14 from the perspective of Petersburg, and of modernization, we will see a new basis for the old reverence. If we see the city itself as a symbolic expression of modernization from above, December 14 represents the first attempt to assert, at the city's spatial and political center, an alternate mode of modernization from below. Till then, every definition and initiative in St. Petersburg emanated from the government; then suddenly the people—at least a segment of the people—were taking initiative into their own hands, defining Petersburg public space and its political life in their own way. Till then, the government had furnished everyone in Petersburg with reasons for being there; indeed, it had forced many of them to be there. On December 14, for the first time, Petersburgers asserted the right to be there for reasons of their own. Rousseau, in one of his most powerful sentences, had written that houses make a town, but citizens a city.[4] December 14, 1825, marked an attempt by the inhabitants of some of Petersburg's grandest houses to transform themselves into citizens, and their town into a city.

The attempt failed, of course, as it was bound to; and it would be decades before such an attempt would be made again. What Petersburgers made instead, over the next half century, was a distinctive and brilliant literary tradition, a tradition that focused obsessively on their city as a symbol of warped and weird modernity, and that struggled to take possession of this city imaginatively on behalf of the peculiar sort of modern men and women that Petersburg had made.

Pushkin's "Bronze Horseman": The Clerk and the Tsar

This tradition begins with Alexander Pushkin's poem "The Bronze Horseman," written in 1833. Pushkin was a close friend of many of the Decembrist leaders; he himself escaped imprisonment only because Nicholas enjoyed keeping him on a string, under constant surveillance and pressure. In 1832 he began a sequel to his "novel in verse" *Evgeny Onegin*, in which his aristocratic hero would participate in the December rising. His new canto was written in a code known only to himself, but he came to feel that even this was too risky, and burned the manuscript. He then began work on "The Bronze Horseman." This poem is written in the same stanza form as *Onegin,* and has a hero with the same first name, but it is shorter and more intense. It is less politically explicit but probably far more explosive than the manuscript Pushkin destroyed. It was banned by Nicholas' censors, of course, and appeared only after Pushkin's death. "The Bronze Horseman" is lamentably unknown in English, but considered by such diverse spirits as Prince Dmitri Mirsky, Vladimir Nabokov and Edmund Wilson to be the greatest Russian poem. This alone might justify the lengthy discussion that is about to follow. But "The Bronze Horseman" is also, like so much Russian literature, a political as well as an artistic act. It points the way not only to great works by Gogol and Dostoevsky and Biely and Eisenstein and Zamyatin and Mandelstam, but also to the collective revolutionary creations of 1905 and 1917, and to the desperate initiatives of Soviet dissidents in our own day.

"The Bronze Horseman" is subtitled "A Petersburg Tale." Its setting is the great flood of 1824, one of the three dreadful floods in Petersburg's history. (They occurred almost precisely at hundred-year intervals, and all at historically crucial moments: the first in 1725, just after Peter's death, the most recent in 1924, just after Lenin's.) Pushkin inscribes a headnote to the poem: "The incident described in this tale is based on fact. The details are taken from contemporary magazines. The curious may verify them from material compiled by V. I. Berkh." Pushkin's insistence on the concrete factuality of his material and his allusion to the journalism of the day connect his poem with the traditions of the nineteenth-century realistic novel.[5] The fact that I will be citing Edmund Wilson's prose translation, the most vivid one I could find, will make the connection even clearer.[6] At the same time, "The Bronze Horseman," like the great tradition it inaugurates, will reveal the surreal quality of Petersburg's real life.

"Beside the desolate waves stood *He* and, thronged with mighty thoughts, stared out." So "The Bronze Horseman" begins: it is a kind of Petersburg Book of Genesis, beginning in the mind of the city's creator-God. "Thought *He:* Here, for our greatness, Nature has ordained that we shall break a window through to Europe; shall stand with feet set firm beside the sea." Pushkin uses the familiar image of a window to Europe; only he sees the window as something broken, made by an act of violence, violence that will recoil against the city as the poem unfolds. There is irony in Peter's "feet set firm beside the sea": Petersburg's foothold will turn out to be far more precarious than its creator could conceive.

"A hundred years went by, and that young city, the beauty and the marvel of northern lands . . . rose up in all its grandeur and its pride." Pushkin evokes this grandeur in proud images: "Today by the bustling docks crowd bulks of tower and palace, strong and shapely; ships swarm from all the earth's ends to that rich port; Neva [literally "mud"] has clothed itself in stone; bridges have spanned her waters; her isles are covered with groves dark green; and now before the younger capital, old Moscow dims—as, before a new Tsarina, the widow of the purple."

He asserts his own presence at this point: "I love thee, master-piece of Peter—I love thine aspect, graceful and severe, Neva's mighty stream, her granite banks, stiff lace of iron fences, the limpid dusk and moonless radiance of nights so full of thought, when lampless in my room I write and read, and sleeping masses of deserted streets show clear, and the Admiralty's needle gleams, and one glow makes haste to take another's place, never suffering the shade of night to dim the golden sky." Pushkin is alluding here to the famous summer "white nights," to magnify Petersburg's aura as a "city of light."

Several dimensions open outward from this point. First of all, Petersburg itself is a product of thought—it is, as Dostoevsky's Underground Man will remark, "the most abstract and premedi-tated city in the world"—and, of course, of Enlightenment. But the image of lampless, solitary rooms and "nights full of thought" suggests something else about Petersburg's intellectual and spiri-tual activity in the years to come: much of its light will be generated in ill-lit lonely rooms, away from the official radiance of the Winter Palace and the government, out of the range of its surveillance (a crucial issue, sometimes a matter of life and death), but also, at times, isolated from its foci of shared and public life.

Pushkin goes on to evoke the beauty of sleighs in winter, the freshness of young girls' faces at festivals and balls, the pomp of great martial processions (Nicholas I loved parades and created immense urban plazas for them), the celebrations of victory, the life force of the Neva breaking through the ice in spring. There is a lyrical loveliness in all this, but also a certain stuffiness; it has the lofty tone of state commissions and official verse. Twentieth-century readers are likely to distrust this rhetoric, and in the context of the poem as a whole we will have every right to distrust it. Nevertheless, there is a sense in which Pushkin—along with all those who follow in the Petersburg tradition, even Eisenstein in *October*—means every word of it. Indeed, it is only in the context of this lyrical celebration that the full horror of Petersburg becomes clear.

Pushkin's introduction to the poem closes with a lofty invocation: "Be splendid, Peter's city, and stand, like Russia, strong; for lo, the very conquered element has made her peace with thee at last; may the Finnish waves forget their ancient hate and bondage, nor vex with impotent rage Peter's eternal sleep." What sounds at first like civic cliché will turn out to be ghastly irony: the narrative that follows will make it clear that the elements have not made their peace with Petersburg—and, indeed, have never really been conquered—that their anger is all too potent, and that Peter's spirit remains vigilantly and vindictively awake.

"A dreadful time there *was*—of that I tell." So the story starts. Pushkin emphasizes the past tense, as if to say that the dread has passed; but the tale he is about to unfold will belie him. "On Petrograd all clouded over, November breathed the autumn cold. Splashing with loud waves against her handsome banks, Neva thrashed about, a sick man on his restless bed. The hour was late and dark; the rain beat angry against the window, the dolorous wind drew howling." At this point, coming through the wind and rain, we meet Pushkin's hero Evgeny. He is the first hero in Russian literature, and one of the first in world literature, to belong to the great anonymous urban mass. "Our hero lodges in a little room, works somewhere or other," a clerk in the lowest ranks of the civil service. Pushkin suggests that his family may once have had standing in Russian society, but the memory, even the fantasy, has been long lost. "And so, come home, he shook his overcoat, undressed and went to bed; but he could not sleep long, disturbed by diverse thoughts. What thoughts? That he was poor; that he had to work for decent independence"—irony here, because we will see how indecently dependent he is forced to be—"that God could have given him more brains and money; that he must wait two years to get promotion; that the river was all bloated, that the weather got no better; that the bridges might be taken up, and his

Parasha would surely miss him. . . . Here he was filled with ardent tenderness; his fancy, like a poet's soared away."

Evgeny is in love with a girl even poorer than he is, who lives on one of the remotest and most exposed of the islands on the city's fringe. As he dreams of her, we see the modesty and ordinariness of his desires: "Get married? Well, why not? . . . I shall make myself a modest little corner, and I shall give Parasha peace. A bed, two chairs, a pot of cabbage soup, and I the master of the house. What more should I want? . . . I'll take Parasha out for country walks on summer Sundays; humble I'll be and sly; they'll give me a snug berth; Parasha will keep house, bring up the children. . . . And so we'll live, and so go down to death, hand in hand, and be buried by our grandchildren." His dreams are almost pathetically limited; and yet, small as they are, they will clash radically and tragically with the reality that is about to break over the city's head.

"All night the Neva had plunged to reach the sea, but, worsted by that fury, she could fight no more." The winds coming off the Gulf of Finland, out of the Baltic, blow the Neva back on itself and over the city. The river "fell back in rage and tumult; flooded the islands; grew fiercer and fiercer; reared up and roared; like a cauldron, boiled, breathed steam; and, frenzied, fell at last upon the town." Pushkin's language erupts with images of cataclysm and doom; Milton is the only poet in English who can write at this pitch. "All fled before her—all was left abandoned—and now the waves were breaking through the streets. . . .

"A siege! A storming! Waves, like savage beasts, climb to the windows. Boats, pell-mell borne along, strike the glass with their sterns. Bridges swept loose by the deluge, fragments of cabins, timbers, roofs, the thrifty merchant's wares, the wretched chattels of the poor, the wheels of city droshkies, the coffins from the graveyard, washed afloat—all these drift through the town.

"The people see the wrath of God and await their execution. All ruined: roof and food! Where will it end?" The elements that Peter's imperial will had supposedly subdued, and whose conquest Petersburg was meant to embody, have taken their revenge. Pushkin's images here express a radical shift in point of view: the language of the people—religious, superstitious, attuned to omens, fired with fears of final judgment and doom—speaks more truly at this moment than the secular, rationalistic language of the rulers who have brought Petersburg's people to this pass.

Where are these rulers now? "The late Tsar [Alexander I] in that terrible year still gloriously ruled." It may seem ironical, even caustic, to speak of imperial glory at a time like this. But if we don't realize that Pushkin believed the Tsar's glory was real, we won't feel the full force of his belief in this glory's futility and emptiness. "Distressed and baffled now, he [Alexander] sought the balcony and spoke: 'To Tsars it is not given to curb the elements, for they belong to God.' " This is obviously true. But what makes the obvious truth outrageous here is the fact that Petersburg's very existence is an assertion that Tsars *can* control the elements. "With mournful brooding eyes he watched the dreadful work. The public squares were lakes, and into them the streets were pouring rivers. The palace seemed a dismal isle." Here, in an image that flows by so fast that it is easy to miss, we see crystallized the political life of St. Petersburg for the next ninety years, up to the revolutions of 1917: the imperial palace as an island cut off from the city that surges violently around it.

At this point we meet Evgeny again, in "Peter's Square"—Senate Square, site of Falconet's *Bronze Horseman*—at the water's edge. He is perched high on an ornamental lion, "hatless, with arms tightly folded, rigid and deathly pale." Why is he there? "Not for himself, poor fellow, did he fear. He did not notice how the greedy billows rose till they lapped his soles, nor did he see how his face was dashed with rain, nor how the wind howling had snatched his hat. His eyes were fixed far out in one desperate stare. There reared and ravaged the waves, like mountains from the outraged deep; *there* raved the storm, *there* broken things were tossed.... And *there*—God! God!—within the billows' reach, by the Gulf's very brink—the paintless fence, the willow, the little flimsy house—and they, the widow and her daughter, *there*—his dear Parasha, all his hope.... Or is it a dream he sees? Or is our life, then, nothingness, as empty as a dream, Fate's mockery of man?"

Now Pushkin steps back from Evgeny's torment and points out his ironic position on the urban stage: he has become a Petersburg statue. "As if bewitched, fast rooted to the marble, he can't dismount! Around him stretches water now and nothing else." Not quite nothing: directly opposite Evgeny, "back turned toward him, steady on its height above defiant Neva, rears on its steed of bronze, with outstretched arm, the idol." The godlike figure who began both the poem and the city now stands revealed as the radical antithesis of a god: "the idol." But this idol has created a city of men in its own image; it has transformed them, like Evgeny, into statues, monuments of despair.

The next day, although "still exulting fiercely in the fullness of their triumph, still wickedly the waters boil," the river recedes enough for people to come out into the streets again, enough for Evgeny to leave his perch opposite the *Bronze Horseman*. As Petersburgers try to pick up the scattered and shattered pieces of their lives, Evgeny, still crazed with fear, hires a boat to take him to Parasha's home at the mouth of the Gulf. He sails past twisted bodies and debris; he reaches the place, but there's nothing there —no house, no gates, no willow, no people—everything has been washed away.

"And, full of black foreboding, he prowls and prowls about, talks loudly to himself—then suddenly, striking his brow, he bursts out laughing." Evgeny's wits give way. The roar of the waves and the winds resounds incessantly in his ears. "Possessed by dreadful thoughts he could not utter, he strayed from place to place. Some dream was preying on him. A week, and then a month passed— he never from that day went home." The world, Pushkin tells us, forgot him soon. "All day he tramped, at night slept on the docks. His shabby clothes were torn and wearing out." Children stoned him, coachmen whipped him, he didn't notice, always submerged in some inner terror. "And so he dragged his miserable life, not beast or man, not this nor that, no dweller on the earth, nor yet departed spirit."

This could be the end of many a heartrending Romantic story —a poem by Wordsworth, say, or a tale of Hoffmann. But Pushkin is not yet ready to let Evgeny go. One night, wandering, not noticing where he was, "suddenly he stopped, and, his face aghast with terror, began to gaze about." He has found his way back to Senate Square: "and right before him, from its fenced-in rock, with outstretched arm, uprearing in the darkness, the idol sat its copper steed." Suddenly his thoughts grew terribly clear. He knew this place; "and him he knew who, fixed and still forever, held in the murk of night his copper head—himself whose fateful will had based this city on the sea. . . . How dreadful now in all-enveloping mist! What power of thought upon his brow! What force within! And in that steed, what fire! Where are you galloping, haughty steed? And where will you plant your hoof? O you who, in your might, did master Destiny! Did you not just so, aloft above the very precipice, make Russia rear?

"The poor fellow prowled about the pedestal, cast wild looks at the image of the lord of half the world." But now, suddenly, "His blood boiled up, a flame swept though his heart. Somber he stood before the arrogant statue, and, clenching his teeth and fists, possessed by some black force: 'Good! wonderworking builder!' with quivering hate he hissed, 'You'll reckon with me yet!'" This is one of the great radical moments of the romantic age: Promethean defiance springing forth from the soul of the oppressed common man.

But Pushkin is a Russian realist as well as a European romantic; and he knows that in the real Russia of the 1820s and 1830s Zeus is bound to have the last word: "You'll reckon with me yet!—And headlong took to flight." It is all one line, one fused instant: for "The terrible Tsar, on the instant hot with wrath, seemed all soundlessly to turn his head. And through the empty square he plunges wildly, and hears behind, like rattling thunderclap, a heavy-ringing gallop against the pounded pavement. And, dark in the pale moon, one arm flung up, the Copper Horseman comes behind, his charger's gallop ringing brass; and all night long, turn where Evgeny will, the Copper Horseman's clattering hoofbeats hammer—pursuing, still impend." Evgeny's first moment of rebellion is his last. "Thereafter, if he chanced upon the Square, his face, dismayed, would darken. Quick he would press his hand against his heart as if to calm its fluttering, remove his shabby cap and slink away." The idol drives him not only out of the city center but out of the city altogether, back to the remotest islands, where his love was swept away in the flood. It is there, the next spring, that his body is washed ashore, "and there for charity's sake they buried his cold corpse."

I have devoted so much time and space to "The Bronze Horseman" because it seems to me that Petersburg's whole life story is here, brilliantly crystallized and compressed: a vision of the city's grandeur and magnificence, and a vision of the madness on which it is based—the mad idea that a volatile nature can be permanently tamed and dominated by imperial will; nature's revenge, erupting cataclysmically, smashing grandeur into rubble, shattering lives and hopes; the vulnerability and terror of Petersburg's common people caught in the midst of the crossfire in a battle of giants; the

special role of the clerk in government service, the educated proletarian—perhaps the first of Nietzsche's "state nomads (civil servants, etc.) without home"—as Petersburg's Everyman; the
revelation that Petersburg's man-god, who dominates the whole
city from its center, is in reality an idol; the audacity of the common man who dares to confront the god-idol and demand a
reckoning; the futility of the first act of protest; the power of
Petersburg's powers that be to crush all challenges and
challengers; the idol's strange and seemingly magical power to
incarnate himself in his subjects' minds, an invisible police silently
trampling them down in the night, driving them at last out of their
minds, creating madness in the city's lower depths to complement
the madness that dominates its commanding heights; a vision of
Peter's successors on the throne as sadly impotent, their palace an
island hopelessly cut off from the city that teems and seethes
around it; the note of defiance that echoes, however faintly,
around Senate Square long after the first rebel has been wiped out
—"You'll reckon with me yet!"

Pushkin's poem speaks for the martyred Decembrists, whose
brief moment in Senate Square would come just a year after Evgeny's. But "The Bronze Horseman" also goes beyond them, for it
reaches far deeper into the city, into the lives of the impoverished
masses whom the Decembrists ignored. In generations to come,
Petersburg's common people would gradually find ways to make
their presence felt, to make the city's great spaces and structures
their own. For the time being, however, they would slink away or
stay out of sight—underground, in Dostoevsky's image of the
1860s—and Petersburg would continue to incarnate the paradox
of public space without public life.

Petersburg Under Nicholas I: Palace vs. Prospect

The reign of Nicholas I (1825–1855), which began with the
repression of the Decembrists and ended with military humiliation
at Sevastopol, is one of the most dismal in modern Russian history.
Nicholas' most lasting contribution to Russian history was the development of a political police, controlled by its secret Third Section, which came to penetrate every area of Russian life, and
established Russia in the European imagination as the archetypal

"police state." But the trouble was not merely that Nicholas' government was cruelly repressive: that it clamped down on the serfs (about four fifths of the population) and crushed all hopes for their liberation, repressed them with horrible brutality (there were more than six hundred peasant uprisings during Nicholas' reign; one of his achievements was to keep nearly all of them, and their repression, secret from the country as a whole); that it condemned thousands of people to death after secret trials, without even a facade of due process of law (Dostoevsky, the most illustrious, was reprieved thirty seconds before execution); that it established multiple layers of censorship, packed schools and universities with informers, eventually paralyzed the whole educational system, finally drove all thought and culture underground, into prison, or out of the country.

What was distinctive here was neither the fact of repression nor its scope—the Russian state had always treated its subjects dreadfully—but its goal. Peter the Great had murdered and terrorized in order to break open a window to Europe, to open the way to Russia's progress and growth; Nicholas and his police were repressing and brutalizing in order to close that window. The difference between the Tsar who was the subject of Pushkin's poem and the Tsar who suppressed the poem was the difference between a "wonderworking builder" and a policeman. The "Bronze Horseman" had pursued his countrymen in order to drive them forward; the current ruler seemed interested only in pressing them down. In Nicholas' Petersburg, Pushkin's Horseman was almost as alienated as his clerk.

Alexander Herzen, writing from exile, gave the classic account of Nicholas' regime. Here is a typical passage:

> Without becoming a Russian, he ceased to be a European. . . . In his system there was no motor. . . . He limited himself to the persecution of any yearning for freedom, any idea of progress. . . . During his long reign he affected in turn nearly all institutions, introducing everywhere the element of paralysis, of death.[7]

Herzen's image of a system without a motor, an image drawn from modern technology and industry, is especially apt. One of the firmest pillars of Tsarist policy from Peter through Catherine the Great was the mercantilist attempt to stimulate economic and industrial growth for the sake of *raison d'état:* to give the system a motor. Under Nicholas, this policy was consciously and decisively abandoned. (It would not be revived until the 1890s, under Count Witte, with spectacular success.) Nicholas and his ministers believed that the government should actually retard economic development, because economic progress might well create demands for political reform, and new classes—a bourgeoisie, an industrial proletariat—capable of taking political initiative into their own hands. Ruling circles had realized since the hopeful early years of Alexander I that serfdom—because it kept the vast majority of the population shackled to the land and its lords, reduced the landowners' incentive to modernize their estates (or in effect rewarded them for not modernizing), and prevented the growth of a free, mobile industrial labor force—was the main force retarding the economic growth of the country. Nicholas' insistence on the sacredness of serfdom ensured that Russian economic development would be held back, just at the moment when the economies of Western Europe and the United States were taking off and surging ahead. Thus the relative backwardness of the country increased considerably during the Nicolavean age. It took a major military defeat to shake the government's monumental complacency. It was only after the disaster at Sevastopol, a political and military as well as an economic disaster, that Russia's official celebration of its backwardness came to an end.[8]

The political and human costs of underdevelopment were clear to thinkers as diverse as the Moscow aristocrat Chadaaev and the Petersburg plebeian Belinsky; both said that what Russia needed most desperately was a new Peter the Great to break the Western window open again. But Chadaaev was officially declared insane and kept for many years under house arrest; as for Belinsky, "We would have rotted him in a fortress," one of the heads of the secret police said regretfully, after he died young of tuberculosis in early 1848. Moreover, Belinsky's views on development—"countries without a middle class are doomed to eternal insignificance"; "the internal process of civil development in Russia will not start until . . . the Russian gentry has been transformed into a bourgeoisie" —were very much in the minority, even within the radical opposition. Even the radical, democratic, socialistic and pro-Western thinkers of Nicholas' time shared many of the government's economic and social biases: agrarianism, celebration of peasant communal traditions, aversion to the bourgeoisie and to industry. When Herzen said, "God save Russia from the bourgeoisie!" he was inadvertently working to keep the system he despised from getting a motor.[9]

During Nicholas' regime, Petersburg acquired a reputation, which it never lost, as a strange, weird, spectral place. These qualities were evoked most memorably in this period by Gogol and Dostoevsky. Here, for instance, is Dostoevsky in 1848, in a short story entitled "A Weak Heart":

> I remember one wintry January evening when I was hurrying home from the Vyborg side. I was still very young then. When I reached the Neva, I stopped for a minute and threw a piercing glance along the river into the smoky, frostily dim distance, which had suddenly turned crimson with the last purple of a sunset that was dying over the hazy horizon. Night lay over the city. . . . Frozen steam poured from tired horses, from running people. The taut air quivered at the slightest sound, and columns of smoke like giants rose from all the roofs on both embankments and rushed upward through the cold sky, twining and untwining on the way, so it seemed that new buildings were rising above the old ones, a new city was forming in the air. . . . It seemed, finally, that this whole world with all its inhabitants, strong and weak, with all their domiciles, the shelters of the poor or gilded mansions, resembled at this twilight hour a fantastic, magic vision, a dream, which would in its turn vanish immediately and rise up as steam toward the dark-blue sky.[10]

We will be exploring the evolution, over a century, of Petersburg's identity as a mirage, a ghost town, whose grandeur and magnificence are continually melting into its murky air. I want to suggest here that in the political and cultural atmosphere of Nicholas' regime the effusion of spectral symbolism made very real sense. This city, whose very existence was a symbol of Russia's dynamism and its determination to be modern, now found itself at the head of a system that prided itself on being a system without a motor; the Bronze Horseman's successors were asleep in the saddle, the reins pulled tight but frozen stiff, horse and rider supported by the static equilibrium of a great dead weight. In Nicholas' Petersburg, Peter's dangerous but dynamic spirit was reduced to a specter, a ghost, powerful enough to haunt the city but powerless to animate it. No wonder, then, that Petersburg should establish itself as the archetypal modern ghost town. Ironically, the very incongruities that arose out of Nicholas' politics—a politics of enforced backwardness in the midst of forms and symbols of enforced modernization—made Petersburg the source and the inspiration for a distinctively weird form of modernism, which we might call the "modernism of underdevelopment."

In the Nicolavean age, while the state slept, the axis and drama of modernity shifted from the magnificent ensemble of state buildings and monuments and enormous squares at the city's center along the Neva, to the Nevsky Prospect. The Nevsky was one of the three radial streets spreading out from Admiralty Square that gave the city its shape. It had always been one of Petersburg's main roads. In the early nineteenth century, however, during Alexander's reign, the Nevsky was almost completely rebuilt by several distinguished neoclassical architects. As its new form emerged in the late 1820s, it came to be distinguished sharply from its competing radials (the Voznesensky Prospect and Gorokhovaya Street), and recognized as a unique urban environment.[11] It was the city's longest, widest, best-lit and best-paved street. From Admiralty Square it moved outward in a straight line for two and three quarter miles to the southwest. (It then turned aside, narrowed, and proceeded in a brief coda to the Alexander Nevsky Monastery; but this section was never really felt to be part of "the Nevsky," and we will not consider it here.) It led, after 1851, to the terminal of the Moscow–Petersburg express train, one of Russia's primary symbols of modern energy and mobility (and, of course, a central character in Tolstoy's *Anna Karenina*). It was crossed by the Moika River, by the Katherine and Fontanka canals, and spanned by graceful bridges that offered fine long perspectives of the city's flowing life.

Splendid buildings lined the street, often built on subsidiary squares and public spaces of their own: the neobaroque cathedral of Our Lady of Kazan; the rococo Mikhailovsky Palace, where the mad Tsar Paul I was strangled by his bodyguards in 1801 to make way for his son Alexander; the neoclassical Alexander Theater; the Public Library, beloved by generations of intellectuals too poor to afford libraries of their own; the Gostiny Dvor (or Les Grands Boutiques, as its signs proclaimed), a square block of glassed-in shopping arcades built on the lines of the Rue de Rivoli and Regent Street, but, like so many Russian adaptations of Western prototypes, far surpassing the originals in scale. From every point on the street the golden needle of the Admiralty Tower (reconstructed 1806–10) could be seen, lifting up the eye, giving the viewer a visual orientation and a sense of place in the city as a whole, inflaming the imagination as the shifting sun lit up the golden spire, transforming real urban space into a magical dreamscape.

The Nevsky Prospect was a distinctively modern environment in many ways. First, the street's straightness, breadth, length and good paving made it an ideal medium for moving people and things, a perfect artery for the emerging modes of fast and heavy traffic. Like the boulevards that Haussmann hacked through Paris in the 1860s, it served as a focus for newly accumulated material and human forces: macadam and asphalt, gaslight and electric light, the railroad, electric trolleys and automobiles, movies and mass demonstrations. But because Petersburg had been planned and designed so well, the Nevsky was in action a full generation before its Parisian counterparts, and it functioned far more smoothly, without devastating any old neighborhoods or lives.

Next, the Nevsky served as a showcase for the wonders of the new consumer economy that modern mass production was just beginning to open up: furniture and silverware, fabrics and clothing, boots and books, all were displayed attractively in the street's multitude of shops. Displayed along with foreign goods—French fashions and furniture, English textiles and saddles, German chinaware and clocks—were foreign styles, foreign men and women, all the forbidden allure of the world outside. A recently reissued series of lithographs from the 1830s shows more than half the shop signs on the Nevsky to be either bilingual or exclusively English or French; very few are in Russian alone. Even in a city as international as Petersburg, the Nevsky was an unusually cosmopolitan zone.[12] Furthermore—and this was especially important under a repressive government like Nicholas'—the Nevsky was the one public space in Petersburg that was not dominated by the state. The government could monitor but it could not generate the actions and interactions that took place here. Hence the Nevsky emerged as a kind of free zone in which social and psychic forces could spontaneously unfold.

Finally, the Nevsky was the one place in Petersburg (and perhaps in all Russia) where all the existing classes came together, from the nobility whose palaces and town houses graced the street at its starting point near the Admiralty and the Winter Palace, to the poor artisans, prostitutes, derelicts and bohemians who huddled in the wretched fleabags and taverns near the railroad station in Znaniemsky Square where the Prospect came to an end. The Nevsky brought them all together, whirled them around in a vortex, and left them to make of their experiences and encounters what they could. Petersburgers loved the Nevsky, and mythologized it inexhaustibly, because it opened up for them, in the heart of an underdeveloped country, a prospect of all the dazzling promises of the modern world.

Gogol: The Real and Surreal Street

The popular mythology of the Nevsky Prospect is first transformed into art by Gogol in his marvelous story "Nevsky Prospect," published in 1835. This story, practically unknown in the English-speaking world,[13] is mostly concerned with a young artist's romantic tragedy and a young soldier's romantic farce. We will discuss their stories soon. More original, however, and more important for our purposes, is Gogol's introduction, in which he frames his protagonists in their natural habitat. The framework is provided by a narrator who, with the ebullience of a carnival barker, introduces us to the street. In these few pages Gogol, without any apparent effort (or even awareness), invents one of the primary genres in modern literature: the romance of the city street, in which the street is itself the hero. Gogol's narrator addresses us with a breathless giddiness:

> There is nothing to compare with the Nevsky Prospect, at least not in Petersburg; for in that city it is everything. The beauty of the capital!—what splendors does this street not know? I'm sure that not one of the town's pale and clerkish inhabitants would exchange the Nevsky for any earthly blessing. . . . And the ladies! Oh, to the ladies the Nevsky Prospect is an even greater delight. But who isn't delighted with it?

He tries to explain to us how this street is different from all other streets:

Even if you had important business, you'd probably forget it all as soon as you stepped into the street. This is one place where people don't show themselves because they have to, where they aren't driven by the necessary and commercial interest that embraces the whole of St. Petersburg. It seems that the man you meet on the Nevsky is less of an egoist than those on the Morskaya, Gorkhovaya, Litenaya, Meshchanskaya and other streets, where greed and self-interest are stamped on passersby and those who flit by in carriages and cabs. The Nevsky is the common meeting ground and communications line of St. Petersburg. No directory or information bureau will furnish such correct information as the Nevsky. Omniscient Nevsky Prospect! . . . How swift the phantasmagoria that develops here in the course of a single day! How many metamorphoses it goes through within twenty-four hours!

The essential purpose of this street, which gives it its special character, is sociability: people come here to see and be seen, and to communicate their visions to one another, not for any ulterior purpose, without greed or competition, but as an end in itself. Their communication, and the message of the street as a whole, is a strange mixture of reality and fantasy: on one hand, it acts as a setting for people's fantasies of who they want to be; on the other hand, it provides true knowledge—for those who can decode it—of who people really are.

There are several paradoxes about the Nevsky's sociability. On one hand, it brings people face to face with each other; on the other hand, it propels people past each other with such speed and force that it's hard for anyone to look at anyone closely—before you can focus clearly, the apparition is gone. Hence much of the vision that the Nevsky affords is a vision not so much of people presenting themselves as of fragmented forms and features flashing by:

How clean-swept are its pavements, and how many feet have left their marks on them! The clumsy, dirty boot of the retired soldier beneath whose weight the very granite seems to crack; the miniature slipper, light as smoke, of the young lady who turns her head to the dazzling shop windows like a sunflower to the sun; the hopeful ensign's rattling saber that draws a sharp scratch over its surface—everything is marked on it by the power of strength or the power of weakness.

This passage, written as if from the point of view of the pavement, suggests that we can grasp the people of the Nevsky only if we break them up into their constituent parts—in this case, their feet —but also that, if we know how to look closely, we can grasp each feature as a microcosm of their whole being.

This fragmented vision is carried to great lengths and depths as Gogol traces a day in the life of the street. "How many metamorphoses it goes through in twenty-four hours!" Gogol's narrator starts slowly just before dawn, at a moment when the street itself is slow: only a few peasants here, trudging in from the countryside to work on the city's vast construction projects, and beggars standing around in front of bakeries whose ovens have been going all night. Around sunrise, life begins to stir, with shopkeepers opening up their stores, goods unloading, old ladies on their way to Mass. Gradually the street becomes crowded with clerks rushing to their offices, and soon with their superiors' carriages. As the day progresses and the Nevsky swells up with multitudes of people, and picks up energy and momentum, Gogol's prose, too, gains in speed and intensity: breathlessly he piles up one group on top of another—tutors, governesses and their children, actors, musicians and their prospective audiences, soldiers, male and female shoppers, office clerks and foreign secretaries, the endless gradations of Russian civil servants—cutting rapidly back and forth, making the street's frantic rhythms his own. Finally, in the late afternoon and early evening, as the Prospect reaches its peak hours, as it is inundated with fashionable and would-be fashionable people, the energy and momentum have become so intense that the planes of vision are shattered and the unity of human form is broken into surreal fragments:

> Here you'll find marvelous mustaches, which neither pen nor brush could depict, to which the best part of a lifetime has been devoted, objects of long vigils by day and midnight; mustaches on which the most ravishing ointments have been poured, which have been anointed with the most precious pomades, and which are the envy of passersby. . . . Here you'll find a thousand varieties of ladies' hats, gowns, kerchiefs, bright and wispy, which sometimes remain their owners' favorites for two whole days. . . . It looks as though a whole sea of butterflies has suddenly arisen from the flowerstalks, and is waving a dazzling cloud above the black beetles of the male sex. Here you'll meet waists such as

you've never dreamed of, so narrow that fear and trembling will assail you that some careless breath of yours might injure this wondrous product of nature and art. And what ladies' sleeves you'll meet on the Nevsky Prospect! sleeves like two balloons, on which a lady might suddenly float up into the air, if not supported by a gentleman. Here you'll meet unique smiles, product of the highest art.

And so on. It is hard to know what Gogol's contemporaries made of passages like this; they certainly didn't say much in print. From the perspective of our century, however, this writing is uncanny: the Nevsky Prospect seems to carry Gogol out of his time and into our own, like that lady floating through the air on her own sleeves. Joyce's *Ulysses*, Döblin's *Alexanderplatz, Berlin*, cubo-futurist cityscapes, dadaist and surrealist montage, the German expressionist cinema, Eisenstein and Dziga Vertov, the Parisian nouvelle vague, all start from this point; Gogol seems to be inventing the twentieth century out of his own head.

Gogol now presents, perhaps for the first time in literature, another archetypally modern theme: the special magical aura of the city at night. "But as soon as twilight falls on the houses and the streets, and the watchman scrambles up the steps to light the lamp, the Nevsky Prospect begins to revive and to move again, and then begins that mysterious time when lamps lend a wondrous, enticing light to all things." Older people, married people, people with solid homes are all off the streets by now; the Nevsky now belongs to the young and avid and, Gogol adds, to the working classes, who are of course the last to leave off their work. "At this time one feels a kind of purpose, or rather something resembling a purpose, something completely involuntary; everyone's pace grows hurried and uneven. Long shadows glimmer on the walls and on the pavement, and nearly top the Police Bridge." At this hour the Nevsky grows at once more real and more unreal. More real in that the street is now animated by direct and intense real needs: sex, money, love; these are the involuntary currents of purpose in the air; the fragmented features are resolved into real people now, as they avidly seek out other people to fulfill their needs. On the other hand, the very depth and intensity of these desires distort people's perceptions of each other, as well as their presentation of themselves. Both self and others are enlarged in the magical light, but their grandeur is as evanescent and baseless as the shadows on the walls.

Till now, Gogol's vision has been sweeping and panoramic. Now, however, he focuses in closely and sharply on two young men whose stories he is about to tell: Pishkarev, an artist, and Pirogov, an officer. As these unlikely comrades promenade together along the Prospect, their eyes are simultaneously captivated by two girls passing by. They separate and rush off in opposite directions, off the Nevsky and into the darkness of the side streets, to pursue the girls of their respective dreams. As Gogol follows them, he shifts from the surreal pyrotechnics of his introduction into a more conventionally coherent vein, typical of nineteenth-century romantic realism, of Balzac and Dickens and Pushkin, oriented toward actual people and their lives.

Lieutenant Pirogov is a great comic creation, a monument of crude conceits and vanities—sexual, class, national—for which his name has become a Russian byword. As Pirogov follows the girl he has seen on the Nevsky, he finds himself in a neighborhood of German craftsmen; the girl turns out to be a Swabian metalworker's wife. This is the world of the Westerners who produce the goods that the Nevsky displays, and that the Russian officer class happily consumes. In fact, the importance of these foreigners to Petersburg's and Russia's economy testifies to the country's incapacity and inner weakness. But Pirogov knows nothing of this. He treats foreigners as he is accustomed to treating serfs. At first he is surprised that the husband, Schiller, is indignant at his flirtation with Schiller's wife: Is he not, after all, a Russian officer? Schiller and his friend, the cobbler Hoffmann, are not impressed: they say they could have been officers themselves, had they chosen to stay at home. Then Pirogov gives the man an order for some work: on one hand, this will give him an excuse for coming around again; at the same time, he seems to understand his order as a kind of bribe, an incentive for the husband to look the other way. Pirogov makes an assignation with Frau Schiller; when he appears, however, Schiller and Hoffmann surprise him, pick him up bodily, and throw him out. The officer is stunned:

Nothing could equal Pirogov's anger and indignation. The very thought of such an insult drove him wild. He considered Siberia and the whip the least punishment Schiller could expect. He rushed home to change and go straight to the general, to whom he could describe this rebellion of the German workmen in the most striking colors. He wanted to make a request in writing to the Chief of Staff. . . .

But all this had a rather peculiar ending: on his way home he entered a confectioner's shop, ate a couple of flaky pastries, glanced through the *Northern Bee*, and left in a less wrathful frame of mind. In addition, the rather cool evening tempted him to stroll along the Nevsky Prospect for a while.

He is humiliated in his quest for conquest, but too stupid to learn from his failure, or even to try to understand it. Within a few minutes Pirogov has forgotten the whole affair; he prowls along the Prospect happily, wondering whom he will conquer next. He fades into the twilight, on the road to Sevastopol. He is perfectly typical of the class that governed Russia until 1917.

Pishkarev, a far more complex figure, may be the one genuinely tragic character in all of Gogol's work, and the character to whom Gogol most completely gives his heart. As the officer chases his blonde, his friend, an artist, is smitten in love with the dark woman he sees. Pishkarev imagines her to be a great lady, and trembles to approach her. When he finally does, however, he finds that she is in fact a whore—and a shallow and cynical one. Pirogov, of course, would have known at once; but Pishkarev, in love with beauty, lacks the experience of life and the worldly wisdom to understand beauty as a mask and a commodity. (In the same way, the narrator tells us, he is unable to exploit his own paintings as commodities: he is so delighted when people appreciate their beauty that he parts with them for far less than their market value.) The young artist recovers from his first rebuff and imagines the girl as a helpless victim: he resolves to rescue her, to inspire her with his love, to carry her off to his garret, where they can live, poor but honest, on love and art. Once again he gathers up his courage, approaches her, and declares himself; and once again, of course, she laughs in his face. Indeed, she doesn't know which to laugh at more—the idea of love or the idea of honest work. Now we see that he is far more in need of rescue than she is. Shattered by the gulf between his dreams and the real life around him, this "Petersburg dreamer" loses his hold on both. He stops painting, plunges into opium visions, then into addiction, finally locks himself in his room and slits his throat.

What is the point of the artist's tragedy, of the soldier's farce? One point is proposed by the narrator at the story's conclusion: "Oh, do not trust the Nevsky Prospect!" But there are ironies wheeling within ironies here. "I always wrap my cloak more tightly about me when I walk in it, and try not to gaze at the objects I meet with." The irony here is that the narrator has been doing nothing but gazing at these objects, and presenting them for our gaze, for the last fifty pages. He goes on in this vein, bringing the story to an end by apparently negating it. "Don't look into the shop windows: the frippery they display is lovely, but smells of assignations." Assignations, of course, are what this whole story has been about. "You think those ladies . . . but trust ladies least of all. May the Lord defend you from gazing under the brims of ladies' hats. However enticingly the cloak of a beautiful woman floats by, I wouldn't let my curiosity follow after her for anything. And for heaven's sake keep away from the lamp! and pass by as quickly as possible!" For—and with this the story ends—

> The Nevsky Prospect always lies, but more than ever when the thick mass of night settles over it and makes the white and yellow walls of houses stand out, and when the whole town becomes thunderous and dazzling, and myriad carriages roll down the street, and postillions shout and mount their horses, and the devil himself lights the lamps in order to show everything in an unreal light.

I have quoted this conclusion at length because it shows Gogol, the author behind the narrator, playing with his readers in a fascinating way. In the act of denying his love for the Nevsky Prospect, the author enacts it; even as he execrates the street for its false allure, he presents it in the most enticing way. The narrator doesn't seem to know what he's saying or doing, but it is clear that the author knows. In fact, this ambivalent irony will turn out to be one of the primary attitudes toward the modern city. Again and again, in literature, in popular culture, in our own everyday conversation, we will encounter voices like this: the more the speaker condemns the city, the more vividly he evokes it, the more attractive he makes it; the more he disassociates himself from it, the more deeply he identifies himself with it, the clearer it is that he can't live without it. Gogol's denunciation of the Nevsky is itself a way of "wrapping my cloak more tightly about me"—a mode of self-concealment and disguise; but he lets us see him peeking seductively from behind the mask.

What binds the street and the artist together is, above all, dreams. "Oh, do not trust the Nevsky . . . It's all a dream." So the narrator says, after showing us how Pishkarev was destroyed by his dreams. And yet, Gogol has shown us, dreams were the motive force of the artist's life as well as of his death. This is made clear with a typically Gogolian twist: "This young man belonged to a class that is rather a strange phenomenon in our midst, and which no more belongs to the citizens of St. Petersburg than a face we see in dreams belongs to real life. . . . He was an artist." The rhetorical tone of this sentence seems to dismiss the Petersburg artist; its substance, for those who notice, turns out to exalt him to great heights: his relation to the city is to represent, and maybe even to personify, "the face we see in dreams." If this is so, then the Nevsky Prospect, as Petersburg's dream street, is not only the artist's natural habitat but his fellow creator on a macrocosmic scale: he articulates with paint and canvas—or with words on the printed page—the collective dreams that the street realizes with human material in time and space. Thus Pishkarev's mistake is not to wander up and down the Prospect but to wander off it: it is only when he confuses the luminous dream life of the Nevsky with the murky and mundane real life of the side streets that he is undone.

If the affinity of artist and Prospect embraces Pishkarev, it embraces Gogol as well: the collective dream life that gives the street its luminosity is a primary source of his own imaginative power. When, in the story's last line, Gogol ascribes the street's weird but alluring light to the devil, he is being playful; but it is clear that if he took the image literally and sought to renounce this devil and turn away from this light, he would extinguish his own life force. Seventeen years later, a world away from the Nevsky—in Moscow, Russia's traditional holy city, and Petersburg's symbolic antithesis —Gogol will do just that. Under the influence of a crooked but fanatical holy man, he will come to believe that all literature, and his own above all, is inspired by the devil. He will then create an ending for himself as dreadful as the one he has written for Pishkarev: he will burn the unfinished second and third books of *Dead Souls,* and then systematically starve himself to death.[14]

One of the main problems in Gogol's story is the relation between its introduction and the two narratives that follow. Pish-karev's and Pirogov's stories are presented in the language of nine-teenth-century realism: clearly articulated characters doing intelligible and coherent things. The introduction, however, is bril-liantly disarrayed surreal montage, closer in style to the twentieth century than to Gogol's own. The connection (and disconnection) between the two languages and experiences may have something to do with the connection between two spatially contiguous but spiritually disparate aspects of modern city life. On the side streets, where Petersburgers live their everyday lives, normal rules of structure and coherence, of space and time, of comedy and trag-edy, apply. On the Nevsky, however, these rules are suspended, the planes of normal vision and the boundaries of normal experi-ence are shattered, people step into a new frame of space and time and possibility. Take, for instance, one of the strikingly modernist moments (this is Nabokov's favorite passage and his translation) in "Nevsky Prospect": the girl who has caught Pishkarev's eye turns to him and smiles at him and all at once

> The pavement rushed away beneath him, the carriages with their galloping horses seemed motionless, the bridge stretched out and broke in the middle of its arch, a house stood upside down, a sentry box toppled towards him, and the sentry's halberd, to-gether with the golden letters of a shop sign and a pair of scissors painted on it, seemed to glitter on the very lash of his eye.

This dazzling, frightening experience is like a moment inside a cubist landscape, or on a hallucinogenic drug. Nabokov sees it as an instance of artistic vision and genius soaring beyond all social and experiential bounds. I would argue that, on the contrary, this is precisely what the Nevsky Prospect is meant to do to those who enter upon it: Pishkarev is getting what he came for. The Nevsky can enrich Petersburgers' lives spectacularly, so long as they know how to take the trips it offers and then come back, to step back and forth between their own century and the next. But those who cannot integrate the city's two worlds are likely to lose their hold on both, and hence on life itself.

Gogol's "Nevsky Prospect," written in 1835, is almost contem-poraneous with "The Bronze Horseman," written two years ear-lier; yet the worlds they present are light-years away. One of the

most striking differences is that Gogol's Petersburg seems utterly
depoliticized: Pushkin's stark and tragic confrontation between the
common man and central authority has no place on Gogol's Prospect. This is not merely because Gogol has a very different sensibility from Pushkin's (though of course he does), but also because
he is trying to express the spirit of a very different urban space.
The Nevsky Prospect was in fact the one place in Petersburg that
had developed and was developing independently of the state. It
was perhaps the one public place where Petersburgers could present themselves and interact with each other without having to
look behind them and listen for the Bronze Horseman's hooves.
This was a primary source of the street's aura of ebullient freedom
—especially during Nicholas' reign, when the presence of the state
was so uniformly grim. But the Nevsky's apoliticality also made its
magical light unreal, its aura of freedom something of a mirage.
On this street Petersburgers could feel like free individuals; in
reality, however, they were clamped cruelly into constricting social
roles imposed by the most rigidly stratified society in Europe. Even
in the midst of the street's deceptive luminosity, this reality could
break through. For one brief moment, like a single frame in a slide
show, Gogol lets us see the latent facts of Russian life:

> He [Lieutenant Pirogov] was very pleased with his rank, to which
> he had only recently been promoted, and although sometimes he
> would say as he stretched on the couch, "Vanity, all is vanity! so
> what if I am a lieutenant?" yet secretly his new dignity was very
> flattering to him: he often tried to give a covert hint of it in
> conversation, and once when he came across a copyist clerk in the
> street who seemed rude to him, he immediately stopped him and
> made him see in a few curt words that he had a lieutenant to deal
> with, and nothing less—he tried to express this, and more elo-
> quently, because at this moment two rather good-looking young
> ladies were passing.

Here, in a typically offhand way, Gogol shows us what will become
the primal scene in Petersburg literature and life: the confrontation between officer and clerk. The officer, representative of Russia's ruling class, demands from the clerk a quality of respect that
he wouldn't dream of giving in return. For now, he succeeds: he
puts the clerk in his place. The clerk promenading on the Prospect

has escaped from the "official" sector of Petersburg, near the Neva and the palace, dominated by the *Bronze Horseman*, only to be trampled by a miniature but malign reproduction of the Tsar even in the city's freest space. Lieutenant Pirogov, in reducing the clerk to submission, forces him to recognize the limitations of the freedom that the Nevsky confers. Its modern fluidity and mobility turn out to be an illusory display, a dazzling screen for autocratic power. The men and women out on the Nevsky might forget Russian politics—indeed, this was part of the joy of being there—but Russian politics was not about to forget them.

And yet, the old order here is less solid than it may seem. The man who made Petersburg was an awesome figure of implacable integrity; the authorities of the nineteenth century, as Gogol sees them here (and in a great deal of his work), are merely silly, so shallow and shaky as to be almost endearing. Thus Lieutenant Pirogov has to prove his potency and primacy not only to his supposed inferiors, and to the ladies, but to his own nervous self. The latter-day Bronze Horsemen are not only miniatures; they are made of tin. If the fluidity of Petersburg's modern street is a mirage, so is the solidity of its ruling caste. This is only the first phase in the confrontation between officers and clerks; there will be more acts, with different endings, as the century goes on.

In Gogol's other Petersburg stories, the Nevsky Prospect continues to exist as a medium for intense, surreal life. The scorned and embittered clerk-protagonist of "Diary of a Madman" (1835) is overwhelmed by its people but feels instantly at home with its dogs, with whom he strikes up animated conversations. Later in the story, he is able to look without quaking, and even to tip his hat, as the Tsar drives by; but this is only because, stark raving mad, he is convinced that he is the Tsar's equal—the King of Spain.[15] In "The Nose" (1836), Major Kovalev finds his lost nose riding up and down the Nevsky, but finds, too, to his horror, that his nose outranks him, and that he dare not claim it as his own. In Gogol's most famous and probably his greatest Petersburg story, "The Overcoat" (1842), the Nevsky Prospect is never mentioned by name, but neither is anyplace else in the city, because the hero, Akaky Akakyevich, is so cut off from life that he is oblivious to everything around him—except the cold that cuts through him. But the Nevsky may be the street on which, dressed in his new coat, Akaky Akakyevich briefly comes alive: for one fleeting moment, on the way to the party that his fellow clerks give for him and his coat, he is thrilled by the brilliant window displays and glittering women flashing by; but in a flash it is all over, as his coat is torn away. The point that emerges from all these stories is that without a minimal sense of one's personal dignity—"necessary egoism," as Dostoevsky will put it in his column for the *Petersburg News*—no man can participate in the Nevsky's distorted and deceptive yet genuine public life.

Many members of the Petersburg lower classes fear the Nevsky. But they are not the only ones. In a magazine article entitled "Petersburg Notes of 1836," Gogol laments:

> In 1836 Nevsky Prospect, the perpetually stirring, hustling and bustling Nevsky, has completely fallen: strolling has shifted over to the English Embankment. The late Emperor [Alexander I] loved the English Embankment. It is, indeed, beautiful. But only when the strolling began did I notice that it is rather short. But the strollers have something to gain, since half of Nevsky Prospect is always taken up by craftsmen and civil servants, which is why on the Nevsky one suffers half again as many jolts as in any other place.[16]

Thus the fashionable set is retreating from the Nevsky Prospect because they are afraid of physical contact with plebeian artisans and clerks. As delightful as the Nevsky may be, they seem to be willing to abandon it for a far less interesting urban space—barely half a mile long as against the Nevsky's two and three quarters; only one side; no cafes or shops—out of fear. In fact, this retreat won't last long: the nobility and gentry will return to the Nevsky's bright lights. But they will remain wary, uncertain of their power to define the street as their own, amid the pressure of jolts from below. They fear that, along with all their other real and imagined enemies, the street itself—even, or especially, the street they love most—may be flowing against them.

Words and Shoes: The Young Dostoevsky

Eventually, the traffic on the Nevsky will start to change direction. But first the poor clerk must find his voice. That voice is first sounded by Dostoevsky in his first novel, *Poor Folk,* published in 1845.[17] Makar Devushkin, Dostoevsky's hero, a copying clerk in a nameless government department, presents himself as a worthy inheritor of the Akakyevich mantle. From his account of his life at work, his real occupation seems to be that of victim. He is honest and conscientious, shy and self-effacing; he holds himself apart from the incessant banter and intrigue that enable his fellow workers to get through the day. Eventually they turn on him and anoint him as a sort of ritual scapegoat; tormenting him comes to energize them, to give the life of the office focus and cohesion. Devushkin describes himself as a mouse, but a mouse others can ride to organizational power and glory. What makes him different from his Gogolian precursor, and what makes his story bearable (can any national literature hold more than one "Overcoat"?), is a complex intelligence, a rich inner life, a spiritual pride. As he writes his life story to Varvara Dobroselova, a young woman who lives across his tenement's courtyard, we see that he is alive enough to resent his victimization, and intelligent enough to see some of the ways in which he colludes in it. But he doesn't see it all: even as he tells his victim's tale, he is continuing to act it out—by telling it to a woman who, we see, couldn't care less.

Devushkin is vaguely aware that, apart from his real poverty, loneliness and bad health, part of his problem is himself. He describes a youthful episode in which, from a theater's fourth balcony, he fell in love with a beautiful actress. Now there is nothing wrong with this sort of love in itself: it is one of the things that the performing arts are for, one of the forces that keep audiences coming back; virtually everyone goes through it at least once. Most people in the audience (today as much as in the 1840s) keep this love on a plane of fantasy, sharply distinct from their real lives. A minority will hang about stage doors, present flowers, write impassioned letters and strive to meet the objects of their love face to face; this will usually mean getting hurt (unless they are unusually beautiful and/or rich), but it enables them to satisfy the desire to bring their fantasy lives and their real lives together. Devushkin, however, follows neither the majority nor the minority route; what he does instead brings him the worst of both worlds:

I had one ruble left in my pocket, and the next payday was still ten days off. So what do you think I did, dear? Well, on my way to the office, I spent the remainder of my money on French perfume and scented soap. . . . Then, instead of going home for dinner, I spent the time walking up and down under her windows. She lived in a house on the Nevsky Prospect, on the fourth floor. I went home, rested for an hour or so, then went back to the Nevsky, just for the sake of passing under her windows. For a month and a half I went on like that, trailing along behind her, hiring cabs and even private carriages to drive me past her windows. I got quite entangled in debt, but later I got over it and stopped loving her—I got bored with the whole thing.[18]

If the Nevsky is (as Gogol said) Petersburg's communications line, Devushkin opens the circuit, and indeed pays for the call, but can't bring himself to make the connection. He prepares himself for an encounter that will be at once personal and public; he makes sacrifices and takes risks—picture this poor clerk in French perfume! —but can't go through with the act in the end. The crucial events in his life are things that don't happen: things he sets his heart on, elaborates with imaginative power, circles around endlessly, but runs away from at the moment of truth. No wonder he gets bored; and even his most sympathetic readers are apt to find themselves bored with him.

Poor Folk gives the poor clerks a voice, but the voice is halting and tremulous at first. It often sounds like the voice of the classic *shlemiehl*, one of the primary figures in Eastern European (Russian, Polish, Yiddish) folklore and literature. But it is also surprisingly similar to the most prominent aristocratic voice in the Russian literature of the 1840s: the "superfluous man." This figure— named and elaborated beautifully by Turgenev ("Diary of a Superfluous Man," 1850; *Rudin,* 1856; the fathers in *Fathers and Sons,* 1862)—is rich in brains, sensitivity and talent, but devoid of the will to work and act; he turns himself into a *shlemiel* even when he is meant to inherit the earth. The politics of the gentry "superfluous men" tended toward an idealistic liberalism, which could see through the pretensions of the autocracy and feel for the common people, but which lacked the will to fight for radical change. These 1840s liberals were sunk in a cloud of boredom and dejection which, in a work like *Poor Folk,* merged with another cloud of liberal despondency and boredom drifting upward from below.

Even if Devushkin wanted to, there is simply no way in the 1840s for a poor clerk to fight. But there is one thing that perhaps he

could do: he could write. As he pours his heart out, even to someone who isn't listening, he comes to feel that he has something to
say. Isn't he, as much as anyone in Petersburg, a representative
man? Instead of the escapist and sentimental drivel that passes for
literature—fantasies of clanking swords, galloping steeds, clinging
virgins abducted in the night—why not confront the public with
the real inner life of a man of Petersburg like themselves? At this
point, the image of the Nevsky Prospect surges up in his mind and
pushes him back into his lowly place:

> But really, one does get ideas sometimes, and I wonder what
> would happen if I just sat down and wrote something? . . . Just
> suppose for one minute that a book has been published. You pick
> it up and it says *Poems*, by Makar Devushkin! I can tell you one
> thing for sure, my dear: if that book were published, I'd never
> dare show myself on the Nevsky Prospect again. For how would
> it feel if everybody started saying, "Here comes Devushkin, the
> author and poet; look, here he comes in person!" What, for in-
> stance, would I do about my shoes then? Because, as perhaps you
> know, my shoes have been patched many times, and the soles
> tend to break away sometimes, which is a very unseemly sight. So
> what would happen if everybody realized that Devushkin, the
> author, had patched shoes? Suppose some duchess or countess
> noticed this, what would the dear lady say about me? Maybe,
> though, she wouldn't notice it at all, because I don't suppose that
> countesses are all that interested in shoes, especially minor offi-
> cials' shoes (because, as they say, there are shoes and shoes).

For the clerk, literate and sensitive but common and poor, the
Nevsky Prospect and Russian literature represent the same elusive
promise: a line on which all men can communicate freely with each
other, and be recognized equally by each other. In the Russia of
the 1840s, however, a society that combines modern mass communications with feudal social relations, this promise is a cruel
mockery. The media that seem to bring people together—street
and print—only dramatize the enormity of the gulf between them.
  The Dostoevskian clerk fears two things: on one hand, that
"some duchess or countess," the ruling class that dominates both
street life and cultural life, will laugh at him, at his tattered soles,
at his tattered soul; on the other hand—and this would probably
be even worse—that his social superiors won't even notice his soles

("because, as they say, there are shoes and shoes") or his soul. Either of these things may indeed happen: the clerk cannot control his rulers' responses. What does fall under his jurisdiction, however, is his own self-respect: his "sense of personal dignity, of necessary egoism." The class of poor clerks must come to accept their shoes and their thoughts, to the point where the look of the other—or the lack of a look from the other—won't turn them to dust. Then, and only then, will they be able to put themselves on the line, in print and in the street, and to create out of Petersburg's vast public spaces a true public life. At this point, 1845, no Russian, real or fictional, can imagine concretely how this might take place. But *Poor Folk* at least defines the problem—a crucial problem in Russian culture and politics—and enables Russians of the 1840s to imagine that the change will take place somehow someday.

In Dostoevsky's second novel, *The Double,* published a year later, the hero, another government clerk, girds himself up to make a grand gesture of self-presentation on the Nevsky Prospect. But this gesture turns out to be so wildly disproportionate to Mr. Golyadkin's actual resources, political or psychic, that it turns into a bizarre nightmare, which propels him into a maelstrom of paranoia in which he will be thrown back and forth for 150 excruciating pages before he is finally, mercifully engulfed.

Golyadkin awakens at the story's start, leaves his wretched dark and narrow room, and ascends into a magnificent carriage, described in loving detail, which he has hired for the day. He orders the driver to take him to his office by way of the Nevsky, lets the windows down, and smiles benignly at the street's pedestrian crowd. But suddenly he is recognized by two young clerks from his office, half his age but of equivalent rank. As they wave and call out his name, he is seized with terror, and shrinks back into the carriage's darkest corner. (We see here the dual character of vehicles in city traffic: for those with personal or class confidence, they can be armored fortresses from which to lord it over the masses on foot; for those who lack the confidence, they are traps, cages, whose occupant becomes supervulnerable to any assassin's fatal glance.) [19] A moment later, something even worse happens: the carriage of his boss pulls alongside, close enough to touch. "Golyadkin, realizing that Andrei Filipovich had recognized him, that he was now staring at him pop-eyed, and that there was no place to hide, blushed to the roots of his being." Golyadkin's terrified response to his superior's stare will carry him across an invisible frontier into the madness that will eventually swallow him up:

> "Should I bow or shouldn't I? Should I acknowledge him? Admit that it is me? Or should I pretend I'm someone else, someone strikingly resembling me, and look completely indifferent?" Golyadkin asked himself in indescribable anguish. "Yes, that's it; I'm not me and that's all there is to it." So he thought, his eyes fixed on Andrei Filipovich as he took off his hat to him.
> "I, I, I . . . no, nothing, sir," he stammered in a whisper. "The fact is, it's not me. . . . Yes, that's all there is to it."[20]

All the surreally cruel twists of the plot follow directly from this self-denial. Golyadkin, caught in the act in the middle of the Nevsky Prospect, cannot look his boss in the face and affirm his own desire to be his peer. The wish for speed, for style, for luxury—and for recognition of his dignity—these guilty desires don't belong to him at all—"I'm not me . . . that's all there is to it"—but, somehow, to "someone else." Dostoevsky then arranges for the desires that have been so radically split off from the self to take on objective form as a real "someone else," as the double. This ambitious, pushy, aggressive person, whom Golyadkin can't face and acknowledge as his own, proceeds to evict him from his life, and to use that life as a springboard to the success and happiness that Golyadkin has craved all along. As Golyadkin's torments multiply (this is where Dostoevsky got his reputation as "a cruel talent"),[21] he becomes convinced that he is being punished for his evil desires. He strives to convince his superiors, and himself as well, that he has never wanted or sought anything for himself at all, that his life's only goal has been submission to their will. He is still denying and punishing himself at the story's end as they take him away.

Imprisoned in his lonely madness, Golyadkin is one of the first in a line of tormented solitary figures who will haunt modern literature, into our own age. But Golyadkin also stands in another line, the line of Pushkin's Evgeny, the tradition of Petersburg common clerks who are driven insane by their claim to dignity in a city and a society that deny their dignity—and, moreover, who get themselves into trouble by dramatizing their claims in the city's public prospects and squares. But there are important differences in their forms of madness. Evgeny has internalized Petersburg's supreme authority, which takes up residence in his soul and subjects his inner life to draconic discipline—as Freud would say, "setting up an agency within [the self] to watch over it, like a garrison in a conquered city."[22] Golyadkin's delusions take an opposite form: rather than introjecting external authority, he projects outward, onto "Golyadkin Junior," his desire to assert his own authority. For the young Hegel and for Feuerbach, whose thought was deeply influential among Russian intellectuals in the 1840s, the movement from Evgeny to Golyadkin would represent a kind of progress in madness: the self recognizing itself, even in a twisted and self-destructive way, as the ultimate source of authority. The truly revolutionary breakthrough would occur, according to this dialectic, if the clerk could affirm both Golyadkins, with all their desires and drives, as his own. Then, and only then, he would be ready to stake his claim to recognition—a moral, psychological and political claim—in Petersburg's immense but hitherto unclaimed public space. But it will take another generation before Petersburg's clerks learn to act.

2.

The 1860s: The New Man in the Street

THE 1860s are a watershed in Russian history. The decisive event is Alexander II's edict of February 19, 1861, freeing the serfs. Politically and culturally, however, the 1860s can be said to have begun a few years earlier, at the start of Alexander's reign, when after the disaster of the Crimean War it became universally clear that Russia would have to go through radical changes. Alexander's early years were marked by a significant liberalization of culture, a new openness in public discussion, and a great ferment of expectation and hope, building up to February 19. But the emancipation decree produced bitter fruits. It was observed very quickly that the peasants remained shackled to their lords, received even less land than they had been allotted before, incurred a whole new network of obligations to their village communes, and in effect found themselves free in name only. But beyond these and other substantive flaws in the emancipation decree, a pervasive sense of disappointment filled the air. So many Russians had hoped fervently that emancipation would usher in an age of brotherhood and social regeneration and make Russia a beacon for the modern world; a modified but basically unchanged caste society was what they got instead. The hopes were unrealistic—it is easy to see this a century afterward. But the bitterness that followed the failure of these hopes was decisive in shaping Russian culture and politics for the next fifty years.

The 1860s are notable for the emergence of a new generation and a new style of intellectuals: the *raznochintsy*, "men of various origins and classes," the administrative term for all Russians who did not belong to the nobility or gentry. This term is more or less equivalent to the French pre-revolutionary Third Estate; it is a measure of Russia's backwardness that the members of this estate —which, of course, included the vast majority of Russians—did not appear as historical actors until this point. When the *raznochintsy* do appear—sons of army sergeants, of tailors, of village priests, of copyist clerks—they burst on the scene with aggressive stridency. They take pride in their plain-spoken vulgarity, their lack of social graces, their contempt for everything genteel. The most memorable portrait of the "new man" of the 1860s is Bazarov, the young medical student in Turgenev's *Fathers and Sons*. Bazarov pours scornful invective on all poetry, art and morality, on all existing beliefs and institutions; he spends his time and energy studying mathematics and dissecting frogs. It is in his honor that Turgenev coins the word "nihilism." In fact, Bazarov's negativity, and that of the 1860s generation, is limited and selective: the "new men" tend, for instance, to adopt an uncritically "positive" attitude toward supposedly scientific and rational modes of thought and of life. Nevertheless, the plebeian intellectuals of the 1860s make a traumatic break with the cultivated liberal humanism that characterized the gentry intellectuals of the 1840s. Their break may be more in behavior than in beliefs: the "men of the sixties" are determined to undertake decisive action, and glad to bring on themselves and their society any embarrassment, heartache and trouble that action may entail.[23]

On September 1, 1861, a mysterious horseman raced full speed up the Nevsky Prospect, flinging leaflets around and behind him as he disappeared. The impact of this gesture was sensational, and the whole city was soon discussing the horseman's message, a proclamation addressed "To the Younger Generation." The message was simple and shockingly fundamental:

> We do not need either a Tsar, an Emperor, the myth of some lord, or the purple which cloaks hereditary incompetence. We want at our head a simple human being, a man of the land who understands the life of the people and who is chosen by the people. We do not need a consecrated Emperor, but an elected leader receiving a salary for his services.[24]

Three weeks later, on September 23, the crowd on the Nevsky saw something even more amazing, perhaps the one thing that this street had never seen before: a political demonstration. A group of hundreds of students (the "younger generation") moved across the Neva from the university and marched up the street to the rector's house. They were protesting a series of new administrative regulations that would bar students and faculty from holding any sort of meetings and—far more devastating—would abolish scholarships and stipends (thus shutting off the flood of poorer students who had been pouring into the university in recent years), thereby making higher education once again the caste privilege it had been under Nicholas I. The demonstration was spontaneous, the mood was gay, the group was sympathetically regarded by the crowd on the street. Here is how a participant remembered it years later:

> A sight like it had never been seen. It was a wonderful September day. . . . In the streets the girls, who were just beginning to go to university, joined in, together with a number of young *razno-chintsy* who knew us or merely agreed with us. . . . When we ap-

peared on the Nevsky Prospect, the French barbers came out of their shops, and their faces lit up, and they waved their arms cheerfully, shouting *"Revolution! Revolution!"*[25]

That night, the government—haunted, no doubt, by those French barbers' cries—arrested dozens of students, including delegates who had been promised immunity. This began months of turmoil on Vasilevsky Island, in and around the university: student and faculty strikes, lockouts and police occupations, mass expulsions, firings and arrests, and finally the closing of the university for two years. After September 23 the young militants kept away from the Nevsky and the center of the city. When they were driven out of the university quarter, they dropped from sight, to form a sophisticated network of underground groups and cells. Many left Petersburg for the countryside, where they sought to follow Herzen's advice and "go to the people,"[26] though this movement did not pick up momentum for another decade. Others left Russia altogether, to pursue their studies in Western Europe, notably in Switzerland, generally in the faculties of science and medicine. Life on the Nevsky returned to normal; it would be more than a decade before the next demonstration there. Nevertheless, for one fleeting moment, Petersburgers had had a taste of political confrontation in the city streets. These streets had been defined irrevocably as political space. The Russian literature of the 1860s would strive to imaginatively fill that space.

Chernyshevsky: The Street as Frontier

The first great confrontation scene of the 1860s was imagined and written from a dungeon cell. In July 1862, the radical critic and editor Nikolai Chernyshevsky was arrested on vague charges of subversion and conspiracy against the state. In fact there was absolutely no evidence against Chernyshevsky, who had been very careful to limit his activity to the realm of literature and ideas. Accordingly, some evidence had to be manufactured. It took some time for the government to arrange this, so Chernyshevsky was held for nearly two years without trial in the depths of the Peter-Paul Fortress, St. Petersburg's oldest structure, and its Bastille until 1917.* A secret tribunal would eventually sentence him to life imprisonment in Siberia, where he would serve twenty years, to be released only when his health was shattered and his mind shaken and his death at hand. His martyrdom would make him one of the saints in the annals of the Russian intelligentsia. While Chernyshevsky shivered in solitary confinement, waiting for his case to be fixed, he read and wrote feverishly. His most substantial prison work was a novel entitled *What Is to Be Done?* The book, which appeared in serial form in 1863, survived only through a bizarre series of events that seem to come directly out of some surreal Petersburg novel—only no novelist could have got away with it. First, the manuscript was given to the prison authorities, who sent it on to the special commission of inquiry that had been created for this case. The two agencies put so many official seals on it that when it arrived at the censor's office he never bothered to read it, thinking it had already been examined and cleared. Next it was passed to the liberal poet Nikolai Nekrasov, Chernyshevsky's friend and co-editor on the *Contemporary* magazine. But Nekrasov lost the manuscript on the Nevsky Prospect. He recovered it only after placing an advertisement in the Petersburg *Police Gazette:* it was handed to him by a young government clerk who had picked it up in the street.

Everyone, including Chernyshevsky, considered *What Is to Be Done?* a failure as a novel: it had no real plot, no substantial characters—or, rather, an array of characters who are indistinguishable from one another—no clear environment, no unity of voice or sensibility. Yet both Tolstoy and Lenin would appropriate Chernyshevsky's title, and the aura of moral grandeur that went with it. They recognized that this clumsy book, for all its blatant flaws, marked a crucial step in the development of the modern Russian spirit.[27]

* The fortress is worth noting for its symbolic resonance as well as its military and political importance. Cf. Trotsky in October 1905, denouncing Nicholas II's Manifesto of October 17, which had promised representative government and a constitution: "Look around, citizens. Has anything changed since yesterday? The Peter and Paul Fortress still dominates the city, doesn't it? Don't you still hear groans and the gnashing of teeth from behind its accursed walls?" In *Petersburg,* Andrei Biely's poetic novel of the same month, "above the white fortress walls, the pitiless spire of Peter and Paul, tormentingly sharp, reached up so coldly to the sky." We see here a symbolic polarity in Petersburgers' perceptions of the two most striking vertical landmarks in an overwhelmingly horizontal cityscape: the golden Admiralty spire crystallized all the city's promise of life and joy; the stone fortress steeple marked the state's threat to that promise, the permanent shadow it cast across the city's sun.

The source of the book's immediate fame and its enduring force is revealed in the subtitle: "Tales of New People." It was only through the emergence and the initiative of a class of "new people," Chernyshevsky believed, that Russia could be propelled into the modern world. *What Is to Be Done?* is at once a manifesto and a manual for this would-be vanguard. It would have been impossible, of course, for Chernyshevsky to show his new men and women engaged in any sort of concrete politics. What he did instead was far more exciting; he portrayed a series of exemplary lives whose personal encounters and relationships were saturated with politics. Here is a typical incident, a day in the life of a "new man":

> What kind of a man was Lopukhov? This is the kind of man he was. He was walking along the Kameny-Ostrovsky Prospect* in a ragged [student's] uniform (on the way back from giving a lesson for a pittance, two miles from the school). Toward him comes a dignitary, taking a constitutional, and, like a dignitary, comes straight at him without moving aside. At that time Lopukhov practiced the rule, "Except in the case of women, I will not move aside first for anyone." They banged into each other's shoulders. The individual, making a half turn, said, "What's the matter with you, pig? Cattle!" and was about to continue in this tone, but Lopukhov turned fully toward the individual, picked him up bodily, and deposited him very carefully in the gutter. He stood over him and said, "If you make a move, I'll push you in further." Two peasants passed by, looked, and praised him. A functionary passed by, looked, did not praise, but smiled broadly. Carriages passed, but no one looked out of them. . . . Lopukhov stood for a while, then picked up the individual again—this time not bodily, but by the hand—raised him, drew him up to the sidewalk, and said, "Alas, dear sir, what have you done? I hope you did not hurt yourself. Will you permit me to wipe you off?" A peasant passed and helped to wipe him off, two townspeople passed and helped to wipe him off, they all wiped the individual and went their ways.[28]

It is hard for readers to know how to respond to this. We are bound to admire Lopukhov's audacity and courage, as well as his

* It is worth noting that the Kameny-Ostrovsky Prospect, the street on which Chernyshevsky stages his confrontation scene, terminated in the Peter-Paul Fortress, in which Chernyshevsky was imprisoned while he wrote. The location of this scene here itself constituted an oblique but powerful challenge to the forces that hoped to keep the author and his ideas locked up.

sheer physical strength. But a reader of Russian literature is bound to wonder about this hero's total lack of inner life, of self-consciousness. Can he really feel no vestige of awe toward his ruling class, no learned deference to conflict with his indignation? Can he be utterly free of anxiety over the consequences of his act? over the dignitary's power to have him expelled from the university and clapped in jail? Isn't he a little worried, at least for an instant, over whether he can actually pick the man up? Chernyshevsky would say, no doubt, that this is precisely what's new about his "new people": they are free from all the endless Hamlet-like doubts and anxieties that have enfeebled the Russian soul till now. Presumably one of these new men would never let any Bronze Horseman push him around: he would simply pitch him into the Neva, horse and all. But this very absence of inner conflict deprives Lopukhov's victory of some of the sweetness it should bring: it's too fast, too easy; the confrontation between officer and clerk, between rulers and ruled, is over before it becomes real.

It is ironic that Chernyshevsky should be known as the most prominent critical advocate of literary "realism," and a lifelong enemy of what he called "phantasmagoria": this is surely one of the most fantastic heroes, and one of the most phantasmagoric scenes, in the history of Russian literature. The literary genres that it resembles are at the remotest pole from realism: the American frontier tale, the Cossack warrior epic, the romance of Deerslayer or Taras Bulba. Lopukhov is a Western gunslinger, or a wild man of the steppes; all he needs is a horse. The stage directions for this scene indicate a Petersburg prospect, but its spirit is much closer to the O.K. Corral. It shows Chernyshevsky as a true "Petersburg dreamer" in his heart of hearts.

One important feature of the mythological frontier world is its classlessness: one man comes up against another, individually, in a void. The dream of a pre-civilized democracy of "natural men" is what makes frontier mythology powerful and attractive. But when frontier fantasies are transported into a real street in St. Petersburg, the results are particularly bizarre. Consider the spectators who form the background of Chernyshevsky's scene: both peasants and functionaries are open in expressing their delight; not even the people in carriages are troubled to see a dignitary dumped in the mud. Not only does the hero not get into trouble; the whole world happily (or insouciantly) supports him. Now this would make perfect sense in the open and atomized world of the mythical American frontier. But in order for it to be even remotely plausible in Petersburg, the dignitaries would have to have ceased to be the city's—and, indeed, the whole society's—ruling class. In other words, the Russian Revolution would have to have already taken place! And in that case, why bother dumping the man at all? Even if there were a point—to humiliate the former ruling class —there surely wouldn't be anything heroic about it.* Thus, if this strange scene were ever possible, it would be unnecessary. It is clearly inadequate, as literature or politics, to the heroic emotions it aims to call forth.

Nevertheless, for all Chernyshevsky's incoherence and ineptitude, he does it: he portrays the plebeians of Petersburg defying the dignitaries in the middle of the street, in the full light of day. This scene is far more subversive than the phony conspiracies for which the state destroyed his life. To have conceived and written it shows not only moral courage but imaginative power. Its setting in St. Petersburg gives it a special resonance and richness. This city was meant to dramatize for the Russian people both the demands and the adventure of modernization from above. *What Is to Be Done?* dramatizes, for the first time in Russian history, the counterdream of modernization from below. Chernyshevsky was aware of the inadequacies of his book as drama and as dream. Nevertheless, as he disappeared into the Siberian emptiness, he left a remarkable challenge to his survivors, in literature and in politics, to work the dream through and make it more real.

The Underground Man in the Street

Dostoevsky's *Notes from Underground,* which appeared in 1864, is full of allusions to Chernyshevsky and to *What Is to Be Done?* The

* It is not hard to imagine a scene like this taking place in a post-revolutionary city anywhere in the world: Tehran, say, or Managua, in 1979. But there would have to be an important change in Chernyshevsky's stage directions: the dignitary, now an ex-dignitary, would be likely to keep a low profile, or even to behave with excessive deference toward his ex-subjects, assuming he wanted to survive. Alternately, we could imagine a confrontation like Chernyshevsky's at the very beginning of a revolution. But then the background figures of various classes would propel themselves into the foreground and confront each other rather than passing serenely on their separate ways.

most famous of these allusions is the image of the Crystal Palace. London's Crystal Palace, built in Hyde Park for the International Exhibition of 1851 and reconstructed on Sydenham Hill in 1854, glimpsed from afar by Chernyshevsky on a brief visit to London in 1859, appears as a magical vision in the dream life of Vera Pavlovna, his novel's heroine. For Chernyshevsky and his vanguard of "new people," the Crystal Palace is a symbol of the new modes of freedom and happiness that Russians can enjoy if they make the great historical leap into modernity. For Dostoevsky and his anti-hero, too, the Crystal Palace stands for modernity; only here it symbolizes everything that is ominous and threatening about modern life, everything against which modern man must stand *en garde*. Commentators on the *Notes* and on the motif of the Crystal Palace tend to appropriate the Underground Man's virulent invective and, in this case at least, to take it at face value. Thus they pour endless scorn on Chernyshevsky for his lack of spiritual depth: how stupid and banal this man must have been to think that mankind is rational, that social relations are perfectible; how delightful that the profound Dostoevsky put him in his place.[29] As it happens, Dostoevsky did not share this complacent condescension. In fact, he was virtually the only figure in respectable Russia to speak out, both before and after Chernyshevsky's arrest, in defense of his intellect, his character, even his spirituality. Although he believed Chernyshevsky to be both metaphysically and politically wrong, he could see how his radicalism sprang from "an abundance of life." Those who derided Chernyshevsky "have only succeeded in displaying the depth of your cynicism," which "serves current material interests, often to the detriment of your fellow men." Dostoevsky insisted that "these outcasts at least try to do something; they delve in order to find a way out; they err and thereby save others; but you"—so he admonished his conservative readers—"you can only grin in a melodramatic posture of unconcern."[30]

We will return to the Crystal Palace. But in order to see this symbol of modernity in its fullness and depth, I want first to look at it from the perspective of another archetypal modern setting: the Petersburg street. From the perspective of the Prospect, we will be able to see the social and spiritual framework that Chernyshevsky and Dostoevsky share. There are, of course, profound metaphysical and moral conflicts between them. But if we compare

Dostoevsky's Underground Man with Chernyshevsky's New Man, as they see themselves and as they present themselves on the Prospect, we will find deep affinities in where they are coming from and where they want to go.

Dostoevsky's confrontation scene, which is hardly ever mentioned in the many commentaries on the *Notes*, takes place in the generally neglected Second Book. It follows the classical Petersburg paradigm: aristocratic officer versus poor clerk. Where it differs radically from Chernyshevsky is that the Underground Man's defiance of authority takes several years of gruelling anguish, unfolded in eight densely and intensely written pages, before it finally takes place. What it shares with Chernyshevsky, and with the radical and democratic initiatives of the 1860s, is that it *does* take place: after seemingly endless Hamlet-like introspective agony, the Underground Man finally goes through with the act, stands up to his social superior and fights for his rights in the street. Moreover, he does it on the Nevsky Prospect, which for a generation has been Petersburg's closest thing to a truly political space—and which in the 1860s is getting closer all the time. Once we explore this scene, it will be obvious how much Chernyshevsky helped to liberate Dostoevsky's imagination, to make the Underground Man's confrontation possible. Without Chernyshevsky, it is hard to imagine such a scene—a scene that is, in fact, at once more realistic and more revolutionary than anything in *What Is to Be Done?*

The story begins in darkness, late at night, in "completely obscure places" far from the Nevsky. This was a stage in his life, our hero explains, when "I was terribly afraid of being seen, of being met, of being recognized. I already had the underground in my soul."[31] But suddenly something happens that takes hold of him and shakes away his solitude. As he passes a tavern, he hears and sees a commotion going on inside. Some men are fighting, and at the climax of the fight a man is thrown through the window. This event seizes the Underground Man's imagination, and arouses his desire to participate in life—even to participate in a painful and degrading way. He feels envy for the man who has been thrown out the window; maybe he can get thrown out the window himself! He recognizes the perversity of this desire, but it makes him feel more alive—this is a crucial thing for him: *"more alive"*—than he can recall. Now, instead of dreading recognition, he desperately hopes to be recognized, even if recognition leads to abuse and broken bones. He enters the pool hall, looks for the aggressor—it is an officer, of course, well over six feet tall—and approaches the man, hoping to provoke trouble. But the officer reacts to him in a way that is far more deeply shattering than physical assault:

> I was standing by the billiard-table, and in my ignorance blocking up the way, and he wanted to pass; he took me by the shoulders, and without a word—without a warning or an explanation—moved me from where I was standing to another spot, and passed by as though he had not noticed me. I could have forgiven blows, but I could not forgive his having moved me, and so completely failing to notice me.

From the officer's commanding heights, the puny clerk is not even there—or no more "there" than a table or chair. "It seemed that I was not even equal to being thrown out the window." Too nonplussed and humiliated to protest, he returns to the anonymous streets.

The first thing that marks the Underground Man as a "new man," a "man of the sixties," is his desire for a head-on clash, an explosive encounter—even if he turns out to be the victim of that encounter. Earlier Dostoevskian characters like Devushkin, or fellow anti-heroes like Goncharov's Oblomov, would pull up their blankets and never leave their rooms at all, in dread of precisely such incidents. The Underground Man is far more dynamic: we see him lurch out of his solitude and hurl himself into action, or at least into an attempt at action; he is thrilled at the prospect of trouble.[32] It is at this point that he learns his first political lesson: it is impossible for men of the clerk class to make trouble for men of the officer class, because their class—the nobility and gentry that, even after February 19, is still ruling Russia—doesn't even know that his class, Petersburg's multitude of educated and self-educated proletarians, is there. Matlaw's translation puts the political point nicely: "I was not even equal to being thrown out the window." There cannot be any sort of encounter, even a violent one, without a minimal equality: the officers must recognize the clerks as human beings who are there.

In the story's next phase, which spans several years, the Underground Man racks his brain in vain in search of ways to bring this recognition about. He follows the officer around, gets to know the man's name, his home, his habits—he pays off the porters for information—while remaining, or keeping himself, invisible. (The officer didn't notice him when he was a foot away, so why should he notice him now?) He concocts inexhaustible fantasies about his oppressor and even, under pressure of this obsession, transforms some of these fantasies into stories, and himself into an author. (But nobody is interested in clerks' fantasies about officers, so he remains an unpublished author.) He decides to challenge the officer to a duel, and goes so far as to write a provocative letter; but then he assures himself that the officer would never fight a low-caste civilian (he might be drummed out of the officer corps if he did), and the note lies unmailed. This is just as well, he concludes, because just beneath the message of rage and rancor he has left a subtext that exudes an abject longing for his enemy's love. In fantasy, he lets himself snuggle up to his tormentor:

> The letter was so composed that if the officer had had the least understanding of "the sublime and the beautiful," he would certainly have rushed to me to fling himself on my neck and offer me his friendship. And how fine that would have been! How we would have gotten along! He would have shielded me with his higher rank, while I could have improved his mind with my culture, and, well—my ideas, and all sorts of things might have happened.

Dostoevsky unfolds this plebeian ambivalence with great brilliance. Any plebeian will feel a shock of recognition, and of shame, to see the abject love and need that so often lie behind our selfrighteous class hate and pride. This ambivalence will be dramatized politically a generation later, in the letters of the first generation of Russian terrorists to the Tsar.[33] The Underground Man's wild leaps from love to hate are worlds away from Lopukhov's serene (or vacuous) self-confidence. Nevertheless, Dostoevsky is fulfilling Chernyshevsky's demand for Russian realism far better than Chernyshevsky could fulfill it himself: he shows us the real depth and volatility of the new man's inner life.

The Nevsky Prospect plays a complex role in the Underground Man's inner life. It has drawn him out of his isolation, into the sun and into the crowd. But life in the light has evoked new intensities of suffering, which Dostoevsky analyzes with his usual virtuosity:

Sometimes on holidays I used to stroll on the sunny side of the Nevsky between three and four in the afternoon. That is, I did not so much stroll as experience innumerable torments, humiliations and resentments; but no doubt that was just what I wanted. I used to wriggle like an eel among the passersby in the most unbecoming fashion, continually moving aside to make way for generals, for officers of the Guards and hussars, or for ladies. In those minutes I used to feel a convulsive twinge at my heart, and hot all the way down my back at the mere thought of the wretchedness of my dress, of the wretchedness and vulgarity of my little wriggling figure. This was a regular martyrdom, a continual, intolerable humiliation at the thought, which passed into an incessant and direct sensation that I was a fly in the eyes of the whole world, a nasty, disgusting fly—more intelligent, more cultured and more noble than any of them, of course, but a fly that was constantly making way for everyone. Why I inflicted this torment on myself, why I went to the Nevsky, I don't know, I felt simply drawn there at every opportunity.

As the Underground Man encounters his old nemesis, the six-foot officer, in the crowd, his social and political humiliation takes on a more personal force:

> . . . people like me, or even neater than I, he simply walked over; he made straight for them as though there were nothing but empty space before him, and never, under any circumstances, moved aside. I gloated over my resentment watching him—and resentfully made way for him every time.

A wriggling eel, a fly, empty space: here, as always in Dostoevsky, the varieties and nuances of abasement are breathtaking. But Dostoevsky is especially trenchant here in showing how the gradations of degradation spring not from his hero's abnormalities but from the normal structure and operation of Petersburg life. The Nevsky Prospect is a modern public space that offers an alluring promise of freedom; and yet for the poor clerk on the street the caste configurations of feudal Russia are more rigid and more humiliating than ever.

The contrast between what the street promises and what it delivers drives the Underground Man not only to frenzies of impotent range but also to rhapsodies of Utopian yearning:

It tormented me that even in the street I could not be on an even footing with him. "Why must you invariably be the first to step aside?" I kept asking myself in hysterical rage, waking up at three o'clock in the morning. "Why precisely you and not he? After all, there's no regulation about it; after all, there's no written law. . . . Let the making way be equal, as it usually is when refined people meet: he moves halfway and you move halfway; there's mutual respect." But that never happened, and I always made way, while he never even noticed that I moved aside for him.

"Let the making way be equal"; "refined people"; "mutual respect": even as the Underground Man invokes these splendid ideals, he knows how hollow they ring in the real Russian world. They are at least as Utopian as anything in Chernyshevsky. "Why must you invariably be the first to step aside?" Even as he asks, he knows the answer: because they live in what is still a caste society, and walking through other people is a perennial caste privilege. "After all, there's no regulation about it . . . there's no written law." Actually, it is only recently—since February 19—that there is "no written law" certifying the officer caste as owners of their fellow Russians' bodies and souls. The Underground Man is discovering for himself what the *Younger Generation* manifesto scattered along the Nevsky by that mysterious horseman was trying to tell him: the letter of serfdom has been repealed, but even on the Nevsky the reality of caste still rules.

But even as the Nevsky inflicts wounds on the poor clerk, it serves as the medium through which the wounds can be healed; even as it dehumanizes him—reduces him to an eel, a fly, an empty space—it gives him the resources to transform himself into a man, a modern man with freedom, dignity, equal rights. As the Underground Man observes his nemesis in action on the Prospect, he notices something startling: even as this officer walks through people of lower rank, "he, too, made way for generals and persons of high rank, and he, too, shifted among them like an eel." It is a remarkable—and revolutionary—discovery. "He, too, made way." Then the officer is not the semi-demonic, semi-divine being that haunts the clerk's fantasy life, but a limited and vulnerable human being like himself, just as subject to caste pressures and social norms. If the officer is also capable of being reduced to an eel, then maybe the gulf between them is not so vast after all; and then

—for the first time—the Underground Man thinks about the unthinkable:

> And lo and behold, the most astounding idea dawned upon me! "What," I thought, "if I meet him and—don't move aside? What if I don't move aside on purpose, even if I were to bump into him? How would that be?" This audacious idea little by little took such a hold on me that it gave me no peace. I dreamt of it continually.

Now the street takes on a new prospect: "I purposely went to the Nevsky more frequently in order to picture more vividly how I would do it when I did do it." Now that he conceives of himself as an active subject, the Nevsky becomes a medium for an array of new meanings, a theater of operations for the self.

The Underground Man begins to plan his action. His project is gradually modified:

> "Of course I will not really bump him," I thought in my joy. "I will simply not turn aside, will bump against him, not very violently, but just shouldering each other—just as much as decency permits. I will bump him just as much as he bumps me."

This is no retreat or evasion: the demand for equality in the street is just as radical as a demand for primacy would be—from the officer's point of view, it is probably even more radical—and will get him in just as much trouble. But it is also more realistic: the officer, after all, is twice his size; and the Underground Man takes material forces far more seriously than do the materialist heroes of *What Is to Be Done?* He worries about his looks and grooming; about his clothes—he borrows money to buy a more respectable-looking coat—yet his dress must not be too respectable or the point of the confrontation will be lost; about how he will attempt to defend himself, both physically and verbally, not only against the officer, but—this is at least as important—in front of the crowd. His assertion will not be merely a personal claim against a particular officer but a political testament addressed to the whole of Russian society. A microcosm of that society will be flowing along the Nevsky Prospect; he wants to bring not only the officer but the society to a stop, until they recognize what he has come to understand as his human dignity.

After many rehearsals the big day arrives. Everything is ready. Slowly, deliberately, like Lopukhov or Matt Dillon, the Underground Man approaches the Nevsky. But somehow, things just don't come off. At first he can't find his man; the officer is nowhere on the street. Then he spies him, but the man disappears like a mirage as soon as our hero gets close. Finally he zeroes in on his target, only to lose his courage and shrink back at the last moment. Once he comes within half a foot of the officer, then pulls back in fear, but trips himself up and falls directly at the officer's feet. The only thing that keeps the Underground Man from dying of humiliation is the fact that the officer has still noticed nothing. Dostoevsky, in his best black comic style, draws out his hero's agony endlessly—until at last, when he has all but given up hope, the officer abruptly appears in the crowd, and:

> Suddenly, three paces from my enemy, I unexpectedly made up my mind—I closed my eyes, and we ran full tilt, shoulder to shoulder, into each other! I did not budge an inch, and passed him on a perfectly equal footing! ... Of course, I got the worst of it—he was stronger—but that was not the point. The point was that I had attained my goal, I had kept up my dignity. I had not yielded a step, and put myself publicly on an equal social footing with him.

He has really done it: risked his body and soul, confronted the ruling caste and insisted on his equal rights, and moreover—"put myself *publicly* on an equal social footing with him"—proclaimed it before the whole world. "I was delighted," says this man who is ordinarily so bitter and cynical about any sort of delight; now his delight is real, and we can share it. "I was triumphant, and sang Italian arias." Here, as in much great Italian opera—which coincides, remember, with Italy's struggles for self-determination—the triumph is political as well as personal. By fighting for his freedom and dignity in the light of day, and fighting not only against the officer but against his own self-doubt and self-hate, the Underground Man has won it.

Of course, since this is Dostoevsky, there are endless second thoughts. Maybe, perhaps, the officer didn't notice that he was being challenged? "He did not even look round, and pretended not to notice; but he was only pretending, I am convinced of that.

I am convinced of that to this day!" The repetition suggests that our hero probably isn't so convinced as he would like to be. Nevertheless, as he says, "that was not the point." The point is that the lower classes are learning to think and to walk in a new way, to assert a new presence and power in the street. It doesn't matter if the nobility and gentry don't notice yet; they are going to be forced to notice soon. It doesn't matter, either, if the poor clerk feels guilty and hates himself in the morning, as the Underground Man says he does; or if he never does anything like this again, as he says he doesn't; or if he tells himself (and us) incessantly that his brains and sensibility reduce him to a mouse—they don't, and he knows it. He has taken decisive action to change his life, and no self-negation or failure to follow through can change it back again. He has become a New Man, whether he likes it or not.

This scene, which dramatizes so powerfully the struggle for human rights—for equality, dignity, recognition—shows why Dostoevsky could never turn himself into a reactionary writer, hard as he sometimes tried, and why crowds of radical students wept over his coffin when he died. It shows, too, the dawn of a new stage in Petersburg's life. Petersburg, the Underground Man declares, is "the most abstract and intentional city in the world." The primary intention behind it was to propel Russia both materially and symbolically into the midst of the modern world. But a century after Peter's death, his intentions are sadly unfulfilled. His city has created a large body of "men of various origins and classes," full of modern desires and ideas, and a magnificent street that incarnates all the most brilliant images and dynamic rhythms of modern life. But the city's political and social life, in the middle of the nineteenth century, remains under control of a caste-bound autocracy that still has the dead weight to push its modern men off the street and drive them underground. In the 1860s, however, we see these men and women beginning to rise and step into the light—this is what's new about the "new people"—and to illuminate the city streets with their own weird but brilliant inner light. *Notes from Underground* marks a great leap forward in spiritual modernization: the moment when the citizens of "the most abstract and intentional city in the world" learn to assert abstractions and intentions of their own, Petersburg's spiritual street light flares up with a new intensity from this point on.

Petersburg vs. Paris: Two Modes of Modernism in the Streets

At this point I want to turn back, and compare Dostoevsky's modernism with Baudelaire's.[34] Both writers are original in creating what I have called primal modern scenes: everyday encounters in the city street that are raised to first intensity (as Eliot put it in his essay on Baudelaire), to the point where they express fundamental possibilities and pitfalls, allures and impasses of modern life. For both writers, too, the sense of political urgency becomes a primary source of energy, and the personal encounter in the street emerges as a political event; the modern city works as a medium in which personal and political life flow together and become one. But there are also fundamental differences in the Baudelairean and Dostoevskian visions of modern life. One vital source of their differences is the form and extent of modernization in the two cities from which these writers spring.

The boulevards of Haussmann's Paris, which we explored in Chapter III, are instruments of a dynamic bourgeoisie and an active state, determined to modernize fast, to develop productive forces and social relations, to speed up the flow of commodities, money and human beings through French society and around the world. Along with this drive toward economic modernization, Baudelaire's Paris has been, since the storming of the Bastille, an arena for the most explosive modes of modern politics. Baudelaire is part of, and proud to be part of, a mass urban population that knows how to organize and mobilize to fight for its rights. Even when he is alone in the midst of this crowd, he nourishes himself on its active traditions, both mythical and real, and its eruptive potentialities. These anonymous multitudes may at any moment resolve themselves into comrades and enemies; the potential for fraternity—and, ipso facto, for enmity—hovers over the Parisian street and boulevard like a gas in the air. Baudelaire, living in the midst of the most revolutionary city in the world, never for an instant doubts his human rights. He may feel like an alien in the universe, but he is at home as a man and a citizen in the Paris streets.

Petersburg's Nevsky Prospect spatially resembles a Parisian boulevard. Indeed, it may be more splendid than any Parisian boulevard. But economically, politically, spiritually, it is worlds away.

Even in the 1860s, after the emancipation of the serfs, the state is more concerned to contain its people than to move them forward.[35] As for the gentry, they are anxious to enjoy the cornucopia of Western consumer goods, but without working toward the Western development of productive forces that has made the modern consumer economy possible. Thus the Nevsky is a kind of stage set, dazzling the population with glittering wares, nearly all imported from the West, but concealing a dangerous lack of depth behind the brilliant facade.* The nobility and gentry are still playing the leading roles in this imperial capital, but since February 19 they are increasingly aware that the people in the streets are no longer their property, to be moved around like props. It is a bitter knowledge, and their spleen overflows against the capital city itself: " 'Progress? Progress would be Petersburg burning down on all four sides!' said the irritable general" in Turgenev's *Smoke* (1866). It makes this caste all the more determined to crash through the crowd of extras who surge up all around them on the Petersburg prospects; but they know now, after February 19, that their arrogant disdain is something of an act.

As for these extras, the "men of various origins and classes," although they constitute the great majority of the urban population, they are still, up to the 1860s, passive and atomized, uneasy in the streets, clinging to their overcoats for dear life. And how should they presume, and where can they begin? Unlike the lower classes of the West—even Baudelaire's beggars and families in rags—they have no tradition of *fraternité* and collective action to lean on. In this context, the Petersburg *raznochintsy* are driven to invent a modern political culture on their own. And they must invent it *ex nihilo*, "underground," because in the Russia of the 1860s modern political thought and action are still not openly allowed. Great changes lie ahead of them—both self-transformations and social transformations—before they can come to be at home in the city they love, and make it their own.

One of the decisive steps in this transformation is the develop-

---

* For instance, the streamlined new Moscow–Petersburg Express, which departed and arrived at the end of the Nevsky after 1851, served as a vivid symbol of dynamic modernity. And yet, if we take 1864, the date of *Notes from Underground*, we learn that there were only 3600 miles of railroads running in the whole immense Russian Empire, compared with about 13,100 in Germany and 13,400 in France. *European Historical Statistics, 1750–1870*, 581–84.

ment of a distinctive Petersburg expressive form, a form that is both artistic and political: the one-man demonstration in the streets. We saw this form make a dramatic debut at the climax of "The Bronze Horseman"—"you'll reckon with me yet!"; but in the Petersburg of Nicholas I it cannot hope to last—"and headlong took to flight." Two generations later, however, on the Nevsky Prospect, amid the abortive but real modernization of the 1860s, it is clear that the form is here to stay. It is suited perfectly to an urban society that stimulates modern patterns of consumption even as it represses modern modes of production and action, that nourishes individual sensibilities without recognizing individual rights, that fills its people with the need and the desire to communicate while restricting communication to official celebration or escapist romance. In such a society, life in the street takes on a special weight, because the street is the only medium in which free communication can take place. Dostoevsky evokes brilliantly the structure and dynamics of the one-man demonstration, and reveals the desperate needs and contradictions out of which this form is born. The confrontation between a "new man," a man just up from the underground, and an old ruling class, in the midst of a spectacular urban prospect, is a vital legacy from Dostoevsky and Petersburg to the modern art and the modern politics of the whole world.*

The contrast of Baudelaire and Dostoevsky, and of Paris and Petersburg in the middle of the nineteenth century, should help us to see a larger polarity in the world history of modernism. At one pole we can see the modernism of advanced nations, building

---

* The one-man street demonstration plays a crucial role in all Dostoevsky's Petersburg writing, and it is particularly striking in *Crime and Punishment*. Raskolnikov and his fellow sufferers are far too ravaged inwardly to expose themselves to the social flow of the Nevsky Prospect as the Underground Man does or, like him, to even begin to assert their rights in a politically coherent way. (This is in fact one of Raskolnikov's problems: between being an insect and being Napoleon he can conceive nothing.) Nevertheless, at climactic moments in their lives, they throw themselves into the streets and confront the strangers they see, to demonstrate where they stand and who they are. Thus, near the book's end, Svidrigailov stops in front of a suburban watchtower which offers a prospect of the whole city. He presents himself to the conscript Jewish soldier who serves as the tower's guard, announces that he is going to America, and puts a bullet through his brain. Simultaneously, at the book's climactic moment, Raskolnikov enters Haymarket Square in the midst of a teeming central city slum, throws himself down and kisses the pavement, before going to his neighborhood police station (recently opened, a product of the legal reforms of the mid-1860s) to confess and turn himself in.

directly on the materials of economic and political modernization and drawing vision and energy from a modernized reality— Marx's factories and railways, Baudelaire's boulevards—even when it challenges that reality in radical ways. At an opposite pole we find a modernism that arises from backwardness and under-development. This modernism first arose in Russia, most dramatically in St. Petersburg, in the nineteenth century; in our own era, with the spread of modernization—but generally, as in old Russia, a truncated and warped modernization—it has spread throughout the Third World. The modernism of underdevelopment is forced to build on fantasies and dreams of modernity, to nourish itself on an intimacy and a struggle with mirages and ghosts. In order to be true to the life from which it springs, it is forced to be shrill, uncouth and inchoate. It turns in on itself and tortures itself for its inability to singlehandedly make history—or else throws itself into extravagant attempts to take on itself the whole burden of history. It whips itself into frenzies of self-loathing, and preserves itself only through vast reserves of self-irony. But the bizarre reality from which this modernism grows, and the unbearable pressures under which it moves and lives—social and political pressures as well as spiritual ones—infuse it with a desperate incandescence that Western modernism, so much more at home in its world, can rarely hope to match.

The Political Prospect

Gogol, in his "Nevsky Prospect" story, had spoken of the Petersburg artist as the face the city sees in its dreams. *What Is to Be Done?* and *Notes from Underground* show Petersburg in the 1860s dreaming of radical encounters on its broad streets. A decade later, these dreams will begin to materialize. On the morning of December 4, 1876, several hundred of the miscellaneous people on the Nevsky will suddenly coalesce into a crowd, and converge collectively on the magnificent baroque colonnade in front of the Kazan Cathedral.[36] About half the crowd consists of students, clerks, unemployed and free-floating intellectuals, direct descendants of Chernyshevsky's and Dostoevsky's *raznochintsy* heroes; formerly "underground," they have become increasingly visible in the past decade. The crowd's other half are people for whom the word "underground" is much more apt: industrial workers from the factory districts that have recently come to form a ring around the city, from the Vyborg side on the Neva's north bank to the Narva and Alexander-Nevsky districts on the city's southern fringe. These workers are a bit hesitant as they cross the Neva or the Fontanka Canal, for they are strangers to the Nevsky and the city center, and virtually invisible to respectable Petersburg, though they are coming to play an increasingly important role in the city's (and the state's) economy.* Groups of workers and intellectuals have met and talked intermittently since the early 1870s—literally underground, in secluded cellars on the Vyborg Side—but they have never appeared together in public. When they come together now, in Kazan Square, they don't quite know what to do. They are a far smaller crowd than the organizers had hoped, and they fill only a little of the colonnade's vast space. They are jittery, and on the point of dissolving, when a young intellectual named Georgi Plekhanov decides to seize the day: he steps out from the midst of the crowd, makes a short, fiery speech, concludes with "Long live the social revolution!" and unfurls a red flag marked *Zemlya i Volya*, "Land and Liberty." Then—the whole thing lasts barely a couple of minutes—the police charge in, aided by a mob hastily recruited on the Nevsky. They have been taken by surprise, and respond with hysterical brutality; they manhandle everybody they can get their hands on, including many people who have nothing to do with the demonstration. Dozens are arrested at random, though in the chaos and confusion the primary organizers escape. Many of

---

* Petersburg's greatest concentration of capital and labor was in metallurgy and textiles. Enormous and ultramodern factories were built here, almost entirely on foreign capital, but with elaborate guarantees and subsidies from the state, to manufacture locomotives and rolling stock, textile looms, steamship parts, advanced weaponry and agricultural machinery. Most prominent was the giant Putilov Iron Works, whose 7000 workers would play a crucial part in the revolutions of 1905 and 1917. Petersburg's industrial development is discussed incisively in Reginald Zelnik, *Labor and Society in Tsarist Russia: The Factory Workers of St. Petersburg, 1855–1870* (Stanford, 1971); see also Roger Portal, "The Industrialization of Russia," in *Cambridge Economic History of Europe*, VI, 831–34. See Zelnik, 239, on the deep isolation of the factory workers, mostly new arrivals from the countryside, who "settled in the industrial border areas of the city, where they lived without families. Their incorporation into the city was only nominal; for all practical purposes they belonged to the industrial suburbs that stood beyond the city limits, rather than to an urban community." Not until St. Petersburg's first industrial strike, at the Nevsky cotton-spinning plant in 1870, which resulted in a mass public trial and extensive newspaper coverage, did the walls between the workers and the city begin to break down.

those arrested are tortured, and a few go mad under torture; others will be banished to Siberia, never to return. Still, on the night of December 4 and the morning after, in the students' garrets and the workers' shacks—and in the cells of the Peter-Paul Fortress—a new spirit of joy and promise fills the air.

Why all the excitement? Many liberal and some radical commentators see the demonstration as a debacle: a small crowd lost in a big space; hardly any time to proclaim the revolutionary message; great suffering at the hands of the police and the mob. Khazov, one of the participants, writes a pamphlet in January 1877, just before his arrest (he will die in Siberia in 1881), that tries to explain the point. For the past twenty years, Khazov says, ever since Nicholas' death, Russian liberals have been calling for freedom of speech and assembly; yet they have never been able to bring themselves to actually assemble and speak out. "The Russian liberals were very learned. They knew that liberty had been *conquered* [Khazov's emphasis] in the West. But obviously one ought not to try to apply this emphasis to Russia." It was precisely this liberal ideal that the radical workers and intellectuals were striving to fulfill on Kazan Square. A dubious form of conquest, critics might say, quixotic at best. Maybe so, Khazov agrees; but under Russian conditions, the only alternative to quixotic speech and action is no speech or action at all. "Russia is led along the road to political freedom not by the liberals but by dreamers who organize ridiculous and childish demonstrations; by men who dare to break the law, who are beaten, sentenced and reviled." In fact, Khazov argues, this "ridiculous and childish demonstration" signifies a new collective seriousness and maturity. The action and suffering on Kazan Square has brought about, for the first time in Russian history, "a union between the intelligentsia and the people."[37] I have shown how, since "The Bronze Horseman," the solitary heroes of Petersburg literature have undertaken such desperate gestures and actions on their own. Now, at last, the dreams of the city's art are taking hold of its waking life. A new, political prospect is opening up in Petersburg.

Demonstrations like the one in Kazan Square are remarkably hard to find in histories of Russia's revolutionary development. This is because, with few exceptions, that history has been written from above, from the perspectives of a series of elites. Thus we have, on one hand, the history of intellectual tendencies—"Slavophiles," "Westernizers," "the Forties," "the Sixties," "Populism," "Marxism"—and, on the other hand, a history of conspiracies. In this elitist perspective, Chernyshevsky stands in the foreground as the maker of what became the standard Russian revolutionary mold: men and women of iron discipline, mechanically programmed minds, and no sensibilities or inner lives at all; the inspiration of Lenin and later of Stalin. Dostoevsky enters this picture only as a severe critic of radical tendencies, in *Notes from Underground,* and of radical conspiracies in *The Possessed.* In the last generation, however, historians have come to understand the history of revolutions, starting with the French Revolution of 1789, from below, as a history of revolutionary crowds: groups of anonymous and ordinary people, of people full of weaknesses and vulnerabilities, torn by fear and self-doubt and ambivalence, but willing at crucial moments to go out into the streets and risk their necks to fight for their rights.[38] The more we grow accustomed to looking at revolutionary movements from below, the more clearly we will see Chernyshevsky and Dostoevsky as part of the same cultural and political movement: a movement of Petersburg plebeians striving, in increasingly active and radical ways, to make Peter's city their own. Nietzsche might have been thinking of Petersburg when he imagined "a history of the modern eclipse: the state nomads (civil servants, etc.) without home." The movement I have traced aims toward a radically modern sunrise after this eclipse: a great dawn in which these modern nomads will make themselves a home in the city that has made them what they are.

Afterword: The Crystal Palace, Fact and Symbol

All forms of modernist art and thought have a dual character: they are at once expressions of and protests against the process of modernization. In relatively advanced countries, where economic, social and technological modernization are dynamic and thriving, the relationship of modernist art and thought to the real world around it is clear, even when—as we have seen in Marx and Baudelaire—that relationship is also complex and contradictory. But in relatively backward countries, where the process of modernization has not yet come into its own, modernism, where it develops, takes on a fantastic character, because it is forced to nourish itself not on social reality but on fantasies, mirages, dreams. For Russians in the middle of the nineteenth century, the Crystal Palace was one of the most haunting and compelling of modern dreams. The extraordinary psychic impact it had on Russians—and it plays a far more important role in Russian than in English literature and thought—springs from its role as a specter of modernization haunting a nation that was writhing ever more convulsively in the anguish of backwardness.

Dostoevsky's symbolic treatment of the Crystal Palace has an indisputable richness and brilliance. And yet, anyone who knows anything about the real building that stood on London's Sydenham Hill—Chernyshevsky saw it in 1859, Dostoevsky in 1862—will be apt to feel that between Russian dreams and nightmares and Western realities falls a very large shadow. Let us recollect some of the qualities of the Dostoevskian Crystal Palace, as the hero of *Notes from Underground* describes it in Book One, Chapters 8, 9 and 10. First of all, it is mechanically conceived and realized: "all ready-made and computed with mathematical exactitude," to the point where, when it is complete, "every possible question will vanish, simply because every possible answer will be provided." The building's tone is pompous and ponderous; the message it proclaims is not merely historic culmination but cosmic totality and immutability: "Must not one accept this as the ultimate truth, and become silent forever? This is all so triumphant, majestic and proud that it takes your breath away . . . you feel that something final has taken place here, taken place and ended." The building is meant to intimidate, to force the spectator to "become silent forever": thus vast audiences, millions of people from every corner of the earth, "quietly and persistently mill around," powerless to respond in any way but to say yes and shut up. "You"—the Underground Man addresses his audience of "gentlemen"—

> you believe in a crystal edifice that can never be destroyed, an edifice at which one would not be able to stick one's tongue out, or to thumb one's nose, even on the sly. And I am afraid of this edifice just because it is of crystal and can never be destroyed, and because one could not stick out one's tongue at it on the sly.

Sticking out one's tongue becomes a demonstration of personal autonomy, an autonomy to which the Crystal Palace represents a radical threat.

Readers who try to visualize the Crystal Palace on the basis of Dostoevsky's language are apt to imagine an immense Ozymandian slab, bearing men down with its heaviness—a heaviness both physical and metaphysical—and brutal implacability; perhaps a shorter version of the World Trade Center. But if we turn from Dostoevsky's words to the multitude of paintings, photographs, lithographs, aquatints and detailed descriptions of the real thing, we are likely to wonder if Dostoevsky ever saw the real thing at all. What we see [39] is a glass structure supported by barely perceptible slender iron beams, a structure with gentle, flowing lines and graceful curves, light almost to the point of weightlessness, looking as if it could float at any instant into the sky. Its color alternates between the color of the sky through the transparent glass, which covers most of the building's volume, and the sky-blue of its narrow iron beams; this combination drenches us in a dazzling radiance, catching the sunlight from the sky and the water, shimmering dynamically. Visually, the building feels like a late Turner painting; it particularly suggests Turner's *Rain, Steam and Speed* (1844), fusing nature and industry in a vividly chromatic and dynamic ambience.

In its relationship to nature, it envelops rather than obliterates: great old trees, rather than being chopped down, are contained within the building, where—as in a greenhouse, which the Palace resembles, and with which its designer, Joseph Paxton, first made his reputation—they grow bigger and healthier than ever. Moreover, far from being designed by arid mechanical calculation, the Crystal Palace is in fact the most visionary and adventurous building of the whole nineteenth century. Only the Brooklyn Bridge and the Eiffel Tower, a generation later, will match its lyrical expression of the potentialities of an industrial age. We can see this lyricism vividly in Paxton's first sketch, dashed off in a couple of minutes on a sheet of blotting paper in the heat of inspiration. We can appreciate it even more if we compare the Palace with the ponderous neo-Gothic, neo-Renaissance and neobaroque enormities that were going up all around it. In addition, the Palace's builders, far from presenting the building as final and indestructible, prided themselves on its transience: utilizing the most advanced modes of prefabrication, it was built in six months in Hyde Park to house the Great International Exhibition of 1851; disassembled in three months when the exhibition closed; and then put together again in an enlarged version halfway across the city on Sydenham Hill in 1854.

Far from reducing its spectators to humble, passive assent, the Crystal Palace provoked the most explosive public controversy. Most of the British cultural establishment condemned it, Ruskin with a special vehemence, as a travesty on architecture and a frontal assault on civilization. The bourgeoisie enjoyed the Exhibition, but rejected the building, and went back to building Arthurian railroad stations and Hellenistic banks; in fact, no more genuinely modern buildings would be built in England for another fifty years. It might be argued that the unwillingness of the British bourgeoisie to accept and live with such a brilliant expression of its own modernity presaged its gradual loss of energy and imagination. In retrospect, 1851 appears as its zenith and the beginning of its gradual decline, a long decline for which the English people are still paying today. In any case, the building was not a grand consummation, as Dostoevsky said, but a courageous and lonely beginning that lay underdeveloped for many decades.

The Crystal Palace would probably not have been built at all, and would surely not have been rebuilt and allowed to stand for eight decades (it perished in a mysterious fire in 1936), had it not been acclaimed enthusiastically both by the English common people and by foreigners from all over the world. Long after the Great International Exhibition was over, the masses embraced it as a site for family outings, for children's play, for romantic encounters and assignations. Far from milling around quietly and being reduced to silence, they seem to have found all their energies aroused and engaged; no building in modern times, up to that point, seems to have had the Crystal Palace's capacity to excite people. As for foreigners, the Palace, more than anything else in London, became the sight they wanted to see first. Contemporary journalists reported that it was London's most cosmopolitan zone, crowded at any given time with Americans, Frenchmen, Germans, Russians (like Chernyshevsky and Dostoevsky), Indians, even Chinese and Japanese. Foreign architects and builders like Gottfried Semper and James Bogardus grasped its long-range possibilities in ways that no Englishman, apart from the builders themselves, was able to do; the world adopted the building immediately as a symbol of England's world vision and leadership, even as England's own ruling classes regarded it with a jaundiced eye.

The most interesting and penetrating account of the Crystal Palace—the real one, that is—was written, of course, by a foreigner, a German named Lothar Bucher. Bucher is a fascinating character: a democratic revolutionary in the 1840s, a refugee journalist eking out a living on Grub Street in the 1850s, a Prussian intelligence agent and intimate of Bismarck in the 1860s and 1870s —he even tried to recruit Marx into the Prussian intelligence service [40]—and, in his last years, an architect of the first great wave of German modernization and industrial growth. Bucher wrote in 1851 that "the impression [the building] produced on those who saw it was of such romantic beauty that reproductions of it were seen hanging on the cottage walls of remote German villages." [41] Bucher, perhaps projecting his own desires outward, sees the German peasants yearning en masse for modernization, a form of modernization that can fulfill German romantic ideals of beauty. To some extent Bucher's text is equivalent to Dostoevsky's: both use the Palace as a symbol to express their own hopes and fears. But Bucher's projections and expressions have a kind of authority that Dostoevsky's lack, because they are set in the context of a vivid and precise analysis of the building as a real space, a real structure, a real experience. It is Bucher we turn to, more than anyone else, for a sense of what it must have actually felt like to be inside the Crystal Palace:

> We see a delicate network of lines, without any clue by means of which we might judge their distance from the eye or their real size. The side walls are too far apart to be embraced in a single glance. Instead of moving from the wall at one end to the wall at the other, the eye sweeps along an unending perspective that fades into the horizon. We cannot tell if this structure towers a hundred or a thousand feet above us, or whether the roof is a flat structure or built up from a succession of ridges, for there is no play of shadows to enable our optic nerves to gauge the measurements.

Bucher continues:

> If we let our gaze travel downward it encounters the blue-painted lattice girders. At first these occur only at wide intervals; then they range closer and closer together until they are interrupted by a dazzling band of light—the transept—which dissolves into a

distant background where all materiality is blended into the atmosphere.

We see here that, although Bucher was unable to recruit Marx into the Prussian intelligence, he did manage to appropriate one of Marx's richest images and ideas: "All that is solid melts into air." Like Marx, Bucher sees the tendency of solid material to decompose and melt as the basic fact of modern life.

The more we are convinced by Bucher's vision of the Crystal Palace as a world in which everything is spectral, mysterious, infinite—and I think it is pretty convincing—the more we must be puzzled by Dostoevsky's denunciation of the same building as the very negation of all uncertainty and mystery, the defeat of adventure and romance.

How can we explain this disparity? Dostoevsky himself provides some ideas. He presents us with a hilarious account of his envy and defensiveness toward the constructive achievements of the West. *Winter Notes on Summer Impressions,* his travel journal of 1862, where he first describes the Crystal Palace, begins with an account of a disastrous sojourn in Cologne.[42] First he goes to see Cologne's legendary medieval monument, its cathedral. He brushes it off in a moment: its spectacular beauty is "too easy." He next proceeds to the city's most impressive modern work, a brand new bridge. "Admittedly it is a magnificent bridge, and the city is justly proud of it—but I felt that it was too proud of it. Naturally, I was not long in becoming indignant." As he pays his toll, Dostoevsky becomes convinced that the toll taker is insulting him "with the look of someone fining me for some unknown offense." After a moment of fervid fantasizing, the offense becomes national: "He must have guessed that I am a foreigner—in fact, that I am a Russian." The guard's eyes were obviously saying to him, "You see our bridge, miserable Russian, and you see that you are a worm before our bridge, and before every German person, because you people don't have such a bridge!"

Dostoevsky is willing to admit that this conjecture is pretty farfetched: the man actually said nothing, made no sign, and in all probability such thoughts never entered his mind. "But that makes no difference: I was so sure then that he meant precisely that, that I lost my temper altogether." In other words, the "backward" Russian is enraged not by the "advanced" German's assertions of superiority—even if the German makes no such assertions, "that makes no difference"—but by his own sense of inferiority. "The devil take you!" Dostoevsky thinks. "We invented the samovar . . . we have journals . . . we do the kind of things officers do . . . we . . ." His shame at his country's backwardness—and envious rage at a symbol of development—drives him not merely off the bridge but out of the country itself. After buying a bottle of eau de Cologne ("there was no escape from that"), he gets on the next train to Paris, "hoping that the French would be much more gracious and interesting." We know, of course, what is going to happen in France, and indeed anywhere else he goes in the West: the more beautiful and impressive the sights around him, the more his rancor will blind him to what is actually there. Something of this blindness might well have struck him on Sydenham Hill.*

So Dostoevsky's assault on the Crystal Palace was not only uncharitable but significantly off the mark. Commentators tend to explain that Dostoevsky wasn't really interested in the fact of the building but only in its symbolism, and that it symbolized for him arid Western rationalism, materialism, the mechanical view of the world, etc.; that, indeed, the dominant impulse in *Notes from Underground* is contempt and defiance toward the facts of modern life. And yet, if we read closely, we can find, in the midst of the Underground Man's diatribe against the Crystal Palace (Book I, Chapter 9) a far more complex and interesting relationship to modern factuality, technology and material construction. "I agree," he says, "that man is pre-eminently a creative animal, predestined to strive consciously toward a goal, and *to engage in engineering, that is, eternally and incessantly, to build new roads, no matter where they might lead.*" The second emphasis here is Dostoev-

* One of the weirdest ironies of this story is the fact that at the time the *Winter Notes* were written what was probably the most advanced suspension bridge in the world was located in Russia itself: the Dnieper Bridge, just outside of Kiev, designed by Charles Vignoles, and built between 1847 and 1853. Nicholas I had a special affection for this bridge, which he had commissioned: he exhibited blueprints, drawings and watercolors at the Great International Exhibition and kept an elaborate model in the Winter Palace (Klingender, *Art and the Industrial Revolution*, 159, 162). But neither Dostoevsky—who had been trained as an engineer and actually knew something about bridges—nor any other Russian intellectual, conservative or radical, seems to have taken the least notice of the project. It is as if the belief that Russia was constitutionally incapable of development—a belief accepted axiomatically by those who wanted development, as well as by those who did not—blinded everybody to the development that was actually going on. This, no doubt, helped to retard development even more.

sky's; the first is mine. What I find remarkable here, and what brings the Underground Man spiritually close to the creators of the Crystal Palace, is that his primary symbol of human creativity is not, say, art or philosophy, but engineering. This has special relevance to the Crystal Palace, which, as both its celebrants and its detractors emphasized, was perhaps the first major public building to be conceived and built exclusively by engineers, with no architects in the works at all.

There is plenty of room for argument about the meaning of this development; but the main point here is that he affirms the development: the primacy of engineering is one of the few things that the Underground Man does not question at all. The idea of engineering as the actual symbol of human creativity is strikingly radical in the nineteenth century, not only for Russia but even for the West. Apart from Saint-Simon and his followers, it is hard to think of anyone in Dostoevsky's century who would assign engineering such a high place in the scheme of human values. The Underground Man does, however, prefigure twentieth-century constructivism, a movement that was active all over Europe in the aftermath of World War I, but nowhere so vital and imaginative as in Russia: the modern romance of construction was ideally suited to a country of immense spiritual energy where virtually nothing had been constructed for a century.

Thus engineering plays a crucial role in Dostoevsky's vision of the good life. But he insists on one essential condition: human engineers must follow the logic of their own visions, *"no matter where they might lead."* Engineering should be a medium for creativity, not computation; but this requires recognition that "the destination it leads to is less important than the process of making it." Now Dostoevsky makes his decisive point, about the Crystal Palace or any other structure:

> Man loves to create and build roads, that is beyond dispute. But . . . may it not be that . . . he is instinctively afraid of attaining his goal and completing the edifice he is constructing? How do you know, perhaps he only likes that edifice from a distance and not at close range, *perhaps he only likes to build it, and does not want to live in it.*

The crucial distinction here is between building a building and living in it: between a building as a medium for the self's development and as a container for its confinement. The activity of engineering, so long as it remains an activity, can bring man's creativity to its highest pitch; but as soon as the builder stops building, and entrenches himself in the things he has made, the creative energies are frozen, and the palace becomes a tomb. This suggests a fundamental distinction between different modes of modernization: modernization as *adventure* and modernization as *routine*. We should be able to see, now, that Dostoevsky is intensely committed to modernization as an adventure. This is what the Underground Man is doing in his encounter with the officer on the Nevsky Prospect. I have tried to show how the creators of the Crystal Palace were engaging in a modernist adventure of their own. But if the adventure were ever transformed into a routine, then the Crystal Palace would become (as the Underground Man fears) a chicken coop, and then modernization would turn into a death sentence for the spirit. Until then, however, modern man can thrive quite happily, and thrive spiritually as well as materially, as an engineer.

Having come this far, if we turn back to Chernyshevsky's *What Is to Be Done?* we will find the apotheosis of modernity as a routine. And we will find, too, that it is Chernyshevsky's Crystal Palace far more than Paxton's—that is, Russian fantasies of modernization rather than Western realities—that Dostoevsky really fears. In "Vera Pavlovna's Fourth Dream,"[43] the scene in which Chernyshevsky invokes and canonizes the Crystal Palace, what we find is a vision of a future world that consists exclusively of crystal palaces. These "huge buildings stand two or three miles from each other, as if they were numerous chessmen on a chessboard"; they are separated by acres of "fields and meadows, gardens and woods." This chessboard configuration stretches as far as the eye can see; if it is meant to coexist with any other mode of building or living space, Chernyshevsky doesn't tell us what or where. (Twentieth-century readers will recognize this model as a precursor of the "towers in the park" of Le Corbusier's *ville radieuse*.) Each building will be what our age calls a megastructure, containing apartments, industrial workshops, communal eating and recreational facilities (Chernyshevsky describes the ballrooms, and the festivals to be held there, in elaborate loving detail), and enhanced by aluminum furniture, sliding walls (to facilitate household rearrangements), and an early form of air conditioning. Each megastructure will contain a community of several thousand people, satisfying all their material needs through a collectivized, technologically advanced agriculture and industry, and satisfied sexually and emotionally through the social policies of a benign, sophisticated and rational administration. The "new Russia," as Chernyshevsky calls it, will be utterly devoid of tension, personal or political; even the dream of trouble is absent from this new world.

Because Chernyshevsky has worked so hard to eliminate all traces of conflict from his vision, it takes a while to understand what his crystal-palace world is defined against. Eventually, however, the point comes through. The heroine, after being given a tour of the "new Russia" of the future, finally remembers what is missing from this world. She asks her guide: "But there must be cities for people who want to live in them?" The guide answers that there are very few such people, and hence far fewer cities than there were in the old days. Cities do continue to exist (far off camera) on a minimal basis, as communications centers and vacation resorts. Thus, "Everyone goes there for a few days, for variety," and the few remaining cities are full of entertaining spectacles for the tourists; but their population is constantly changing. "But what," Vera Pavlovna asks, "if someone wants to live there constantly?" Her guide answers with amused contempt:

> They can live there, as you [in the present] live in your St. Petersburgs, Londons, Parises—what business is it of anyone's? Who would stop them? Let everyone live as he likes. Only the overwhelming majority, ninety-nine out of a hundred, live in the manner shown to you [i.e., in crystal-palace communities], because it is more pleasant and advantageous for them.

Thus the Crystal Palace is conceived as the antithesis of the city. Chernyshevsky's dream, we can see now, is a dream of modernization without urbanism. The new antithesis to the city is no longer the primitive countryside, but a highly developed, super-technological, self-contained exurban world, comprehensively planned and organized—because created *ex nihilo* on virgin soil—more thoroughly controlled and administered, and hence "more pleasant and advantageous," than any modern metropolis could ever be. As a vision of hope for Russia, Vera Pavlovna's dream is an ingenious variation on the familiar populist hope for a "leap" from feudalism to socialism, skipping the bourgeois and capitalist society of the modern West. Here, the leap will be from a tranquil and underdeveloped rural life to a tranquil and abundantly developed exurban life, without ever having to go through a life of turbulent urbanism. For Chernyshevsky, the Crystal Palace symbolizes a death sentence against "your St. Petersburgs, Londons, Parises"; these cities will be, at best, museums of backwardness in the brave new world.

This vision should help us locate the terms of Dostoevsky's quarrel with Chernyshevsky. The Underground Man says he is afraid of this edifice, because "one would not be able to stick one's tongue out, or to thumb one's nose, even on the sly." He is wrong, of course, about Paxton's Crystal Palace, at which thousands of genteel and cultivated tongues were stuck out, but right about Chernyshevsky's; wrong, in other words, about the Western reality of modernization, which is full of dissonance and conflict, but right about the Russian fantasy of modernization as an end to dissonance and conflict. This point should clarify one of the primary sources of Dostoevsky's love for the modern city, and especially for Petersburg, *his* city: this is the ideal environment for the sticking out of tongues—that is, for the acting out and working out of personal and social conflict. Again, if the Crystal Palace is a denial of "suffering, doubt and negation," the streets and squares and bridges and embankments of Petersburg are precisely where these experiences and impulses find themselves most at home.

The Underground Man thrives on Petersburg's infinite prospects of suffering, doubt, negation, desire, struggle of every kind. These experiences are precisely what make him, as he says (and Dostoevsky underlines, on the book's last page), "more alive" than the genteel readers—he calls them "gentlemen"—who recoil from him and his world. (" 'Progress would be Petersburg burning down on all four sides,' said the irritable general" in Turgenev's *Smoke*.) We should be able to see now how it is possible for *Notes from Underground* to be at once a scathing attack on the ideologues of Russian modernization and one of the great canonical works of modernist thought. Dostoevsky, in his critique of the Crystal Palace, is attacking the modernity of the suburbs and exurbs—still, in the 1860s, only an ideal—in the name of the modernity of the city. Another way to put it: he is affirming modernization as a human adventure—a frightening and dangerous adventure, as any real adventure must be—against a modernization of trouble-free but deadening routines.

There is one more ironic postscript to the Crystal Palace story. Joseph Paxton was one of the great urbanists of the nineteenth century: he designed vast, wild city parks that prefigured and inspired Olmsted's work in America; he conceived and planned a comprehensive mass transit plan for London, including a network of subways, forty years before anyone dared to build a subway anywhere. His Crystal Palace, too—especially in its post-Exhibition incarnation on Sydenham Hill—was meant to enrich the possibilities of urban life: it would be a new kind of social space, an archetypally modern environment that could bring all London's fragmented and opposed social strata together. It might be seen as a brilliant equivalent for the Parisian boulevards or Petersburg prospects that London conspicuously lacked. Paxton would have resisted vehemently any attempt to use his great building against the city.

At the very end of the nineteenth century, however, Ebenezer Howard grasped the anti-urban potentialities of the Crystal Palace–type structure, and exploited them far more effectively than Chernyshevsky had done. Howard's enormously influential work, *Garden Cities of To-Morrow* (1898, revised 1902), developed very powerfully and cogently the idea, already implicit in Chernyshevsky and in the French Utopians he had read, that the modern city was not merely spiritually degraded but economically and technologically obsolete. Howard repeatedly compared the metropolis in the twentieth century to the stagecoach in the nineteenth, and argued that suburban development was the key to both material prosperity and spiritual harmony for modern man. Howard grasped the Crystal Palace's formal potentialities as a human hothouse—it had been initially modeled on the greenhouses Paxton had built in his youth—a supercontrolled environment; he appropriated its name and form for a vast glass-enclosed shopping arcade and cultural center that would be the heart of the new suburban complex.* *Garden Cities of To-Morrow* had tremendous

---

*Garden Cities of To-Morrow, 1902 (MIT, 1965, with introductions by F. J. Osborn and Lewis Mumford); on the metropolis as stagecoach, 146; on the Crystal Palace as a suburban model, 53–4, 96–8. Ironically, although the Crystal Palace was one of the most popular features of Howard's ideal design, the men in charge of building the first Garden City at Letchworth excluded it from the plan as being un-English (Mr. Podsnap would surely have agreed), too daringly modern, and excessively expensive. They substituted a neo-medieval market street which they said was more "organic" (Fishman, *Urban Utopias in the Twentieth Century*, 67–8).

impact on the architects, planners and developers of the first half of the twentieth century; they directed all their energies to the production of "more pleasant and advantageous" environments that would leave the turbulent metropolis behind.

It would take us too far afield to explore in any detail the metamorphosis of the Underground Man and the Crystal Palace in Soviet culture and society. But I can at least suggest how such an exploration might proceed. It should be noted, first of all, that the brilliant first generation of Soviet architects and planners, though they disagreed about many things, were nearly unanimous in their belief that the modern metropolis was a wholly degenerate effusion of capitalism, and that it must go. Those who believed that modern cities contained anything worth preserving were stigmatized as anti-Marxist, right-wing and reactionary.[44] Second, even those who favored some sort of urban environments agreed that the city street was entirely pernicious, and had to go, to be replaced by a more open, greener and presumably more harmonious public space. (Their arguments were similar to those of Le Corbusier, who made several trips to Moscow and was extremely influential in the early Soviet period.) The most trenchantly critical literary work of the Soviet 1920s, Evgeny Zamyatin's futuristic and anti-Utopian novel, *We*, was notably responsive to this emerging landscape. Zamyatin reincarnates Chernyshevsky's Crystal Palace, and Dostoevsky's critical vocabulary, in a brilliantly realized visionary landscape of steel-and-glass skyscrapers and glassed-in arcades. The dominant motif in Zamyatin's crystalline new world is ice, which symbolizes for him the freezing of modernism and modernization into solid, implacable, life-devouring forms. Against the coldness and uniformity of these newly crystallized structures, and their newly rigidified ruling class, Zamyatin's hero and heroine of the future invoke a nostalgic vision of "the avenue of *their* 20th-century days, a deafeningly jangling motley, confused crush of people, wheels, animals, posters, trees, colors, birds." Zamyatin feared that the "new" modernity of cold steel and regimentation was extinguishing the "old" modernity of the spontaneous, vibrant city street.[45]

As it turned out, Zamyatin's fears were not fulfilled to the letter, though their spirit was only too well realized. The early U.S.S.R. simply lacked the resources—the capital, the labor skills, the technology—to build dazzling crystal-palace buildings; but it was sufficiently modernized, alas, to construct, maintain and extend the solid structures of a totalitarian state. The real twentieth-century reincarnation of the Crystal Palace turned out to take place half a world away, in the U.S.A. There, in the generation after World War Two, Paxton's lyrical and gently flowing building would emerge, in travestied but recognizable form, endlessly and mechanically reproduced in a legion of steel and glass corporate headquarters and suburban shopping malls that covered the land.[46] Much has recently been said, in increasingly anguished retrospect, about this pervasive style of building. The only point relevant here is that one of its fundamental impulses was a desire to flee the modern metropolis, "a deafeningly jangling motley, confused crush of people, wheels, animals, posters, trees, colors, birds," and to create a far more enclosed, controlled, orderly world. Paxton, a lover of the modern city, would be appalled to find himself in one of the crystalline suburban IBM "campuses" of our day. But Chernyshevsky would almost certainly feel at home here: this is precisely the "more pleasant and advantageous" environment that his dream of modernization was all about.

All this suggests how good a prophet Dostoevsky really was. His critical vision of the Crystal Palace suggests how even the most heroic expression of modernity as an adventure may be transformed into a dismal emblem of modernity as a routine. As the postwar dynamism of American and Western European and Japanese capital drove—irresistibly, it seemed for a while—toward the creation of a crystal-palace world, Dostoevsky became urgently relevant, in ways he was never relevant before, to everyday modern life.

3.

The Twentieth Century: The City Rises, the City Fades

To EVEN attempt to do justice to Petersburg's political and cultural upheavals over the following half century would throw the structure of this book into hopeless disarray. But it should be worthwhile to give at least flashes of the city's life and literature in the early twentieth century, to show some of the weird and tragic ways in which Petersburg's nineteenth-century themes and impulses will be worked out.

1905: More Light, More Shadows ·

Petersburg in 1905 has become a major industrial center, with close to 200,000 factory workers, more than half of whom have migrated from the countryside since 1890. Now descriptions of the city's industrial districts have begun to have a nervous ring: "The factories surrounded the city as if they were a ring, squeezing the administrative-commercial center in their embrace."[47] Since 1896, the date of a remarkably disciplined and coordinated city-wide textile strike, Petersburg's workers have held an important point on the European political map.

Now, on Sunday, January 9, 1905, an immense crowd of these workers, as many as 200,000 men, women and children, moves en masse from every direction toward the center of the city, determined to reach the palace where all Petersburg prospects end. They are led by the handsome and charismatic Father George Gapon, a state-approved chaplain at the Putilov Iron Works, and organizer of the Assembly of St. Petersburg Factory Workers. The people are explicitly unarmed (Gapon's ushers have searched the crowd and disarmed some) and nonviolent. Many carry icons and mounted pictures of Tsar Nicholas II, and crowds sing "God Save the Tsar" along the way. Father Gapon has entreated the Tsar to appear before the people at the Winter Palace, and to respond to their needs, which he carries inscribed on a scroll:

> SIRE—We, workers and residents of the city of St. Petersburg of various ranks and stations, our wives, our children, and our helpless old parents, have come to Thee, Sire, to seek justice and protection. We have become beggars; we are oppressed and burdened by labor beyond our strength; we are not recognized as human beings, but treated as slaves who must endure their bitter fate in silence. We have endured it, and we are being pushed further and further into the depths of poverty, injustice and ignorance. We are being so stifled by justice and arbitrary rule that we cannot breathe. Sire, we have no more strength! Our endurance is at an end. We have reached that awful moment when death is preferable to the continuation of intolerable suffering.
>
> Therefore we have stopped work and told our employers that we would not resume until they complied with our demands.

The petition then demands an eight-hour day, a minimum wage of one ruble per day, the abolition of compulsory unpaid overtime, and the workers' freedom to organize. But these first demands are addressed primarily to the workers' employers, and only indirectly to the Tsar himself. Immediately following them, however, is a series of radical political demands that only the Tsar could fulfill: a democratically elected constituent assembly ("This is our chief request; in it and on it all else is based; it is . . . the only plaster for our painful wounds"); guarantees of freedom of speech, press and assembly; due process of law; a system of free education for all; finally, an end to the disastrous Russo-Japanese War. The petition then concludes:

> These, Sire, are our chief needs, concerning which we have come to Thee. We are seeking here the last salvation. Do not refuse assistance to Thy people. Give their destiny into their own hands. Cast away from them the intolerable oppression of the officials. Destroy the wall between Thyself and Thy people, and let them rule the country together with Thyself. . . .

Order and take an oath to carry out these measures, and Thou wilt make Russia happy and famous, and Thy name will be engraved in our hearts and in the hearts of our posterity forever.

If Thou wilt not order and will not answer our prayer, we shall die here on this Square before Thy Palace. We have nowhere else to go and no purpose in going. We have only two roads: one leading to freedom and happiness, the other to the grave. . . . Let our lives be a sacrifice for suffering Russia. We offer this sacrifice, not grudgingly, but with joy.[48]

Father Gapon never got to read his petition to the Tsar: Nicholas and his family had left the capital hastily, and left his officials in charge. They planned a confrontation very different from the one for which the workers had hoped. As the people approached the palace, detachments of troops, 20,000 strong, fully armed, surrounded them, then fired at close range directly into the crowd. No one ever found out how many people were killed that day—the government admitted 130, but respectable estimates ranged up to a thousand—but everyone knew at once that a whole epoch of Russian history had come to an abrupt end and that a revolution had begun.

With the events of "Bloody Sunday," according to Bertram Wolfe, "millions of primitive minds took the leap from the Middle Ages to the Twentieth Century. In love and reverence they had come to lay their troubles at the feet of their Dear Father Tsar. The bullets and the shared blood swept away all the vestiges of love and credulity. Now they knew themselves fatherless and knew they would have to solve their problems themselves." This is the general judgment on January 9, and it is generally right. But it is wrong in underestimating the evolution of the Petersburg crowd *before* the bullets and the blood. Trotsky, in his participant account of the 1905 Revolution, describes the Gapon demonstration as "the *attempted dialogue* between the proletariat and the monarchy in the city streets."[49] A people's demand for dialogue with its ruler in the streets is not the work of "primitive minds" or of childlike souls; it is an idea that expresses both a people's modernity and its maturity. The demonstration of January 9 is a form of modernity that springs from Petersburg's distinctive soil. It expresses the deepest needs and ambivalences of the common people that this city has made: their volatile mixture of deference and defiance, of ardent devotion to their superiors and equally ardent determination to be themselves; their willingness to risk everything, even their lives, for the sake of a direct encounter in the streets, an encounter at once personal and political, through which they will at last be—as the Underground Man said in the 1860s, and as Gapon's petition repeats on a mass scale in 1905—"recognized as human beings."

Petersburg's most original and enduring contribution to modern politics was born nine months later: the soviet, or workers' council. The Petersburg Soviet of Workers' Deputies burst on the scene virtually overnight in early October 1905. It died young, with the 1905 Revolution, but sprang up again, first in Petersburg and then all over Russia, in the revolutionary year of 1917. It has been an inspiration to radicals and to oppressed peoples all over the world throughout the twentieth century. It is hallowed by the U.S.S.R.'s name, even as it is profaned by that state's reality. Many of those who have opposed the Soviet Union in Eastern Europe, including those who revolted against it in Hungary and Czechoslovakia and Poland, have been inspired by a vision of what a true "soviet society" might be.

Trotsky, one of the moving spirits of that first Petersburg Soviet, described it as "an organization which was authoritative, and yet had no traditions; which could immediately involve a scattered mass of thousands of people, while having virtually no organizational machinery; which united the revolutionary currents within the proletariat; which was capable of spontaneous initiative and self-control—and, most important of all, which could be brought out from underground in twenty-four hours." The soviet "paralyzed the autocratic state by means of [an] insurrectionary strike," and proceeded to "introduce its own free democratic order into the life of the laboring urban population."[50] It was perhaps the most radically participatory form of democracy since ancient Greece. Trotsky's characterization, although somewhat idealized, is generally apt—except for one thing. Trotsky says that the Petersburg Soviet "had no traditions." But this chapter should make it clear how the soviet comes directly out of the rich and vibrant Petersburg tradition of personal politics, of politics through direct personal encounters in the city's streets and squares. All the courageous, futile gestures of Petersburg's generations of common clerks—"You'll reckon with me yet!—and headlong took to flight"—all the "ridiculous and childish demonstrations" of the *raznochintsy* Underground Men, are redeemed here, for a little while.

But if 1905 in Petersburg is a year for confrontations in the street and epiphanies face to face, it is also a year of deepening ambiguities and mysteries, of wheels within wheels, of doors turning in on themselves and slamming shut. No figure is more profoundly ambiguous than Father Gapon himself. Gapon, a son of Ukrainian peasants, an intermittent wanderer and Tolstoyan, actually did his union organizing under the auspices of the secret police. Zubatov, chief of its Moscow section, had developed the idea of organizing industrial workers into moderate unions that would deflect the workers' anger onto their employers and away from the government; his experiment was baptized "police socialism." Gapon was an eager and brilliant recruit. However, just as Zubatov's critics had anticipated, the police agent was carried away by the needs and energies of his workers, and worked to carry the movement far beyond the bounds of decorum that the police had set. Gapon's own naive faith in the Tsar—not shared by his worldly and cynical superiors—helped to propel the city and the nation toward the disastrous collision of January 9.

No one was more deeply shocked than Gapon at the events of Bloody Sunday, and no one, it seemed, was more inflamed overnight with revolutionary zeal. From the underground, and then from exile, he issued a series of explosive manifestos. "There is no Tsar anymore!" he proclaimed. He called for "bombs and dynamite, terror by individuals and by masses—everything that may contribute to a national uprising." Lenin met Gapon in Geneva (after Plekhanov had refused to see him), and was fascinated by his naive and intensely religious radicalism—far more typical of the Russian masses, Lenin said later, than his own Marxism. But he urged the priest to read and study, to clarify and solidify his political thinking, and, above all, to avoid being carried away by flattery and instant fame.

Gapon, in coming to Geneva, had initially hoped to use his prestige to unite all revolutionary forces, but was soon overwhelmed by their sectarian quarrels and intrigues. At this point, he sailed for London, where he was taken up as a celebrity, wined and dined by millionaires and adored by society ladies. He managed to raise a great deal of money for the revolutionary cause, but didn't know what to do with the money, because he had no coherent ideas of what was to be done. After a failed attempt at gunrunning, he found himself isolated and helpless, and, as the Revolution gradually ran aground, increasingly beset by depression and despair. He returned secretly to Russia in early 1906—and sought to re-enter the police! He offered to betray anyone and everyone for lavish sums of money; but Pincus Rutenberg, one of his closest comrades during and after January 1905 (and co-author of his manifesto), discovered his duplicity and handed him over to a secret workers' tribunal, which killed him in a lonely house in Finland in April 1906. The masses still revered Gapon, and persisted for years in the belief that he had been murdered by the police.[51] A story worthy of Dostoevsky in his darkest moments: an Underground Man who comes out into the sunlight for one heroic moment, only to sink back in, to sink himself deeper by his own flailing about, till he is buried in the end.

One of the enduring mysteries in Gapon's story is this: If the police and the Ministry of the Interior knew what he was doing in the weeks and days before January 9, why didn't they stop the demonstration before it could get started—for instance, by arresting all the organizers—or else press the government to make a conciliatory gesture that would keep the workers within bounds? Some historians believe that the police had come to relax their vigilance in late 1904, trusting Gapon to keep the workers in line, foolishly underestimating the volatility of their own agent, as well as that of the workers in his charge. Others argue, on the contrary, not only that the police knew what was going to happen on January 9, but that they wanted it to happen, and indeed encouraged both Gapon and the government to make it happen—because, by helping to plunge the country into revolutionary chaos, they could create a pretext and a suitable atmosphere for the draconic repression and reaction that they were hoping to unleash.

This image of the Tsarist police might seem absurd and paranoid, had it not been proven beyond a doubt that between 1902 and 1908 the police had been subsidizing a wave of political terrorism. A secret offshoot of the populist Social Revolutionary Party, which carried out a series of dramatic assassinations of high officials—its most prominent victim was the Grand Duke Sergei, the Tsar's uncle, military governor of Moscow—was working all along, unknown to its members, under the direction of a police agent, Evny Azef, with the knowledge and collusion of Azef's superiors. What makes the story especially bizarre is that the group's most spectacular assassination, and the one that won widest public acclaim, was directed against its own employer, the dreaded Vyacheslav von Plehve, the Tsar's Minister of the Interior, the official in charge of the secret police, and the man under whose auspices the group had been formed! In between assassination attempts, Azef turned over many terrorists to the police; at the same time, he delivered other police agents into the terrorists' hands. Azev's activities were finally unmasked in 1908, and the whole policy (and mystique) of terrorism was decisively discredited on the left. But this did not prevent another police agent, again acting in revolutionary guise, from assassinating another Minister of the Interior, Peter Stolypin, in the summer of 1911.

Azev, another character out of Dostoevsky, has been a source of endless fascination to everyone who has ever studied the 1905 period. But no one has ever unraveled his remarkable machinations, or penetrated to the center—if there was a center—of his being.[52] But the fact that his murderous initiatives, intended to paralyze the government and plunge the country into chaos, emanated from within the government itself, confirms an argument I made earlier in this book: that the nihilism of modern revolutionaries is a pale shadow of the nihilism of the forces of Order. The one thing that is clear about Azev and his fellow double agents, and their official sponsors, is that together they created a political atmosphere hopelessly shrouded in mystery, an atmosphere in which anything might turn out to be its radical opposite, in which action was desperately necessary, yet the meaning of every action was fatally obscure. At this point, Petersburg's traditional reputation as a spectral and surreal city took on a new immediacy and urgency.

Biely's *Petersburg:* The Shadow Passport

This surreal reality is the inspiration for Andrei Biely's novel *Petersburg*, set at the climax of the Revolution of 1905, written and published between 1913 and 1916, revised in 1922. This novel has never been allowed to find its public in the U.S.S.R., and is only just beginning to find one in the U.S.A.[53] Its reputation rested for years on adulation from the *emigré* avant-garde: Nabokov, for instance, considered it, along with Joyce's *Ulysses*, Kafka's *Metamorphosis* and Proust's *Recherche*, "one of the four great masterpieces of 20th-century prose." A reader without Russian cannot seriously evaluate Biely's prose; but it is perfectly clear in translation that the book is a masterpiece, worthy of the finest traditions of modern literature.

A random glance at any couple of pages of Biely's *Petersburg* will reveal that it is, in all the most obvious senses, a modernist work. It contains no unified narrative voice, as nearly all nineteenth-century literature does, but moves instead by continuous rapid jump-cutting, cross-cutting and montage. (In Russian terms, it is contemporaneous with, and related to, Mayakovsky and the futurists in poetry, Kandinsky and Malevitch, Chagall and Tatlin in painting and visual arts. It anticipates Eisenstein, Rodchenko and constructivism by a few years.) It consists almost entirely of broken and jagged fragments: fragments of social and political life in the city's streets, fragments of the inner lives of the people on those streets, dazzling leaps back and forth between them—as Baudelaire said, *soubresauts de conscience*. Its planes of vision, like those in cubist and futurist painting, are shattered and askew. Even Biely's punctuation goes wild; sentences break off in midair, while periods, commas, question marks and exclamation points float alone, in the middle of the page, lost in empty space. We, the readers, are kept constantly off balance; we must work from line to line and moment to moment to grasp where we are and what is going on. But the bizarre and chaotic quality of Biely's style is not an end in itself: Biely is forcing us to experience the dazzling but mystifying atmosphere in which the people of Petersburg in 1905 were forced to live:

> Petersburg is the fourth dimension that is not indicated on maps.
> . . . It's not customary to mention that *our* capital city belongs to
> the land of spirits when reference books are compiled. Karl Baedeker keeps mum about it. A man from the provinces who hasn't
> been informed of this takes only the visible administrative apparatus into account; he has no shadow passport. [5, 205–07]

These images serve to define the novel itself as a kind of four-dimensional map or Baedeker, as a shadow passport. But this means that *Petersburg* is a work of realism as well as of modernism.

Its triumph shows how realism in literature and thought must develop into modernism, in order to grasp the unfolding, fragmenting, decomposing and increasingly shadowy realities of modern life.[54]

If Petersburg is a modernist work, and a realist one, it is also a novel of tradition, of Petersburg tradition. Every page is drenched in the accumulated traditions of the city's history, literature and folklore. Real and imaginary figures—Peter the Great and various successors, Pushkin, his clerk and his Bronze Horseman, Gogolian overcoats and noses, superfluous men and Russian Hamlets, doubles and devils, tsars who were murderers and murderers of tsars, the Decembrists, the Underground Man, Anna Karenina, Raskolnikov, along with assorted Persians, Mongols, the Flying Dutchman, and many more—not only haunt the minds of Biely's characters, but actually materialize on his city streets. At times it appears that the book is about to sink under the accumulated weight of Petersburg tradition; at other moments, it seems that the book will blow apart from that tradition's increasing pressures. But the problems that pervade the book perplex the city as well: Petersburg's citizens themselves are being blown up and dragged down by the weight and intensity of their city's traditions—including its traditions of rebellion.

Biely's principal characters are these: Apollon Apollonovich Ableukhov, a high imperial official modeled loosely on the icy and sinister archreactionary Konstantin Pobedonostsev, ideologue of the fin-de-siècle extreme right, patron of pogroms; his son Nikolai, a handsome, languid, imaginative, weak youth in the superfluous man tradition, who alternates between moping and meditating in his room, appearing in weird costumes that startle high society, and delivering papers on the destruction of all values; Alexander Dudkin, a poor ascetic *raznochinets* intellectual and member of the revolutionary underground; and the mysterious Lippanchenko, a double agent loosely modeled on Azev (who used the name Lipchenko as one of his aliases), who contrives the vicious plot that gives Biely's narrative much of its motive force; and finally, seething and swirling around them all, pushing them on and pulling them back, the city of Petersburg itself.

The Nevsky Prospect is still, in 1905, mysterious and lovely, and it still evokes lyrical response: "Of an evening the Prospect is flooded with fiery obfuscation. Down the middle, at regular intervals, hang the apples of electric lights. While along the sides plays the changeable glitter of shop signs. Here the sudden flare of ruby lights, there the flare of emeralds. A moment later the rubies are there, the emeralds here." (1, 31) And the Nevsky is still, as much as in Gogol's or Dostoevsky's time, Petersburg's communication line. Only now, in 1905, new kinds of messages are coming through. They are coming primarily from the city's self-conscious and intensely active working class:

> Petersburg is surrounded by a ring of many-chimneyed factories.
>
> A many-thousand swarm plods toward them in the morning, and the suburbs are all aswarm. All the factories were then [October 1905] in a state of terrible unrest. The workers had turned into prating shady types. Amidst them circulated Browning revolvers. And something else.
>
> The agitation that ringed Petersburg then began penetrating to the very centers of Petersburg. It first seized the islands, then crossed the Liteny and Nikolaevsky bridges. On Nevsky Prospect circulated a human myriapod. However, the composition of the myriapod kept changing; and an observer could now note the appearance of a shaggy black fur hat from the fields of blood-stained Manchuria [demobilized soldiers from the Russo-Japanese War]. There was a sharp drop in the percentage of passing top hats. Now were heard the disturbing anti-government cries of street urchins running full tilt from the railway station to the Admiralty waving gutter rags.

Now, too, one can hear the strangest sound on the Nevsky, a faint humming, impossible to pin down, "the same importunate note, 'Oooo—oooo—ooo! . . . But was it a sound? It was the sound of some other world." And "it had a rare strength and clarity" in the fall of 1905. (2, 51–2; 7, 224) This is a rich and complex image; but one of its crucial meanings points to the "other world" of the Petersburg working class, who now, in 1905, are determined to assert themselves in "this world," the world of prospect and palace at the center of the city and the state. "Don't let the crowd of shadows in from the islands!" Senator Ableukhov urges himself and the government (1, 13); but in 1905, his heart's cry is in vain.

Let us see how Biely situates his figures in this landscape. His first dramatic scene is a version of what I have called the Petersburg primal scene: the encounter between officer and clerk, between gentry and *raznochintsy*, on the Nevsky Prospect. (1, 10–14) Biely's rendering of this archetypal scene makes it shockingly clear how much Petersburg life has changed since the era of the Underground Man. Senator Ableukhov, we are told, loves the Nevsky: "Inspiration took possession of the senator's soul whenever the lacquered cube [of his coach] cut along the line of the Nevsky. There the enumeration of the houses was visible. And the circulation went on. There, from there, on clear days, from far, far away, came the blinding blaze of the gold [Admiralty] needle, the clouds, the crimson ray of the sunset." But we find that he loves it in a peculiar way. He loves the prospect's abstract geometric forms— "his tastes were distinguished by their harmonious simplicity. Most of all he loved the rectilineal prospect; this prospect reminded him of the flow of time between two points"—but he can't stand the real people on it. Thus, in his coach, "gently rocking on the satin seat cushions," he is relieved to be "cut off from the scum of the streets by four perpendicular walls. Thus he was isolated from people and from the red covers of the damp trashy rags on sale right there at the intersection."

We see here the Tsarist bureaucracy, in its last phase, trying to leave behind its past obscurantism, so as to be able to develop the country according to rational methods and ideas. But this rationalism is unfortunately suspended in a void: it stops short of any attempt to deal rationally with the myriad of people who occupy its vast rectilineal space. Insulated from "the scum of the streets" on the Nevsky, the senator begins to think about "the islands," site of Petersburg's factories and its most concentrated proletariat, and concludes that "the islands must be crushed!" Comfortable with this thought, he drifts off into daydreams, into cosmic rhapsodies of rectilinear prospects "expanding into the abysses of the universe in planes of squares and cubes."

As the senator floats dreamily on,

Suddenly—
—his face grimaced and began to twitch, his blue-rimmed eyes rolled back convulsively. His hands flew up to his chest. And his torso reeled back, while his top hat struck the wall and fell on his lap. . . .

Contemplating the flowing silhouettes, Apollon Apollonovich

likened them to shining dots. One of these dots broke loose from
its orbit and hurtled at him with dizzying speed, taking the form
of an immense crimson sphere.

We are shocked almost as badly as the senator himself: What has
happened here? Has he been shot? Has his coach been struck by a
bomb? Is he dying? In fact, we find to our comic relief, nothing of
the sort has happened. All that has happened is that, "hemmed in
by a stream of vehicles, the carriage has stopped at an intersection.
A stream of *raznochintsy* had pressed against the senator's carriage,
destroying the illusion that he, in flying along the Nevsky, was
flying billions of miles away from the human myriapod." At this
point, as he was stuck in traffic, "among the bowler [hats] he
caught sight of a pair of eyes. And the eyes expressed the inadmis-
sible. They recognized the senator and, having recognized him,
they grew rabid, dilated, lit up, and flashed."

The most striking thing about this encounter, especially if we
contrast it with the street encounters of Petersburg's past, is the
defensiveness of the ruling class. This high official recoils in fright
from an obscure *raznochinets'* eyes, as if the other could kill him
with a look. Now it is true that in the ambience of 1905 imperial
officials have every right to fear attempts on their lives, not least
from their own police. But Ableukhov, like many of his real-life
counterparts, goes beyond rational fear: he seems to feel that any
contact with his subjects, even eye contact, would be lethal. Although the Ableukhovs are still Russia's rulers, they know the
precariousness of their hold on power and authority. Hence the
senator in his coach on the Nevsky feels as vulnerable as that poor
clerk, Mr. Golyadkin, a half century before, prey to any malicious
pedestrian's fatal glance.

Even as the senator recoils from that *raznochinets'* eyes, he has an
obscure feeling that he has seen those eyes somewhere. Indeed, he
soon remembers, to his horror, he has seen them in his own house.
For Nikolai, the senator's son, has embraced precisely the people
and experiences that his father most dreads. He has left his cold
marble mansion and wandered through Petersburg's streets, sordid taverns, underground cellars, in search of an "other world"
more vibrant and authentic than his own. There he has encountered Dudkin, a political prisoner many times escaped—he is
known as "the Uncatchable One"—who lives in hiding in a miser-

able hovel on Vasilevsky Island. Dudkin, who introduces Nikolai to the revolutionary underground, is a precarious and highly explosive fusion of all Petersburg's revolutionary traditions and all its "Underground Man" traditions. He is visited in his hovel not only by revolutionaries and police agents—and double and triple agents—but by hallucinatory visions of the devil, and of the bronze Peter the Great, who blesses him as a son.

Dudkin and Nikolai become friends; they lose themselves together in interminable accounts of their extrabodily experiences and existential anguish. Here, at last, we see a sort of intimacy and mutuality, weird but real, between a Petersburg officer and clerk. But this modest success opens the way to disaster, for even as Nikolai discovers a genuine revolutionary, he is discovered by a false and monstrous one, Lippanchenko. Lippanchenko—who, remember, is secretly working for the police—exploits his anger, guilt and inner weakness, and intimidates him into agreeing to murder his father with a bomb that he will plant in the house they share. This bomb, constructed inside a sardine tin, has been designed to go off twenty-four hours after it is set. As the lives of a dozen desperate characters unfold simultaneously, along with the Revolution that embraces them all (and embraces its enemies most tightly), we know that the bomb in the senator's study is ticking, and its inexorable movement gives this immensely complex novel a precise and dreadful unity of time and action.

It is impossible here to do more than dip into the text of *Petersburg* at a few arbitrarily chosen points, to explore its rich interplay between the city's people and its landscape, at a moment when people and cityscape together are going through a state of radical upheaval and plummeting into the unknown. Let us take a scene about halfway through the book (5, 171–84), at a point when Nikolai has inwardly recoiled from the deal he has made, yet lacks the courage to call it off on his own. (The bomb is ticking, of course.) He heads for the islands in search of Dudkin, to shriek hysterically at him for forcing a man into so foul a deed. But Dudkin, it turns out, knows nothing of the plot, and is just as horrified as he is. Dudkin may be even more profoundly distraught: first, because the crime is monstrous in itself—he may be a metaphysical nihilist, but, he insists, in concrete human life he draws a line; second, because the parricide plot shows either that the Party is being used and betrayed, in ways that might wreck it as a political force, or else that, without his noticing it, the Party has become hideously cynical and corrupt overnight; finally—and the title of the agent who gave Nikolai his dreadful order, "the Unknown One," underscores this—it suggests that Dudkin really doesn't know what is going on in a movement to which he has devoted his whole life, and apart from which he has no life at all. Nikolai's revelation not only outrages his sense of decency but shatters his sense of reality. The two men stagger together deliriously across the Nikolaevsky Bridge, floundering to find themselves in the ruins of a world they had thought they shared:

"The Unknown One," a baffled Nikolai Apollonovich insisted, "is your Party comrade. Why are you so surprised? What surprises you?"

"But I assure you there is no *Unknown One* in the Party."

"What? There is no Unknown One in the Party?"

"Not so loud. . . . No."

"For three months I've been receiving notes."

"From whom?"

"From him."

Each fixed goggling eyes on the other, and one let his drop in horror, while a shadow of faint hope flickered in the eyes of the other.

"I assure you, on my word of honor, I had no part in this business."

Nikolai Apollonovich does not believe him.

"Well, then, what does this all mean?"

At this point, as they cross the Neva, the landscape begins to suggest meanings of its own; the two men take up its suggestions and carry them off. They head in different directions, but both ways are bleak.

"Well, then, what does this all mean?"

And [Nikolai] looked with unseeing eyes off into the recesses of the street. How the street had changed, and how these grim days had changed it!

A wind from the seashore swept in, tearing off the last leaves, and Alexander Ivanovich knew it all by heart:

There will be, oh yes, there will be, bloody days full of horror. And then—all will crash into ruins. Oh, whirl, oh swirl, last days!

For Nikolai, this world is running down, losing its color and vibrancy, sinking into entropy. For Dudkin, it is blowing up, hurling toward an apocalyptic crash. For both, however, the drift is toward death, and they stand together here, the poor *raznochinets* and the high official's son, united in their sense of doomed passivity, helpless as leaves in a gale. For both, the waning of the year 1905 presages the death of all the hopes that this revolutionary year brought to life. Yet they must hang on, to meet the crisis that confronts them both more starkly than ever—as the bomb ticks on —to save what life and honor can still be saved.

But now, as they pass the Winter Palace and enter the Nevsky Prospect, the dynamism of the street hits them with a hallucinatory force:

> Rolling toward them down the street were many-thousand swarms of bowlers. Rolling toward them were top hats, and froth of ostrich feathers.
>
> Noses sprang out from everywhere.
>
> Beaklike noses: eagles' and roosters', ducks' and chickens'; and —so on and on—greenish, green, and red. Rolling toward them senselessly, hastily, profusely.
>
> "Consequently, you suppose that error has crept into everything?"
>
> . . . Alexander Ivanovich tore himself away from the contemplation of noses.
>
> "Not error, but charlatanism of the vilest kind is at work here. This absurdity has been maintained in order to stifle the Party's public action."
>
> "Then help me. . . ."
>
> "An impermissible mockery"—Dudkin interrupted him— "made up of gossip and phantoms."

The floating hats and noses are a marvelous Gogolian touch—and, since Gogol's "The Nose" and "Nevsky Prospect," a vital part of Petersburg comic folklore. Now, however, in the highly charged atmosphere of October 1905, traditional images take on new and menacing meanings: bullets or projectiles flying at Dudkin and Nikolai; intimations of people coming apart, both emotionally, as these two men are, and physically, like people blown apart by bombs. The Prospect hurtles more meanings at them: the people of Petersburg metamorphosing into animals and birds, human crowds devolving into insect swarms; human forms dissolving into blobs of pure color—"greenish, green, and red"—as is happening even as Biely writes, in the avant-garde art of the 1910s. Dudkin takes Nikolai's hand and promises to resolve a mystery that he hasn't even begun to understand—and, as he stands and shakes, his world undergoes a still more radical devolution, into a sort of primal ooze:

> All the shoulders formed a viscous and slowly flowing sediment. The shoulder of Alexander Ivanovich stuck to the sediment, and was, so to speak, sucked in. In keeping with the laws of the organic wholeness of the body, he followed the shoulder and thus was cast out onto the Nevsky.
>
> What is a grain of caviar?
>
> There the body of each individual that streams onto the pavement becomes the organ of a general body, an individual grain of caviar, and the sidewalks of the Nevsky are the surface of an open-faced sandwich. Individual thought was sucked into the cerebration of the myriapod that moved along the Nevsky.... The sticky sediment was composed of individual segments; and each individual segment was a torso.
>
> There were no people on the Nevsky, but there was a crawling, howling myriapod there. The damp space poured a myria-distinction of voices into a myria-distinction of words. All the words jumbled and again wove into a sentence; and the sentence seemed meaningless. It hung above the Nevsky, a black haze of phantasmata.
>
> And swelled by those phantasmata, the Neva roared and thrashed between its massive granite banks.

We have been hearing since Gogol about the Nevsky as a catalyst and communications line for fantasies of alternate worlds and lives. Biely makes us feel how, in a year of radical hopes and frightful realities, this street can generate a new surreality: a vision of itself as a primal swamp in which the anguished modern individual can merge and submerge himself, forget his personality and his politics, and drown.

But Biely does not allow Dudkin to drown: Nikolai pursues him, and drags him out of the flow in which he was nearly lost. "Do you understand? Do you understand me, Alexander Ivanovich? Life has been stirring"—it is not clear if this black humor is meant to be Nikolai's or merely Biely's—"in the tin. The mechanism has been ticking in a strange manner." At first Dudkin, still half submerged in the Nevsky's swamp, has not the slightest idea of what Nikolai is talking about. But when he hears that Nikolai has set the bomb in motion, he flings up his hands in horror, and shouts, "What have you done? Throw it in the river at once!"

The encounter and the scene could easily end here. But Biely has learned from Dostoevsky the art of constructing scenes with a seemingly endless series of climaxes and endings, scenes that, just when the characters and the reader seem ready to come to a resolution, force all parties to work themselves up to a frenzied pitch again and again. Moreover, equally important, Biely is determined to show us that the actual scenes of Petersburg in 1905 do not resolve themselves at the points where it appears logical that they should. If the encounter between Nikolai and Dudkin ended here, it would lead not only to a dramatic resolution but to a human one. But neither Petersburg nor *Petersburg* is willing to let its people go without a fight.

What keeps this scene going, even as the bomb ticks, is a new transformation that Nikolai suddenly goes through. He begins to talk, in an almost caressing way, about the bomb as a human subject: "It was, how shall I put it? dead. I turned the little key—and you know, it even began sobbing, I assure you, like a body being awakened. . . . It made a face at me. . . . It dared to chatter something at me." Finally, he confesses raptly, "I became the bomb, with a ticking in my belly." This bizarre lyricism startles the reader, and forces us to worry seriously about Nikolai's sanity. For Dudkin, however, Nikolai's monologue has a fatal allure: it is another imaginative swamp in which he can sink, to wash himself clean of the terror that is clinging to him. The two men push off into a stream of consciousness and free association on their favorite subject—and ultimate common ground—the feeling of existential despair. Nikolai gives an interminable (and inadvertently hilarious) account of his sensations of nothingness: "In place of the sense organs there was a zero. I was aware of something that wasn't even a zero, but a zero minus something, say five for example." Dudkin serves as a combination metaphysical sage and psychoanalytic therapist, directing Nikolai both to various mystical theories and to the specificities of his childhood. After several pages of this, both parties are happily lost, as they apparently want to be.

Finally, however, Dudkin lifts himself out of the swamp they share, and tries to put Nikolai's lyrical effusions of despair into some sort of perspective:

> "Nikolai Apollonovich, you've been sitting over your Kant in a shut-up airless room. You've been hit by a squall. You've listened to it carefully, and what you've heard in it is yourself. Anyway, your states of mind have been described, and they're the subject of observations."
> "Where, where?"
> "In fiction, in poetry, in psychiatry, in research into the occult."
> Alexander Ivanovich smiled at how illiterate this mentally developed scholastic was, and he continued.

At this point Dudkin offers an extremely important comment, one that can easily get lost amid all the rhetorical and intellectual pyrotechnics, but that illuminates the overall strategy and meaning of *Petersburg*, and that suggests Biely's ultimate vision of what modern literature and thought should be. Dudkin says:

> "Of course, a modernist would call it the sensation of the abyss, and he would search for the image that corresponds to the symbolic sensation."
> "But that is allegory."
> "Don't confuse allegory with symbol. Allegory is a symbol that has become common currency. For example, the usual understanding of your [sense of being] 'beside yourself.' A symbol is your act of appealing to what you experienced there, over the tin."

Dudkin, surely speaking here for Biely, offers a brilliant and compelling interpretation of modernism. First of all, modernism is preoccupied with the dangerous impulses that go by the name of "sensation of the abyss." Second, the modernist imaginative vision is rooted in images rather than abstractions; its symbols are direct, particular, immediate, concrete. Finally, it is vitally concerned to explore the human contexts—the psychological, ethical and political contexts—from which sensations of the abyss arise. Thus modernism seeks a way into the abyss, but also a way out, or rather a way *through*. The depth of Nikolai's abyss, Dudkin tells him, is "what you experienced there, over the tin"; he will find deliverance from the abyss if he can "throw the tin into the Neva, and everything . . . will return to its proper place." The way out of the labyrinth into which his mind has locked itself—the only way out—will be to do what is morally, politically and psychologically right.

> "But why are we standing here? We've gone on and on. You need to go home and . . . throw the tin into the river. Sit tight, and don't set foot inside the house (you're probably being watched). Keep taking bromides. You're horribly worn out. No, better not take bromides. People who abuse bromides become incapable of doing anything. Well, it's time for me to dash—on a matter involving you."
> Alexander Ivanovich darted into the flow of bowlers, turned, and shouted out of the flow:
> "And throw the tin into the river!"
> His shoulder was sucked into the shoulders. He was rapidly borne off by the headless myriapod.

This is a man who has been in the abyss, and has come through it. Dudkin's second disappearance into the Nevsky Prospect crowd is radically different from his first. Before, he sought to drown his consciousness; now he wants to use it, to discover "the Unknown One" who has entrapped Nikolai, and stop him in his tracks. Before, the Nevsky was a symbol of oblivion, a swamp into which the despairing self could sink; now it is a source of energy, an electric wire along which the renewed and newly active self can move when it's time to dash.

The few scenes on which I have focused give only a hint of *Petersburg*'s great richness and depth. And the relatively happy ending of the scene just above is a long way from the book's conclusion. We will have to live through many more actions and reactions, complexities and contradictions, revelations and mystifications, labyrinths within labyrinths, internal and external eruptions—what Mandelstam called "the feverish babble of constant digressions . . . the delirium of the Petersburg influenza"—before the story ends. Nikolai will fail to get the bomb out of the house, it will explode, the senator will not be killed, but the lives of father and son both will be shattered. Dudkin will discover Lippanchenko's treachery and kill him; he will be found next morning, quite mad, mounted on the agent's naked, bloody corpse, frozen in the pose of Peter the Great astride his bronze horse. The Nevsky Prospect itself, and its human myriapod, will go through more spectacular upheavals and metamorphoses before the Revolution runs down. But there is a point in stopping here. The encounter between Nikolai and Dudkin, which began with mystification, hysteria and terror, has evolved dialectically toward a real epiphany and human triumph; and modernism turns out to be the key. Modernism, as Biely portrays it here, shows modern men how they can hold themselves together in the midst of a sea of futility and absurdity that threatens to engulf their cities and their minds. Thus Biely's modernism turns out to be a form of humanism. It is even a kind of optimism: it insists that, in the end, modern man can salvage himself and his world if he summons up the self-knowledge and courage to throw his parricidal bomb away.

It is not customary in the 1980s to judge modernist works of art by their fidelity to any sort of "real life." Nevertheless, when we encounter a work that is so deeply saturated in historical reality as *Petersburg*, so intensely committed to that reality, and intent on bringing its shadows into light, we must take special notice wherever the work seems to diverge sharply from the reality in which it moves and lives. In fact, as I have argued, there are surprisingly few points of divergence in Biely's novel. But one point seems to me to require special discussion: Was Petersburg really so chaotic and mysterious in the revolutionary year of 1905 as *Petersburg* suggests? It could be argued that October 1905, when the novel's action unfolds, is one of the relatively few clear moments in Petersburg's whole history. All through 1905, first in Petersburg but soon all over Russia, millions of people were going into the city streets and village squares to confront the autocracy in the clearest possible way. On Bloody Sunday the government made its own position only too clear to the people who faced it. In the next few months, millions of workers went out on strike against the autocracy—often with the support of their bosses, who paid their wages while they demonstrated and fought. Meanwhile, millions of peasants seized the lands they had worked, and burned the manor houses of their lords; many units of soldiers and sailors mutinied, most memorably on the battleship *Potemkin;* middle classes and professionals joined the action; students poured out of their schools in joyous support, while professors opened their universities to the workers and their cause.

By October, the whole empire was caught up in a general strike —"the great all-Russian strike," it was called. Tsar Nicholas wanted to call out his armies to crush the uprising; but his generals and ministers warned him that there was no guarantee that the soldiers would obey, and that even if they did, it was impossible to crush a hundred million people in revolt. At that point, with his back to the wall, Nicholas issued his October Manifesto, which proclaimed freedom of speech and assembly, and promised universal suffrage, government by representative assembly, and due process of law. The October Manifesto threw the revolutionary movement into disarray, gave the government time and space to quell the flash points of insurrection, and enabled the autocracy to save itself for another decade. The Tsar's promises were false, of course, but it would take the people time to find that out. Meanwhile, however, the sequence of events from Bloody Sunday to the end of October revealed the structures and contradictions of Petersburg's life with remarkable clarity; this was one of the few years in Petersburg's history when the shadows were *not* in charge, when open human realities seized and held the streets.[55]

Biely might well have accepted this account of Petersburg in 1905. But he would have pointed out how soon after the October "days of freedom" the workers and intellectuals alike were thrown into confusion and devouring self-doubt; how the government became more elusive and enigmatic than ever—even to its own cabinet ministers, who often found themselves as much in the dark as the man in the street on matters of national policy; and how, amid all this, the Azevs came into their own and took over the Petersburg prospects once again. From the perspective of 1913–16, when *Petersburg* was written, the dazzling clarity of 1905 could plausibly appear as just one more seductive, deceptive Petersburg dream.

There is one more realistic objection to *Petersburg* that is worth mentioning here. For all the book's panoramic scope, it never really gets close to the workers who compose so much of the city's "myriapod," and who are the driving force of the 1905 Revolution. There is something to this critique; Biely's workers do tend to remain, as Senator Ableukhov puts it, shadows in from the islands. And yet, if we compare *Petersburg* with its only serious competition in the literature of 1905, Gorky's *Mother* (1907), it is clear that Biely's shadowy figures and spectral cityscapes are far more real and alive than Gorky's proletarian "positive heroes," who in fact are not flesh-and-blood people at all, but neo-Chernyshevskian cutouts and cartoons.[56] We could argue, too, that Dudkin's heroism is not only more authentic than that of Gorky's models but more "positive" as well: decisive action means so much more for him because he has so much more to fight against, both around him and inside him, before he can pull himself together to do what must be done.

Far more can be said about Biely's *Petersburg*, and I have no doubt that far more will be said about it in the generation to come. I have tried to suggest how this book is at once an exploration of the failure of the first Russian Revolution and an expression of its creativity and enduring success. *Petersburg* develops a great nineteenth-century cultural tradition into a mode of twentieth-century modernism that is more relevant and powerful than ever today, amid the continued chaos, promise and mystery of personal and political life in our century's streets.

Mandelstam: The Blessed Word with No Meaning

"But if Petersburg is not the capital," Biely wrote in the Prologue to his novel, "there is no Petersburg. It only appears to exist." Even as Biely wrote, in 1916, Petersburg had in some sense ceased to exist: Nicholas II had transformed it overnight into Petrograd—a pure Russian name, he said—amid the chauvinist hysteria of August 1914. For those with a sense of symbolism, it was an ominous sign, the autocracy slamming shut the window to the West, but also, perhaps unconsciously, closing the door on itself. Within a year, Biely's prophecy would be fulfilled in a far deeper way: Petersburg would reach its apotheosis—as the scene and the source of two revolutions—and its end. In March 1918, with German armies surrounding the city on three sides, the new Bolshevik government departed for Moscow, five hundred miles to the south. Abruptly, almost incidentally, Russia's Petersburg Period was over, its Second Moscow Age had begun.

How much of Petersburg survived under the new Moscow regime? There was a stronger emphasis than ever on the Petrine drive for economic and industrial development—along with the Petrine stress on heavy industry and military hardware, ruthless subjugation of the masses, extravagant brutality, and utter indifference to any sort of human happiness that modernization might bring.[57] Peter was glorified endlessly for his ability to get Russia moving again, to push and press it to catch up with the West. Of course, Peter had already had a long career as a revolutionary hero, going back to Belinsky and the radical opposition to Nicholas I. Biely developed this theme when he had Falconet's (and Pushkin's) Bronze Horseman pay Dudkin a midnight call (*Petersburg*, 6, 214), and bless him as his son.

The most memorable apotheosis of Peter as a revolutionary occurred in Pudovkin's film *The End of St. Petersburg* (1927), in which, through brilliant use of montage, the Bronze Horseman appeared as part of the Bolshevik force that charged forward to storm the Winter Palace. On the other hand, the despotic, inquisitorial, fratricidal, hysterically xenophobic and anti-Western regime that came to dominate Moscow within a decade struck many people, including Sergei Eisenstein, as a throwback to the Moscow of Ivan the Terrible. "The culture of the Stalin era," James Billington argues, "seems more closely linked with ancient Muscovy than with even the rawest stages of St. Petersburg–based radicalism. . . . With Stalin in the Kremlin, Moscow at last wreaked its revenge on St. Petersburg, seeking to wipe out the restless reformism and critical cosmopolitanism which this 'window on the West' has always symbolized."[58]

Would Soviet history have turned out any differently if Petersburg had remained its focal point? Probably not much. But it is worth noting that Petersburg in 1917 contained the most intensely conscious and independently active urban population in the world. Recent historians have made it clear that, contrary to the claims of Soviet hagiography, Lenin and the Bolsheviks did not create or even direct Petersburg's mass revolutionary movement; they recognized the dynamism and potentiality of this spontaneous movement, attached themselves tenaciously to it, and rode to power on its crest.[59] When the Bolsheviks consolidated their power and suppressed all spontaneous popular initiative after 1921, they were far from the city and the population that had brought them to power—a city and a people that might have been able to confront them and call them to account. It might at any rate have been more difficult for a Petersburg government to force Petersburg's active and audacious masses into the helpless passivity of old Tsarist times.

No writer was more obsessed with Petersburg's passing away, or more determined to remember and redeem what was lost, than Osip Mandelstam. Mandelstam, born in 1891, killed in one of Stalin's labor camps in 1938, has been recognized in the past decade as one of the great modern poets. At the same time, Mandelstam is a profoundly traditional writer, in the Petersburg tradition —a tradition that, as I have tried to show, is distinctively modern from the start, but modern in a twisted, gnarled, surreal way. Mandelstam cherished and proclaimed the modernism of Petersburg, at a historical moment when Moscow was dictating and imposing its own mode of modernity, a modernity that was supposed to make all the traditions of Petersburg obsolete.

Throughout his life, Mandelstam identified himself and his sense of his destiny with Petersburg and the city's own changing fate. In his youthful pre–World War One poems like "The Admiralty" (48, 1913),[60] Petersburg appears remarkably like a Mediterranean city, sometimes a Hellenic one, akin to Athens and Venice, dying slowly yet living forever, proclaiming eternal artistic forms and universal humanistic values. Before long, however, as Petersburg is swept by war, revolution, civil war, terror, starvation, Mandelstam's picture of his city and himself grows darker and more anguished. In Poem 101, written in 1918,

> A wandering fire at a terrible height—
> can it be a star shining like that?
> Transparent star, wandering fire,
> your brother, Petropolis, is dying.
>
> The dreams of earth blaze at a terrible height,
> a green star is burning.
> O if you are a star, this brother of water and sky,
> your brother, Petropolis, is dying.
>
> A giant ship at a terrible height
> is rushing on, spreading its wings,
> Green star, in splendid poverty
> your brother, Petropolis, is dying.

Above the black Neva transparent spring
has broken, the wax of immortality is melting.
O if you are a star, Petropolis, your city,
your brother, Petropolis, is dying.

Two years later, in Poem 118,

We shall meet again in Petersburg,
as though we had buried the sun there,
and then we shall pronounce for the first time
the blessed word with no meaning.
In the Soviet night, in the velvet dark,
in the black velvet Void, the loved eyes
of blessed women are still singing,
flowers are blooming that will never die.

The "blessed word with no meaning" is surely "Petersburg" itself,
which has been emptied of meaning by "the black velvet Void" of
the Soviet night. But somewhere in nonexistent Petersburg, perhaps through memory and art, it might be possible to recover the
buried sun.

Mandelstam's identification of himself with Petersburg is as
deep and complex as Dostoevsky's; it has the richness of Baudelaire's identification of himself with Paris, Dickens' with London,
Whitman's with New York. It is impossible here to do more than
focus on a couple of points of identity. The Mandelstamian theme
that develops most clearly from the themes we have been exploring here, and that will best enable us to bring this chapter to an
end, is the poet's representation of the Petersburg "little man." We
have traced this figure's metamorphoses in literature, in Pushkin,
Gogol, Chernyshevsky, Dostoevsky and Biely, but also in politics,
in the "ridiculous and childish demonstrations" that begin in
Kazan Square in 1876 and reach the Winter Palace in 1905. The
Petersburg "little man" is always a victim. In the course of the
nineteenth century, however, he becomes, as I have tried to show,
an increasingly bold, active, intransigent victim; when he falls, as
he must, he goes down fighting for his rights. This little man is
always both a strange and a subversive figure. What makes him
even stranger and more subversive in Mandelstam's work is his
appearance in a Soviet context, that is, after a revolution that he
and his fellows have supposedly won, in a new order where he

allegedly enjoys all the rights and dignity a man could possibly need. "Could I ever betray," Mandelstam asks himself repeatedly, "the great vow to the Fourth Estate / and vows solemn enough for tears?" (140, "1 January 1924") "Did those *raznochintsy* wear out the dried leather of their boots, / that I should now betray them?" (260, "Midnight in Moscow," 1932)[61] Mandelstam's radicalism lies in his insistence that, even in the midst of Soviet Moscow's drive for revolutionary modernization, the basic structures and oppositions of Tsarist Petersburg—the little man versus a gigantic, brutal political and social order—are still intact.

Mandelstam captures the drama and agony of the post-revolutionary little man most vividly in his 1928 novella, *The Egyptian Stamp*.[62] Reading this work today, it is amazing to find that it passed through Soviet censorship intact. There are several possible reasons why. First of all, the book is set in the summer of 1917, in the interval between the February and October revolutions, so that a generous censor might have construed the work's critical force as directed not against the Bolsheviks, but against the Kerensky government that the Bolsheviks overthrew. Second, there was Mandelstam's style, full of weird ironic juxtapositions and disjunctions, alternately whimsical, vaguely ominous and desperately intense:

> It was the Kerensky summer, and the lemonade government was in session.
> Everything had been prepared for the grand cotillion. At one point it appeared as if the citizens would remain this way forever, like tomcats in turbans.
> But the Assyrian bootblacks, like ravens before the eclipse, were already becoming alarmed, and dentists began to run out of false teeth. [3, 161]

> Rosy-fingered Dawn has broken her colored pencils. Now they lie scattered about like nestlings with empty, gaping beaks. Meanwhile I seem to see in everything the advance deposit of my dear prosaic delirium.
> Are you familiar with this condition? When it's just as if every object were running a fever, when they are all joyously excited and ill: barriers in the street, posters shedding their skin, grand pianos thronging at the depot like an intelligent, leaderless herd, born for frenzies of the sonata and for boiled water. [6, 186–87]

Perhaps a stupid censor hadn't the slightest idea what Mandelstam was talking about, and luckily didn't care. Or perhaps a kindly censor, recognizing the insignia of Petersburg modernism, concluded that the book's very elusiveness was insurance against its explosiveness, that those few readers likely to comply with the great demands that Mandelstam made on his readers would be unlikely to make their demands in the streets.

"Our life is a tale without a plot or a hero," Mandelstam writes, "made up . . . out of the feverish babble of constant digressions, out of the delirium of the Petersburg influenza." (6, 186) In fact, his tale does have a plot and a hero. At the same time, he takes care to saturate them, and nearly drown them, in a flood of Petersburg detail: history, geography, houses, streets, rooms, sounds, smells, legends and folklore, people—Mandelstam's own family and friends, and figures from his childhood. This stream of Petersburg nostalgia serves as a powerful digressive force, because it is fascinating and beautifully realized in its own right. The Egyptian Stamp is especially evocative of the city's rich musical life, and —what is more original in the Petersburg tradition—of the life of its 100,000 Jews, overwhelmingly "little men," tailors and dressmakers and leather dealers (like Mandelstam's father) and watchmakers and music teachers and insurance salesmen, dreaming as they sip their tea in their little shops or in ghetto cafes ("memory is a sick Jewish girl who steals away in the night to the Nicholas Station, thinking that perhaps someone will turn up to carry her off"), providing the city with so much of its warmth and vibrancy.

What gives Mandelstam's river of memory a special pathos and poignancy is that in the late 1920s so much of what he evoked was gone: the shops emptied and boarded up, the furniture carted away or burnt for firewood during the disastrous winters of the Civil War, the people scattered or dead—Petersburg lost two thirds of its population during the Civil War, and a decade later had only begun to recover from the shock. Even the streets were gone with the wind: the Kameny-Ostrovsky Prospect, where Mandelstam's hero lived in 1917 (and where Chernyshevsky's hero threw the dignitary in the mud half a century before), had become, as he wrote in 1928—he does not mention it, but it can be found on the period's maps, as on today's—the Street of the Red Dawn. Petersburg, home to so many generations of dreamers, had itself become a dream.

Mandelstam's tale does have a hero: "There lived in Petersburg a little man with patent leather shoes, who was despised by doormen and women. His name was Parnok. In early spring he would run out onto the street and patter along the still wet sidewalks with his little sheep hooves." Parnok's story begins almost like a fairy tale, and this little hero is endowed with an appropriate ethereality. "From childhood he had been devoted to whatever was useless, metamorphosing the streetcar rattle of life into events of consequence, and when he began to fall in love he tried to tell women about this, but they didn't understand him, for which he avenged himself by speaking to them in a wild, bombastic, birdy language, and exclusively about the loftiest matters." (2, 156–58) This "shy, concert-going soul belonging to the raspberry kingdom of contrabasses and drones" (5, 173) is a Jew, but also, in his imagination, a Hellene; his fondest dream is to obtain a minor diplomatic post at the Russian Embassy in Greece, where he can serve as a translator and interpreter between two worlds; but he is pessimistic about his prospects, for he knows he lacks the proper family tree.

Parnok would be happy to be left to enjoy his Petersburg dreams —and so, it seems, would Mandelstam—only Petersburg will not let him. As he sits in the dentist's chair one fine summer morning and gazes through the window that overlooks Gorokhovaya Street, he discovers, to his horror, what looks like a lynch mob in the street. (4, 163–69) It appears that somebody has been caught stealing a watch from somebody. The crowd bears the culprit along in a solemn procession: they are going to drown him in the Fontanka Canal.

> Could one say that this figure [the prisoner] was faceless? No, there was a face, although faces in the crowd have no significance; only napes of necks and ears have an independent life.
> Thus advanced the shoulders, like a coat hanger stuffed with wadding, the secondhand jacket richly bestrewn with dandruff, the irritable napes and dog ears.

The fragmentation of people through the dynamism of the street is a familiar theme of Petersburg modernism. We saw it for the first time in Gogol's "Nevsky Prospect"; it is renewed in the twentieth century by Alexander Blok and Biely and Mayakovsky, by cubist and futurist painters, and by Eisenstein in *October*, his 1927 Petersburg romance. Mandelstam adapts this modernist visual experience, but gives it a moral dimension that has been missing until now. As Parnok sees the moving street, it is dehumanizing the people in it, or rather offering them an opportunity to dehumanize themselves, to strip themselves of their faces, and hence of their personal responsibility for their actions. Faces and persons are submerged in "that terrible order which welded the mob together." Parnok feels certain that anyone who tried to confront this mob or help this man "would himself land in the soup, would be suspect, declared an outlaw and dragged into the empty square." Nevertheless, he springs from his perch above the street —"Parnok spun like a top down the gap-toothed stair, leaving the dumfounded dentist before the sleeping cobra of his drill"—and plunges into the midst of the crowd. "Parnok ran, tripping along the paving blocks with the little sharp hooves of his patent leather shoes," trying frantically to attract attention and stop the movement of the mob. But he fails to make the slightest impact on the crowd—who knows if he is even noticed?—and, at the same time, feels very vividly the resemblance between the condemned man and himself:

> You have had your stroll, my dear fellow, along Shcherbakov Lane, you have spat at the bad Tartar butcher-shops, hung for a bit on the hand-rails of a streetcar, taken a trip to see your friend Serezhka in Gatchina, frequented the public baths and the Ciniselli Circus; you have done a bit of living, little man—enough!

Something has come over Petersburg; Parnok doesn't understand what it is, but it terrifies him. "The innumerable swarm of human locusts (God knows where they were coming from) blackened the banks of the Fontanka," where they have come to see a man killed. "Petersburg has declared itself Nero, and was as loathsome as if it were eating a soup of crushed flies." Here, as in Biely's *Petersburg*, the magnificent city has devolved into an insect horde, murderers and victims alike. Once again, Mandelstam's biological imagery takes on a political force: it is as if the people's revolutionary ascent has precipitated its moral decline; having just become sovereign, they rush to re-enact the darkest chapters in the history of sovereignty. And Petersburg's archetypal common man has become a stranger, if not a fugitive ("There are people who for some reason or other displease mobs"), in his own home city at precisely the historical moment when the city's common men are supposed to have taken command.

There are two more brief phases in this scene. Parnok tries desperately to find a telephone, to alert someone in the government. In the twentieth century, after all, electronic mass media mediate between the individual and the state. Finally he finds a phone—only to find himself more lost than he was before: "he telephoned from a pharmacy, telephoned the police, telephoned the government, the state, which had vanished, sleeping like a carp." Electronic media may at times facilitate communication, but they can also block communication with a new effectiveness: it is now possible for the state to simply not answer, to be more elusive than ever, to let its subjects, like Kafka's K., ring forever without response. "He might with equal success have telephoned Proserpine or Persephone, who had not yet had a telephone installed."

In the midst of his search for help, Parnok has a weird encounter that abruptly plunges him, and us, back into the depths of the Petersburg past. "At the corner of Voznesensky Prospect there appeared Captain Krzyzanowski himself with his pomaded mustache. He was wearing a military topcoat, but with a saber, and was nonchalantly whispering to his lady the sweet nothings of the Horse Guard." This pompous figure has stepped directly out of the world of Nicholas I and Gogol and Dostoevsky. His appearance in 1917 at first appears bizarre; nevertheless, "Parnok raced up to him as though he were his best friend and implored him to draw his weapon." But all in vain: "I respect the moment, the bowlegged captain coldly replied, but pardon me, I am with a lady." He neither approves nor disapproves of the murder going on around him; he is called to higher duties. "And skillfully seizing his companion, he jingled his spurs and disappeared into a cafe."

Who is Captain Krzyzanowski? He is the most surreal feature of *The Egyptian Stamp,* yet, we will see, the key to its real political point. Mandelstam's brief description identifies him at once as a symbol of all the archetypal stupidity and brutality of the old officer class, and as the Petersburg little man's archetypal enemy. The Revolution of February 1917 ought to have finished him off, or at least driven him underground. Yet he flaunts his traditional qualities more boldly than ever. As Parnok is informed by a laundress, "That gentleman hid for only three days, and then the soldiers themselves"—in the new revolutionary democratic army—"the soldiers themselves elected him to the regimental committee, and now they carry him above their heads." (3, 162) Thus, it appears, the February Revolution has not got rid of Russia's traditional ruling class, but only entrenched it further and endowed it with a democratic legitimacy. Now there is nothing here to which any Soviet communist could seriously object; indeed, Bolsheviks would say that the point of the October Revolution was precisely to get rid of these types for good. (This may have been the thought of whatever censor passed Mandelstam's story on.) But Mandelstam is up to more than this. It turns out, in what at first seems another surreal twist, that the captain has designs on Parnok's clothes: he wants his shirts, his underwear, his overcoat. Moreover, everyone in the story seems to feel that he is entitled to them. In the end— and the story ends with him—

> At 9:30 P.M. the former Captain Krzyzanowski was planning to board the Moscow express. He had packed in his suitcase Parnok's morning coat and his best shirts. The morning coat, having tucked in its fins, fit into the suitcase especially well, almost without a wrinkle. . . .
> In Moscow he stopped at the Hotel Select—an excellent hotel on the Malaia Lubianka—where he was given a room that had formerly been used as a store; in place of a regular window it had a fashionable shop window, heated by the sun to an improbable degree. [8, 189]

What do these Gogolian goings-on mean in 1928? Why should the officer want the little man's clothes, and why should he take them to Moscow? In fact, if we place this episode in the context of Soviet politics and culture, the answers are almost embarrassingly simple. Since 1918, Moscow has become headquarters for a new Soviet elite (the Hotel Select), protected and sometimes led by a dreaded secret police that operates out of the Lubianka Prison (Malaia Lubianka)—where six years later Mandelstam himself will be interrogated and held. This new ruling class in the 1920s claims descent from Petersburg's fraternity of little men and *raznochintsy* intellectuals (Parnok's clothes), but exudes all the crude and complacent brutality of Petersburg's old ruling caste of Tsarist officers and police.

Because Mandelstam cares so deeply about Petersburg's pathetic but noble little men, he is intent on protecting their memory from the Moscow *apparatchiki* who would appropriate it to legitimize their power. Consider this passage, remarkable for its intensity of feeling, in which Mandelstam describes Parnok's Petersburg roots. It begins with Parnok lamenting that he will probably never get that job in Greece, because of his lack of a noble (or at least a Christian) "pedigree." At this point, the narrator breaks into Parnok's stream of consciousness to remind him and us how noble his ancestry is:

> But—wait a moment—how is that not a pedigree? What about Captain Golyadkin? and the Collegiate Assessor [Evgeny in "The Bronze Horseman"] to whom "the Lord God might have given more brains and more money"? All the people shown down the stairs, disgraced, insulted in the forties and fifties of the last century, all those mutterers, windbags in capes, with gloves that have been laundered to shreds, all those who do not "live" but "reside" on the Sadovaya and the Podyacheskaya in houses made of stale sections of petrified chocolate, and grumble to themselves: "How is that possible? Not a penny to my name, and me with a university education?"

It is so urgent for Mandelstam to clarify Parnok's lineage because the men who are walking around in his clothes are precisely the men who pushed all Petersburg's little men off the Nevsky Prospect in the nineteenth century, and who are ready to drown them in the Fontanka or torture them in the Lubianka today. This work of unmasking is a crucial force in Mandelstam's life: "One has only to remove the film from the Petersburg air, and then its hidden meaning will be laid bare . . . there will be revealed something completely unexpected." This vocation is a source of pride, but also of dread: "But the pen that removes this film is like a doctor's teaspoon, contaminated with a touch of diphtheria. It is better not to touch it." (8, 184) A moment before the novella ends, Mandelstam warns himself, prophetically: "Destroy your manuscript." But he cannot bring himself to end on this note:

> Destroy your manuscript, but save whatever you have inscribed in the margin out of boredom, out of helplessness, and, as it were, in a dream. These secondary and involuntary creations of your fantasy will not be lost in the world, but will take their place behind shadowy music stands, like third violins at the Maryinsky Theater, and out of gratitude to their author strike up the overture to *Leonore* or the *Egmont* of Beethoven. [187–88]

Mandelstam asserts his faith that the dream of Petersburg's radiance will take on a life of its own, that it will create its own passionate music—a music of overtures, of new beginnings—out of the shadows of the city's warped and lost light.

Two years after *The Egyptian Stamp*, with Stalin firmly in power in Moscow and terror under way, Mandelstam returned with his wife, Nadezhda, to his home city, hoping to settle there for good. While he waited for police authorization to live and work, he wrote one of his most heartrending poems (221) on the changes that he and his city had gone through:

LENINGRAD

I've come back to my city. These are my own old tears,
my own little veins, the swollen glands of my childhood.

So you're back. Open wide. Swallow
the fish-oil from the river lamps of Leningrad.

Open your eyes. Do you know this December day,
the egg-yolk with the deadly tar beaten into it?

Petersburg! I don't want to die yet!
You know my telephone numbers.

Petersburg! I've still got the addresses:
I can look up dead voices.

I live on the back stairs, and the bell,
torn out nerves and all, jangles in my temples.

And I wait till morning for guests that I love,
And rattle the door in its chains.

                                        Leningrad, December 1930

But the Party hack who ran the Leningrad writers' union, and who controlled both jobs and living space, drove them out, saying that Mandelstam was not wanted in Leningrad, that he belonged perhaps in Moscow, in any case somewhere else. This did not prevent Mandelstam from being attacked in Moscow, in *Pravda*, in an article entitled "Shades of Old Petersburg," as a typical Petersburg snob who used fancy language and failed to appreciate the achievements of the new socialist order.[63]

"Lord!" Mandelstam wrote in *The Egyptian Stamp*. "Do not make me like Parnok! Give me the strength to distinguish myself from him. For I, also, have stood in that terrifying, patient line which creeps toward the yellow window of the box office. . . . And I, too, am sustained by Petersburg alone." (5, 171) It will not be immediately clear to the reader how the Petersburg author is to be distinguished from his hero; and Mandelstam himself may not have been entirely clear about it when he wrote this in 1928. But one distinction emerged five years later, after the Mandelstams had been forced out of Leningrad and back to Moscow. In November 1933, in the midst of the Stalinist collectivization campaign that would claim up to four million peasant lives, and on the verge of the Great Purge that would kill even more, Mandelstam composed a poem (286) on Stalin:

> We live, deaf to the land beneath us,
> Ten steps away no one hears our speeches.
>
> All we hear is the Kremlin's mountaineer,
> The murderer and peasant-slayer.
>
> His fingers are fat as grubs,
> And the words, final as lead weights, fall from his lips.
>
> His cockroach whiskers leer
> And his boot tops gleam.
>
>
> Ringed with a scum of chicken-necked bosses
> he toys with the tributes of half-men.
>
> One whistles, another meows, a third snivels.
> He pokes out his finger and he alone goes boom.
>
> He forges decrees in a line like horseshoes,
> One for the groin, one the forehead, temple, eye.
>
> He rolls the executions on his tongue like berries.
> He wishes he could hug them like big friends from home.[64]

Mandelstam differed from Parnok here in that he didn't turn to Captain Krzyzanowski for help, didn't try to phone "the police, the government, the state"; his action consisted simply in speaking the truth about them all. Mandelstam never wrote this poem down ("Destroy your manuscript"), but spoke it aloud in several tight, closed Moscow rooms. One of those who heard it denounced the poet to the secret police. They came for him one night in May 1934. Four years later, after excruciating physical and mental anguish, he died in a transit camp near Vladivostok.

Mandelstam's life and death illuminate some of the depths and paradoxes of the Petersburg modern tradition. Logically, this tradition should have died a natural death after the October Revolution and the departure of the new government for Moscow. But the increasingly sordid betrayal of that Revolution by that government served, ironically, to give the old modernism a new life and force. In the neo-Muscovite totalitarian state, Petersburg became "the blessed word with no meaning," a symbol of all the human promise that the Soviet order had left behind. In the Stalin era, that promise was scattered to the Gulag and left for dead; but its resonance proved deep enough to survive many murders and, indeed, to outlive its murderers as well.

In Brezhnev's Russia, as the Soviet state edges ever further from even the vestiges of international Marxism, and ever closer to a blustering, bigoted "official nationality" of which Nicholas I would have approved, the surreal visions and desperate energies that burst from the Petersburg underground in Nicholas' era have once again come into their own. These visions and energies have been renewed in the great effusion of *samizdat* literature and, indeed, in the very idea of *samizdat,* a literature that springs from underground sources, a culture that is at once more shadowy and more real than the official culture propagated by party and state. The neo-Petersburg literature of surreal radicalism made a brilliant debut in 1959–60, with Andrei Sinyavsky's *On Socialist Realism;*[65] it lives on in Alexander Zinoviev's enormous, weird, luminous work, *The Yawning Heights.* ("It was on this basis that the sociologist Ibanov produced his original but far from new hypothesis on the overthrow of the Tartar-Mongol yoke. According to this theory, far from our destroying the Tartar-Mongol hordes and driving them from our territory, the very opposite happened: they destroyed us, drove us out, and stayed behind in our place forever.")[66]

Another form of *samizdat* has emerged in the political demonstrations that began to take place in the mid-1960s in Moscow, Leningrad and Kiev, after being stifled by the Soviet state for forty years. One of the first large demonstrations in Moscow, on Constitution Day in December 1965, was ignored by passersby, who apparently took it for an outdoor filming of some movie about the Revolution of 1917![67] Most of these actions have been undertaken by pitifully small groups, and instantly crushed by the KGB and vigilante mobs, followed by savage reprisals against participants, who have been tortured, banished to labor camps, sealed up in "special" psychiatric institutions run by the police. Nevertheless, these actions, like the "ridiculous and childish demonstration" on Kazan Square a century before, have proclaimed not merely ideas and messages that Russia badly needs to hear but also modes of expression and action and communication that their countrymen once knew well, and need to learn again. Here is the final plea of Vladimir Dremlyuga, a railway electrician from Leningrad who was arrested along with six other people for demonstrating on the old Execution Platform in Moscow's Red Square to protest the Soviet invasion of Czechoslovakia in August 1968:

> All my conscious life I have wanted to be a citizen—that is, a person who proudly and calmly speaks his mind. For ten minutes I was a citizen, during the demonstration. My voice will, I know, sound a false note in the universal silence which goes by the name of "unanimous support for the policy of Party and Government." I am glad that there proved to be others to express their protest together with me. Had there not been, I would have entered Red Square alone.[68]

"For ten minutes I was a citizen": this is the true note of Petersburg modernism, always self-ironical, but clear and strong when it counts most. It is the lonely but persistent voice of the little man in the immense public square: "You'll reckon with me yet!"

Conclusion: The Petersburg Prospect

I HAVE tried to trace in this essay some of the sources and transformations of Petersburg tradition in the nineteenth and twentieth centuries. The traditions of this city are distinctively modern, growing out of the city's existence as a symbol of modernity in the midst of a backward society; but Petersburg traditions are modern in an unbalanced, bizarre way, springing from the imbalance and unreality of the Petrine scheme of modernization itself. In response to more than a century of brutal but abortive modernization from above, Petersburg will engender and nourish, through the nineteenth century and into the twentieth, a marvelous array of experiments in modernization from below. These experiments are both literary and political; such a distinction makes little sense here, in a city whose very existence is a political statement, a city where political drives and relations saturate everyday life.

Petersburg's originality and dynamism, after the noble failure of December 14, 1825, will spring from the common life of its legion of "little men." These men live in and through a series of radical contradictions and paradoxes. On one hand, they are, as Nietzsche says in his projected "history of the modern eclipse," a class of "state nomads (civil servants, etc.) without home." On the other hand, they are deeply rooted in the city that has uprooted them from all else. Trapped in servitude to tyrannical superiors or deadening routines, returning from their offices and factories to cramped, dark, cold, solitary rooms, they seem to incarnate everything that the nineteenth century will say about alienation from nature, from other men and from oneself. And yet, at crucial moments, they emerge from their various undergrounds to assert their right to the city; they seek solidarity with other solitaries, to make Peter's city their own. They are endlessly tormented and paralyzed by the richness and complexity of their inner lives, yet, to everyone's surprise, most of all to their own, they can step into the streets and prospects to take action in a public world. They are exquisitely and painfully sensitive to the shifting strangeness of this city's air, in which "all that is solid melts," both ultimate morality and everyday reality come apart.

In this climate, their imaginative power is bound to plunge them into abysses of nihilism and delusion, "the delirium of the Petersburg influenza." But somehow they find the strength to pull themselves up from the fatal depths of their inner Neva, and to see with luminous clarity what is real, what is healthy, what is right: stand up to the officer, throw the bomb in the river, save the man from the mob, fight for the right to the city, confront the state. The moral imagination and courage of these little men surge up suddenly, like the Admiralty's golden needle piercing through the Petersburg fog. In a moment it is gone, swallowed up by dark and murky history; but its vividness and radiance remain to haunt the bleak air.

This trip through the mysteries of St. Petersburg, through its clash and interplay of experiments in modernization from above and below, may provide clues to some of the mysteries of political and spiritual life in the cities of the Third World—in Lagos, Brasilia, New Delhi, Mexico City—today. But the clash and fusion of modernities goes on even in the most fully modernized sectors of today's world; the Petersburg influenza infuses the air of New York, of Milan, of Stockholm, of Tokyo, of Tel Aviv, and it blows on and on. Petersburg's little men, its "state nomads without home," find themselves at home everywhere in the contemporary world.[69] The Petersburg tradition, as I have presented it, can be uniquely valuable to them. It can provide them with shadow passports into the unreal reality of the modern city. And it can inspire them with visions of symbolic action and interaction that can help them to act as men and citizens there: modes of passionately intense encounter and conflict and dialogue through which they can at once assert themselves and confront each other and challenge the powers that control them all. It can help them to become, as Dostoevsky's Underground Man claimed (and desperately hoped) to be, both personally and politically "more alive" in the elusively shifting light and shadow of the city streets. It is this prospect above all that Petersburg has opened up in modern life.

In the Forest of Symbols: Some Notes on Modernism in New York

The City of the Captive Globe . . . is the capital of Ego, where science, art, poetry and forms of madness compete under ideal conditions to invent, destroy and restore the world of phenomenal reality.

. . . Manhattan is the product of an unformulated theory, **Manhattanism,** *whose program [is] to exist in a world totally fabricated by man, to live* inside *fantasy. . . . The entire city became a factory of manmade experience, where the real and natural ceased to exist.*

. . . The Grid's two-dimensional discipline creates undreamt-of freedom for three-dimensional anarchy . . . the city can be at the same time ordered and fluid, a metropolis of rigid chaos.

. . . a mythical island where the invention and testing of a metropolitan life-style, and its attendant architecture, could be pursued as a collective experiment . . . a Galapagos Island of new technologies, a new chapter in the survival of the fittest, this time a battle among species of machines. . . .

—**Rem Koolhaas,** *Delirious New York*

287

Out for a walk, after a week in bed,
I find them tearing up part of my block
And, chilled through, dazed and lonely, join the dozen
In meek attitudes, watching the huge crane
Fumble luxuriously in the filth of years. . . .

As usual in New York, everything is torn down
Before you have had time to care for it. . . .

You would think the simple fact of having lasted
Threatened our cities like mysterious fires.

—James Merrill, "An Urban Convalescence"

"You trace out straight lines, fill up the holes and level up the
ground, and the result is nihilism!" (From an angry speech of a great
authority who was presiding on a Commission to report on plans for
extension.)
I replied: "Excuse me, but that, properly speaking, is just what our
work should be."

—Le Corbusier, *The City of Tomorrow*

ONE OF the central themes of this book has been the fate of "all that is solid" in modern life to "melt into air." The innate dynamism of the modern economy, and of the culture that grows from this economy, annihilates everything that it creates—physical environments, social institutions, metaphysical ideas, artistic visions, moral values—in order to create more, to go on endlessly creating the world anew. This drive draws all modern men and women into its orbit, and forces us all to grapple with the question of what is essential, what is meaningful, what is real in the maelstrom in which we move and live. In this final chapter, I want to put myself in the picture, to explore and chart some of the currents that have flowed through my own modern environment, New York City, and given form and energy to my life.

For more than a century, New York has served as a center for international communications. The city has become not merely a theater but itself a production, a multimedia presentation whose audience is the whole world. This has given a special resonance and depth to much of what is done and made here. A great deal of New York's construction and development over the past century needs to be seen as symbolic action and communication: it has been conceived and executed not merely to serve immediate economic and political needs but, at least equally important, to demonstrate to the whole world what modern men can build and how modern life can be imagined and lived.

Many of the city's most impressive structures were planned specifically as symbolic expressions of modernity: Central Park, the Brooklyn Bridge, the Statue of Liberty, Coney Island, Manhattan's many skyscrapers, Rockefeller Center and much else. Other areas of the city—the harbor, Wall Street, Broadway, the Bowery, the Lower East Side, Greenwich Village, Harlem, Times Square, Madison Avenue—have taken on symbolic weight and force as time went by. The cumulative impact of all this is that the New Yorker finds himself in the midst of a Baudelairean forest of symbols. The presence and profusion of these giant forms make New York a rich and strange place to live in. But they also make it a dangerous place, because its symbols and symbolisms are endlessly fighting each other for sun and light, working to kill each other off, melting each other along with themselves into air. Thus, if New York is a forest of symbols, it is a forest where axes and bulldozers are always at work, and great works constantly crashing down; where pastoral dropouts encounter phantom armies, and *Love's Labour's Lost* interplays with *Macbeth;* where new meanings are forever springing up with, and falling down from, the constructed trees.

I will begin this section with a discussion of Robert Moses, whose career in public life stretched from the early 1910s to the late 1960s, who is probably the greatest creator of symbolic forms in twentieth-century New York, whose constructions had a destructive and disastrous impact on my early life, and whose specter still haunts my city today. Next, I will explore the work of Jane Jacobs and some of her contemporaries, who, locked in combat with Moses, created a radically different order of urban symbolism in the 1960s. Finally, I will delineate some of the symbolic forms and environments that have sprung up in the cities of the 1970s. As I develop a perspective on the urban metamorphoses of the past four decades, I will be painting a picture in which I can locate myself, trying to grasp the modernizations and modernisms that have made me and many of the people around me what we are.

I.

Robert Moses: The Expressway World

When you operate in an overbuilt metropolis, you have to hack your way with a meat ax.

I'm just going to keep right on building. You do the best you can to stop it.

—**Maxims of Robert Moses**

> *. . . She it was put me straight*
> *about the city when I said, it*
>
> *makes me ill to see them run up*
> *a new bridge like that in a few months*
>
> *and I can't find time even to get*
> *a book written. They have the power,*
>
> *that's all, she replied. That's what you all*
> *want. If you can't get it, acknowledge*
>
> *at least what it is. And they're not*
> *going to give it to you.*
> —**William Carlos Williams, "The Flower"**

What sphinx of cement and aluminum hacked open their skulls
 and ate up their brains and imagination? . . .
Moloch whose buildings are judgment!
 —**Allen Ginsberg, "Howl"**

AMONG THE many images and symbols that New York has contributed to modern culture, one of the most striking in recent years has been an image of modern ruin and devastation. The Bronx, where I grew up, has even become an international code word for our epoch's accumulated urban nightmares: drugs, gangs, arson, murder, terror, thousands of buildings abandoned, neighborhoods transformed into garbage- and brick-strewn wilderness.

The Bronx's dreadful fate is experienced, though probably not understood, by hundreds of thousands of motorists every day, as they negotiate the Cross-Bronx Expressway, which cuts through the borough's center. This road, although jammed with heavy traffic day and night, is fast, deadly fast; speed limits are routinely transgressed, even at the dangerously curved and graded entrance and exit ramps; constant convoys of huge trucks, with grimly aggressive drivers, dominate the sight lines; cars weave wildly in and out among the trucks: it is as if everyone on this road is seized with a desperate, uncontrollable urge to get out of the Bronx as fast as wheels can take him. A glance at the cityscape to the north and south—it is hard to get more than quick glances, because much of the road is below ground level and bounded by brick walls ten feet high—will suggest why: hundreds of boarded-up abandoned buildings and charred and burnt-out hulks of buildings; dozens of blocks covered with nothing at all but shattered bricks and waste.

Ten minutes on this road, an ordeal for anyone, is especially dreadful for people who remember the Bronx as it used to be: who remember these neighborhoods as they once lived and thrived, until this road itself cut through their heart and made the Bronx, above all, a place to get out of. For children of the Bronx like myself, this road bears a load of special irony: as we race through our childhood world, rushing to get out, relieved to see the end in sight, we are not merely spectators but active participants in the process of destruction that tears our hearts. We fight back the tears, and step on the gas.

Robert Moses is the man who made all this possible. When I heard Allen Ginsberg ask at the end of the 1950s, "Who was that sphinx of cement and aluminum," I felt sure at once that, even if the poet didn't know it, Moses was his man. Like Ginsberg's "Moloch, who entered my soul early," Robert Moses and his public works had come into my life just before my Bar Mitzvah, and helped bring my childhood to an end. He had been present all along, in a vague subliminal way. Everything big that got built in or around New York seemed somehow to be his work: the Triborough Bridge, the West Side Highway, dozens of parkways in Westchester and Long Island, Jones and Orchard beaches, innumerable parks, housing developments, Idlewild (now Kennedy) Airport, a network of enormous dams and power plants near Niagara Falls; the list seemed to go on forever. He had generated an event that had special magic for me: the 1939–40 World's Fair, which I had attended in my mother's womb, and whose elegant logo, the trylon and perisphere, adorned our apartment in many forms—programs, banners, postcards, ashtrays— and symbolized human adventure, progress, faith in the future, all the heroic ideals of the age into which I was born.

But then, in the spring and fall of 1953, Moses began to loom over my life in a new way: he proclaimed that he was about to ram an immense expressway, unprecedented in scale, expense and difficulty of construction, through our neighborhood's heart. At first we couldn't believe it; it seemed to come from another world. First of all, hardly any of us owned cars: the neighborhood itself, and the subways leading downtown, defined the flow of our lives. Besides, even if the city needed the road—or was it the state that needed the road? (in Moses' operations, the location of power and authority was never clear, except for Moses himself)—they surely couldn't mean what the stories seemed to say: that the road would be blasted directly through a dozen solid, settled, densely populated neighborhoods like our own; that something like 60,000 working- and lower-middle-class people, mostly Jews, but with many Italians, Irish and Blacks thrown in, would be thrown out of their homes. The Jews of the Bronx were nonplussed: could a fellow-Jew really want to do this to us? (We had little idea of what kind of Jew he was, or of how much we were all an obstruction in his path.) And even if he did want to do it, we were sure it couldn't happen here, not in America. We were still basking in the afterglow of the New Deal: the government was *our* government, and it would come through to protect us in the end. And yet, before we knew it, steam shovels and bulldozers were there, and people were getting notice that they had better clear out fast. They looked numbly at the wreckers, at the disappearing streets, at each other, and they went. Moses was coming through, and no temporal or spiritual power could block his way.

For ten years, through the late 1950s and early 1960s, the center of the Bronx was pounded and blasted and smashed. My friends and I would stand on the parapet of the Grand Concourse, where 174th Street had been, and survey the work's progress—the immense steam shovels and bulldozers and timber and steel beams, the hundreds of workers in their variously colored hard hats, the giant cranes reaching far above the Bronx's tallest roofs, the dynamite blasts and tremors, the wild, jagged crags of rock newly torn, the vistas of devastation stretching for miles to the east and west as far as the eye could see—and marvel to see our ordinary nice neighborhood transformed into sublime, spectacular ruins.

In college, when I discovered Piranesi, I felt instantly at home. Or I would return from the Columbia library to the construction site and feel myself in the midst of the last act of Goethe's *Faust*. (You had to hand it to Moses: his works gave you ideas.) Only there was no humanistic triumph here to offset the destruction. Indeed, when the construction was done, the real ruin of the Bronx had just begun. Miles of streets alongside the road were choked with dust and fumes and deafening noise—most strikingly, the roar of trucks of a size and power that the Bronx had never seen, hauling heavy cargoes through the city, bound for Long Island or New England, for New Jersey and all points south, all through the day and night. Apartment houses that had been settled and stable for twenty years emptied out, often virtually overnight; large and impoverished black and Hispanic families, fleeing even worse slums, were moved in wholesale, often under the auspices of the Welfare Department, which even paid inflated rents, spreading panic and accelerating flight. At the same time, the construction had destroyed many commercial blocks, cut others off from most of their customers and left the storekeepers not only close to bankruptcy but, in their enforced isolation, increasingly vulnerable to crime. The borough's great open market, along Bathgate Avenue, still flourishing in the late 1950s, was decimated; a year after the road came through, what was left went up in smoke. Thus depopulated, economically depleted, emotionally shattered—as bad as the physical damage had been the inner wounds were worse—the Bronx was ripe for all the dreaded spirals of urban blight.

Moses seemed to glory in the devastation. When he was asked, shortly after the Cross-Bronx road's completion, if urban expressways like this didn't pose special human problems, he replied impatiently that "there's very little hardship in the thing. There's a little discomfort and even that is exaggerated." Compared with his earlier, rural and suburban highways, the only difference here was that "There are more houses in the way . . . more people in the way—that's all." He boasted that "When you operate in an overbuilt metropolis, you have to hack your way with a meat ax."[1] The subconscious equation here—animals' corpses to be chopped up and eaten, and "people in the way"—is enough to take one's breath away. Had Allen Ginsberg put such metaphors into his Moloch's mouth, he would have never been allowed to get away with it: it would have seemed, simply, too much. Moses' flair for extravagant cruelty, along with his visionary brilliance, obsessive energy and megalomaniac ambition, enabled him to build, over the years, a quasi-mythological reputation. He appeared as the latest in a long line of titanic builders and destroyers, in history and in cultural mythology: Louis XIV, Peter the Great, Baron Haussmann, Joseph Stalin (although fanatically anti-communist, Moses loved to quote the Stalinist maxim "You can't make an omelette without breaking eggs"), Bugsy Siegel (master builder of the mob, creator of Las Vegas), "Kingfish" Huey Long; Marlowe's Tamburlaine, Goethe's Faust, Captain Ahab, Mr. Kurtz, Citizen Kane. Moses did his best to raise himself to gigantic stature, and even came to enjoy his increasing reputation as a monster, which he believed would intimidate the public and keep potential opponents out of the way.

In the end, however—after forty years—the legend he cultivated helped to do him in: it brought him thousands of personal enemies, some eventually as resolute and resourceful as Moses himself, obsessed with him, passionately dedicated to bringing the man and his machines to a stop. In the late 1960s they finally succeeded, and he was stopped and deprived of his power to build. But his works still surround us, and his spirit continues to haunt our public and private lives.

It is easy to dwell endlessly on Moses' personal power and style. But this emphasis tends to obscure one of the primary sources of his vast authority: his ability to convince a mass public that he was the vehicle of impersonal world-historical forces, the moving spirit of modernity. For forty years, he was able to pre-empt the vision of the modern. To oppose his bridges, tunnels, expressways, housing developments, power dams, stadia, cultural centers, was—or so it seemed—to oppose history, progress, modernity itself. And few people, especially in New York, were prepared to do that. "There are people who like things as they are. I can't hold out any hope to them. They have to keep moving further away. This is a great big state, and there are other states. Let them go to the

Rockies."[2] Moses struck a chord that for more than a century has been vital to the sensibility of New Yorkers: our identification with progress, with renewal and reform, with the perpetual transformation of our world and ourselves—Harold Rosenberg called it "the tradition of the New." How many of the Jews of the Bronx, hotbed of every form of radicalism, were willing to fight for the sanctity of "things as they are"? Moses was destroying our world, yet he seemed to be working in the name of values that we ourselves embraced.

I can remember standing above the construction site for the Cross-Bronx Expressway, weeping for my neighborhood (whose fate I foresaw with nightmarish precision), vowing remembrance and revenge, but also wrestling with some of the troubling ambiguities and contradictions that Moses' work expressed. The Grand Concourse, from whose heights I watched and thought, was our borough's closest thing to a Parisian boulevard. Among its most striking features were rows of large, splendid 1930s apartment houses: simple and clear in their architectural forms, whether geometrically sharp or biomorphically curved; brightly colored in contrasting brick, offset with chrome, beautifully interplayed with large areas of glass; open to light and air, as if to proclaim a good life that was open not just to the elite residents but to us all. The style of these buildings, known as Art Deco today, was called "modern" in their prime. For my parents, who described our family proudly as a "modern" family, the Concourse buildings represented a pinnacle of modernity. We couldn't afford to live in them—though we did live in a small, modest, but still proudly "modern" building, far down the hill—but they could be admired for free, like the rows of glamorous ocean liners in port downtown. (The buildings look like shell-shocked battleships in drydock today, while the ocean liners themselves are all but extinct.)

As I saw one of the loveliest of these buildings being wrecked for the road, I felt a grief that, I can see now, is endemic to modern life. So often the price of ongoing and expanding modernity is the destruction not merely of "traditional" and "pre-modern" institutions and environments but—and here is the real tragedy—of everything most vital and beautiful in the modern world itself. Here in the Bronx, thanks to Robert Moses, the modernity of the urban boulevard was being condemned as obsolete, and blown to pieces, by the modernity of the interstate highway. *Sic transit!* To be modern turned out to be far more problematical, and more perilous, than I had been taught.

What were the roads that led to the Cross-Bronx Expressway? The public works that Moses organized from the 1920s onward expressed a vision—or rather a series of visions—of what modern life could and should be. I want to articulate the distinctive forms of modernism that Moses defined and realized, to suggest their inner contradictions, their ominous undercurrents—which burst to the surface in the Bronx—and their lasting meaning and value for modern mankind.

Moses' first great achievement, at the end of the 1920s, was the creation of a public space radically different from anything that had existed anywhere before: Jones Beach State Park on Long Island, just beyond the bounds of New York City along the Atlantic. This beach, which opened in the summer of 1929, and recently celebrated its fiftieth anniversary, is so immense that it can easily hold a half million people on a hot Sunday in July without any sense of congestion. Its most striking feature as a landscape is its amazing clarity of space and form: absolutely flat, blindingly white expanses of sand, stretching forth to the horizon in a straight wide band, cut on one side by the clear, pure, endless blue of the sea, and on the other by the boardwalk's sharp unbroken line of brown. The great horizontal sweep of the whole is punctuated by two elegant Art Deco bathhouses of wood, brick and stone, and halfway between them at the park's dead center by a monumental columnar water tower, visible from everywhere, rising up like a skyscraper, evoking the grandeur of the twentieth-century urban forms that this park at once complements and denies. Jones Beach offers a spectacular display of the primary forms of nature—earth, sun, water, sky—but nature here appears with an abstract horizontal purity and a luminous clarity that only culture can create.

We can appreciate Moses' creation even more when we realize (as Caro explains vividly) how much of this space had been swamp and wasteland, inaccessible and unmapped, until Moses got there, and what a spectacular metamorphosis he brought about in barely two years. There is another kind of purity that is crucial to Jones Beach. There is no intrusion of modern business or commerce here: no hotels, casinos, ferris wheels, roller coasters, parachute jumps, pinball machines, honky-tonks, loudspeakers, hot-dog stands, neon signs; no dirt, random noise or disarray.* Hence, even when Jones Beach is filled with a crowd the size of Pittsburgh, its ambience manages to be remarkably serene. It contrasts radically with Coney Island, only a few miles to the west, whose middle-class constituency it immediately captured on its opening. All the density and intensity, the anarchic noise and motion, the seedy vitality that is expressed in Weegee's photographs and Reginald Marsh's etchings, and celebrated symbolically in Lawrence Ferlinghetti's "A Coney Island of the Mind," is wiped off the map in the visionary landscape of Jones Beach.†

What would a Jones Beach of the mind be like? It would be hard to convey in poetry, or in any sort of symbolic language that depended on dramatic movement and contrast for its impact. But we can see its forms in the diagrammatic paintings of Mondrian, and later in the minimalism of the 1960s, while its color tonalities belong in the great tradition of neoclassical landscape, from Poussin to the young Matisse to Milton Avery. On a sunny day, Jones Beach transports us into the great romance of the Mediterranean, of Apollonian clarity, of perfect light without shadows, cosmic geometry, unbroken perspectives stretching onward toward an infinite horizon. This romance is at least as old as Plato. Its most passionate and influential modern devotee is Le Corbusier. Here, in the same year that Jones Beach opened, just before the Great Crash, he delineates his classic modern dream:

> If we compare New York with Istanbul, we may say that the one is a cataclysm, and the other a terrestrial paradise.
> New York is exciting and upsetting. So are the Alps; so is a tempest; so is a battle. New York is not beautiful, and if it stimulates our practical activities, it wounds our sense of happiness. . . .

* But American enterprise never gives up. On weekends a continuous procession of small planes cruise just above the shoreline, skywriting or bearing banners to proclaim the glories of various brands of soda or vodka, or roller discos and sex clubs, of local politicians and propositions. Not even Moses has devised ways to zone business and politics out of the sky.

† Coney Island epitomizes what the Dutch architect Rem Koolhaas calls "the culture of congestion." *Delirious New York: A Retrospective Manifesto for Manhattan,* especially 21–65. Koolhaas sees Coney Island as a prototype, a kind of rehearsal, for Manhattan's intensely vertical "city of towers"; compare the radically horizontal sweep of Jones Beach, which is only accentuated by the water tower, the one vertical structure allowed.

A city can overwhelm us with its broken lines; the sky is torn by its ragged outline. Where shall we find repose? . . .

As you go North, the crocketed spires of the cathedrals reflect the agony of the flesh, the poignant dreams of the spirit, hell and purgatory, and forests of pines seen through pale light and cold mist.

Our bodies demand sunshine.

There are certain shapes that cast shadows.[3]

Le Corbusier wants structures that will bring the fantasy of a serene, horizontal South against the shadowed, turbulent realities of the North. Jones Beach, just beyond the horizon of New York's skyscrapers, is an ideal realization of this romance. It is ironic that, although Moses thrived on perpetual conflict, struggle, *Sturm und Drang,* his first triumph, and the one of which he seems to be proudest half a century later, was a triumph of *luxe, calme et volupté.* Jones Beach is the giant Rosebud of this Citizen Cohen.

Moses' Northern and Southern State parkways, leading from Queens out to Jones Beach and beyond, opened up another dimension of modern pastoral. These gently flowing, artfully landscaped roads, although a little frayed after half a century, are still among the world's most beautiful. But their beauty does not (like that of, say, California's Coast Highway or the Appalachian Trail) emanate from the natural environment around the roads: it springs from the artificially created environment of the roads themselves. Even if these parkways adjoined nothing and led nowhere, they would still constitute an adventure in their own right. This is especially true of the Northern State Parkway, which ran through the country of palatial estates that Scott Fitzgerald had just immortalized in *The Great Gatsby** (1925). Moses' first Long Island roadscapes represent a modern attempt to recreate what Fitzgerald's narrator, on the novel's last page, described as "the old island here that flowered once for Dutch sailors' eyes—a fresh, green breast of the new world." But Moses made this breast avail-

---

* This generated bitter conflict with the estate owners, and enabled Moses to win a reputation as a champion of the people's right to fresh air, open space and the freedom to move. "It was exciting working for Moses," one of his engineers reminisced half a century later. "He made you feel you were a part of something big. It was you fighting for the people against these rich estate owners and reactionary legislators. . . . It was almost like a war." (Caro, 228, 273) In fact, however, as Caro shows, virtually all the land Moses appropriated consisted of small homes and family farms.

able only through the mediation of that other symbol so dear to Gatsby: the green light. His parkways could be experienced only in cars: their underpasses were purposely built too low for buses to clear them, so that public transit could not bring masses of people out from the city to the beach. This was a distinctively techno-pastoral garden, open only to those who possessed the latest modern machines—this was, remember, the age of the Model T—and a uniquely privatized form of public space. Moses used physical design as a means of social screening, screening out all those without wheels of their own. Moses, who never learned to drive, was becoming Detroit's man in New York. For the great majority of New Yorkers, however, his green new world offered only a red light.

Jones Beach and Moses' first Long Island parkways should be seen in the context of the spectacular growth of leisure activities and industries during the economic boom of the 1920s. These Long Island projects were meant to open up a pastoral world just beyond the city limits, a world made for holidays and play and fun —for those who had the time and the means to step out. The metamorphoses of Moses in the 1930s need to be seen in the light of a great transformation in the meaning of construction itself. During the Great Depression, as private business and industry collapsed, and mass unemployment and desperation increased, construction was transformed from a private into a public enterprise, and into a serious and urgent public imperative. Virtually everything serious that was built in the 1930s—bridges, parks, roads, tunnels, dams—was built with federal money, under the auspices of the great New Deal agencies, the CWA, PWA, CCC, FSA, TVA. These projects were planned around complex and well-articulated social goals. First, they were meant to create business, increase consumption and stimulate the private sector. Second, they would put millions of unemployed people back to work, and help to purchase social peace. Third, they would speed up, concentrate and modernize the economies of the regions in which they were built, from Long Island to Oklahoma. Fourth, they would enlarge the meaning of "the public," and give symbolic demonstrations of how American life could be enriched both materially and spiritually through the medium of public works. Finally, in their use of exciting new technologies, the great New Deal projects dramatized the promise of a glorious future just emerging over the horizon, a new day not merely for a privileged few but for the people as a whole.

Moses was perhaps the first person in America to grasp the immense possibilities of the Roosevelt administration's commitment to public works; he grasped, too, the extent to which the destiny of American cities was going to be worked out in Washington from this point on. Now holding a joint appointment as City and State Parks Commissioner, he established close and lasting ties with the most energetic and innovative planners of the New Deal bureaucracy. He learned how to free millions of dollars in federal funds in a remarkably short time. Then, hiring a staff of first-rate planners and engineers (mostly from off the unemployment lines), he mobilized a labor army of 80,000 men and went to work with a great crash program to regenerate the city's 1700 parks (even more rundown at the nadir of the Depression than they are today) and create hundreds of new ones, plus hundreds of playgrounds and several zoos. Moses got the job done by the end of 1934. Not only did he display a gift for brilliant administration and execution, he also understood the value of ongoing public work as public spectacle. He carried on the overhauling of Central Park, and the construction of its reservoir and zoo, twenty-four hours a day, seven days a week: floodlights shined and jackhammers reverberated all through the night, not only speeding up the work but creating a new showplace that kept the public enthralled.

The workers themselves seem to have been caught up in the enthusiasm: they not only kept up with the relentless pace that Moses and his straw bosses imposed but actually outpaced the bosses, and took initiative, and came up with new ideas, and worked ahead of plans, so that the engineers were repeatedly forced to run back to their desks and redesign the plans to take account of the progress the workers had made on their own.[4] This is the modern romance of construction at its best—the romance celebrated by Goethe's Faust, by Carlyle and Marx, by the constructivists of the 1920s, by the Soviet construction films of the Five-Year Plan period, and the TVA and FSA documentaries and WPA murals of the later 1930s. What gave the romance a special reality and authenticity here is the fact that it inspired the men who were actually doing the work. They seem to have been able to find meaning and excitement in work that was physically gruelling and ill-paying, because they had some vision of the work as a whole, and believed in its value to the community of which they were a part.

The tremendous public acclaim that Moses received for his work on the city's parks served him as a springboard for something that meant far more to him than parks. This was a system of highways, parkways and bridges that would weave the whole metropolitan area together: the elevated West Side Highway, extending the length of Manhattan, and across Moses' new Henry Hudson Bridge, into and through the Bronx, and into Westchester; the Belt Parkway, sweeping around the periphery of Brooklyn, from the East River to the Atlantic, connected to Manhattan through the Brooklyn-Battery Tunnel (Moses would have preferred a bridge), and to the Southern State; and—here was the heart of the system—the Triborough Project, an enormously complex network of bridges and approaches and parkways that would link Manhattan, the Bronx and Westchester with Queens and Long Island.

These projects were incredibly expensive, yet Moses managed to talk Washington into paying for most of them. They were technically brilliant: the Triborough engineering is still a classic text today. They helped, as Moses said, to "weave together the loose strands and frayed edges of the New York metropolitan arterial tapestry," and to give this enormously complex region a unity and coherence it had never had. They created a series of spectacular new visual approaches to the city, displaying the grandeur of Manhattan from many new angles—from the Belt Parkway, the Grand Central, the upper West Side—and nourishing a whole new generation of urban fantasies.* The uptown Hudson riverfront, one of Moses' finest urban landscapes, is especially striking when we realize that (as Caro shows, in pictures) it was a wasteland of hoboes' shacks and garbage dumps before he got there. You cross the George Washington Bridge and dip down and around and

* On the other hand, these projects made a series of drastic and near-fatal incursions into Manhattan's grid. Koolhaas, Delirious New York, 15, explains incisively the importance of this system to the New York environment: "The Grid's two-dimensional discipline creates undreamt-of freedom for three-dimensional anarchy. The Grid defines a new balance between control and decontrol. . . . With its imposition, Manhattan is forever immunized against any [further] totalitarian intervention. In the single block—the largest possible area that can fall under architectural control —it develops a maximum unit of urbanistic Ego." It is precisely these urban ego-boundaries that Moses' own ego sought to sweep away.

slide into the gentle curve of the West Side Highway, and the lights and towers of Manhattan flash and glow before you, rising above the lush greenness of Riverside Park, and even the most embittered enemy of Robert Moses—or, for that matter, of New York —will be touched: you know you have come home again, and the city is there for you, and you can thank Moses for that.

At the very end of the 1930s, when Moses was at the height of his creativity, he was canonized in the book that, more than any other, established the canon of the modern movement in architecture, planning and design: Siegfried Giedion's *Space, Time and Architecture*. Giedion's work, first delivered in lecture form at Harvard in 1938–39, unfolded the history of three centuries of modern design and planning—and presented Moses' work as its climax. Giedion presented large photos of the recently completed West Side Highway, the Randall's Island cloverleaf, and the "pretzel" interchange of the Grand Central Parkway. These works, he said, "proved that possibilities of a great scale are inherent in our period." Giedion compared Moses' parkways to cubist paintings, to abstract sculptures and mobiles, and to the movies. "As with many of the creations born out of the spirit of this age, the meaning and beauty of the parkway cannot be grasped from a single point of observation, as was possible from a window of the château at Versailles. It can be revealed only by movement, by going along in a steady flow, as the rules of traffic prescribe. The space-time feeling of our period can seldom be felt so keenly as when driving."[5]

Thus Moses' projects marked not only a new phase in the modernization of urban space but a new breakthrough in modernist vision and thought. For Giedion, and for the whole generation of the 1930s—Corbusierian or Bauhaus formalists and technocrats, Marxists, even agrarian neopopulists—these parkways opened up a magical realm, a kind of romantic bower in which modernism and pastoralism could intertwine. Moses seemed to be the one public figure in the world who understood "the space-time conception of our period"; in addition, he had "the energy and enthusiasm of a Haussmann." This made him "uniquely equal, as Haussmann himself had been equal, to the opportunities and needs of the period," and uniquely qualified to build "the city of the future" in our time. Hegel in 1806 had conceived of Napoleon as "the *Weltseele* on horse"; for Giedion in 1939, Moses looked like the *Weltgeist* on wheels.

Moses received a further apotheosis at the 1939–40 New York World's Fair, an immense celebration of modern technology and industry: "Building the World of Tomorrow." Two of the fair's most popular exhibits—the commercially oriented General Motors Futurama and the utopian Democracity—both envisioned elevated urban expressways and arterial parkways connecting city and country, in precisely the forms that Moses had just built. Spectators on their way to and from the fair, as they flowed along Moses' roads and across his bridges, could directly experience something of this visionary future, and see that it seemed to work.*

Moses, in his capacity as Parks Commissioner, had put together the parcel of land on which the fair was being held. With lightning speed, at minimal cost, with his typical fusion of menace and finesse, he had seized from hundreds of owners a piece of land the size of downtown Manhattan. His proudest accomplishment in this affair was to have destroyed the notorious Flushing ash heaps and mounds of garbage that Scott Fitzgerald had immortalized as one of the great modern symbols of industrial and human waste:

> a valley of ashes—a fantastic farm where ashes grow like wheat into ridges and hills and grotesque gardens; where ashes take the forms of houses and chimneys and rising smoke and, finally, with a transcendent effort, of men who move dimly and already crumbling through the powdery air. Occasionally a line of gray cars crawls along an invisible track, gives out a ghastly creak, and comes to rest, and immediately the ash-gray men swarm up with leaden spades and stir up an impenetrable cloud, which screens their obscure operations from your sight. [*The Great Gatsby*, Chapter 2]

Moses obliterated this dreadful scene and transformed the site into the nucleus of the fairgrounds, and later of Flushing Meadow Park. This action moved him to a rare effusion of Biblical lyricism:

---

* Walter Lippmann seems to have been one of the few who saw the long-range implications and hidden costs of this future. "General Motors has spent a small fortune to convince the American public," he wrote, "that if it wishes to enjoy the full benefit of private enterprise in motor manufacturing, it will have to rebuild its cities and its highways by public enterprise." This apt prophecy is quoted by Warren Susman in his fine essay "The People's Fair: Cultural Contradictions of a Consumer Society," included in the Queens Museum's catalogue volume, *Dawn of a New Day: The New York World's Fair, 1939/40* (NYU, 1980), 25. This volume, which includes interesting essays by several hands, and splendid photographs, is the best book on the fair.

he invoked the beautiful passage from Isaiah (61:1–4) in which "the Lord has anointed me to bring good tidings to the afflicted; he has sent me to bind up the brokenhearted, to proclaim liberty to the captives, and the opening of the prison to those that are bound; . . . to give unto them beauty for ashes . . . [so that] they shall repair the ruined cities, the devastations of many generations." Forty years later, in his last interviews, he still pointed to this with special pride: I am the man who destroyed the Valley of Ashes and put beauty in its place. It is on this note—with the fervent faith that modern technology and social organization could create a world without ashes—that the modernism of the 1930s came to an end.

Where did it all go wrong? How did the modern visions of the 1930s turn sour in the process of their realization? The whole story would require far more time to unravel, and far more space to tell, than I have here and now. But we can rephrase these questions in a more limited way that will fit into the orbit of this book: How did Moses—and New York and America—move from the destruction of a Valley of Ashes in 1939 to the development of far more dreadful and intractable modern wastelands a generation later only a few miles away? We need to seek out the shadows within the luminous visions of the 1930s themselves.

The dark side was always there in Moses himself. Here is the testimony of Frances Perkins, America's first Secretary of Labor under FDR, who worked closely with Moses for many years and admired him all her life. She recalls the people's heartfelt love for Moses in the early years of the New Deal, when he was building playgrounds in Harlem and on the Lower East Side; however, she was disturbed to discover, "he doesn't love the people" in return:

> It used to shock me because he was doing all these things for the welfare of the people. . . . To him, they were lousy, dirty people, throwing bottles all over Jones Beach. "I'll get them! I'll teach them!" He loves the public, but not as people. The public is . . . a great amorphous mass to him; it needs to be bathed, it needs to be aired, it needs recreation, but not for personal reasons—just to make it a better public.[6]

"He loves the public, but not as people": Dostoevsky warned us repeatedly that the combination of love for "humanity" with hatred for actual people was one of the fatal hazards of modern politics. During the New Deal period, Moses managed to maintain a precarious balance between the poles and to bring real happiness not only to "the public" he loved but also to the people he loathed. But no one could keep up this balancing act forever. "I'll get them! I'll teach them!" The voice here is unmistakably that of Mr. Kurtz: "It was very simple," Conrad's narrator says, "and at the end of every idealistic sentiment it blazed at you, luminous and terrifying, like a flash of lightning in a serene sky: 'Exterminate all the brutes!' " We need to know what was Moses' equivalent for Mr. Kurtz's African ivory trade, what historical chances and institutional forces opened up the floodgates of his most dangerous drives: What was the road that led him from the radiance of "give unto them beauty for ashes" to "you have to hack your way with a meat ax" and the darkness that cleft the Bronx?

Part of Moses' tragedy is that he was not only corrupted but in the end undermined by one of his greatest achievements. This was a triumph that, unlike Moses' public works, was for the most part invisible: it was only in the late 1950s that investigative reporters began to perceive it. It was the creation of a network of enormous, interlocking "public authorities," capable of raising virtually unlimited sums of money to build with, and accountable to no executive, legislative or judicial power.[7]

The English institution of a "public authority" had been grafted onto American public administration early in the twentieth century. It was empowered to sell bonds to construct particular public works—e.g., bridges, harbors, railroads. When its project was completed, it would charge tolls for use until its bonds were paid off; at that point it would ordinarily go out of existence and turn its public work over to the state. Moses, however, saw that there was no reason for an authority to limit itself in time or space: so long as money was coming in—say, from tolls on the Triborough Bridge—and so long as the bond market was encouraging, an authority could trade in its old bonds for new ones, to raise more money, to build more works; so long as money (all of it tax-exempt) kept coming in, the banks and institutional investors would be only too glad to underwrite new bond issues, and the authority could go on building forever. Once the initial bonds were paid off, there would be no need to go to the city, state or federal governments, or to the people, for money to build. Moses proved in court that no government had any legal right even to look into an authority's books. Between the late 1930s and the late 1950s, Moses created or took over a dozen of these authorities—for parks, bridges, highways, tunnels, electric power, urban renewal and more—and integrated them into an immensely powerful machine, a machine with innumerable wheels within wheels, transforming its cogs into millionaires, incorporating thousands of businessmen and politicians into its production line, drawing millions of New Yorkers inexorably into its widening gyre.

Kenneth Burke suggested in the 1930s that whatever we might think of the social value of Standard Oil and U.S. Steel, Rockefeller's and Carnegie's work in creating these giant complexes had to be rated as triumphs of modern art. Moses' network of public authorities clearly belongs in this company. It fulfills one of the earliest dreams of modern science, a dream renewed in many forms of twentieth-century art: to create a system in perpetual motion. But Moses' system, even as it constitutes a triumph of modern art, shares in some of that art's deepest ambiguities. It carries the contradiction between "the public" and the people so far that in the end not even the people at the system's center—not even Moses himself—had the authority to shape the system and control its ever-expanding moves.

If we go back to Giedion's "bible," we will see some of the deeper meanings of Moses' work which Moses himself never really grasped. Giedion saw the Triborough Bridge, the Grand Central Parkway, the West Side Highway, as expressions of "the new form of the city." This form demanded "a different scale from that of the existing city, with its *rues corridors* and rigid divisions into small blocks." The new urban forms could not function freely within the framework of the nineteenth-century city: hence, "It is the actual structure of the city that must be changed." The first imperative was this: "There is no longer any place for the city street; it cannot be permitted to persist." Giedion took on an imperial voice here that was strongly reminiscent of Moses' own. But the destruction of the city streets was, for Giedion, only a beginning: Moses' highways "look ahead to the time when, after the necessary surgery has been performed, the artificially swollen city will be reduced to its natural size."

Leaving aside the quirks in Giedion's own vision (What makes any urban size more "natural" than any other?), we see here how modernism makes a dramatic new departure: the development of modernity has made the modern city itself old-fashioned, obsolete. True, the people, visions and institutions of the city have created the highway—"To New York . . . must go the credit for the creation of the parkway."[8] Now, however, by a fateful dialectic, because the city and the highway don't go together, the city must go. Ebenezer Howard and his "Garden City" disciples had been suggesting something like this since the turn of the century (see above, Chapter IV). Moses' historical mission, from the standpoint of this vision, is to have created a new superurban reality that makes the city's obsolescence clear. To cross the Triborough Bridge, for Giedion, is to enter a new "space-time continuum," one that leaves the modern metropolis forever behind. Moses has shown that it is unnecessary to wait for some distant future: we have the technology and the organizational tools to bury the city here and now.

Moses never meant to do this: unlike the "Garden City" thinkers, he genuinely loved New York—in his blind way—and never meant it any harm. His public works, whatever we may think of them, were meant to add something to city life, not to subtract the city itself. He would surely have recoiled at the thought that his 1939 World's Fair, one of the great moments in New York's history, would be the vehicle of a vision which, taken at face value, would spell the city's ruin. But when have world-historical figures ever understood the long-range meaning of their acts and works? In fact, however, Moses' great construction in and around New York in the 1920s and 30s served as a rehearsal for the infinitely greater reconstruction of the whole fabric of America after World War Two. The motive forces in this reconstruction were the multibillion-dollar Federal Highway Program and the vast suburban housing initiatives of the Federal Housing Administration. This new order integrated the whole nation into a unified flow whose lifeblood was the automobile. It conceived of cities principally as obstructions to the flow of traffic, and as junkyards of substandard housing and decaying neighborhoods from which Americans should be given every chance to escape. Thousands of urban neighborhoods were obliterated by this new order; what happened to my Bronx was only the largest and most dramatic instance of something that was happening all over. Three decades of massively capitalized highway construction and FHA suburbanization would serve to draw millions of people and jobs, and billions of dollars in investment capital, out of America's cities, and plunge these cities into the chronic crisis and chaos that plague their inhabitants today. This wasn't what Moses meant at all; but it was what he inadvertently helped to bring about.*

Moses' projects of the 1950s and 60s had virtually none of the beauty of design and human sensitivity that had distinguished his early works. Drive twenty miles or so on the Northern State Parkway (1920s), then turn around and cover those same twenty miles on the parallel Long Island Expressway (1950s/60s), and wonder and weep. Nearly all he built after the war was built in an indifferently brutal style, made to overawe and overwhelm: monoliths of steel and cement, devoid of vision or nuance or play, sealed off from the surrounding city by great moats of stark empty space, stamped on the landscape with a ferocious contempt for all natural and human life. Now Moses seemed scornfully indifferent to the human quality of what he did: sheer quantity—of moving vehicles, tons of cement, dollars received and spent—seemed to be all that drove him now. There are sad ironies in this, Moses' last, worst phase.

The cruel works that cracked open the Bronx ("more people in the way—that's all") were part of a social process whose dimensions dwarfed even Moses' own megalomaniac will to power. By the 1950s he was no longer building in accord with his own visions; rather, he was fitting enormous blocks into a pre-existing pattern of national reconstruction and social integration that he had not made and could not have substantially changed. Moses at his best had been a true creator of new material and social possibilities. At his worst, he would become not so much a destroyer—though he destroyed plenty—as an executioner of directives and imperatives not his own. He had gained power and glory by opening up new forms and media in which modernity could be experienced as an adventure; he used that power and glory to institutionalize modernity into a system of grim, inexorable necessities and crushing routines. Ironically, he became a focus for mass personal obsession and hatred, including my own, just when he had lost personal

---

* Moses at least was honest enough to call a meat ax by its real name, to recognize the violence and devastation at the heart of his works. Far more typical of postwar planning is a sensibility like Giedion's, for whom, "after the necessary surgery has been performed, the artificially swollen city will be reduced to its natural size." This genial self-delusion, which assumes that cities can be hacked to pieces without blood or wounds or shrieks of pain, points the way forward to the "surgical precision" bombing of Germany, Japan, and, later, Vietnam.

vision and initiative and become an Organization Man; we came to know him as New York's Captain Ahab at a point when, although still at the wheel, he had lost control of the ship.

The evolution of Moses and his works in the 1950s underscores another important fact about the postwar evolution of culture and society: the radical splitting-off of modernism from modernization. Throughout this book I have tried to show a dialectical interplay between unfolding modernization of the environment—particularly the urban environment—and the development of modernist art and thought. This dialectic, crucial all through the nineteenth century, remained vital to the modernism of the 1920s and 1930s: it is central in Joyce's *Ulysses* and Eliot's *Waste Land* and Doblin's *Berlin, Alexanderplatz* and Mandelstam's *Egyptian Stamp*, in Léger and Tatlin and Eisenstein, in William Carlos Williams and Hart Crane, in the art of John Marin and Joseph Stella and Stuart Davis and Edward Hopper, in the fiction of Henry Roth and Nathanael West. By the 1950s, however, in the wake of Auschwitz and Hiroshima, this process of dialogue had stopped dead.

It is not that culture itself stagnated or regressed: there were plenty of brilliant artists and writers around, working at or near the peak of their powers. The difference is that the modernists of the 1950s drew no energy or inspiration from the modern environment around them. From the triumphs of the abstract expressionists to the radical initiatives of Davis, Mingus and Monk in jazz, to Camus' *The Fall*, Beckett's *Waiting for Godot*, Malamud's *The Magic Barrel*, Laing's *The Divided Self*, the most exciting work of this era is marked by radical distance from any shared environment. The environment is not attacked, as it was in so many previous modernisms: it is simply not there.

This absence is dramatized obliquely in what are probably the two richest and deepest novels of the 1950s, Ralph Ellison's *Invisible Man* (1952) and Günter Grass's *The Tin Drum* (1959): both these books contained brilliant realizations of spiritual and political life as it had been lived in the cities of the recent past—Harlem and Danzig in the 1930s—but although both writers moved chronologically forward, neither one was able to imagine or engage the present, the life of the postwar cities and societies in which their books came out. This absence itself may be the most striking proof of the spiritual poverty of the new postwar environment. Ironically, that poverty may have actually nourished the development of modernism by forcing artists and thinkers to fall back on their own resources and open up new depths of inner space. At the same time, it subtly ate away at the roots of modernism by sealing off its imaginative life from the everyday modern world in which actual men and women had to move and live.[9]

The split between the modern spirit and the modernized environment was a primary source of anguish and reflection in the later 1950s. As the decade dragged on, imaginative people became increasingly determined not only to understand this great gulf but also, through art and thought and action, to leap across it. This was the desire that animated books as diverse as Hannah Arendt's *The Human Condition*, Norman Mailer's *Advertisements for Myself*, Norman O. Brown's *Life Against Death*, and Paul Goodman's *Growing Up Absurd*. It was a consuming but unconsummated obsession shared by two of the most vivid protagonists in the fiction of the late 1950s: Doris Lessing's Anna Wolf, whose notebooks overflowed with unfinished confessions and unpublished manifestos for liberation, and Saul Bellow's Moses Herzog, whose medium was unfinished, unmailed letters to all the great powers of this world.

Eventually, however, the letters did get finished, signed and delivered; new modes of modernist language gradually emerged, at once more personal and more political than the language of the 1950s, in which modern men and women could confront the new physical and social structures that had grown up around them. In this new modernism, the gigantic engines and systems of postwar construction played a central symbolic role. Thus, in Allen Ginsberg's "Howl":

> What sphinx of cement and aluminum hacked open their skulls and ate up their brains and imagination? . . .
> Moloch the incomprehensible prison! Moloch the crossbone soulless jailhouse and Congress of sorrows! Moloch whose buildings are judgment! . . .
> Moloch whose eyes are a thousand blind windows! Moloch whose skyscrapers stand in the long streets like endless Jehovahs! Moloch whose factories dream and croak in the fog! Moloch whose smokestacks and antennae crown the cities!
> Moloch! Moloch! Robot apartments! invisible suburbs! skeleton treasuries! blind capitals! demonic industries! spectral nations! invincible madhouses! granite cocks!
> They broke their backs lifting Moloch to Heaven! Pavements,

> trees, radios, tons! lifting the city to Heaven which exists and is
> everywhere about us! . . .
> Moloch who entered my soul early! Moloch in whom I am a
> consciousness without a body! Moloch who frightened me out
> of my natural ecstasy! Moloch whom I abandon! Wake up in
> Moloch! Light streaming out of the sky!

There are many remarkable things happening here. Ginsberg is urging us to experience modern life not as a hollow wasteland but as an epic and tragic battle of giants. This vision endows the modern environment and its makers with a demonic energy and a world-historical stature that probably exceed even what the Robert Moseses of this world would claim for themselves. At the same time, the vision is meant to arouse us, the readers, to make ourselves equally great, to enlarge our desire and moral imagination to the point where we will dare to take on the giants. But we cannot do this until we recognize their desires and powers in ourselves— "Moloch who entered my soul early." Hence Ginsberg develops structures and processes of poetic language—an interplay between luminous flashes and bursts of desperate imagery and a solemn, repetitive, incantatory piling up of line upon line—that recall and rival the skyscrapers, factories and expressways he hates. Ironically, although the poet portrays the expressway world as the death of brains and imagination, his poetic vision brings its underlying intelligence and imaginative force to life—indeed, brings it more fully to life than the builders were ever able to do on their own.

When my friends and I discovered Ginsberg's Moloch, and thought at once of Moses, we were not only crystallizing and mobilizing our hate; we were also giving our enemy the world-historical stature, the dreadful grandeur, that he had always deserved but never received from those who loved him most. They could not bear to look into the nihilistic abyss that his steam shovels and pile drivers opened up; hence they missed his depths. Thus it was only when modernists began to confront the shapes and shadows of the expressway world that it became possible to see that world for all it was.*

Did Moses understand any of this symbolism? It is hard to know.

---

* For a slightly later version of this confrontation, very different in sensibility but equal in intellectual and visionary power, compare Robert Lowell's "For the Union Dead," published in 1964.

In the rare interviews he gave during the years between his enforced retirement [10] and his death at ninety-two, he could still explode with fury at his detractors, overflow with wit and energy and tremendous schemes, refuse, like Mr. Kurtz, to be counted out ("I'll carry out my ideas yet. . . . I'll show you what can be done. . . . I will return . . . I . . ."). Driven restlessly up and down his Long Island roads in his limousine (one of the few perquisites he has kept from his years of power), he dreamt of a glorious hundred-mile ocean drive to whip the waves, or of the world's longest bridge connecting Long Island with Rhode Island across the Sound.

This old man possessed an undeniable tragic grandeur; but it is not so clear that he ever achieved the self-awareness that is supposed to go with that grandeur. Replying to *The Power Broker*, Moses appealed plaintively to us all: Am I not the man who blotted out the Valley of Ashes and gave mankind beauty in its place? It is true, and we owe him homage for it. And yet, he did not really wipe out the ashes, only moved them to another site. For the ashes are part of us, no matter how straight and smooth we make our beaches and freeways, no matter how fast we drive—or are driven—no matter how far out on Long Island we go.

2.

The 1960s: A Shout in the Street

—History, Stephen said, is a nightmare from which I am trying to awake.

From the playfield the boys raised a shout. A whirring whistle: goal. What if that nightmare gave you a back kick?

—The ways of the Creator are not our ways, Mr. Deasy said. All history moves toward one goal, the manifestation of God.

Stephen jerked his thumb toward the window, saying:

—That is God.

Hooray! Ay! Whrrwhee!

—What? Mr. Deasy asked.
—A shout in the street, Stephen answered.
                    —James Joyce, *Ulysses*

I am for an art that tells you the time of day, or where such and
such a street is. I am for an art that helps old ladies across the street.
                    —Claes Oldenburg

THE EXPRESSWAY world, the modern environment that emerged after World War Two, would reach a pinnacle of power and self-confidence in the 1960s, in the America of the New Frontier, the Great Society, Apollo on the moon. I have been focusing on Robert Moses as the New York agent and incarnation of that world, but Secretary of Defense McNamara, Admiral Rickover, NASA Director Gilruth, and many others, were fighting similar battles with equal energy and ruthlessness, far beyond the Hudson, and indeed beyond the planet Earth. The developers and devotees of the expressway world presented it as the only possible modern world: to oppose them and their works was to oppose modernity itself, to fight history and progress, to be a Luddite, an escapist, afraid of life and adventure and change and growth. This strategy was effective because, in fact, the vast majority of modern men and women do not want to resist modernity: they feel its excitement and believe in its promise, even when they find themselves in its way.

Before the Molochs of the modern world could be effectively fought, it would be necessary to develop a modernist vocabulary of opposition. This is what Stendhal, Buechner, Marx and Engels, Kierkegaard, Baudelaire, Dostoevsky, Nietzsche, were doing a century ago; it is what Joyce and Eliot, the dadaists and surrealists, Kafka, Zamyatin, Babel and Mandelstam, were doing earlier in our century. However, because the modern economy has an infinite capacity for redevelopment and self-transformation, the modernist imagination, too, must reorient and renew itself again and again. One of the crucial tasks for modernists in the 1960s was to confront the expressway world; another was to show that this was not the only possible modern world, that there were other, better directions in which the modern spirit could move.

I invoked Allen Ginsberg's "Howl" at the end of the last chapter to show how, toward the end of the 1950s, modernists were beginning to confront and combat the expressway world. But this project could not go very far unless the new modernists could generate affirmative visions of alternate modern lives. Ginsberg and his circle were in no position to do this. "Howl" was brilliant in unmasking the demonic nihilism at the heart of our established society, and revealing what Dostoevsky a century ago called "the disorder that is in actuality the highest degree of bourgeois order." But all Ginsberg could suggest as an alternative to lifting Moloch to Heaven was a nihilism of his own. "Howl" began with a desperate nihilism, a vision of "angelheaded hipsters . . . the best minds of my generation destroyed by madness, starving hysterical naked, / dragging through the negro streets at dawn looking for an angry fix." It ended with a sentimental and sappy nihilism, an all-embracing mindless affirmation: "The world is holy! The soul is holy! . . . The tongue and cock and hand and asshole holy! / Everything is holy! everybody's holy! everywhere is holy!" etc., etc. But if the emerging modernists of the 1960s were going to turn the world of Moloch and Moses around, they would have to offer something more.

Before long they would find something more, a source of life and energy and affirmation that was just as modern as the expressway world, but radically opposed to the forms and motions of that world. They would find it in a place where very few of the modernists of the 1950s would have dreamt of looking for it: in the everyday life of the street. This is the life that Joyce's Stephen Dedalus points to with his thumb, and invokes against the official history taught by Mr. Deasy, representative of Church and State: God is absent from that nightmarish history, Stephen implies, but present in the apparently inchoate random shouts that drift in from the streets. Wyndham Lewis was scandalized by this conception of truth and meaning, which he disparagingly called "plainmanism." But this was exactly Joyce's point: to sound the untapped depths of the cities of the plain. From Dickens' and Gogol's and Dostoevsky's time, up to our own, this is what modernist humanism has been all about.

If there is one work that perfectly expresses the modernism of the street in the 1960s, it is Jane Jacobs' remarkable book *The Death and Life of Great American Cities*. Jacobs' work has often been appreciated for its role in changing the whole orientation of city and community planning. This is true, and admirable, but it suggests only a small part of what the book contains. By quoting Jacobs at length in the next few pages, I want to convey the richness of her thought. I believe that her book played a crucial role in the development of modernism: its message was that much of the meaning for which modern men and women were desperately searching in fact lay surprisingly close to home, close to the surface and immediacy of their lives: it was all right there, if we could only learn to dig.[11]

Jacobs develops her vision with a deceptive modesty: all she is doing is talking about her everyday life. "The stretch of Hudson Street where I live is each day the scene of an intricate sidewalk ballet." She goes on to trace twenty-four hours in the life of her street and, of course, of her own life on that street. Her prose often sounds plain, almost artless. In fact, however, she is working within an important genre in modern art: the urban montage. As we go through her twenty-four-hour life cycle, we are likely to experience a sense of déjà vu. Haven't we been through this somewhere before? Yes, we have, if we have read or heard or seen Gogol's "Nevsky Prospect," Joyce's *Ulysses*, Walter Ruttmann's *Berlin, Symphony of a Great City*, Dziga Vertov's *Man with the Movie Camera*, Dylan Thomas' *Under Milk Wood*. Indeed, the better we know this tradition, the more we will appreciate what Jacobs does with it.

Jacobs begins her montage in the early morning: she enters the street to put out her garbage and to sweep up the candy wrappers that are being dropped by junior high school students on their way to school. She feels a ritual satisfaction from this, and, as she sweeps, "I watch the other rituals of morning: Mr. Halpert unlocking the laundry's handcart from its mooring to a cellar door, Joe Cornacchia's son-in-law stacking out the empty crates from the delicatessen, the barber bringing out his sidewalk folding chair, Mr. Goldstein arranging the coils of wire that proclaim that the hardware store is open, the wife of the tenement's superintendent depositing her chunky three-year-old with a toy mandolin on the stoop, the vantage point from which he is learning the English his mother cannot speak."

Interwoven with these known and friendly faces, there are hundreds of strangers passing through: housewives with baby carriages, teenagers gossiping and comparing their hair, young secretaries and elegant middle-aged couples on their way to work, workers coming off the night shift and stopping by the corner bar. Jacobs contemplates and enjoys them all: she experiences and evokes what Baudelaire called the "universal communion" available to the man or woman who knows how to "take a bath of multitude."

By and by, it is time for her to rush off to work, "and I exchange my ritual farewell with Mr. Lofaro, the short, thick-bodied, white-aproned fruit man who stands outside his door a little up the street, his arms folded, his feet planted, looking solid as earth itself. We nod; we each glance quickly up the street, then look back to each other and smile. We have done this many a morning for more than ten years, and we both know what it means: All is well." So it goes as Jacobs takes us through the day and into the night, bringing the children home from school and the adults back from work, bringing forth an abundance of new characters—businessmen, longshoremen, young and old bohemians, scattered solitaries—as they come to and pass along the street in search of food or drink or play or sex or love.

Gradually the life of the street subdues, but it never stops. "I know the deep night ballet and its seasons best from waking long after midnight to tend a baby, and sitting in the dark, seeing the shadows and hearing the sounds of the sidewalk." She attunes herself to these sounds. "Sometimes there is sharpness and anger, or sad, sad weeping . . . about three in the morning, singing, very good singing." Is that a bagpipe out there? Where can the piper be coming from, and where is he going? She'll never know; but this very knowledge, that her street's life is inexhaustibly rich, beyond her (or anyone's) power to grasp, helps her sleep well.

This celebration of urban vitality, diversity and fullness of life is in fact, as I have tried to show, one of the oldest themes in modern culture. Throughout the age of Haussmann and Baudelaire, and well into the twentieth century, this urban romance crystallized around the street, which emerged as a primary symbol of modern life. From the small-town "Main Street" to the metropolitan "Great White Way" and "Dream Street," the street was experienced as the medium in which the totality of modern material and spiritual forces could meet, clash, interfuse and work out their ultimate meanings and fates. This was what Joyce's Stephen Dedalus had in mind in his cryptic suggestion that God was out there, in the "shout in the street."

However, the makers of the post–World War One "modern movement" in architecture and urbanism turned radically against this modern romance: they marched to Le Corbusier's battle cry, "We must kill the street." It was their modern vision that triumphed in the great wave of reconstruction and redevelopment that began after World War Two. For twenty years, streets everywhere were at best passively abandoned and often (as in the Bronx) actively destroyed. Money and energy were rechanneled to the new highways and to the vast system of industrial parks, shopping centers and dormitory suburbs that the highways were opening up. Ironically, then, within the space of a generation, the street, which had always served to express dynamic and progressive modernity, now came to symbolize everything dingy, disorderly, sluggish, stagnant, worn-out, obsolete—everything that the dynamism and progress of modernity were supposed to leave behind.*

In this context, the radicalism and originality of Jacobs' work should be clear. "Under the seeming disorder of the old city," she says—and "old" here means nineteenth-century modern, the remains of the city of the Haussmann age—

> Under the seeming disorder of the old city is a marvelous order for maintaining the safety of the streets and the freedom of the city. It is a complex order. Its essence is intricacy of sidewalk use, bringing with it a constant succession of eyes. This order is all composed of movement and change, and although it is life, not art, we may fancifully call it the art form of the city, and liken it to the dance.

Thus we must strive to keep this "old" environment alive, because it is uniquely capable of nourishing modern experiences and val-

---

* In New York, this irony had a special twist. Probably no American politician incarnated the romance and the hopes of the modern city as well as Al Smith, who used as the anthem for his 1928 presidential campaign the popular song "East Side, West Side, All around the town . . . We'll trip the light fantastic on the sidewalks of New York." It was Smith, however, who appointed and ardently supported Robert Moses, the figure who did more than anyone else to destroy those sidewalks. The 1928 election returns showed that Americans were not ready or willing to accept the sidewalks of New York. On the other hand, as it turned out, America was only too glad to embrace "the highways of New York" and to pave itself over in their image.

ues: the freedom of the city, an order that exists in a state of perpetual motion and change, the evanescent but intense and complex face-to-face communication and communion, of what Baudelaire called the family of eyes. Jacobs' point is that the so-called modern movement has inspired billions of dollars' worth of "urban renewal" whose paradoxical result has been to destroy the only kind of environment in which modern values can be realized. The practical corollary of all this—which sounds paradoxical at first, but in fact makes perfect sense—is that in our city life, for the sake of the modern we must preserve the old and resist the new. With this dialectic, modernism takes on a new complexity and depth.

Reading *The Death and Life of Great American Cities* today, we can find many apt prophecies and intimations of where modernism would be going in the years to come. These themes were not generally noticed when the book came out, and, indeed, Jacobs may not have noticed them herself; still, they are there. Jacobs chose, as a symbol for the vibrant fluidity of street life, the activity of dance: "we may . . . call it the art form of the city, and liken it to dance," specifically "to an intricate ballet in which the individual dancers and ensembles all have distinctive parts which miraculously reinforce each other and compose an orderly whole." In fact, this image was seriously misleading: the years of elite disciplined training required for this sort of dance, its precise structures and techniques of movement, its intricate choreography, were worlds away from the spontaneity, openness and democratic feeling of the Jacobean street.

Ironically, however, even as Jacobs assimilated the life of the street to the dance, the life of modern dance was striving to assimilate the street. Throughout the 1960s and into the 1970s, Merce Cunningham and then younger choreographers like Twyla Tharp and the members of the Grand Union built their work around non-dance (or, as it was later called, "anti-dance") movements and patterns; randomness and chance were often incorporated into choreography, so that the dancers would not know at the start how their dance was going to end; music was sometimes dropped, to be replaced by silence, static from the radio or random street noise; found objects played a central role in the scene—and sometimes found subjects as well, as when Twyla Tharp brought in a street brotherhood of graffitists to fill up the walls in counterpoint to her dancers filling up the floors; sometimes dancers would move directly into New York's streets, and onto its bridges and roofs, interacting spontaneously with whoever and whatever was there.

This new intimacy between the life of the dance and the life of the street was only one aspect of a great upheaval that was going on through the 1960s in nearly every genre of American art. Down on the Lower East Side, across town from Jacobs' neighborhood, though apparently unknown to her, just as she was finishing her book, imaginative and adventurous artists were working to create an art that would be, as Allen Kaprow said in 1958, "preoccupied and even dazzled by the space and objects of everyday life, either our bodies, clothes, rooms, or, if need be, the vastness of Forty-Second Street."[12] Kaprow, Jim Dine, Robert Whitman, Red Grooms, George Segal, Claes Oldenburg and others were moving away not only from the pervasive 1950s idiom of abstract expressionism but from the flatness and confinement of painting as such.

They experimented with a fascinating array of art forms: forms that incorporated and transformed non-art materials, junk, debris, and objects picked up in the street; three-dimensional environments that combined painting, architecture and sculpture—and sometimes theater and dance as well—and that created distorted (usually in an expressionistic way) but vividly recognizable evocations of real life; "happenings" that reached out of the studios and galleries directly into the streets, to assert their presence and undertake actions that would both incorporate and enrich the streets' own spontaneous and open life. Grooms's *Burning Building* of 1959 (which prefigures his spectacular *Ruckus Manhattan* of the mid-1970s) and Oldenburg's *The Street: A Metamorphic Mural* of 1960, long since disassembled but preserved on film, are among the most exciting works of those heady days. In a note to *The Street*, Oldenburg said with a bittersweet irony typical of this art, "The city is a landscape well worth enjoying—damn necessary if you live in the city." His quest for urban enjoyment took him in peculiar directions: "Dirt has depth and beauty. I love soot and scorching." He embraced "the city filth, the evils of advertising, the disease of success, popular culture."

The essential thing, Oldenburg said, was to "look for beauty where it is not supposed to be found."[13] Now this last injunction has been an abiding modernist imperative since the days of Marx and Engels, Dickens and Dostoevsky, Baudelaire and Courbet. It took on a special resonance in the New York of the 1960s because, unlike the physically and metaphysically expansive "Empire City" that had inspired earlier generations of modernists, this was a New York whose whole fabric was beginning to decay. But this very transformation that made the city appear rundown and archaic, especially when compared with its more "modern" suburban and Sunbelt competitors, gave it a special poignancy and radiance for the emerging makers of modern art.

"I am for an art," Oldenburg wrote in 1961, "that is political-erotical-mystical, that does something other than sit on its ass in a museum. I am for an art that embroils itself with the everyday crap and comes out on top. I am for an art that tells you the time of day, or where such and such a street is. I am for an art that helps old ladies across the street."[14] A remarkable prophecy of the metamorphoses of modernism in the 1960s, when an enormous amount of interesting art in a great many genres would be both *about* the street and, sometimes, directly *in* the street. In the visual arts, I have already mentioned Oldenburg, Segal, Grooms, et al.; Robert Crumb would emerge in this company toward the end of the decade.

Meanwhile, Jean-Luc Godard, in *Breathless, Vivre sa Vie, Une Femme Est Une Femme,* made the Paris street an active and central character, and captured its fluctuating light and jagged or fluid rhythms in ways that astounded everyone and opened up a whole new dimension in film. Such diverse poets as Robert Lowell, Adrienne Rich, Paul Blackburn, John Hollander, James Merrill, Galway Kinnell, placed the city streets (especially but not exclusively those of New York) at the center of their imaginative landscapes: indeed, it can be said that the streets erupted into American poetry at a crucial moment, just before they would erupt into our politics.

Streets also played crucial dramatic and symbolic roles in the increasingly serious and sophisticated popular music of the 1960s: in Bob Dylan (42nd Street after a nuclear war in "Talkin' World War Three Blues," "Desolation Row"), Paul Simon, Leonard Cohen ("Stories of the Street"), Peter Townshend, Ray Davies, Jim Morrison, Lou Reed, Laura Nyro, many of the Motown writers, Sly Stone and many more.

Meanwhile, a multitude of performing artists surged into the streets playing and singing music of every kind, dancing, performing or improvising plays, creating happenings and environments and murals, saturating the streets with "political-erotical-mystical" images and sounds, embroiling themselves with "the everyday crap" and at least sometimes coming out on top, though sometimes mystifying themselves and everyone else as to which way was up. Thus modernism returned to its century-old dialogue with the modern environment, with the world that modernization had made.*

The emerging New Left learned much from this dialogue, and eventually contributed much to it. So many of the great demonstrations and confrontations of the 1960s were remarkable works of kinetic and environmental art, in whose creation millions of anonymous people took part. This has often been noticed, but it must also be noticed that the artists were there first—here, as elsewhere, unacknowledged legislators of the world. Their initiatives showed that obscure and decaying old places could turn out to be—or could be turned into—remarkable public spaces; that urban America's nineteenth-century streets, so inefficient for moving twentieth-century traffic, were ideal media for moving twentieth-century hearts and minds. This modernism gave a special richness and vibrancy to a public life that was growing increasingly abrasive and dangerous as the decade went on.

Later, when the radicals of my generation sat down in front of troop trains, stopped business at hundreds of city halls and draft boards, scattered and burned money on the floor of the Stock Exchange, levitated the Pentagon, performed solemn war memorials in the midst of rush hour traffic, dropped thousands of cardboard cluster bombs on the Park Avenue headquarters of the company that made the real ones, and did innumerable other brilliant or stupid things, we knew that the experiments of our gen-

* The claim that the street, missing from the modernism of the 1950s, becomes an active ingredient in the modernism of the '60s, does not hold up in all media. Even in the forlorn '50s, photography continued to nourish itself on the life of the streets, as it had done since its inception. (Note, too, the debuts of Robert Frank and William Klein.) The second-best street scene in American fiction was written in the '50s—though it was written about the '30s: 125th Street before and during the Harlem riot of 1935, in Ralph Ellison's *Invisible Man*. The best scene, or series of scenes, was written in the '30s: East 6th Street, heading toward the river, in Henry Roth's *Call It Sleep*. The street becomes a vital presence in the very different sensibilities of Frank O'Hara and Allen Ginsberg at the very end of the decade, in poems like Ginsberg's "Kaddish" and O'Hara's "The Day Lady Died," which both belong to the transitional year 1959. Exceptions like these should be noted, but I don't think they negate my argument that a big change went on.

eration's modern artists had shown us the way: shown how to recreate that public dialogue which, since ancient Athens and Jerusalem, has been the city's most authentic reason for being. Thus modernism in the 1960s was helping to renew the embattled and abandoned modern city, even as it renewed itself.

There is another crucial prophetic theme in Jacobs' book that no one seems to have noticed at the time. *The Death and Life of Great American Cities* gives us the first fully articulated woman's view of the city since Jane Addams. In one sense Jacobs' perspective is even more fully feminine: she writes out of an intensely lived domesticity that Addams knew only at second hand. She knows her neighborhood in such precise twenty-four-hour detail because she has been around it all day, in ways that most women are normally around all day, especially when they become mothers, but hardly any men ever are, except when they become chronically unemployed. She knows all the shopkeepers, and the vast informal social networks they maintain, because it is her responsibility to take care of her household affairs. She portrays the ecology and phenomenology of the sidewalks with uncanny fidelity and sensitivity, because she has spent years piloting children (first in carriages and strollers, then on roller skates and bikes) through these troubled waters, while balancing heavy shopping bags, talking to neighbors and trying to keep hold of her life. Much of her intellectual authority springs from her perfect grasp of the structures and processes of everyday life. She makes her readers feel that women know what it is like to live in cities, street by street, day by day, far better than the men who plan and build them.*

Jacobs never uses expressions like "feminism" or "women's rights"—in 1960 there were few words that were remoter from current concerns. Nevertheless, in unfolding a woman's perspective on a central public issue, and in making that perspective rich and complex, trenchant and compelling, she opened the way for the great wave of feminist energy that burst at the end of the decade. The feminists of the 1970s would do much to rehabilitate the domestic worlds, "hidden from history," which women had created and sustained for themselves through the ages. They would argue, too, that many of women's traditional decorative

---

* Contemporaneous with Jacobs' work, and similar in texture and richness, is the urban fiction of Grace Paley (whose stories are set in the same neighborhood), and, an ocean away, Doris Lessing.

patterns, textiles, quilts and rooms possessed not only aesthetic value in their own right but also the power to enrich and deepen modern art. For anyone who had encountered the Jacobs persona, the author of *The Death and Life*, at once lovingly domestic and dynamically modern, this possibility made instant sense. Thus she nourished not only a renewal of feminism but also an increasingly widespread male realization that, yes, women had something to tell us about the city and the life we shared, and that we had impoverished our own lives as well as theirs by not listening to them till now.

Jacobs' thought and action heralded a great new wave of community activism, and activists, in all dimensions of political life. These activists have very often been wives and mothers, like Jacobs, and they have assimilated the language—celebration of the family and neighborhood, and their defense against outside forces that would shatter their life—that she did so much to create. But some of their activities suggest that a shared language and emotional tone may conceal radically opposed visions of what modern life is and what it should be. Any careful reader of *The Death and Life of Great American Cities* will realize that Jacobs is celebrating the family and the block in distinctively modernist terms: her ideal street is full of strangers passing through, of people of many different classes, ethnic groups, ages, beliefs and life-styles; her ideal family is one in which women go out to work, men spend a great deal of time at home, both parents work in small and easily manageable units close to home, so that children can discover and grow into a world where there are two sexes and where work plays a central role in everyday life.

Jacobs' street and family are microcosms of all the diversity and fullness of the modern world as a whole. But for some people who seem at first to speak her language, family and locality turn out to be symbols of radical anti-modernism: for the sake of the neighborhood's integrity, all racial minorities, sexual and ideological deviants, controversial books and films, minority modes of music and dress, are to be kept out; in the name of the family, woman's economic, sexual and political freedom must be crushed—she must be kept in her place on the block literally twenty-four hours a day. This is the ideology of the New Right, an inwardly contradictory but enormously powerful movement as old as modernity itself, a movement that utilizes every modern technique of publicity and mass mobilization to turn people against the modern ideals of life, liberty and the pursuit of happiness for all.

What is relevant and disturbing here is that ideologues of the New Right have more than once cited Jacobs as one of their patron saints. Is this connection entirely fraudulent? Or is there something in Jacobs that leaves her open to this misuse? It seems to me that beneath her modernist text there is an anti-modernist subtext, a sort of undertow of nostalgia for a family and a neighborhood in which the self could be securely embedded, *ein'feste Burg*, a solid refuge against all the dangerous currents of freedom and ambiguity in which all modern men and women are caught up. Jacobs, like so many modernists from Rousseau and Wordsworth to D. H. Lawrence and Simone Weil, moves in a twilight zone where the line between the richest and most complex modernism and the rankest bad faith of modernist anti-modernism is very thin and elusive, if indeed there is a line at all.

There is another order of difficulty in Jacobs' perspective. Sometimes her vision seems positively pastoral: she insists, for instance, that in a vibrant neighborhood with a mixture of shops and residences, with constant activity on the sidewalks, with easy surveillance of the streets from within houses and stores, there will be no crime. As we read this, we wonder what planet Jacobs can possibly have been thinking of. If we look back a little skeptically at her vision of her block, we may see the trouble. Her inventory of the people in her neighborhood has the aura of a WPA mural or a Hollywood version of a World War Two bomber crew: every race, creed and color working together to keep America free for you and me. We can hear the roll call: "Holmstrom . . . O'Leary . . . Scagliano . . . Levy . . . Washington . . ." But wait—here is the problem: there is no "Washington" in Jacobs' bomber, i.e., no blacks on her block. This is what makes her neighborhood vision seem pastoral: it is the city before the blacks got there. Her world ranges from solid working-class whites at the bottom to professional middle-class whites at the top. There is nothing and no one above; what matters more here, however, is that there is nothing and no one below—there are no stepchildren in Jacobs' family of eyes.

In the course of the 1960s, however, millions of black and Hispanic people would converge on America's cities—at precisely the moment when the jobs they sought, and the opportunities that

earlier poor immigrants had found, were departing or disappearing. (This was symbolized in New York by the closing of the Brooklyn Navy Yard, once the city's largest employer.) Many of them
found themselves desperately poor, chronically unemployed, at
once racial and economic outcasts, an enormous *lumpenproletariat*
without prospects or hopes. In these conditions, it is no wonder
that rage, despair and violence spread like plagues—and that
hundreds of formerly stable urban neighborhoods all over
America disintegrated completely. Many neighborhoods, including Jacobs' own West Village, remained relatively intact, and even
incorporated some blacks and Hispanics into their families of eyes.
But it was clear by the late 1960s that, amid the class disparities
and racial polarities that skewered American city life, no urban
neighborhood anywhere, not even the liveliest and healthiest,
could be free from crime, random violence, pervasive rage and
fear. Jacobs' faith in the benignness of the sounds she heard from
the street in the middle of the night was bound to be, at best, a
dream.

What light does Jacobs' vision shed on the life of the Bronx?
Even if she misses some of the shadows of neighborhood life, she
is marvelous at capturing its radiance, an inner as well as outer
radiance that class and ethnic conflict might complicate but could
not destroy. Any child of the Bronx who goes through Hudson
Street with Jacobs will recognize, and mourn for, many streets of
our own. We can remember attuning ourselves to their sights and
sounds and smells, and feeling ourselves in harmony with them—
even if we knew, perhaps better than Jacobs knew, that there was
plenty of dissonance out there as well. But so much of this Bronx,
our Bronx, is gone today, and we know we will never feel so much
at home anywhere again. Why did it go? Did it have to go? Was
there anything we could have done to keep it alive? Jacobs' few
fragmentary references to the Bronx display a Greenwich Vil-
lager's snobbish ignorance: her theory, however, clearly implies
that shabby but vibrant neighborhoods like those of the central
Bronx should be able to find the inner resources to sustain and
perpetuate themselves. Is the theory right?

Here is where Robert Moses and his Expressway come in: he
turned potential long-range entropy into sudden inexorable catastrophe; destroying scores of neighborhoods from without, he left
it forever unknown whether they would have collapsed or re-

newed themselves from within. But Robert Caro, working from a Jacobean perspective, makes a powerful case for the inner strength of the central Bronx, had it only been left to itself. In two chapters of *The Power Broker,* both entitled "One Mile," Caro describes the destruction of a neighborhood about a mile from my own. He begins by painting a lovely panorama of this neighborhood, a sentimental but recognizable blend of Jacobs' Hudson Street with *Fiddler on the Roof.* Caro's evocative power sets us up for shock and horror when we see Moses on the horizon moving inexorably ahead. It appears that the Cross-Bronx Expressway could have been slightly curved around this neighborhood. Even Moses' engineers found it feasible to reroute. But the great man would not have it: he deployed every form of force and fraud, intrigue and mystification, at his command, obsessively determined to grind this little world into dust. (When Caro asked him twenty years later how come a leader of the people's protest had suddenly caved in, Moses' reply was cryptic but gloating: "After he was hit over the head with an ax.") [15] Caro's prose becomes incandescent, and utterly devastating, as he shows the blight spreading outward from the Expressway, block by block, year by year, while Moses, like a reincarnated General Sherman run wild in the streets of the North, blazed a path of terror from Harlem to the Sound.

All Caro says here seems to be true. And yet, and yet, it is not the whole truth. There are more questions we need to ask ourselves. What if the Bronxites of the 1950s had possessed the conceptual tools, the vocabulary, the widespread public sympathy, the flair for publicity and mass mobilization, that residents of many American neighborhoods would acquire in the 1960s? What if, like Jacobs' lower Manhattan neighbors a few years later, we had managed to keep the dread road from being built? How many of us would still be in the Bronx today, caring for it and fighting for it as our own? Some of us, no doubt, but I suspect not so many, and in any case—it hurts to say it—not me. For the Bronx of my youth was possessed, inspired, by the great modern dream of mobility. To live well meant to move up socially, and this in turn meant to move out physically; to live one's life close to home was not to be alive at all. Our parents, who had moved up and out from the Lower East Side, believed this just as devoutly as we did—even though their hearts might break when we went. Not even the radicals of my youth disputed this dream—and the Bronx of my childhood was full of radicals—their only complaint was that the dream wasn't being fulfilled, that people weren't able to move fast or freely or equally enough. But when you see life this way, no neighborhood or environment can be anything more than a stage along life's way, a launching pad for higher flights and wider orbits than your own. Even Molly Goldberg, earth goddess of the Jewish Bronx, had to move. (After Philip Loeb, who played Molly's husband, had been moved—by the Blacklist—off the air and, soon after, off the earth.) Ours was, as Leonard Michaels put it, "the mentality of neighborhood types who, quick as possible, got the hell out of their neighborhoods." Thus we had no way to resist the wheels that drove the American dream, because it was driving us ourselves—even though we knew the wheels might break us. All through the decades of the postwar boom, the desperate energy of this vision, the frenzied economic and psychic pressure to move up and out, was breaking down hundreds of neighborhoods like the Bronx, even where there was no Moses to lead the exodus and no Expressway to make it fast.

Thus there was no way a Bronx boy or girl could avoid the drive to move on: it was planted within us as well as outside. Moses entered our soul early. But it was at least possible to think about what directions to move in, and at what speed, and with what human toll. One night in 1967, at an academic reception, I was introduced to an older child of the Bronx who had grown up to be a famous futurologist and creator of scenarios for nuclear war. He had just come back from Vietnam, and I was active in the anti-war movement, but I didn't want trouble just then, so I asked about his years in the Bronx instead. We talked pleasantly enough, till I told him that Moses' road was going to blow every trace of both our childhoods away. Fine, he said, the sooner the better; didn't I understand that the destruction of the Bronx would fulfill the Bronx's own basic moral imperative? What moral imperative? I asked. He laughed as he bellowed in my face: "You want to know the morality of the Bronx? 'Get out, schmuck, get out!' " For once in my life, I was stunned into silence. It was the brutal truth: I had left the Bronx, just as he had, and just as we were all brought up to, and now the Bronx was collapsing not just because of Robert Moses but also because of all of us. It was true, but did he have to laugh? I pulled back and went home as he began to explain Vietnam.

Why did the futurologist's laughter make me want to cry? He was laughing off what struck me as one of the starkest facts of modern life: that the split in the minds and the wound in the hearts of the men and women on the move—like him, like me—were just as real and just as deep as the drives and dreams that made us go. His laughter carried all the easy confidence of our official culture, the civic faith that America could overcome its inner contradictions simply by driving away from them.

As I thought this over, it made me see more clearly what my friends and I were up to when we blocked traffic throughout the decade. We were trying to open up our society's inner wounds, to show that they were still there, sealed but never healed, that they were spreading and festering, that unless they were faced fast they would get worse. We knew that the glittering lives of the people in the fast lane were just as deeply maimed as the battered and buried lives of the people in the way. We knew, because we ourselves were just learning to live in that lane, and to love the pace. But this meant that our project was shot through with paradox from the start. We were working to help other people, and other peoples—blacks, Hispanics, poor whites, Vietnamese—to fight for their homes, even as we fled our own. We, who knew so well how it felt to pull up roots, were throwing ourselves against a state and a social system that seemed to be pulling up, or blowing up, the roots of the whole world. In blocking the way, we were blocking our own way. So long as we grasped our self-divisions, they infused the New Left with a deep sense of irony, a tragic irony that haunted all our spectacular productions of political comedy and melodrama and surreal farce. Our political theater aimed to force the audience to see that they, too, were participants in a developing American tragedy: all of us, all Americans, all moderns, were plunging forward on a thrilling but disastrous course. Individually and collectively, we needed to ask who we were and what we wanted to be, and where we were racing to, and at what human cost. But there was no way to think any of this through under pressure of the traffic that was driving us all on: hence the traffic had to be brought to a halt.

So the 1960s passed, the expressway world gearing itself up for ever more gigantic expansion and growth, but finding itself attacked by a multitude of passionate shouts from the street, individual shouts that could become a collective call, erupting into the heart of the traffic, bringing the gigantic engines to a stop, or at least radically slowing them down.

3.

The 1970s: Bringing It All Back Home

I am a patriot—of the Fourteenth Ward, Brooklyn, where I was raised. The rest of the United States doesn't exist for me except as idea, or history, or literature. . . .

In my dreams I come back to the Fourteenth Ward, as a paranoiac returns to his obsessions. . . .

The plasm of the dream is the pain of separation. The dream lives on after the body is buried.

—Henry Miller, *Black Spring*

To pull yourself up by your own roots; to eat the last meal in your old neighborhood. . . .

To reread the instructions on your palm; to find there how the lifeline, broken, keeps its direction.

—Adrienne Rich, "Shooting Script"

Philosophy is really homesickness, an urge to be at home everywhere. Where, then, are we going? Always to our home.

—Novalis, *Fragments*

I HAVE depicted the conflicts of the 1960s as a struggle between opposed forms of modernism, which I described symbolically as "the expressway world" and "a shout in the street." Many of us who demonstrated in those streets allowed ourselves to hope, even as the trucks and police bore down on us, that out of all these struggles a new synthesis might someday be born, a new mode of modernity through which we all could harmoniously move, in which we all could feel at home. That hope was one of the vital signs of the '60s. It did not last long. Even before the decade ended, it was clear that no dialectical synthesis was in the works, and that we should have to put all such hopes on "Hold," a long hold, if we were going to get through the years ahead.

It was not just that the New Left fell apart: that we lost our knack for being simultaneously on the road and in the way, and so, like all the brave modernisms of the 1960s, broke down. The trouble went deeper than that: it soon became clear that the expressway world, on whose initiative and dynamism we had always counted, was itself beginning to break down. The great economic boom that had gone on beyond all expectations, for a quarter of a century after the Second World War, was coming to a close. The combination of inflation and technological stagnation (for which the still-unending Vietnam war was largely to blame), plus a developing world energy crisis (which we could ascribe in part to our spectacular success), was bound to take its toll—though no one could tell in the early 1970s how high that toll would be.

The end of the boom did not endanger everyone—the very rich were pretty well insulated, as they usually are—but everyone's vision of the modern world and its possibilities has come to be reshaped. Horizons for expansion and growth abruptly shrank: after decades of being flooded with energy cheap enough and abundant enough to create and recreate the world endlessly anew, modern societies would now have to learn fast how to use their diminishing energies to protect the shrinking resources they had and keep their whole world from running down. During the prosperous decade after the First World War, the reigning symbol of modernity was the green light; during the spectacular boom that followed the Second World War, the central symbol was the federal highway system, in which the driver could go from coast to coast without encountering any traffic lights at all. But the modern societies of the 1970s were forced to live in the shadow of the speed limit and the stop sign. In these years of reduced mobility, modern men and women everywhere had to think deeply about how far and in what directions they wanted to go, and to search for new media in which they could move. It is out of this process of thought and searching—a process that has only just begun— that the modernisms of the 1970s have come.

To show how things have changed, I want briefly to go back to the extensive debate over the meaning of modernity in the 1960s. One of the last interesting entries in this debate, and perhaps a kind of memorial to it, was entitled "Literary History and Literary Modernity," by the literary critic Paul De Man. For De Man, writing in 1969, "the full power of the idea of modernity" lay in a "desire to wipe out whatever came earlier," so as to achieve "a radically new departure, a point that could be a true present." De Man used as a touchstone of modernity the Nietzschean idea (developed in *The Use and Abuse of History*, 1873) that one needs to willfully forget the past in order to achieve or create anything in the present. "Nietzsche's ruthless forgetting, the blindness with which he throws himself into action lightened of all previous experience, captures the authentic spirit of modernity." In this perspective, "modernity and history are diametrically opposed to one another."[16] De Man gave no contemporary examples, but his scheme could easily embrace all sorts of modernists working in the 1960s in a great variety of media and genres.

There was Robert Moses, of course, hacking his expressway world through the cities, obliterating every trace of the life that was there before; Robert McNamara, paving over the jungles of Vietnam for instant cities and airports, and bringing millions of villagers into the modern world (Samuel Huntington's strategy of "forced modernization") by bombing their traditional world into rubble; Mies van der Rohe, whose modular glass boxes, identical everywhere, were coming to dominate every metropolis, equally oblivious to every environment, like the giant slab that springs up in the midst of the primitive world in Stanley Kubrick's *2001*. But we must not forget the apocalyptic wing of the New Left in its terminal delirium *circa* 1969–70, glorying in visions of barbarian hordes destroying Rome, writing "Tear Down the Walls" on all the walls, and going to the people with the slogan "Fight the People."

Of course, this was not the whole story. I argued above that some of the most creative modernism of the 1960s consisted of "shouts in the street," visions of worlds and values that the triumphant march of modernization was trampling down or leaving behind. Nevertheless, those artists, thinkers and activists who challenged the expressway world took for granted its inexhaustible energy and inexorable momentum. They saw their works and actions as antitheses, locked in a dialectical duel with a thesis that was striving to silence all the shouts and wipe all the streets off the modern map. This struggle of radically opposed modernisms gave the life of the 1960s much of its coherence and excitement.

What happened in the 1970s was that, as the gigantic motors of economic growth and expansion stalled, and the traffic came close to a stop, modern societies abruptly lost their power to blow away their past. All through the 1960s, the question had been whether they should or shouldn't; now, in the 1970s, the answer was that they simply couldn't. Modernity could no longer afford to throw itself into "action lightened of all previous experience" (as De Man put it), to "wipe away whatever came earlier in the hope of reaching at last a true present . . . a new departure." The moderns of the 1970s couldn't afford to annihilate the past and present in order to create a new world *ex nihilo;* they had to learn to come to terms with the world they had, and work from there.

Many modernisms of the past have found themselves by forgetting; the modernists of the 1970s were forced to find themselves by remembering. Earlier modernists have wiped away the past in order to reach a new departure; the new departures of the 1970s lay in attempts to recover past modes of life that were buried but not dead. This project in itself was not new; but it took on a new urgency in a decade when the dynamism of the modern economy and technology seemed to collapse. At a moment when modern society seemed to lose the capacity to create a brave new future, modernism was under intense pressure to discover new sources of life through imaginative encounters with the past.

In this final section, I will try to characterize several of these imaginative encounters, in various media and genres. Once again, I will organize my discussion around symbols: the symbol of home, and the symbol of ghosts. The modernists of the 1970s tended to be obsessed with the homes, the families and neighborhoods they left in order to be modern in the modes of the 1950s and '60s. Hence I have entitled this section "Bringing It All Back Home."*

---

* I have borrowed this title from a work of the 1960s, Bob Dylan's album *Bringing It All Back Home*, Columbia Records, 1965. This brilliant album, perhaps Dylan's best, is full of the surreal radicalism of the late '60s. At the same time, its title and the titles of some of its songs—"Subterranean Homesick Blues," "It's Alright, Ma, I'm Only Bleeding"—express an intense bond with the past, parents, home, that was almost entirely missing in the culture of the 1960s, but centrally present a decade later. This album may be re-experienced today as a dialogue between the '60s and the '70s. Those of us who grew up on Dylan's songs can only hope that he might learn as much from his 1960s work as we have learned from it.

The homes toward which today's modernists orient themselves are far more personal and private spaces than the expressway or the street. Moreover, the look toward home is a look "back," backward in time—once again radically different from the forward movement of the modernists of the highway, or the free movement in all directions of the modernists of the street—back into our own childhood, back into our society's historical past. At the same time, modernists do not try to blend or merge themselves with their past —this distinguishes modernism from sentimentalism—but rather to "bring it all back" into the past, that is, to bring to bear on their past the selves they have become in the present, to bring into those old homes visions and values that may clash radically with them— and maybe to re-enact the very tragic struggles that drove them from their homes in the first place. In other words, modernism's rapport with the past, whatever it turns out to be, will not be easy. My second symbol is implicit in the title of this book: *All That Is Solid Melts into Air.* This means that our past, whatever it was, was a past in the process of disintegration; we yearn to grasp it, but it is baseless and elusive; we look back for something solid to lean on, only to find ourselves embracing ghosts. The modernism of the 1970s was a modernism with ghosts.

One of the central themes in the culture of the 1970s was the rehabilitation of ethnic memory and history as a vital part of personal identity. This has been a striking development in the history of modernity. Modernists today no longer insist, as the modernists of yesterday so often did, that we must cease to be Jewish, or black, or Italian, or anything, in order to be modern. If whole societies can be said to learn anything, the modern societies of the 1970s seemed to have learned that ethnic identity—not only one's own but everyone's—was essential to the depth and fullness of self that modern life opens up and promises to all. This awareness brought to Alex Haley's *Roots* and, a year later, Gerald Green's *Holocaust* audiences that were not only immense—the largest in the history of television—but actively involved and genuinely moved. The responses to *Roots* and *Holocaust,* not only in America but around the world, suggested that, whatever qualities contemporary mankind may lack, our capacity for empathy was great. Unfortunately, presentations like *Roots* and *Holocaust* lack the depth to transform empathy into real understanding. Both works present extravagantly idealized versions of the familial and ethnic past, in which all ancestors are beautiful, noble and heroic, and all pain and hate and trouble spring from groups of oppressors "outside." This contributes less to a modern ethnic awareness than to the traditional genre of family romance.

But the real thing could also be found in the 1970s. The single most impressive exploration of ethnic memory in this period, I believe, was Maxine Hong Kingston's *Woman Warrior*. For Kingston, the essential image of the familial and ethnic past is not roots but ghosts: her book is subtitled "Memoirs of a Girlhood Among Ghosts."[17] Kingston's imagination is saturated with Chinese history and folklore, mythology and superstition. She conveys a vivid sense of the beauty and wholeness of Chinese village life—her parents' life—before the Revolution. At the same time, she makes us feel the horrors of that life: the book begins with the lynching of her pregnant aunt, and proceeds through a nightmarish series of socially enforced cruelties, abandonments, betrayals and murders. She feels haunted by the ghosts of victims past, whose burdens she takes on herself by writing of that past; she shares her parents' myth of America as a country of ghosts, multitudes of white shadows at once unreal and magically powerful; she fears her parents themselves as ghosts—after thirty years, she is still not sure that she knows these immigrants' real names, and hence remains uncertain of her own—haunted by ancestral nightmares that it will take her whole life to wake up from; she sees herself metamorphosing into a ghost, losing her embodied actuality even as she learns to walk tall in the ghost world, "to do ghost things even better than ghosts can"—to write books like this.

Kingston has the ability to create individual scenes—whether actual or mythical, past or present, imagined or directly experienced—with a remarkable directness and luminous clarity. But the relationship between the different dimensions of her being is never integrated or worked out; as we lurch from one plane to another, we feel that the work of life and art is still in process, that she is still working it through, shuffling her vast cast of ghosts around in the hope of finding some meaningful order in which she can stand firmly at last. Her personal, sexual and ethnic identities remain elusive to the end—in just the way that modernists have always shown that modern identity is bound to be elusive—but she shows great courage and imagination in looking her ghosts in the face and fighting to find their proper names. She remains split or diffused in a dozen directions, like a cubist mask, or Picasso's *Girl Before a Mirror;* but, in their tradition, she transforms disintegration into a new form of order that is integral to modern art.

An equally powerful confrontation with home, and with ghosts, took place in the Performance Group's trilogy, *Three Places in Rhode Island,* developed between 1975 and 1978. These three plays are organized around the life of one member of the company, Spalding Gray; they dramatize his development as a person, a character, an actor, an artist. The trilogy is a kind of *Recherche du Temps Perdu* in the tradition of Proust and Freud. The second and most powerful play, *Rumstick Road,*[18] first performed in 1977, focuses on the malaise and gradual disintegration of Gray's mother, Elizabeth, culminating in her suicide in 1967; the play enacts Gray's attempts to understand his mother, his family, and himself as a child and as an adult, to live with what he knows and with what he will never know.

This anguished quest has two outstanding precursors, Allen Ginsberg's long poem "Kaddish" (1959) and Peter Handke's novella *A Sorrow Beyond Dreams* (1972). What makes *Rumstick Road* especially striking, and gives it the distinctive stamp of the 1970s, is the way it uses the ensemble acting techniques and multimedia art forms of the 1960s to open up new depths of personal inner space. *Rumstick Road* incorporates and integrates live and recorded music, dance, slide projection, photography, abstract movement, complex lighting (including strobes), videotaped sights and sounds, to evoke different but intersecting modes of consciousness and being. The action consists of direct addresses by Gray to the audience; dramatizations of his reveries and dreams (in which he sometimes plays one of the phantoms that haunt him); taped interviews with his father, his grandmothers, with old friends and neighbors from Rhode Island, with his mother's psychiatrist (in which he mimes his words as they come over the tape); a slide show depicting the family and its life over the years (Gray is both a character in the pictures and a sort of *Our Town* narrator and commentator); some of the music that meant most to Elizabeth Gray, accompanied by dance and narration.

All this goes on in an extraordinary environment. The stage is divided into three equal compartments; at any given moment action will be going on simultaneously in two, and sometimes in all.

At the center, brought forward, is an audiovisual control booth inhabited by a shadowy technical director; directly beneath the booth is a bench that sometimes functions as a psychiatrist's couch, where Gray alternately plays a therapist (or "examiner") and various patients. On the audience's left, recessed in depth to form a room, is an enlargement of the Gray family house on Rumstick Road, where many scenes take place; sometimes the wall becomes blank, and the room appears to be an inner chamber of Gray's mind in which various ominous scenes are played out; but even when the house's image is absent, its aura lingers on. On the audience's right is another deep room with a large picture window, representing Gray's own room in the old house. Dominating this room for most of the play is a huge red-domed inflatable tent, lit from inside, magically and menacingly suggestive (a whale's belly? a mother's womb? a brain?); much action goes on, in or around this tent, which looms forth as a spectral character in its own right. Late in the play, after Gray and his father have finally talked about his mother and her suicide, the two of them together lift the tent through the window and out of the room: it is still visible, and weirdly luminous, like the moon, but it is at a distance now, and in perspective.

Rumstick Road suggests that this is the kind of liberation and reconciliation that is possible for human beings in the world. For Gray, and for us insofar as we can identify ourselves with him, the liberation is never total; but it is real, and earned: he has not merely looked into the abyss but gone into it and brought its depths up into the light for us all. Gray's fellow actors have helped him: their intimacy and mutuality, developed through years of work as a close ensemble, are absolutely vital in his labor of discovering and facing and being himself. Their collective production dramatizes the ways in which theatrical collectives have evolved over the past decade. In the intensely political ambience of the 1960s, when ensemble groups like the Living Theater, the Open Theater and the San Francisco Mime Troupe were among the most exciting things in American theater, their collective works and lives were presented as ways out of the trap of privacy and bourgeois individuality, as models of the communist society of the future. In the relatively apolitical 1970s, they evolved from communist sects into something like therapeutic communities whose collective strength could enable each member to grasp and embrace the depths of his or her individual life. Works like *Rumstick Road* show the creative directions in which this evolution can go.

One of the central themes in the modernism of the 1970s was the ecological idea of recycling: finding new meanings and potentialities in old things and forms of life. Some of the most creative recycling of the 1970s, all over America, went on in the sort of dilapidated neighborhoods that Jane Jacobs celebrated in the early 1960s. The difference a decade makes is that the initiatives that seemed like a delightful alternative in the boom times of 1960 have come to be felt as a desperate imperative today. Our largest and perhaps our most dramatic urban recycling has gone on precisely where Spalding Gray's life cycle was first publicly performed: the lower Manhattan neighborhood now known as SoHo. This district of nineteenth-century workshops, warehouses and small factories between Houston and Canal streets was literally anonymous; it had no name until about a decade ago. After World War Two, with the development of the expressway world, this district was widely written off as obsolete, and the planners of the 1950s slated it for destruction.

It was scheduled to be razed for one of Robert Moses' most cherished projects, the Lower Manhattan Expressway. This road would have slashed clean across Manhattan Island, from the East River to the Hudson, and torn down or sealed off large parts of the South and West Village, Little Italy, Chinatown, and the Lower East Side. As plans for the expressway gathered momentum, many industrial tenants left the area, anticipating its destruction. But then, in the early and mid-1960s, a remarkable coalition of diverse and generally antagonistic groups—young and old, radical and reactionary, Jews, Italians, WASPs, Puerto Ricans and Chinese—fought fervidly for years and finally, to their amazement, won and wiped Moses' project off the map.

This epic triumph over Moloch left a sudden abundance of prime loft space available at unusually low rents, which turned out to be ideal for New York's rapidly growing artist population. In the late 1960s and early 1970s, thousands of artists moved in and, within a few years, turned this anonymous space into the world's leading center for the production of art. This amazing transformation infused SoHo's dreary and crumbling streets with a unique vitality and intensity.

Much of the neighborhood's aura arises from its interplay between its nineteenth-century-modern streets and buildings and the late-twentieth-century-modern art that is created and displayed inside them. Another way to see it might be as a dialectic of the neighborhood's old and new modes of production: factories that produce cord and rope and cardboard boxes and small engine and machine parts, that collect and process used paper and rags and scrap, and modes of art that collect and compress and connect and recycle these materials in very special ways of their own.

SoHo has also emerged as an arena for the liberation of women artists, who have burst on the scene with unprecedented numbers, talent and self-confidence, and fought to establish their identity in a neighborhood that was fighting to establish its own. Their individual and collective presence is at the heart of SoHo's aura. Early one fall evening, I saw a lovely young woman in a glamorous red-wine-colored suit, clearly returning from "Uptown" (a show? a grant? a job?) and climbing the long flights of stairs to her loft. In one arm she supported a big bag of groceries, with protruding French bread, while on the other, balanced delicately on her shoulder, was a great bundle of stretchers five feet long: a perfect expression, it seemed to me, of the modern sexuality and spirituality of our time. But just around the corner, alas, has lurked another archetypally modern figure, the real estate man, whose frantic speculations in the 1970s have made many fortunes in SoHo, and driven from their homes many artists who could not hope to afford the prices that their presence helped to create. Here, as in so many modern scenes, the ambiguities of development roll on.

Just below Canal Street, SoHo's downtown boundary, the walker heading north or south, or coming up out of the IRT subway at Franklin Street, may be startled to glimpse what first appears to be a ghost building. It is a large vertical three-dimensional mass, shaped vaguely like the skyscrapers around it; only, as we approach, we find that as we switch angles it seems to move. At one moment it seems to be tilting over like the Leaning Tower of Pisa; move over to the left, and it seems to be pitching forward almost on top of us; swing around a little more, and it is gliding ahead like a ship sailing into Canal Street. It is Richard Serra's new cor-ten steel sculpture, named *TWU* in honor of the Transit Workers' Union, which was on strike when the work was installed in the spring of 1980. It consists of three immense steel rectangles, each about ten feet across and about thirty-five feet high, aligned like a jagged "H." It is as solid as sculpture can get, yet ghostly in several ways: its capacity to change shapes, depending on our point of view; its metamorphoses of color, luminous bronze gold at one angle or moment, turning into an ominous leaden gray a brief moment or movement away; its evocation of the steel skeletons of all the skyscrapers around it, of the dramatic skyward thrust that modern architecture and engineering made possible, of the expressive promise that all these buildings once made during their brief skeletal phase, but that most of them blatantly betrayed once they were complete. Once we can touch the sculpture, we nestle into the corners of its H-form and feel ourselves inside a city within a city, perceiving the urban space around and above us with a special clarity and vividness, yet protected from the city's shocks by the piece's mass and strength.

TWU is sunken into a small triangular plaza on which there is nothing else—except for a little tree, apparently planted when the sculpture was installed, and oriented to it, frail in its branches yet lush in its leaves, and bearing a single large, lovely white flower at the summer's end. This work is located a little off the beaten path, but its presence has begun to create a new path, drawing people magnetically into its orbit. Once there, they look, touch, lean, nestle, sit. Sometimes they insist on participating more actively in the work, and inscribe their names or beliefs on its sides—"NO FUTURE" was recently inscribed in letters three feet high; in addition, the lower facades have turned into something of a kiosk, decked with innumerable pleasant and unpleasant signs of the times.

Some people are angry at what seems to them the desecration of a work of fine art. It seems to me, however, that all that the city has added to *TWU* has brought out its special depths, which would never have emerged if it had lain untouched. The accumulated layers of signs, periodically torn or burned off (whether by the city, by Serra himself, or by solicitous spectators, I cannot tell) but perpetually renewed, have created a new configuration, whose contours suggest a jagged urban skyline six or seven feet high, far darker and denser than the vast field above. The density and intensity of the lower level (the part that people can reach) has transformed this section into a parable of the building-up of the modern city itself. People are constantly reaching higher, striving to make their marks—do they stand on each other's shoulders?—and there are even, twelve or fifteen feet high, a couple of gobs of red and yellow paint, flung dramatically from somewhere below —are they parodies of "action painting"?

But none of these efforts can be more than glimmers in Serra's great bronze sky soaring above us all, a sky made more glorious than ever in opposition to the darker world we construct below. *TWU* generates a dialogue between nature and culture, between the city's past and present—and its future, the buildings still in girder form, still infinite in potential—between the artist and his audience, between all of us and the urban environment that ties all our lifelines together. This process of dialogue is what the modernism of the 1970s at its best was about.

Having come this far, I want to use this modernism to generate a dialogue with my own past, my own lost home, my own ghosts. I want to go back to where this essay started, to my Bronx, vital and thriving only yesterday, ruins and ashen wilderness today. Can modernism make these bones live? In a literal sense, obviously not: only massive federal investment, along with active and energetic popular participation, can really bring the Bronx back to life. But modernist vision and imagination can give our maimed inner cities something to live for, can help or force our non-urban majority to see their stake in the city's fate, can bring forth its abundance of life and beauty that are buried but not dead.

As I confront the Bronx, I want to use and fuse two distinct media which flourished in the 1970s, one only recently invented, the other quite old but lately elaborated and developed. The first medium is called "earthworks" or "earth art." It goes back to about the beginning of the 1970s, and its most creative spirit was Robert Smithson, who was killed tragically at the age of thirty-five in a plane crash in 1973. Smithson was obsessed with man-made ruins: slag heaps, junkyards, abandoned strip mines, exhausted quarries, polluted pools and streams, the junk heap that occupied the site of Central Park before Olmsted arrived. Throughout the early 1970s, Smithson traveled up and down the country trying in vain to interest corporate and government bureaucrats in the idea that

> One practical solution for the utilization of devastated areas would be land and water re-cycling in terms of "earth art." . . .
> Art can become a resource that mediates between the ecologist

and the industrialist. Ecology and industry aren't one-way streets. Rather, they should be crossroads. Art can help to provide the needed dialectic between them.[19]

Smithson was forced to travel great distances into America's Midwestern and Southwestern wilderness; he didn't live to see an immense wasteland open up in the Bronx, an ideal canvas for his art, virtually at his front door. But his thought is full of clues as to how we might proceed there. It is essential, he would surely say, to accept the process of disintegration as a framework for new kinds of integration, to use the rubble as a medium in which to construct new forms and make new affirmations; without such a framework and such a medium, no real growth can take place.* The second medium I want to use is the historical mural. Murals thrived in the WPA period, when they were commissioned to dramatize political and generally radical ideas. They came back strong in the 1970s, often financed by federal CETA money. In accord with the general spirit of the 1970s, recent murals emphasized local and communal history rather than world ideology. Moreover—and this appears to be a 1970s innovation—these murals were often executed by members of the community whose history they evoke, so that people can be at once the subjects, objects and audience of art, uniting theory and practice in the best modernist tradition. The most ambitious and interesting community mural of the '70s seems to be Judith Baca's emerging Great Wall of Los Angeles. Earthworks and community murals provide the media for my Bronx modernist dream: The Bronx Mural.

The Bronx Mural, as I imagine it, would be painted onto the brick and concrete retaining walls that run alongside most of the eight miles of the Cross-Bronx Expressway, so that every automobile trip through and out of the Bronx would become a trip into its buried depths. In the places where the road runs close to or above ground level, and the walls recede, the driver's view of the Bronx's past life would alternate with sweeping vistas of its present

---

* Finally, at the end of the 1970s, some local authorities and art commissions began to respond, and some impressive works of earth art have begun to get built. This emerging great opportunity also presents great problems, puts artists in conflict with environmentalists, and leaves them open to a charge of creating a merely cosmetic beauty that disguises corporate and political rapacity and brutality. For a lucid account of the ways in which earth artists have posed and responded to these issues, see Kay Larson, "It's the Pits," *Village Voice*, 2 September 1980.

ruin. The mural might depict cross-sections of streets, of houses, even of rooms full of people just as they were before the Expressway cut through them all.

But it would go back before this, to our century's early years, at the height of the Jewish and Italian immigration, with the Bronx growing along the rapidly expanding subway lines, and (in the words of the *Communist Manifesto*) whole populations conjured out of the ground: to tens of thousands of garment workers, printers, butchers, house painters, furriers, union militants, socialists, anarchists, communists. Here is D. W. Griffith, whose old Biograph Studio building still stands, solid but battered and neglected, at the Expressway's edge; here is Sholem Aleichem, seeing the New World and saying that it was good, and dying on Kelly Street (the block where Bella Abzug was born); and there is Trotsky on East 164th Street, waiting for his revolution (did he really play a Russian in obscure silent films? we will never know). Now we see a modest but energetic and confident bourgeoisie, springing up in the 1920s near the new Yankee Stadium, promenading on the Grand Concourse for a brief moment in the sun, finding romance in the swan boats in Crotona Park; and not far away, "the coops," a great network of workers' housing settlements, cooperatively building a new world beside Bronx and Van Cortlandt parks. We move on to the bleak adversity of the 1930s, unemployment lines, home relief, the WPA (whose splendid monument, the Bronx County Courthouse, stands just above the Yankee Stadium), radical passions and energies exploding, street-corner fights between Trotskyites and Stalinists, candy stores and cafeterias ablaze with talk all through the night; then to the excitement and anxiety of the postwar years, new affluence, neighborhoods more vibrant than ever, even as new worlds beyond the neighborhoods begin to open up, people buy cars, start to move; to the Bronx's new immigrants from Puerto Rico, South Carolina, Trinidad, new shades of skin and clothes on the street, new music and rhythms, new tensions and intensities; and finally, to Robert Moses and his dread road, smashing through the Bronx's inner life, transforming evolution into devolution, entropy into catastrophe, and creating the ruin on which this work of art is built.

The mural would have to be executed in a number of radically different styles, so as to express the amazing variety of imaginative visions that sprang from these apparently uniform streets, apartment houses, schoolyards, kosher butcher shops, appetizing and candy stores. Barnett Newman, Stanley Kubrick, Clifford Odets, Larry Rivers, George Segal, Jerome Weidman, Rosalyn Drexler, E. L. Doctorow, Grace Paley, Irving Howe, would all be there; along with George Meany, Herman Badillo, Bella Abzug and Stokely Carmichael; John Garfield, Tony Curtis' Sidney Falco, Gertrude Berg's Molly Goldberg, Bess Myerson (an iconic monument to assimilation, the Bronx's Miss America, 1945), and Anne Bancroft; Hank Greenberg, Jake La Motta, Jack Molinas (was he the Bronx's greatest athlete, its most vicious crook, or both?); Nate Archibald; A. M. Rosenthal of the *New York Times* and his sister, the communist leader Ruth Witt; Phil Spector, Bill Graham, Dion and the Belmonts, the Rascals, Laura Nyro, Larry Harlow, the brothers Palmieri; Jules Feiffer and Lou Meyers; Paddy Chayevsky and Neil Simon; Ralph Lauren and Calvin Klein, Garry Winogrand, George and Mike Kuchar; Jonas Salk, George Wald, Seymour Melman, Herman Kahn—all these, and so many more.

Children of the Bronx would be encouraged to return and put themselves in the picture: the Expressway wall is big enough to hold them all; as it got increasingly crowded, it would approach the density of the Bronx at its peak. To drive past and through all this would be a rich and strange experience. Drivers might feel captivated by the figures, environments and fantasies on the mural, ghosts of their parents, their friends, even of themselves, like sirens enticing them to plunge into the abyss of the past. On the other hand, so many of these ghosts would be urging and driving them on, dying to leap into a future beyond the Bronx's walls and join the stream of traffic on the way out. The Bronx Mural would end at the end of the Expressway itself, where it interchanges on the way to Westchester and Long Island. The end, the boundary between the Bronx and the world, would be marked with a gigantic ceremonial arch, in the tradition of the colossal monuments that Claes Oldenburg conceived in the 1960s. This arch would be circular and inflatable, suggesting both an automobile tire and a bagel. When fully pumped up, it would look indigestibly hard as a bagel, but ideal as a tire for a fast getaway; when soft, it would appear leaky and dangerous as a tire but, as a bagel, inviting to settle down and eat.

I have portrayed the Bronx of today as a scene of disaster and despair. All that is certainly there, but there is much more. Get off the Expressway, and go south a mile or so, or half a mile north toward the Zoo; drive in and out through streets whose names are posted at the soul's intersections—Fox, Kelly, Longwood, Honeywell, Southern Boulevard—and you will find blocks that feel so much like blocks you left long ago, blocks you thought had vanished forever, that you will wonder if you are seeing ghosts— or if you yourself are a ghost haunting these solid streets with the phantoms of your inner city. The faces and signs are Spanish, but the vibrancy and friendliness—the old men in the sun, women with shopping bags, kids playing ball in the street—feel so close to home that it is easy to feel as if you had never left home at all.

Many of these blocks are so comfortably ordinary that we can almost feel ourselves blending in, nearly lulled to sleep—till we turn a corner and the full nightmare of devastation—a block of black burnt-out hulks, a street of rubble and glass where no man goes—surges up in front of us and jars us awake. Then we may begin to understand what we saw on the street before. It has taken the most extraordinary labors to rescue these ordinary streets from death, to begin everyday life here again from the ground up. This collective work springs from a fusion of the government's money with the people's labor—"sweat equity," it is called—and spirit.[20] It is a risky and precarious enterprise—we can feel the risks when we see the horror just around the corner—and it takes a Faustian vision, energy and courage to carry through. These are the people of Faust's new town, who know that they must win their life and freedom every day anew.

Modern art is active in this work of renewal. Among the pleasant resurrected streets we find an enormous steel sculpture towering several stories into the sky. It suggests the forms of two palm trees leaning expressionistically against each other and forming a gateway arch. This is Rafael Ferrer's "Puerto Rican Sun," the newest tree in New York's forest of symbols. The arch leads us to a network of garden plots, the Fox Street Community Garden. This piece is at once imposing and playful; standing back, we can admire its Calderesque fusion of massive forms and sensuous curves. But Ferrer's work gains special resonance and depth from its relationship to its site. In this mostly Puerto Rican and overwhelmingly Caribbean neighborhood, it evokes a tropical paradise lost. Fabricated of industrial materials, it suggests that the joy and sensuality that are available here in America, in the Bronx, must come

—and indeed, are coming—through industrial and social reconstruction. Manufactured in black, but painted over in broad, vivid abstract-expressionist slashes and flecks—hot red, yellow and green on one side, facing west, and pink, sky-blue and white on the sunrise side—it symbolizes the ways, different but perhaps equally valid ways, in which the people of the South Bronx, working within their new forms, can bring the world to life. These people, unlike the downtown audience for Serra's *TWU,* have left Ferrer's gateway undisturbed by graffiti; but it appears to be a popular object of proud contemplation on the street. It may be helping people who are going through a crucial, excruciating passage in their history—and in ours—get a grip on where they are going and who they are. I hope it is helping them; I know it is helping me. And it seems to me that this is what modernism is all about.[21]

I could go on talking about more exciting modernist works of the past decade. Instead, I thought to end up with the Bronx, with an encounter with some ghosts of my own. As I come to the end of this book, I see how this project, which consumed so much of my time, blends into the modernism of my times. I have been digging up some of the buried modern spirits of the past, trying to open up a dialectic between their experience and our own, hoping to help the people of my time create a modernity of the future that will be fuller and freer than the modern lives we have known till now.

Should works so obsessed with the past be called modernist at all? For many thinkers, the whole point of modernism is to clear the decks of all these entanglements so that the self and the world can be created anew. Others believe that the really distinctive forms of contemporary art and thought have made a quantum leap beyond all the diverse sensibilities of modernism, and earned the right to call themselves "post-modern." I want to respond to these antithetical but complementary claims by reviewing the vision of modernity with which this book began. To be modern, I said, is to experience personal and social life as a maelstrom, to find one's world and oneself in perpetual disintegration and renewal, trouble and anguish, ambiguity and contradiction: to be part of a universe in which all that is solid melts into air. To be a modern*ist* is to make oneself somehow at home in the maelstrom, to make its rhythms one's own, to move within its currents in search of the forms of reality, of beauty, of freedom, of justice, that its fervid and perilous flow allows.

The modern world has changed radically in many ways over the past two hundred years; but the situation of the modernist, trying to survive and create in the maelstrom's midst, has remained substantially the same. This situation has generated a language and culture of dialogue, bringing together modernists of the past, the present and the future, enabling modernist culture to live and thrive even in the most dreadful of times. All through this book, I have tried not only to describe modernism's life of dialogue but to carry it on. But the primacy of dialogue in the ongoing life of modernism means that modernists can never be done with the past: they must go on forever haunted by it, digging up its ghosts, recreating it even as they remake their world and themselves.

If modernism ever managed to throw off its scraps and tatters and the uneasy joints that bind it to the past, it would lose all its weight and depth, and the maelstrom of modern life would carry it helplessly away. It is only by keeping alive the bonds that tie it to the modernities of the past—bonds at once intimate and antagonistic—that it can help the moderns of the present and the future to be free.

This understanding of modernism should help us clarify some of the ironies of the contemporary "post-modern" mystique.[22] I have argued that the modernism of the 1970s was distinguished by its desire and power to remember, to remember so much of what modern societies—regardless of what their ideologies and who their ruling classes are—want to forget. But when contemporary modernists lose touch with and deny their own modernity, they only echo the ruling class self-delusion that it has conquered the troubles and perils of the past, and meanwhile they cut themselves off, and cut us off, from a primary source of their own strength.

There is another disturbing question that needs to be asked about the modernisms of the 1970s: Taken together, do they add up to anything? I have been showing how a number of individuals and small groups have confronted their own ghosts, and how, out of these inner struggles, they created meaning, dignity and beauty for themselves. All well and good; but can these personal, familial, local and ethnic explorations generate any sort of larger vision or collective hope for us all? I have tried to describe some of the diverse initiatives of the past decade in a way that would bring out their common core and would help some of our multitude of isolated people and groups realize that they have more kindred spirits than they think. But whether they will in fact affirm these human bonds, and whether their affirmation will lead to any sort of communal or collective action, I cannot pretend to know. Maybe the moderns of the 1970s will rest content in the artificial inner light of their inflated domes. Or maybe, someday soon, they will lift the domes through their picture windows, open their windows to one another, and work to create a politics of authenticity that will embrace us all. If and when this should happen, it will mark the point when the modernism of the 1980s will be under way.

Twenty years ago, at the end of another unpolitical decade, Paul Goodman heralded a great wave of radicals and radical initiatives that were just coming to life. What was the relationship of this emerging radicalism, including his own, to modernity? Goodman argued that if young people today found themselves "growing up absurd," with no honorable or even meaningful life to grow into, the source of the trouble "is not the spirit of modern society"; rather, he said, "it is that this spirit has not sufficiently realized itself."[23] The agenda of modern possibilities that Goodman brought together under the title of "The Missed Revolutions" is as open and as pressing as ever today. In my presentation of modernities of yesterday and today, I have tried to point out some of the ways in which the modern spirit may go on to realize itself tomorrow.

What about the day after tomorrow? Ihab Hassan, ideologue of post-modernism, laments modernity's stubborn refusal to fade out: "When will the Modern Period end? Has a period ever waited so long? Renaissance? Baroque? Classical? Romantic? Victorian? Perhaps only the Dark Middle Ages. When will Modernism cease and what comes thereafter?"[24] If the overall argument of this book is right, then those who are waiting for the end of the modern age can be assured of steady work. The modern economy is likely to go on growing, though probably in new directions, adapting itself to the chronic energy and environmental crises that its success has created. Future adaptations will require great social and political turmoil; but modernization has always thrived on trouble, on an atmosphere of "everlasting uncertainty and agitation" in which, as

the *Communist Manifesto* says, "all fixed, fast-frozen relations . .
are swept away." In such an ambience, the culture of modernism
will go on developing new visions and expressions of life: for the
same economic and social drives that endlessly transform the
world around us, both for good and for evil, also transform
the inner lives of the men and women who fill this world and make
it go. The process of modernization, even as it exploits and torments us, brings our energies and imaginations to life, drives us to
grasp and confront the world that modernization makes, and to
strive to make it our own. I believe that we and those who come
after us will go on fighting to make ourselves at home in this world,
even as the homes we have made, the modern street, the modern
spirit, go on melting into air.

Notes

INTRODUCTION: MODERNITY—YESTERDAY, TODAY AND TOMORROW

1. *Emile, ou De l'Education*, 1762, in the Bibliothèque de la Pléiade edition of Rousseau's *Oeuvres Complètes* (Paris: Gallimard, 1959ff.), Volume IV. For Rousseau's image of *le tourbillon social*, and how to survive in it, Book IV, page 551. On the volatile character of European society, and the revolutionary upheavals to come, *Emile*, I, 252; III, 468; IV, 507–08.

2. *Julie, ou la Nouvelle Héloïse*, 1761, Part II, Letters 14 and 17. In *Oeuvres Complètes*, Volume II, 231–36, 255–56. I have discussed these Rousseauan scenes and themes from a slightly different perspective in *The Politics of Authenticity* (Atheneum, 1970), especially 113–19, 163–77.

3. "Speech at the Anniversary of the *People's Paper*," in Robert C. Tucker, editor, *The Marx-Engels Reader*, 2nd edition (Norton, 1978), 577–78. This volume will be cited hereafter as *MER*.

4. *MER*, 475–76. I have slightly altered the standard translation, which was made by Samuel Moore in 1888.

5. The passages quoted are from Sections 262, 223 and 224. Translations are by Marianne Cowan (1955; Gateway, 1967), pages 210–11, 146–50.

6. "Manifesto of the Futurist Painters, 1910," by Umberto Boccioni et al. Translated by Robert Brain, in Umbro Apollonio, editor, *Futurist Manifestos* (Viking, 1973), 25.

7. F. T. Marinetti, "The Founding and Manifesto of Futurism, 1909," translated by R. W. Flint, in *Futurist Manifestos*, 22.

8. Marinetti, "Multiplied Man and the Reign of the Machine," from *War, the World's Only Hygiene*, 1911–15, in R. W. Flint, editor and translator, *Marinetti: Selected Writings* (Farrar, Straus and Giroux, 1972), 90–91. For a spirited (if partisan) treatment of futurism in the context of the evolution of modernity, see Reyner Banham, *Theory and Design in the First Machine Age* (Praeger, 1967), 99–137.

9. *Understanding Media: The Extensions of Man* (McGraw-Hill paperback, 1965), 80.

10. "The Modernization of Man," in Myron Weiner, editor, *Modernization: The Dynamics of Growth* (Basic Books, 1966), 149. This collection gives a good picture of the mainstream American paradigm of modernization in its heyday.

Seminal works in this tradition include Daniel Lerner, *The Passing of Traditional Society* (Free Press, 1958) and W. W. Rostow, *The Stages of Economic Growth: A Non-Communist Manifesto* (Cambridge, 1960). For an early radical critique of this literature, see Michael Walzer, "The Only Revolution: Notes on the Theory of Modernization," in *Dissent*, 11 (1964), 132–40. But this body of theory also evoked much criticism and controversy within the mainstream of Western social science. The issues are incisively summarized in S. N. Eisenstadt, *Tradition, Change and Modernity* (Wiley, 1973). It is worth noting that when Inkeles' work eventually appeared in book form, as Alex Inkeles and David Smith, *Becoming Modern: Individual Change in Six Developing Countries* (Harvard, 1974), the Panglossian image of modern life had given way to far more complex perspectives.

11. *The Protestant Ethic and the Spirit of Capitalism*, translated by Talcott Parsons (Scribner, 1930), 181–83. I have slightly altered the translation, in accord with Peter Gay's far more vivid version, in Columbia College, *Man in Contemporary Society* (Columbia 1953), II, 96–97. Gay, however, substitutes "strait jacket" for "iron cage."

12. *One-Dimensional Man: Studies in the Ideology of Advanced Industrial Society* (Beacon Press, 1964), 9.

13. Ibid., 256–57. See my critique of this book in the *Partisan Review*, Fall 1964, and the exchange between Marcuse and me in the following number, Winter 1965. Marcuse's thought would grow more open and dialectical in the late 1960s and, in a different vein, in the middle 1970s. The most striking landmarks are *An Essay on Liberation* (Beacon, 1969) and his last book, *The Aesthetic Dimension* (Beacon, 1978). However, by some perverse historical irony, it is the rigid, closed, "one-dimensional" Marcuse who has attracted the greatest attention and exerted the most influence till now.

14. "Modernist Painting," 1961, in Gregory Battcock, editor, *The New Art* (Dutton, 1966), 100–10.

15. *Writing Degree Zero*, 1953, translated by Annette Lavers and Colin Smith (London: Jonathan Cape, 1967), 58. I associate this book with the 1960s because that is when its impact came to be felt on a large scale, in France as well as in England and the U.S.A.

16. *The Tradition of the New* (Horizon, 1959), 81.

17. *Beyond Culture*, Preface (Viking, 1965). This idea is elaborated most vividly in Trilling's 1961 *Partisan Review* piece, "The Modern Element in Modern Literature," reprinted in *Beyond Culture*, 3–30, but retitled "On the Teaching of Modern Literature."

18. *The Theory of the Avant-Garde*, 1962, translated from the Italian by Gerald Fitzgerald (Harvard, 1968), 111.

19. "Contemporary Art and the Plight of Its Public," a lecture given at the Museum of Modern Art in 1960, printed in *Harper's*, 1962, reprinted in Battcock, *The New Art*, 27–47, and in Steinberg's *Other Criteria: Confrontations with Twentieth Century Art* (Oxford, 1972), 15.

20. Irving Howe discusses critically the off-and-on, phony-and-genuine "war between modernist culture and bourgeois society," in "The Culture of Modernism," *Commentary*, November 1967; reprinted, under the title of "The Idea of the Modern," as the Introduction to Howe's anthology, *Literary Modernism* (Fawcett Premier, 1967). This conflict is a central theme in Howe's collection, which reprints the four writers cited just above, along with many other interesting contemporaries, and splendid manifestos by Marinetti and Zamyatin.

21. See the perceptive discussion in Morris Dickstein, *Gates of Eden: American Culture in the Sixties* (Basic Books, 1977), 266–67.

22. Bell, *Cultural Contradictions of Capitalism* (Basic Books, 1975), 19; "Modernism and Capitalism," *Partisan Review*, 45 (1978), 214. This latter essay became the Preface to the paperback edition of *Cultural Contradictions*, 1978.

23. Cage, "Experimental Music," 1957, in *Silence* (Wesleyan, 1961), 12. "Cross the Border, Close the Gap," 1970, in Fiedler's *Collected Essays* (Stein and Day, 1971), Volume 2; also in this volume, "The Death of Avant-Garde Literature," 1964, and "The New Mutants," 1965. Susan Sontag, "One Culture and the New Sensibility," 1965, "Happenings," 1962, and "Notes on 'Camp,'" 1964, all in her *Against Interpretation* (Farrar, Straus & Giroux, 1966). Actually, all three modes of 1960s modernism can be found in the various essays of which this book consists; but they lead separate lives. Sontag never tries to contrast or confront them with one another. Richard Poirier, *The Performing Self: Compositions and Decompositions in Everyday Life* (Oxford, 1971). Robert Venturi, *Complexity and Contradiction in Architecture* (Museum of Modern Art, 1966); and Venturi, Denise Scott Brown and David Izenour, *Learning from Las Vegas* (MIT, 1972). On Alloway, Richard Hamilton, John McHale, Reyner Banham, and other British contributors to pop aesthetics, see John Russell and Suzi Gablik, *Pop Art Redefined* (Praeger, 1970), and Charles Jencks, *Modern Movements in Architecture* (Anchor, 1973), 270–98.

24. The most energetic early exponents of post-modernism were Leslie Fiedler and Ihab Hassan: Fiedler, "The Death of Avant-Garde Literature," 1964, and "The New Mutants," 1965, both in *Collected Essays*, Volume II; Hassan, *The Dismemberment of Orpheus: Toward a Postmodern Literature* (Oxford, 1971), and "POSTmodernISM: A Paracritical Bibliography," in *Paracriticisms: Seven Speculations of the Times* (Illinois, 1973). For later post-modern instances, Charles Jencks, *The Language of Post-Modern Architecture* (Rizzoli, 1977); Michel Benamou and Charles Calleo, *Performance in Post-Modern Culture* (Milwaukee: Coda Press, 1977); and the ongoing *Boundary 2: A Journal of Postmodern Literature*. For critiques of the whole project, see Robert Alter, "The Self-Conscious Moment: Reflections on the Aftermath of Post-Modernism," in *Triquarterly* #33 (Spring 1975), 209–30, and Matei Calinescu, *Faces of Modernity* (Indiana, 1977), 132–44. Recent numbers of *Boundary 2* suggest some of the problems inherent in the notion of post-modernism. This often fascinating magazine has come increasingly to feature writers like Melville, Poe, the Brontës, Wordsworth, even Fielding and Sterne. Fine, but if these writers belong to the post-modern period, when did the modern era take place? In the Middle Ages? Different problems are unfolded, in the context of visual arts in Douglas Davis, "Post-Post Art," I and II, and "Symbolismo Meets the Faerie Queene," in *Village Voice*, 24 June, 13 August, and 17 December 1979. See also, in a theatrical context, Richard Schechner, "The Decline and Fall of the [American] Avant-Garde," in *Performing Arts Journal* 14 (1981), 48–63.

25. The mainstream justification for abandoning the concept of modernization is given most clearly in Samuel Huntington, "The Change to Change: Modernization, Development and Politics," in *Comparative Politics*, 3 (1970–71), 286–322. See also S. N. Eisenstadt, "The Disintegration of the Initial Paradigm," in *Tradition, Change and Modernity* (cited in note 10), 98–115. Despite the general tendency, a few social scientists in the 1970s sharpened and deepened the concept of modernization. See, for instance, Irving Leonard Markowitz, *Power and Class in Africa* (Prentice-Hall, 1977).

The theory of modernization is likely to develop further in the 1980s as the seminal work of Fernand Braudel and his followers in comparative history is assimilated. See Braudel, *Capitalism and Material Life, 1400–1800*, translated by Miriam Kochan (Harper & Row, 1973), and *Afterthoughts on Material Civili-*

zation and Capitalism, translated by Patricia Ranum (Johns Hopkins, 1977); Immanuel Wallerstein, *The Modern World-System*, Volumes I & II (Academic Press, 1974, 1980).

26. *The History of Sexuality*, Volume I: an Introduction, 1976, translated by Michael Hurley (Pantheon, 1978), 144, 155, and the whole of this final chapter.

27. *Discipline and Punish: The Birth of the Prison*, 1975, translated by Alan Sheridan (Pantheon, 1977), 217, 226–28. The whole chapter entitled "Panopticism," 195–228, shows Foucault at his most compelling. Occasionally in this chapter a less monolithic and more dialectical vision of modernity appears, but the light is soon snuffed out. All this should be compared with the earlier and deeper work of Goffman, e.g., the essays on "Characteristics of Total Institutions" and "The Underlife of a Public Institution," in *Asylums: Essays on the Social Situation of Mental Patients and Other Inmates* (Anchor, 1961).

28. *Alternating Current*, 1967, translated from the Spanish by Helen Lane (Viking, 1973), 161–62.

I. GOETHE'S *FAUST:* THE TRAGEDY OF DEVELOPMENT

1. *The New Yorker,* 9 April 1979, "Talk of the Town," 27–28.

2. *Captain America* #236, Marvel Comics, August 1979. I owe this reference to Marc Berman.

3. Cited in Georg Lukács, *Goethe and His Age* (Budapest, 1947; translated by Robert Anchor, Merlin Press, London, 1968, and Grosset & Dunlap, New York, 1969), 157. This book seems to me, after *History and Class Consciousness*, the best work of Lukács' whole communist period. Readers of *Goethe and His Age* will recognize how much of the essay that follows is a dialogue with it.

4. After the supposedly complete version, which appeared in 1832, additional fragments, often quite lengthy and brilliant, kept emerging all through the nineteenth century. For a short history of the many stages of *Faust*'s composition and publication, see the excellent critical edition by Walter Arndt and Cyrus Hamlin (Norton, 1976), 346–55. This edition, translated by Arndt and edited by Hamlin, contains abundant background material and many perceptive critical essays.

5. In citations from *Faust,* numbers designate the lines. Here, and generally, I have used Walter Kaufmann's translation (New York: Anchor Books, 1962). I have also occasionally drawn on Walter Arndt's version, cited above, and on Louis MacNeice's (1951: New York, Oxford University Press, 1961). Sometimes I have made translations of my own, using the German text of *Faust: Eine Tragödie,* edited by Hanns W. Eppelsheimer (München: Deutscher Taschenbuch Verlag, 1962).

6. This is not quite true. In 1798 and 1799 Goethe inserted before this first scene ("Night") a Prelude in the Theater and a Prologue in Heaven, totaling between them about 350 lines. Both are apparently meant as framing devices, to dilute the searing intensity of the first scene, to create what Brecht called an alienation effect between the audience and the hero's drives and yearnings. The delightful but easily forgettable Prelude, which is almost always left out of performances, succeeds in this; the unforgettable Prologue, which introduces God and the devil, clearly fails to generate alienation, and only whets our appetite for the intensities of "Night."

7. Ernst Schachtel's beautiful essay "Memory and Childhood Amnesia" makes it clear why experiences like Faust's bells should have such miraculous and magical power in adult lives. This 1947 essay appears as the last chapter of Schachtel's book *Metamorphosis: On the Development of Affect, Perception, Attention and Memory* (Basic Books, 1959), 279–322, especially 307ff.

8.   This tradition is brought to life sensitively and sympathetically, though not uncritically, in Raymond Williams, *Culture and Society, 1780–1950* (1958; Anchor Books, 1960).

9.   Lukács draws here on one of Marx's brilliant early essays, "The Power of Money in Bourgeois Society" (1844), which uses the *Faust* passage above and a similar one from *Timon of Athens* as its points of departure. The Marx essay is most conveniently available in *Marx-Engels Reader*, translated by Martin Milligan, 101–05.

10.   *Goethe and His Age*, 191–2.

11.   Ibid., 196–200, 215–16.

12.   On this fertile and fascinating movement, the most interesting works in English are Frank Manuel, *The New World of Henri Saint-Simon* (1956; Notre Dame, 1963), and *The Prophets of Paris* (1962; Harper Torchbooks, 1965), Chapters 3 and 4. See also Durkheim's classic 1895 study, *Socialism and Saint Simon,* translated by Charlotte Sattler, introduced by Alvin Gouldner (1958; Collier paperback, 1962), which makes clear the Saint-Simonian component in the theory and practice of the twentieth-century welfare state; and the penetrating discussions of Lewis Coser, *Men of Ideas* (Free Press, 1965), 99–109; George Lichtheim, *The Origins of Socialism* (Praeger, 1969), 39–59, 235–44; and Theodore Zeldin, *France, 1848–1945: Ambition, Love and Politics* (Oxford, 1973), especially 82, 430–38, 553.

13.   *Conversations of Goethe with Eckermann,* translated by John Oxenford, edited by J. K. Moorehead, introduced by Havelock Ellis (Everyman's Library, 1913), 21 February 1827, pages 173–74.

14.   Andrew Shonfield, *Modern Capitalism: The Changing Balance of Public and Private Power* (Oxford, 1965), sees the primacy of public authorities, and their capacity for internationally coordinated long-range planning, as the main ingredient in contemporary capitalism's success.

15.   "Goethe as a Representative of the Bourgeois Age," in *Essays of Three Decades*, translated by Harriet Lowe-Porter (Knopf, 1953), 91.

16.   In *Isaac Babel: The Lonely Years, 1925–1939,* edited by Nathalie Babel, translated by Max Hayward (Noonday, 1964), 10–15.

17.   *Life Against Death: The Psychoanalytic Meaning of History* (Wesleyan, 1959), 18–19, 91.

18.   "A Course in Film-Making," in *New American Review* #12 (1971), 241. On the Pentagon and its exorcists, *The Armies of the Night* (Signet, 1968), especially 135–45; my own memoir and meditations in an early version of this essay, "Sympathy for the Devil: Faust, the 1960s, and the Tragedy of Development," in [*New*] *American Review* #19 (1974), especially 22–40, 64–75; and Morris Dickstein, *Gates of Eden*, 146–48, 260–61.

19.   Gunther Stent, *The Coming of the Golden Age: A View of the End of Progress,* originally delivered as a course of lectures at Berkeley in 1968, and published by the American Museum of Natural History (Natural History Press, 1969), 83–87, 134–38.

20.   Bernard James, *The Death of Progress* (Knopf, 1973), xiii, 3, 10, 55, 61.

21.   See, for instance, the influential E. F. Schumacher, *Small Is Beautiful: Economics as if People Mattered* (Harper & Row, 1973); L. S. Stavrianos, *The Promise of the Coming Dark Age* (W. H. Freeman, 1976); Leopold Kohr, *The Overdeveloped Nations: The Diseconomies of Scale* (Schocken, 1977, but published in German and Spanish in 1962); Ivan Illich, *Toward a History of Needs* (Pantheon, 1977).

22.   This awareness can be found most clearly in the work of Barry Commoner: *The Closing Circle* (1971), *The Poverty of Power* (1976), and most recently *The Politics of Energy* (1979; all published by Knopf).

23.   This story is told with great dramatic power in Robert Jungk, *Brighter Than a*

Thousand Suns: A Personal History of the Atomic Scientists, 1956, translated by James Cleugh (Harcourt Brace, 1958), and elaborated with a wealth of fascinating detail in Alice Kimball Smith, *A Peril and a Hope: The Scientists' Movement in America, 1945–47* (MIT, 1965). Jungk gives special emphasis to the nuclear pioneers' knowledge of Goethe's *Faust*, and their awareness of its specific dire implications for them and their enterprise. He also uses the Faust theme skillfully in interpreting the rise, fall and ambiguous redemption of J. Robert Oppenheimer.

24. "Social Institutions and Nuclear Energy," delivered before the American Association for the Advancement of Science in 1971, and reprinted in *Science*, 7 (July 1972), 27–34. For a typical critique, Garrett Hardin, "Living with the Faustian Bargain," along with a reply by Weinberg, in *Bulletin of the Atomic Scientists*, November 1976, 21–29. More recently, in the wake of Three Mile Island, see the anonymous "Talk of the Town" columns in *The New Yorker*, 9 and 23 April 1979, and various columns in the *New York Times* by Anthony Lewis, Tom Wicker and John Oakes.

II. ALL THAT IS SOLID MELTS INTO AIR

1. See W. W. Rostow, *The Stages of Economic Growth: A Non-Communist Manifesto* (Cambridge, 1960). Alas, Rostow's account of Marx is garbled and shallow, even for an opponent. A more perceptive account of the relationship between Marx and recent studies of modernization can be found in Robert C. Tucker, *The Marxian Revolutionary Idea* (Norton, 1969), Chapter 5. See also Shlomo Avineri, *The Social and Political Thought of Karl Marx* (Cambridge, 1968), and Anthony Giddens, *Capitalism and Modern Social Theory* (Cambridge, 1971), especially Parts 1 and 4.

2. The one really striking exception is Harold Rosenberg. I owe a great deal to three of his brilliant essays: "The Resurrected Romans" (1949), reprinted in *The Tradition of the New;* "The Pathos of the Proletariat" (1949), and "Marxism: Criticism and/or Action" (1956), both reprinted in *Act and the Actor: Making the Self* (Meridian, 1972). See also Henri Lefebvre, *Introduction à la Modernité* (Gallimard, 1962), and, in English, *Everyday Life in the Modern World*, 1968, translated by Sacha Rabinovitch (Harper Torchbooks, 1971); Octavio Paz, *Alternating Current;* and Richard Ellman's and Charles Feidelson's anthology, *The Modern Tradition: Backgrounds of Modern Literature* (Oxford, 1965), which includes generous selections from Marx.

3. Most of my citations from the *Manifesto* are drawn from Samuel Moore's classic translation (London, 1888), authorized and edited by Engels, and universally reprinted. It may be conveniently found in *Marx-Engels Reader*, 331–62. Page numbers in parentheses in this chapter are drawn from this edition. I have sometimes deviated from Moore, in the direction of more literalism and concreteness, and of a diction less Victorian and more vivid. These changes are generally but not always indicated by bracketed citations from the German. For a convenient edition of the German text, see *Karl Marx–Friedrich Engels Studienausgabe*, 4 volumes, edited by Irving Fetscher (Frankfurt am Main: Fischer Bücherei, 1966). The *Manifesto* is in Band III, 59–87.

4. See Marx's 1845 image of "practical-critical activity, revolutionary activity" (Theses on Feuerbach, #1–3; reprinted in *Marx-Engels Reader*, 143–45.) This image has spawned an enormous literature in the twentieth century, a literature that is at once tactical, ethical and even metaphysical, oriented toward a search for the ideal synthesis of theory and practice in the Marxist model of the good life. The most interesting writers in this vein are Georg Lukács (especially in *History and Class Consciousness, 1919–23)* and Antonio Gramsci.

5. The theme of universal forced development, but development that is warped by the imperatives of competition, was first elaborated by Rousseau in the *Discourse on the Origins of Inequality*. See my *Politics of Authenticity*, especially 145–59.

6. From "Economic and Philosophical Manuscripts of 1844," translated by Martin Milligan; reprinted in *MER*, 74. The German word that can be translated as either "mental" or "spiritual" is *geistige*.

7. *The German Ideology*, Part I, translated by Roy Pascal; *MER*, 191, 197.

8. *Capital*, Volume I, Chapter 15, Section 9, translated by Charles Moore and Edward Aveling; *MER*, 413–14.

9. *Modernity and self-development in Marx's later writings:* In the *Grundrisse*, the 1857–58 notebooks that became the basis for *Capital*, Marx makes a distinction between "the modern epoch" or "the modern world" and "its limited bourgeois form." In communist society, the narrow bourgeois form will be "stripped away," so that the modern potentiality can be fulfilled. He begins this discussion with a contrast of classical (specifically Aristotelian) and modern views of economy and society. "The old view, in which the human being appears as the aim of production . . . seems to be very lofty when contrasted with the modern world, where production appears as the aim of mankind, and wealth as the aim of production.

"In fact, however," Marx says, "when the narrow bourgeois form is stripped away, what is wealth other than the universality of individual needs, capacities, pleasures, productive forces, etc., created through universal exchange? The full development of human mastery over the forces of nature, those of [external] nature as well as humanity's own nature? The absolute working-out of his creative potentialities, with no presupposition other than the previous historic development . . . which makes this the totality of development, i.e., the development of all human powers as the end in itself, not as measured on any predetermined yardstick? Where he does not reproduce himself in one specificity, but produces his totality? Strives not to remain something he has become, but is in the absolute movement of becoming?"

In other words, Marx wants a truly infinite pursuit of wealth for everyone: not wealth in money—"the narrow bourgeois form"—but wealth of desires, of experiences, capacities, sensitivities, of transformations and developments. The fact that Marx follows these formulations with question marks may suggest a certain hesitancy about this vision. Marx closes the discussion by returning to his distinction between ancient and modern modes and ends of life. "The childish world of antiquity . . . really is loftier [than the modern world] in all matters where closed shapes, forms and given limits are sought for. It is satisfaction from a limited standpoint; while the modern gives no satisfaction; or where it appears satisfied with itself, it is vulgar and mean." *Grundrisse: Introduction to the Critique of Political Economy*, translated by Martin Nicolaus (Penguin, 1973), 487–88. In the last sentence, Marx states his variation on Goethe's Faustian bargain: in exchange for the possibility of infinite self-development, modern (communist) man will give up the hope for "satisfaction," which requires closed, fixed, limited personal and social forms. The modern bourgeoisie "is vulgar and mean" because it "appears satisfied with itself," because it does not grasp the human possibilities that its own activities have opened up.

In *Capital*, Chapter 15, the passage quoted in the text (note 8) that ends with "the fully developed individual" begins with a distinction between "modern industry" and "its capitalist form," the form in which it first appears. "Modern industry never views the existing form of a productive process as the definitive form. Its technical basis is revolutionary, whereas all earlier modes of production were essentially conservative. By means of machinery, chemical processes and other methods, it is continually causing changes, not only in the technical basis of production, but also in the functions of the worker, and in the social combinations of the labor process. At the same time it also revolutionizes the division of labor." *(MER, 413)* At this point, Marx quotes in a footnote the passage from the *Manifesto* that begins with "The bourgeoisie cannot exist without constantly revolutionizing the means of production," and ends with "All that is solid melts into air . . ." Here, as in the *Manifesto* and elsewhere, capitalist production and exchange is the force that has made the world modern; now, however, capitalism has become a fetter, a drag on modernity, and it has got to go in order for the permanent revolution of modern industry to keep developing, and in order for the "fully developed individual" to emerge and thrive.

Veblen will pick up this dualism in *The Theory of Business Enterprise* (1904), which distinguishes between a narrowly avaricious "Business" and, interwoven with it, an open-ended and revolutionary "Industry." But Veblen lacks Marx's interest in the relationship between the development of industry and the development of the self.

10. In the first chapter of *Capital*, "Commodities," Marx never tires of reiterating that "the value of commodities is the very opposite of the coarse materiality of their substance; not an atom of materiality enters into its composition." Cf. *MER*, 305, 312–14, 317, 328, 343.

11. The values, critical themes and paradoxes of this paragraph are developed brilliantly in the East European dissident tradition of "Marxist humanism" that runs from thinkers like Kolakowski in his post-Stalin (and pre-Oxonian) phase and the thinkers of the "Prague Spring" in the 1960s, to George Konrad and Alexander Zinoviev in the 1970s. Russian variations on this theme will be discussed in Chapter IV.

12. *The Persian Letters* (1721), translated by J. Robert Loy (Meridian, 1961), Letters 26, 63, 88. The eighteenth-century themes sketched on this page are explored at length in my *The Politics of Authenticity*.

13. *Discourse on the Arts and Sciences* (1750), Part I, translated by G. D. H. Cole (Dutton, 1950), 146–49. In *Oeuvres Complètes*, III, 7–9.

14. *Reflections on the Revolution in France* (1790), reprinted in a joint edition with Thomas Paine's *Rights of Man* (Dolphin, 1961), 90.

15. To clarify this problem, compare two of Marx's statements about life in communist society. First, from the "Critique of the [German Social-Democratic Party] Gotha Program," 1875: "In a higher phase of communist society, after the enslaving subordination of the individual to the division of labor, and thereby the antithesis between mental and physical labor, has vanished; after labor has become not only a means of life, but life's prime want; after productive forces have also increased, along with the all-around development of the individual, and all the springs of cooperative wealth flow more abundantly— only then can the narrow horizon of bourgeois right be crossed in its entirety, and society inscribe on its banner: From each according to his ability, to each according to his needs!" *(MER, 531)*

Consider this in the light of the *Grundrisse* (note 9, above), in which communism will realize the modern ideal of the infinite pursuit of wealth, "stripping the narrow bourgeois form [of wealth] away"; thus communist society will liberate "the universality of needs, capacities, pleasures, productive forces . . . the development of all human powers as the end in itself"; man will "produce his totality," and live "in the absolute movement of becoming." If this vision is taken seriously, it is obvious that everybody's universal needs are going to be hard to satisfy, and that the pursuit of infinite development for everybody is bound to produce serious human conflicts; they may differ from the class conflicts endemic to bourgeois society, but they are likely to be at least as deep. Marx acknowledges the possibility of this sort of trouble only in the most oblique way, and says nothing about how a communist society might deal with it. This may be why Octavio Paz (*Alternating Current,* 121) says that Marx's thought, "although it is Promethean, critical, and philanthropic in spirit . . . is nonetheless nihilistic," but that, alas, "Marx's nihilism is not aware of its own nature."

16. *Capital,* Volume I, Chapter 1, Section 4; *MER,* 319–29. The landmark account of Marx's strategy and originality here is in Lukács' *History and Class Consciousness.*

17. On "art for art's sake," see Arnold Hauser, *The Social History of Art* (1949; Vintage, 1958), Volume III; Cesar Graña, *Bohemian Versus Bourgeois: Society and the French Man of Letters in the Nineteenth Century* (Basic Books, 1964; 1967 paperback edition retitled *Modernity and Its Discontents);* T. J. Clark, *The Absolute Bourgeois: Artists and Politics in France, 1848–51* (New York Graphic Society, 1973). The best introduction to the Comte circle can be found in Frank Manuel, *The Prophets of Paris* (1962; Harper Torchbooks, 1965).

18. Hans Magnus Enzensberger, in his brilliant 1969 essay "The Industrialization of the Mind," develops a similar perspective in the context of a theory of the mass media. In *The Consciousness Industry* (Seabury, 1970), 3–15.

19. From Gramsci's posthumous manuscript, "The Modern Prince." Reprinted in his *Prison Notebooks,* selected, edited and translated by Quintin Hoare and Geoffrey Nowell Smith (International Publishers, 1971), 173.

20. Lukács is the most notorious and fascinating example: forced by the Comintern to denounce all his early modernist works, he spent decades and volumes vilifying modernism and all its works. See, for example, his essay "The Ideology of Modernism," in *Realism in Our Time: Literature and the Class Struggle* (1957), translated by John and Necke Mander (Harper & Row, 1964).

21. "Modernism has been the seducer": *Cultural Contradictions of Capitalism,* 19. Bell's writing, here as elsewhere, is full of unreconciled and apparently unrecognized contradictions. His analysis of the nihilism of modern advertising and salesmanship (65–69) fits perfectly into the overall argument of this book—only Bell seems not to notice how high-pressure advertising and salesmanship arise out of the imperatives of capitalism; rather, these activities, and their accompanying webs of deceit and self-deception, are laid at the door of the modern/modernist "life-style."

A later piece, "Modernism and Capitalism" (1978), incorporates further perspectives close to the ones above: "What became distinctive about capitalism—its very dynamic—was its boundlessness. Propelled by the dynamo of technology, there were no asymptotes to its exponential growth. No limits. Nothing was sacred. Change was the norm. By the middle of the 19th century, this was the trajectory of the economic impulse." But this insight does not last: in a moment capitalist nihilism is forgotten, and the familiar demonology clicks back into place; thus "the modern movement . . . disrupts the unity of culture," shatters "the 'rational cosmology' that underlay the bourgeois world view of an ordered relationship of space and time," etc., etc. In *Partisan Review,* 45 (1978), 213–15, reprinted the following year as a Preface to the paperback edition of *Cultural Contradictions.* Bell, unlike some of his neoconservative friends, at least has the courage of his incoherence.

22. Adorno's remark is quoted by Martin Jay in his history of the Frankfurt School, *The Dialectical Imagination* (Little, Brown, 1973), 57. See also Jean Bau-

drillard, *The Mirror of Production*, translated by Mark Poster (Telos Press, 1975), and various critiques of Marx in *Social Research*, 45.4 (Winter 1978).

23. Marcuse, *Eros and Civilization: A Philosophical Inquiry into Freud* (1955; Vintage, 1962), 146–47, and the whole of Chapter 8, "Orpheus and Narcissus."

24. Arendt, *The Human Condition: A Study of the Central Dilemmas Facing Modern Man* (1958: Anchor, 1959), 101–02, 114–16. Note that in Marx's thought the public realm of shared discourse and values would subsist and thrive, so long as communism remained an opposition *movement;* it would wither away only where that movement triumphed and strove (in vain, with no public realm) to inaugurate a communist *society*.

III. BAUDELAIRE: MODERNISM IN THE STREETS

1. Quoted by Marcel Ruff, editor, *Baudelaire: Oeuvres Complètes* (Editions de Seuil, 1968), 36–7, from an article by Verlaine in the magazine *L'Art*. All French texts cited here are from Ruff's edition.

2. Quoted by Enid Starkie, *Baudelaire* (New Directions, 1958), 530–1, from a paraphrase in the Paris newspaper *L'Etandard*, 4 September 1867.

3. *The Painter of Modern Life, and Other Essays*, translated and edited by Jonathan Mayne, with extensive illustrations (Phaidon, 1965), 1–5, 12–14.

4. Pontus Hulten, *Modernolatry* (Stockholm, Modena Musset, 1966); Fritz Stern, *The Politics of Cultural Despair: A Study in the Rise of the Germanic Ideology* (University of California, 1961).

5. Baudelaire's *Salons* critiques are all in *Art in Paris, 1845–62*, the companion volume to *The Painter of Modern Life*, also translated and edited by Jonathan Mayne, and published by Phaidon, 1965. "To the Bourgeois," 41–3. Note: I have occasionally altered Mayne's translations, generally in the direction of greater precision; where the alterations are important, the French is given.

6. This stereotype is presented exhaustively, and uncritically, in Cesar Graña, *Bohemian Versus Bourgeois*, 90–124. A more balanced and complex account of Baudelaire, the bourgeoisie and modernity is given in Peter Gay, *Art and Act* (Harper & Row, 1976), especially 88–92. See also Matei Calinescu, *Faces of Modernity*, 46–58, 86, and passim.

7. Baudelaire's faith in bourgeois receptivity to modern art may derive from his acquaintance with the Saint-Simonians. This movement, discussed briefly in my chapter on *Faust* above, seems to have generated the modern idea of the avant-garde in the 1820s. Historians emphasize Saint-Simon's *De l'organization Sociale*, and his disciple Olinde Rodriguez' *Dialogue between an Artist, a Scientist and an Industrialist*, both written in 1825. See Donald Drew Egbert, "The Idea of 'Avant-Garde' in Art and Politics," *American Historical Review*, 73 (1967), 339–66; also Calinescu, *Faces of Modernity*, 101–08, and his larger history and analysis of the avant-garde idea, 95–148.

8. *The Painter of Modern Life*, 11. An interesting treatment of this essay, more sympathetic than mine, can be found in Paul De Man, "Literary History and Literary Modernity," in *Blindness and Insight: Essays in the Rhetoric of Contemporary Criticism* (Oxford, 1971), especially 157–61. See also Henri Lefebvre, *Introduction à la Modernité*, Chapter 7, for a critical perspective similar to the one here.

9. *Painter of Modern Life*, 24.

10. The best account of Baudelaire's politics in this period is in T. J. Clark, *The Absolute Bourgeois: Artists and Politics in France, 1848–51* (New York Graphic Society, 1973), especially 141–77. See also Richard Klein, "Some Notes on Baudelaire and Revolution," *Yale French Studies*, 39 (1967), 85–97.

11. *Art in Paris*, 121–9. This essay appears as Part I of a lengthy critical discussion of the 1855 Paris Exposition Universelle.

12. Ibid., 125–7.

13. *Salon of 1859*, Part II. *Art in Paris*, 149–55.

14. Ibid., 125, 127.

15. *Art in Paris*, 31–2.

16. "Heroism of Modern Life," ibid., 116–20.

17. *Painter of Modern Life*, 9, 18.

18. These essays have been brought together under the title of *Charles Baudelaire: Lyric Poet in the Era of High Capitalism*, translated by Harry Zohn (London: New Left Books, 1973), but scandalously unavailable in the U.S.A. as of 1981.

19. *Paris Spleen*, translated by Louise Varèse (New Directions, 1947, 1970). In the poems below, however, translations are my own.

20. On the *feuilleton*, and its connections with some of the greatest of nineteenth-century literature, see Benjamin, *Baudelaire*, 27ff., and Donald Fanger, *Dostoevsky and Romantic Realism* (University of Chicago Press, 1965), throughout.

21. My picture of the Napoleon III–Haussmann transformation of Paris has been put together from several sources: Siegfried Giedion, *Space, Time and Architecture* (1941; 5th edition, Harvard, 1966), 744–775; Robert Moses, "Haussmann," in *Architectural Forum*, July 1942, 57–66; David Pinkney, *Napoleon III and the Rebuilding of Paris* (1958; Princeton, 1972); Leonardo Benevolo, *A History of Modern Architecture* (1960, 1966; translated from the Italian by H. J. Landry, 2 volumes, MIT, 1971), I, 61–95; Françoise Choay, *The Modern City: Planning in the Nineteenth Century* (George Braziller, 1969), especially 15–26; Howard Saalman, *Haussmann: Paris Transformed* (Braziller, 1971); and Louis Chevalier, *Laboring Classes and Dangerous Classes: Paris in the First Half of the Nineteenth Century*, 1970, translated by Frank Jellinek (Howard Fertig, 1973). Haussmann's projects are skillfully placed in the context of long-term European political and social change by Anthony Vidler, "The Scenes of the Street: Transformations in Ideal and Reality, 1750–1871," in *On Streets*, edited by Stanford Anderson (MIT, 1978), 28–111. Haussmann commissioned a photographer, Charles Marville, to photograph dozens of sites slated for demolition and so preserve their memory for posterity. These photographs are preserved in the Musée Carnavalet, Paris. A marvelous selection was exhibited in New York and other American locations in 1981. The catalogue, French Institute/Alliance Française, *Charles Marville: Photographs of Paris, 1852–1878*, contains a fine essay by Maria Morris Hamburg.

22. Haussmann's engineers invented a tree-lifting machine that enabled them to transplant thirty-year-old trees in full leaf, and thus to create shady avenues overnight, seemingly ex nihilo. Giedion, *Space, Time and Architecture*, 757–59.

23. *Art in Paris*, 127.

24. This connection is explicated, in very different terms from the ones here, by Irving Wohlfarth, "*Perte d'Auréole* and the Emergence of the Dandy," *Modern Language Notes*, 85 (1970), 530–71.

25. Pinkney, *Napoleon III*, on census figures, 151–54; on traffic counts and estimates, and conflict between Napoleon and Haussmann over macadam, 70–72; on dual function of boulevards, 214–15.

26. On the distinctively international quality of twentieth-century modernist language and literature, see Delmore Schwartz, "T. S. Eliot as International Hero," in Howe, *Literary Modernism*, 277–85. This is also one of Edmund Wilson's central themes in *Axel's Castle* and *To the Finland Station*.

27. *The City of Tomorrow*, translated by Frederick Etchells (1929; MIT, 1971), 3–4.

I have sometimes used my own translations, based on the French text of *L'Urbanisme* (10th edition, G. Crès, 1941).

28. Ibid., 123, 131.
29. *Towards a New Architecture* (1923), translated by Frederick Etchells (1927; Praeger, 1959), 56–9.
30. Quoted in Sybil Moholy-Nagy, *Matrix of Man: An Illustrated History of Urban Environment* (Praeger, 1968), 274–75.

IV. PETERSBURG: THE MODERNISM OF UNDERDEVELOPMENT

1. Thus Hugh Seton-Watson, in an article on "Russia and Modernization," describes Imperial Russia as "the prototype of the 'underdeveloped society' whose problems are so familiar in our own age." *Slavic Review*, 20 (1961), 583. Seton-Watson's piece is a contribution to an extended discussion and controversy, 565—600, which includes Cyril Black, "The Nature of Imperial Russian Society," and Nicholas Riasanovsky, "Russia as an Underdeveloped Country." For further development of this theme, see Theodore von Laue, *Why Lenin? Why Stalin?* (Lippincott, 1964); I. Robert Sinai, *In Search of the Modern World* (New American Library, 1967), 67–74, 109–24, 163–78; and various discussions of the Russian economy to be discussed below. These sources show how in the course of the 1960s the global theme of modernization came to supersede the far narrower traditional framework of Russian studies, "Russia and/versus the West." This tendency has continued in the 1970s, though 1970s writing on modernization has tended to narrow its focus to the problems of state and nation building. See, for instance, Perry Anderson, *Lineages of the Absolute State* (London: New Left Books, 1974), 328–60, and Reinhard Bendix, *Kings or People: Power and the Mandate to Rule* (California, 1978), 491–581.

2. Virtually every Russian writer from 1830 to 1930 offered some variation on this theme. The best general treatments in English are T. G. Masaryk, *The Spirit of Russia: Studies in History, Literature and Philosophy* (1911), translated from the German by Eden and Cedar Paul (2 volumes, Allen & Unwin/Macmillan, 1919); and, more recently, James Billington, *The Icon and the Axe: An Interpretive History of Russian Culture* (Knopf, 1966).

3. For vivid detailed accounts of the city's construction, see Iurii Egorov, *The Architectural Planning of St. Petersburg*, translated by Eric Dluhosch (Ohio University Press, 1969), especially Translator's Note and Chapter 1, and Billington, *The Icon and the Axe*, 180–92 and throughout. For a comparative perspective, see Fernand Braudel, *Capitalism and Material Life, 1400–1800*, 418–24; in the context of his overall treatment of cities, 373–440.

4. *Social Contract*, Book I, Chapter 6, *Oeuvres Complètes*, III, 361.

5. This point is made by Prince D. S. Mirsky in his seminal *History of Russian Literature*, edited by Francis J. Whitfield (1926; Vintage, 1958) 91ff., and developed by Edmund Wilson in his 1937 essay on the centenary of Pushkin's death, reprinted in *The Triple Thinkers* (1952; Penguin, 1962), 40ff.

6. Published simultaneously with his essay "In Honor of Pushkin," and reprinted in *The Triple Thinkers*, 63–71. I have occasionally altered Wilson's sentence structure where his poetic inversions resulted in English sentences that were stilted to the point of unintelligibility.

7. Quoted in Michael Cherniavsky, *Tsar and People: Studies in Russian Myths* (Yale, 1961), 151–52. This book is particularly illuminating on the age of Nicholas I. Herzen saved some of his most brilliant invective for Nicholas. *My Past and Thoughts*, his memoirs, and *The Russian People and Socialism* contain many such

passages, which equal the very best political rhetoric of the nineteenth century. On the increasing brutality of Nicholas' last years, and the ultimate failure of his repressions, see Isaiah Berlin's classic essays, "Russia and 1848" (1948) and "A Remarkable Decade: The Birth of the Russian Intelligentsia" (1954), both reprinted in his *Russian Thinkers* (Viking, 1978), 1–21, 114–35. Also Sidney Monas, *The Third Section: Police and Society in Russia Under Nicholas I* (Harvard, 1961).

8. Alexander Gerschenkron, "Agrarian Policies and Industrialization: Russia, 1861–1917," in the *Cambridge Economic History of Europe* (Cambridge, 1966), 706–800; on the government's fears of and resistance to modernization, 708–11. Also in the same volume, Roger Portal, "The Industrialization of Russia," 801–72; on stagnation, retrogression and relative backwardness before 1861, 802–10. Note also Gerschenkron's earlier essay, more compressed and perhaps more incisive, "Russia: Patterns and Problems of Economic Development, 1861–1958," in his *Economic Backwardness in Historical Perspective* (1962; Praeger, 1965), 119–51.

9. Gerschenkron, "Economic Development in Russian Intellectual History of the 19th Century," in *Economic Backwardness*, 152–97. This essay is a spirited indictment of nearly all the writers and thinkers of Russia's Golden Age. On Belinsky vs. Herzen, 165–69. See also Isaiah Berlin's essays on Herzen and Belinsky in his *Russian Thinkers*.

10. Quoted in Donald Fanger, *Dostoevsky and Romantic Realism*, 149–50; see all of Chapter 5, "The Most Fantastic City," 137–51. Dostoevsky's best-known evocation of Petersburg as a ghost or dream city is in *White Nights* (1848). Fanger is excellent on the literary and popular traditions that underlay this Dostoevskian theme.

11. On the reconstruction of the Nevsky, Egorov, *Architectural Planning of St. Petersburg*, 204–08.

12. V. Sadovinkov, *Panorama of the Nevsky Prospect* (Leningrad, Pluto Press, 1976), with texts in English, French, German and Russian. This marvelous series traces the Nevsky block by block and house by house. But Sadovinkov worked in a static compositional style, which, while it captures the street's diversity, misses its fluidity and dynamism.

    The Nevsky as an arena for the encounter between Russia and the West is the theme of what appears to be the first literary work in which the street plays a central role: Prince Vladimir Odoevsky's short story of 1833, "A Tale of Why It Is Dangerous for Young Girls to Go Walking in a Group Along Nevsky Prospect," translated by Samuel Cioran, in *Russian Literature Triquarterly* #3 (Spring 1972), 89–96. Odoevsky's style here is semi-satirical, semi-surreal— and, as such, may have influenced Gogol's evocations of the Nevsky—but ultimately conventional, conservative and patriotically complacent in his view of the street and the world.

13. I have drawn mainly on a translation by Beatrice Scott (London: Lindsay Drummond, 1945). See also David Magarshack (Gogol, *Tales of Good and Evil*, Anchor, 1968) and Donald Fanger's translations of long excerpts in *Dostoevsky and Romantic Realism*, 106–12. Fanger insists on the merit and importance of this story, and offers a perceptive discussion. Drawing extensively on the work of the Soviet scholar and critic Leonid Grossman, he is excellent on the mystery and romance of the Petersburg landscape, and on this city as the natural habitat for a "fantastic realism." However, Fanger's Petersburg romance leaves out the political dimension which I am trying to unfold.

14. See Nabokov, *Nikolai Gogol* (New Directions, 1944), Chapter 1, for a magnificently lurid account of Gogol's last act. Nabokov also discusses "Nevsky Pros-

pect," brilliantly of course, but misses the connection between imaginative vision and real space.

15. This passage, and many others, were excised by Nicholas' censors, who worked this story over with extreme vigilance, apparently afraid that the uninhibited bitterness and fantastic yearnings even of a madman might prompt irreverence and dangerous thoughts among the sane. Laurie Asch, "The Censorship of Gogol's *Diary of a Madman*," *Russian Literature Triquarterly* #14 (Winter 1976), 20–35.

16. "Petersburg Notes of 1836," translated by Linda Germano, in *Russian Literature Triquarterly* #7 (Fall 1973), 177–86. The first half of this piece presents one of the classic symbolic contrasts of Petersburg and Moscow.

17. *Poor Folk* and the works that immediately followed it—most strikingly *The Double* and *White Nights*—at once established Dostoevsky as one of the world's great urban writers. This book will be able to explore only a few relatively uncharted aspects of Dostoevsky's rich and complex urban vision. The best general approach to his urbanism can be found in the pioneering work of Leonid Grossman. Most of this is untranslated, but see *Dostoevsky: His Life and Work* (1962), translated by Mary Sackler (Bobbs-Merrill, 1975), and *Balzac and Dostoevsky*, translated by Lydia Karpov (Ardis, 1973). Grossman stresses Dostoevsky's urban journalism of the 1840s, in the feuilleton genre, and points out its echoes in his novels, especially *White Nights, Notes from Underground* and *Crime and Punishment*. Some of these feuilletons are translated by David Magarshack in *Dostoevsky's Occasional Writings* (Random House, 1963); they are discussed perceptively by Fanger, 137–51, and by Joseph Frank, *Dostoevsky: The Seeds of Revolt, 1821–1849* (Princeton, 1976), especially 27–39.

18. Translated by Andrew MacAndrew, in *Three Short Novels of Dostoevsky* (Bantam, 1966). There is also a translation by David Magarshack, *Poor People* (Anchor, 1968).

19. Of course, no amount of confidence can save a victim from a real assassin. Tsar Alexander II would be murdered in a carriage, just off the Nevsky, in 1881, by terrorists who placed themselves at intervals along the prescribed imperial route and waited for the inevitable traffic jam.

20. *The Double*, translated by Andrew MacAndrew, in *Three Short Novels of Dostoevsky*, cited in note 18, and by George Bird, in *Great Short Works of Dostoevsky* (Harper & Row, 1968). I have drawn on both.

21. This phrase itself was coined in 1882, just after Dostoevsky's death, by the populist thinker and leader Nikolai Mikhailovsky. Mikhailovsky argued that Dostoevsky's sympathy with "the insulted and injured" was gradually eclipsed by a perverse joy in their suffering. Mikhailovsky claimed that this fascination with degradation became increasingly prominent and alarming in Dostoevsky's work, but that it could be found as early as *The Double*. See Mirsky, *History of Russian Literature*, 184, 337; Vladimir Seduro, *Dostoevski in Russian Literary Criticism, 1846–1956* (Octagon, 1969), 28–38.

22. *Civilization and Its Discontents*, 1931, translated by James Strachey (Norton, 1962), 71; cf. 51. Russian literature of the nineteenth and early twentieth centuries, especially that emanates from Petersburg, is remarkably rich in images and ideas of a police state within the self. Freud believed that psychoanalytic therapy must strive to strengthen the ego against an overly punitive superego, a "cultural superego" as well as a personal one. We might see the literary tradition that stems from "The Bronze Horseman" performing this task for Russian society.

23. The best general work on the "men of the sixties" is Eugene Lampert's *Sons*

Against Fathers (Oxford, 1965). Franco Venturi's classic study, *Roots of Revolution: A History of the Populist and Socialist Movements in Nineteenth Century Russia* (1952), translated from the Italian by Francis Haskell (Knopf, 1961), provides a marvelous wealth of detail on the activities of this generation, and gives us a feeling for its human complexity. See also Avrahm Yarmolinsky, *Road to Revolution* (1956; Collier, 1962).

24. Venturi, *Roots of Revolution*, 247.

25. Ibid., 227.

26. For Herzen's ringing appeal, Venturi, 35.

27. The best accounts of Chernyshevsky's life and work can be found in Venturi, Chapter 5; in Eugene Lampert's *Sons Against Fathers*, Chapter 3; and in Francis Randall, *Nikolai Chernyshevsky* (Twayne, 1970). See also Richard Hare, *Pioneers of Russian Social Thought* (1951; Vintage, 1964), Chapter 6; Rufus Mathewson, Jr., *The Positive Hero in Russian Literature* (1958; Stanford, 1975), especially 63–83, 101; and, on *What Is to Be Done?*, Joseph Frank, "N. G. Chernyshevsky: A Russian Utopia," in *Southern Review*, 1968, 68–84. Note the curious biographical sketch by the hero of Nabokov's novel *The Gift* (1935–37; translated by Michael Scammell, Capricorn, 1970), Chapter 4.

28. Translated by Benjamin Tucker, 1913; reprinted, Vintage, 1970. The passage quoted above is from Book III, Chapter 8.

29. This spiritual complacency mars some of the best discussions of the *Notes*, including Joseph Frank, "Nihilism and *Notes from Underground*," in *Sewanee Review*, 1961, 1–33; Robert Jackson, *Dostoevsky's Underground Man in Russian Literature* (The Hague: Mouton, 1958); Ralph Matlaw's Introduction to his splendid edition and translation of the *Notes* (Dutton, 1960); Philip Rahv, "Dostoevsky's Underground," in *Modern Occasions*, Winter 1972, 1–13. See also Grigory Pomerants, "Euclidean and Non-Euclidean Reasoning in the Works of Dostoevsky," in the Soviet dissident periodical *Kontinent*, 3 (1978), 141–82. But Soviet citizens have a special motive—and perhaps a special justification—for attacking Chernyshevsky, who was praised by Lenin as a Bolshevik *avant le lettre*, and later canonized as a martyred church father of the Soviet establishment.

30. Quoted in Lampert, *Sons Against Fathers*, 132, 164–65. See also Dostoevsky's *Diary of a Writer*, 1873, entry 3, translated by Boris Brasol (1949; Braziller, 1958), 23–30.

31. *Notes from Underground*, Book II, Chapter 1; translated by Ralph Matlaw (Dutton, 1960), 42–49.

32. It is worth noting that two of the most prominent *raznochintsy* "men of the sixties," Nikolai Dobrolyubov and Dmitri Pisarev, had high praise for Dostoevsky, and saw his work as part of the Russian people's developing struggle for their rights and human dignity; his bitterness and rancor was, for them, a necessary phase of self-emancipation. Seduro, *Dostoevski in Russian Literary Criticism*, 15–27.

33. See "A Letter from the Executive Committee to Alexander III," published March 10, 1881, by the leaders of the *Narodnya Volya* ("People's Will") group, which had assassinated Alexander II on March 1. Venturi, *Roots of Revolution*, 716–20. See also Father Gapon's 1905 petition, quoted and discussed in Section 3 of this chapter.

34. Comparisons of Dostoevsky with Baudelaire, also stressing the urban theme, but with perspectives very different from mine (and from each other's), can be found in Fanger, *Dostoevsky and Romantic Realism*, 253–58, and Alex de Jonge, *Dostoevsky and the Age of Intensity* (St. Martin's Press, 1975), 33–65, 84–5, 129–30.

35. Gerschenkron, in *Economic Backwardness in Historical Perspective*, 119–25, explains how the 1861 reforms, by freezing the peasants on the land and enmeshing them in new obligations to their village communes, intentionally retarded the creation of a free, mobile industrial labor force, and so hampered rather than facilitated economic growth. This theme is developed at greater length in his *Cambridge Economic History* chapter, cited in note 8 above. See also Portal's chapter in the same volume, 810–23.

36. This story is told in Venturi, *Roots of Revolution*, 544–46, 585–86, 805.

37. Ibid., 585.

38. On the French Revolution, see, for example, Albert Soboul, *The Sans-Culottes: Popular Movements and Revolutionary Government, 1793–94*, 1958; abridged version, 1968, translated by Remy Inglis Hall (Anchor, 1972); and George Rudé, *The Crowd in the French Revolution* (Oxford, 1959). On Russia, the landmark work is Venturi's. In recent years, as Soviet archives have opened (slowly and haltingly), a younger generation of historians has begun to work on twentieth-century movements with a sense of detail and depth that approaches what Venturi brought to bear on the nineteenth century. See, for example, Leopold Haimson, "The Problem of Social Stability in Urban Russia, 1905–1917," in *Slavic Review*, 23 (1964), 621–43, and 24 (1965), 1–2; Marc Ferro, *The Russian Revolution of February 1917*, 1967, translated from the French by J. L. Richards (Prentice-Hall, 1972); G. W. Phillips, "Urban Proletarian Politics in Tsarist Russia: Petersburg and Moscow, 1912–1914," in *Comparative Urban Research*, III, 3 (1975–76), II, 2; and Alexander Rabinowitch, *The Bolsheviks Come to Power: The Revolution of 1917 in Petrograd* (Norton, 1976).

39. The most visually detailed treatment of the Crystal Palace is Patrick Beaver, *The Crystal Palace, 1851–1936: A Portrait of Victorian Enterprise* (London: Hugh Evelyn, 1970). See also Giedion, *Space, Time and Architecture*, 249–55; Benevolo, *History of Modern Architecture* I, 96–102; F. D. Klingender, *Art and the Industrial Revolution*, 1947, edited and revised by Arthur Elton (Schocken, 1970).

40. This darkly comic story is told in Franz Mehring, *Karl Marx: The Story of His Life*, 1918, translated by Edward Fitzgerald (London: Allen and Unwin, 1936, 1951), 342–49.

41. Bucher's account is excerpted, and accepted as standard, by Giedion, 252–54, and Benevolo, 101–02.

42. *Winter Notes on Summer Impressions*, translated by Richard Lee Renfield, with an Introduction by Saul Bellow (Criterion, 1955), 39–41.

43. This scene, inexplicably omitted from Tucker's translation, is translated by Ralph Matlaw and included, along with other Chernyshevskian scenes, in his edition of *Notes from Underground*, 157–77.

44. See Anatol Kopp, *Town and Revolution*, 1967, translated by Thomas Burton (Braziller, 1970), and Kenneth Frampton, "Notes on Soviet Urbanism, 1917–32," in *Architects' Year Book* #12 (London: Elek Books, 1968), 238–52. The idea that Marxism demanded the destruction of the city was, of course, a grotesque distortion. For a concise, incisive account of the complexities and ambivalences of Marxism toward the modern city, see Carl Schorske, "The Idea of the City in European Thought: Voltaire to Spengler," 1963, reprinted in Sylvia Fava, editor, *Urbanism in World Perspective* (Crowell, 1968), 409–24.

45. Zamyatin's *We*, written between 1920 and 1927, is translated by Bernard Guilbert Guerney, and included in Guerney's fine anthology, *Russian Literature in the Soviet Period* (Random House, 1960). It is the primary source for both Huxley's *Brave New World* and Orwell's *1984* (Orwell acknowledged the debt;

Huxley did not), but immeasurably superior to both, and one of the modernist masterpieces of the century.

Jackson, in *Dostoevsky's Underground Man in Russian Literature*, 149–216, gives a fascinating account of the importance of *Notes from Underground* in the 1920s for many Soviet writers who were striving to keep the critical spirit alive—Zamyatin, Yuri Olesha, Ilya Ehrenburg, Boris Pilnyak—before the Stalinist darkness covered them all.

46. Alan Harrington seems to have been the first to make this connection explicit, in his novel of exurban and corporate malaise, *Life in the Crystal Palace* (Knopf, 1958). Eric and Mary Josephson juxtaposed a selection from Harrington's book with Part I of *Notes from Underground* in their anthology *Man Alone: Alienation in Modern Society* (Dell, 1962), a best-seller among American students throughout the 1960s.

47. Quoted in Zelnik, *Labor and Society in Tsarist Russia*, 60.

48. There are several versions of this document, none of them definitive. I have assembled the one above from Bertram Wolfe, *Three Who Made a Revolution* (1948; Beacon, 1957), 283–86, and the longer version in Sidney Harcave, *First Blood: The Russian Revolution of 1905* (Macmillan, 1964). See also the fascinating participant account of Solomon Schwarz, *The Russian Revolution of 1905* (U. of Chicago, 1967), 58–72, 268–84.

For background in 1905: on the economic and industrial upsurge of the 1890s, Gerschenkron, *Economic Backwardness in Historical Perspective*, 124–33, and Portal, in *Cambridge Economic History*, VI, 824–43; on the political explosions, Theodore von Laue, *Why Lenin? Why Stalin?*, Chapters 3 and 4; Richard Pipes, *Social Democracy and the St. Petersburg Labor Movement, 1885–1897* (Harvard, 1963); and Allan Wildman, *The Making of a Workers' Revolution: Russian Social Democracy, 1891–1903* (Chicago, 1967).

49. Wolfe, 286; Trotsky, *1905*, translated by Anya Bostock (Vintage, 1972), 253. My italics.

50. Ibid., 104–05, 252–53.

51. See Wolfe, Chapter 16, on "police socialism," and 301–04 on Gapon after January 9, including his encounter with Lenin; Harcave, *First Blood*, 24–5, 65–6, 94–5. For the historic resonance of "There is no Tsar anymore!" Cherniavsky, *Tsar and People*, 191–92, and the whole of the chapter that follows. A vivid account of Gapon's end is found in Boris Nicolaevsky, *Aseff the Spy: Russian Terrorist and Police Stool* (Doubleday, Doran, 1934), 137–48.

52. See, for example, Nicolaevsky, *Aseff the Spy*, cited in note 51; Michael Florinsky, *Russia: A History and an Interpretation* (1947; Macmillan, 1966), II, 1153–54, 1166–67, 1172, 1196, 1204; Wolfe, 266, 479; and the fascinating contemporary account (1911) of Thomas Masaryk, in his classic study, *The Spirit of Russia*, I, 193–94; II, 299–300, 364–69, 454–58. Masaryk offers extensive discussion of the philosophy and world view of Russian terrorism, and distinguishes the nihilism and existential bleakness of Azev's contemporaries from the self-sacrificing humanistic idealism of the *Zemlya i Volya* generation.

Masaryk is particularly intrigued by Azev's lieutenant Boris Savinkov, who, shortly after his (as it turned out, temporary) retirement from the field, published two novels that vividly recapture the terrorists' inner world. The novels, published under the name of V. Ropshin, and entitled *The Pale Horse* and *The Tale of What Was Not*, created a sensation in Europe (English translations 1918–19); they are known to have influenced Lukacs, Ernst Bloch and other Central European intellectuals to make their "leap of faith" into Bolshevism. See *The Spirit of Russia*, II, 375–77, 444–61, 474, 486, 529, 535, 546, 581. See also the recent work of Michael Löwy, *Georg Lukacs: From Romanticism to Bol-*

shevism, 1976, translated from the French by Patrick Cammiller (London, New Left Books, 1979), *passim*, and Andrew Arato and Paul Breines, *The Young Lukács and the Origins of Western Marxism* (Continuum, 1979). Masaryk, like Lukács a few years later, extravagantly compares Savinkov to Ivan Karamazov and Goethe's Faust.

Bolsheviks and Mensheviks alike condemned left terrorism, as all good Marxists must, and suggested that it was being instigated by the police. On the other hand, it should be noted that the police had their agents among their top leaders too. See, for instance, Wolfe, "The Case of Roman Malinovsky," 534–58.

53. An English translation appeared by John Cournos (Grove Press) in 1960, but it did not get the attention it deserved and went out of print for many years. In 1978, however, a new translation appeared, by Robert Maguire and John Malmstad (Indiana University Press), with lavish historical and critical notes, and particularly good discussion of the novel's urbanism, including Petersburg history, folklore, maps, and helpful hints for travelers from the 1913 Baedeker. The success of this new edition seems to have induced Grove Press to reissue the Cournos translation. The fact that American readers can now choose between two versions of *Petersburg* bodes well for the novel's future in this country. I have used the Maguire-Malmstad translation; citations in parenthesis, within my text, designate chapter and page numbers.

54. Donald Fanger perceptively situates *Petersburg* within "The City of Russian Modernist Fiction," in *Modernism*, edited by Malcolm Bradbury and James MacFarlane (Penguin, 1976), 467–80. On Biely's all-pervasive "shadow" theme, and its political relevance, see Lubomir Dolezel, "The Visible and the Invisible Petersburg," in *Russian Literature*, VII (1979), 465–90.

For general discussions, in the Penguin *Modernism* volume, see the interesting essays by Eugene Lampert, "Modernism in Russia: 1893–1917," and G. M. Hyde, "Russian Futurism" and "The Poetry of the City"; the collection edited by George Gibian and H. W. Tjalsma, *Russian Modernism: Culture and the Avant-Garde, 1890–1930* (Cornell, 1976); and Robert C. Williams, *Artists in Revolution: Portraits of the Russian Avant-Garde, 1905–1925* (Indiana, 1977).

55. Harcave, *First Blood*, 168–262, offers the clearest narrative of the October days and their aftermath; 195–96 for the Tsar's manifesto of October 17. But Trotsky's *1905* is especially vivid and brilliant on the Revolution's climax and the beginning of its end. Trotsky's speech of October 18 (quoted in text) and some of his newspaper articles provide a trenchant analysis of the October manifesto, in which, as he said, "Everything is given—and nothing is given." But Trotsky was also one of the first revolutionaries to realize that the Russian masses would have to find this out for themselves, and that until they did—and it might take them years—the Revolution was over.

56. Mathewson, in *The Positive Hero in Russian Literature*, 172, argues that Gorky's treatment of Revolution is far deeper in novels like *The Artamonov Business* and plays where he portrays its impact on nonrevolutionary and nonheroic intellectuals and bourgeoisie.

57. Gerschenkron, in *Economic Backwardness in Historical Perspective*, 124–33, locates communist development and industrialization policies in the context of Russia's Petrine tradition.

58. Billington, *The Icon and the Axe*, 534–36.

59. See the work of Leopold Haimson, Mark Ferro, Alexander Rabinowitch and others, cited in detail in notes 38 and 52. As their work is assimilated and extended, we are gradually accumulating the knowledge and developing a

perspective from which the story of Petersburg in 1917, the city's ultimate romance and tragedy, can be grasped in its full depth. Maybe in the next generation this story will at last be adequately told.

60. Mandelstam's poems, largely untitled, are numbered according to the standard Russian edition, edited by Gleb Struve and Boris Filippov, and published in New York in 1967. Translations here are by Clarence Brown and W. S. Merwin, from *Osip Mandelstam: Selected Poems* (Atheneum, 1974).

61. "Midnight in Moscow," omitted from the *Selected Poems*, can be found in the *Complete Poetry of Osip Emilevich Mandelstam*, translated by Burton Raffel and Alan Burago (State University of New York Press, 1973). But I have used Max Hayward's version, from his translation of Nadezhda Mandelstam's magnificent *Hope Against Hope: a Memoir* (Atheneum, 1970), 176. Mandelstam's widow placed special emphasis on his (and her own) commitment to this tradition, 176–78; see 146–54 for a contrast of Mandelstam, the Petersburg "ordinary man," with Pasternak, the "Moscow aristocrat."

62. Translated by Clarence Brown in his edition of the selected *Prose of Osip Mandelstam* (Princeton, 1967), 149–89, with a perceptive critical essay, 37–57.

63. Clarence Brown, *Mandelstam* (Cambridge, 1973), 125, 130.

64. For the first eight lines, I have used Max Hayward's translation, in *Hope Against Hope*, 13, which includes "the murderer and peasant-slayer." I have used Merwin and Brown's more powerful rendition of the last eight lines. Their translation derives from a later version of the poem with a different line 4. The one above is the one that passed into the hands of the police.

65. *On Socialist Realism*, published under the pseudonym of Abram Tertz, appeared in *Dissent* magazine, translated by George Dennis, in 1959, and in book form (Pantheon, 1960), with an introduction by Czeslaw Milosz.

66. Alexander Zinoviev, *The Yawning Heights*, published in *samizdat* in 1974–75, translated by Gordon Clough (Random House, 1979), 25.

67. Cornelia Gerstenmaier, *The Voices of the Silent*, translated from the German by Susan Hecker (Hart, 1972), 127. This volume, along with Abraham Brumberg, *In Quest of Justice: Protest and Dissent in the Soviet Union Today* (Praeger, 1970), provide a fascinating account, with abundant documentation, of the revival of dissent on paper and in the streets.

68. Quoted in Natalia Gorbanevskaya, *Red Square at Noon*, translated by Alexander Lieven, introduction by Harrison Salisbury (Holt, Rinehart, Winston, 1972), 11–12, 221–22. Gorbanevskaya, herself a participant in this demonstration, was afterward incarcerated in a KGB hospital for several years.

69. Indeed, they may find themselves too much at home for some of the other inhabitants of this world. Thus Simon Karlinsky, Professor of Russian Literature at Berkeley, let loose a trumpet blast against Dostoevsky in September of 1971, in a front-page essay in the *New York Times Book Review*. After quoting an array of cultural authorities, from Nabokov to Lenin, on Dostoevsky's depravity, loathsomeness and artistic ineptitude, Karlinsky made it clear that the real object of his wrath was his radical students, who loved Dostoevsky with a desperate passion, but who cared little for truly "civilized" Russian writers. Karlinsky recounted how he had recently turned on his radio hoping to get a rest from the "overheated universe" of Dostoevskians around him—only to hear a motley assortment of typically Dostoevskian militants and crazies engaged in a discussion with the ultra-Dostoevskian Herbert Marcuse! One had to pity Karlinsky; was it for this that he had fought for tenure in the California sunshine? Nevertheless, he should have remembered Svidrigailov's prophetic last words, delivered as he shoots himself through the head: "Tell them I'm going to America." (His sole witness, it should be noted, is a poor conscript

Jewish soldier, whose great-grandchildren might well have followed that specter to haunt Karlinsky in his class.)

V. IN THE FOREST OF SYMBOLS

1. These statements are quoted by Robert Caro in his monumental study, *The Power Broker: Robert Moses and the Fall of New York* (Knopf, 1974), 849, 876. The "meat ax" passage is from Moses' memoir, *Public Works: A Dangerous Trade* (McGraw-Hill, 1970). Moses' appraisal of the Cross-Bronx Expressway occurs in an interview with Caro. *The Power Broker* is the main source for my narrative of Moses' career. See also my article on Caro and Moses, "Buildings Are Judgment: Robert Moses and the Romance of Construction," *Ramparts*, March 1975, and a further symposium in the June issue.
2. Speech to the Long Island Real Estate Board, 1927, quoted in Caro, 275.
3. *The City of Tomorrow*, 64–66. See Koolhaas, 199–223, on Le Corbusier and New York.
4. For details of this episode, Caro, 368–72.
5. *Space, Time and Architecture*, 823–32.
6. Frances Perkins, Oral History Reminiscences (Columbia University Collection), quoted in Caro, 318.
7. A definitive analysis of public authorities in America can be found in Annemarie Walsh, *The Public's Business: The Politics and Practices of Government Corporations* (MIT, 1978), especially Chapters 1, 2, 8, 11, 12. Walsh's book contains much fascinating material on Moses, but she places his work in a broad institutional and social context that Caro tends to leave out. Robert Fitch, in a perceptive 1976 essay, "Planning New York," tries to deduce all Moses' activities from the fifty-year agenda that was established by the financiers and officials of the Regional Plan Association; it appears in Roger Alcaly and David Mermelstein, editors, *The Fiscal Crisis of American Cities* (Random House, 1977), 247–84.
8. *Space, Time and Architecture*, 831–32.
9. On the problems and paradoxes of that period, the best recent discussion is Morris Dickstein's essay "The Cold War Blues," which appears as Chapter 2 in his *Gates of Eden*. For interesting polemic on the 1950s, see Hilton Kramer's attack on Dickstein, "Trashing the Fifties," in the *New York Times Book Review*, 10 April 1977, and Dickstein's reply in the issue of 12 June.
10. A detailed account of this affair can be found in Caro, 1132–44.
11. *The Death and Life of Great American Cities* (Random House and Vintage, 1961). The passages that follow are from pages 50–54. For interesting critical discussion of Jacobs' vision, see, for instance, Herbert Gans, "City Planning and Urban Realities," *Commentary*, February 1962; Lewis Mumford, "Mother Jacobs' Home Remedies for Urban Cancer," *The New Yorker*, 1 December 1962, reprinted in *The Urban Prospect* (Harcourt, 1966); and Roger Starr, *The Living End: The City and Its Critics* (Coward-McCann, 1966).
12. Quoted in Barbara Rose, *Claes Oldenburg* (MOMA/New York Graphic Society, 1970), 25, 33.
13. Note to *The Street* exhibition, quoted in Rose, 46.
14. Statement for the catalogue of his "Environments, Situations, Spaces" exhibition, 1961, quoted in Rose, 190–91. This statement, a marvelous fusion of Whitman with dada, is also reprinted in Russell and Gablik, *Pop Art Redefined*, 97–99.
15. Quoted in Caro, 876.
16. In *Blindness and Insight*, 147–48.

17. *Woman Warrior: Memoirs of a Girlhood Among Ghosts* (Knopf, 1976; Vintage, 1977). The themes of this book are further developed, with more historical sweep but less personal intensity, in a sort of sequel, *China Men* (Knopf, 1980).

18. A script of *Rumstick Road* is reprinted, along with directorial notes by Elizabeth LeCompte and a few dim photographs, in *Performing Arts Journal*, III, 2 (Fall 1978). *The Drama Review* #81 (March 1979) offers notes on all three plays by Gray and James Bierman, along with excellent photographs.

19. Untitled Proposals, 1971–72, in *The Writings of Robert Smithson: Essays and Illustrations,* edited by Nancy Holt (NYU, 1979), 220–21. For Smithson's urban visions, see his essays "Ultra-Moderne," "A Tour of the Monuments of Passaic, New Jersey," and "Frederick Law Olmsted and the Dialectical Landscape," all in this volume.

20. See the volume *Devastation/Resurrection: The South Bronx*, prepared by the Bronx Museum of the Arts in the winter of 1979–80. This volume gives an excellent account both of the dynamics of urbicide and of the beginnings of reconstruction.

21. See Carter Ratcliff, "Ferrer's Sun and Shade," in *Art in America* (March 1980), 80–86, for a perceptive discussion of this piece. But Ratcliff does not notice that, intertwined with the dialectics of Ferrer's work, this work's site—Fox Street in the South Bronx—has an inner dialectic of its own.

22. For a brief discussion, see Introduction, note 24.

23. *Growing Up Absurd: Problems of Youth in Organized Society* (Random House, 1960), 230.

24. *Paracriticisms: Seven Speculations of the Times*, 40.

Index